LIBRARIES, TECHNOLOGY, AND THE INFORMATION MARKETPLACE

SELECTED PAPERS

Libraries, Technology, and the Information Marketplace

Selected Papers

Richard De Gennaro

G.K. Hall & Co. • Boston, Massachusetts

Libraries, Technology and the Information Marketplace:
Selected Papers

by G.K. Hall & Co.
70 Lincoln Street
Boston, Massachusetts 02111

Special acknowledgment to R.R. Bowker, The American Library Association, and Journal of Academic Librarianship for permission to republish copyrighted materials.

Book design and production by Barbara Anderson

Copyedited by Michael Sims

Printed on acid-free paper and bound in The United States of America

10 9 8 7 6 5 4 3 2 1

LIBRARY OF CONGRESS CATALOGING IN PUBLICATION DATA
De Gennaro, Richard.
Libraries, technology, and the information marketplace.

Includes index.
1. Information services. 2. Library science—Technological innovastions. 3. Library science—Data processing. 4. Libraries—Automation. 5. Library information networks. I. Title.
Z674.4.D43 1987b 025'.02'0285 87-7568
ISBN 0-8161-1855-8 (alk. paper)
ISBN 0-8161-1869-8 (paperback)

CONTENTS

FOREWORD

Discriminating readers of the library press have learned to look forward eagerly to Richard De Gennaro's annual contributions to the professional literature. Once, or sometimes twice, a year for the past several years, this distinguished and articulate academic library administrator could be relied upon to produce an article of opinion for *Library Journal, American Libraries,* or one of the other major journals. His articles were sure to be well written, likely to be rather controversial, and certain to be widely discussed by librarians. "Have you seen De Gennaro's latest article?" has become something of a conversational staple whenever librarians gather.

If the measure of an author's influence is the extent to which what he writes is read and talked about, then Richard De Gennaro ranks unquestionably among our most important librarian-authors. As this collection of his papers reveals, he has an instinct for choosing topics that are timely, but not transient. Even in those few instances in this volume where the specific issue being addressed has shifted with the passage of time (as for example, in the article "Providing Bibliographic Services from Machine-Readable Data Bases: The Library's Role"), the problem analysis remains both cogent and remarkably relevant.

The enduring value of many of these papers derives in large measure, I think, from their author's unusual talent for penetrating below the surface of a current issue to address the underlying problem in a way that enhances our collective understanding of its significance. "Research Libraries Enter the Information Age," for example, obliges the reader to contemplate the profound implications of the inescapable reality that recorded knowledge is *indeed* cumulative—a characteristic that librarians often refer to casually, but only rarely think very deeply about.

De Gennaro reminds us that it is important to penetrate below the surface of our daily professional and institutional environments so as to confront the fundamental and persistent characteristics of the library as a social institution. He teaches us as well to be suspicious of single, simple solutions to complex professional problems. In "Austerity, Technology, and Resource Sharing: Research Libraries Face the Future," he warns that our naive confidence in the capacity of technology alone to resolve the dilemma of research library growth is not only misplaced but also, in fact, diverts our attention away from the urgent need to formulate and implement more realistic acquisitions policies.

Like most ordinary mortals, librarians do not much enjoy being reminded that complex problems are rarely, if ever, amenable to simple solutions. But De Gennaro is a skilled docent whose carefully crafted prose keeps us coming back for repeated applications of reality therapy. We delight in his wry characterization of "research," in "Copyright, Resource Sharing, and Hard Times: A View from the Field," as a word "much overused to describe what professors do and what libraries support." And we nod in reluctant agreement when he speculates in "Libraries and Networks in Transition" on the existence of "a fundamental law of cataloging . . . that the effort required to catalog any particular book is inversely proportional to the amount of use it will receive."

But it is more than graceful prose that makes these papers worth collecting, preserving, and rereading. What is most valuable here for both students and practitioners of librarianship is the consistent vision of the social mission of the research library that unifies these essays on divergent themes. De Gennaro is clearly a man who understands both who he is and what it is that he, as a professional, is about in life. In a time when it is easy for even the best to lack all conviction, that is at once refreshing and inordinately useful.

De Gennaro's writings group themselves naturally under the three central themes that serve to organize this volume: the social role of the library, managing the library in a time of rapid change, and the impact of technology on library operations and services. All three themes are closely interrelated, as these essays make apparent. Indeed, it is precisely the nature and the extent of that interrelatedness that is one of the most important understandings to be derived from reading this volume in its entirety.

This book reflects, as well, a unified and a unifying managerial perspective. It is not a systematic treatise on research library administration, although such a text from this author would indeed be a welcome future addition to the professional literature. Rather, *Libraries, Technology, and the Information Marketplace* does for the student of library management what textbooks are almost never able to do. It reveals how a thoughtful and effective library administrator comes to terms with the range of managerial decisions, both large and small, that are the actual substance and content of the library director's working day. De Gennaro's writings enhance our understanding of what it really means to devote a professional lifetime to *doing* library management, to filling the administrative role. As the author addresses a series of major technological developments over the past eighteen years, the reader comes to understand how an experienced library manager responds to, reacts to, and accommodates change within a context of institutional continuity.

These essays span nearly two decades of dramatic technological change in all types of libraries. The reader is able to trace in these pages the evolution of library computer systems from early mainframe-centered experiments with library automation at Harvard through the emergence of timesharing-based bibliographic utilities to the current era of networking and decentralization. The author exhibits a consistent talent for identifying and anticipating what have turned out to be dominant trends and directions in the development of technology to support research library operations. Not only does this volume provide a wealth of useful information about library technology but, far more important, it presents a useful way of *looking at technology* from a management perspective.

Richard De Gennaro has been no casual observer of the research library scene. His career has placed him at the center of development in three of the world's greatest research libraries: the New York Public Library, Harvard University, and, for the past sixteen years, the University of Pennsylvania. He has served as president of the Association of Research Libraries, as president of the American Library Association's Library and Information Technology Association, and as chairman of the Board of Governors of The Research Libraries Group, Inc. He was the 1986 recipient of the American Library Association's Melvil Dewey Medal and is recognized nationally and internationally as a leader in the academic and research library community. Such a record of professional accomplishment alone would justify the publication of a collection like this one.

But this book is far more than a tribute to a distinguished career. No apology or justification is needed for the preservation of these papers beyond their own intrinsic quality and value. They are quite simply good and valuable reading for all who are concerned about the nation's research libraries—past, present and future.

Dr. Thomas J. Galvin
Executive Director,
American Library Association

PREFACE

This book is divided into two parts. The first part contains six previously unpublished pieces that give the reader some current perspectives on the principal subjects covered in the thirty-three papers that constitute the second part of the book.

The papers in the second part of the book span a twenty-year period and are largely about the implementation of new technology in libraries and the changing environment in which libraries operate. They are grouped in four categories and are arranged in reverse chronological order. They have all been published before, many have been reprinted in other compilations over the years, and several have been translated and republished abroad. The older ones from the early years of library automation and networking are clearly outdated in their original context. Why then should they be compiled and published again in this volume? Because I believe that the essays and papers taken together as a collection provide a unique and useful record of how librarians viewed and implemented the new technology during this critical transition period when libraries were entering the information age.

These writings document the evolution of our ideas and attitudes on a number of the important issues of the time such as relations between librarians and publishers and the emerging information industry, library automation and networking, and library management, among others. The twenty years covered in the collection was a time of unparalleled development for libraries, library networks, and the publishing and information industries.

Obviously, these essays and papers represent only a single

viewpoint and some of the views expressed turned out in retrospect to have been naive, shortsighted, or mistaken. It makes little difference at this point, however, whether the views were right or wrong. What is more interesting now is that this body of published material can contribute to our understanding of the various currents and forces that were shaping the future of libraries during these two crucial and exciting decades.

The principal audience for this book is practicing librarians, library school teachers and students, and anyone who wants to stand back from the plethora of confusing current trends, issues, and concerns and get a useful perspective on the changing role of libraries in the early stages of the information age.

This book is dedicated to my wife, Birgit, with love and gratitude.

Richard De Gennaro
Director, New York Public Library

PART ONE

THE FUTURE IN PERSPECTIVE

SURVIVING TECHNOLOGICAL REVOLUTIONS

I read somewhere once that when the aging Prince Talleyrand was asked what he did during the tumultuous years of the French Revolution, the Terror, and the Napoleonic Wars, he replied simply that he had survived.

When I look back on all the technological revolutions that I have lived through since I became a librarian thirty years ago, I marvel at the fact that, like Talleyrand, I survived. Not only did I survive, but all the libraries that I have worked in have also survived, despite the many predictions to the contrary that I have heard over those years. When I think about the revolutions in technology that are coming in the years ahead, I am confident that libraries and librarians are going to survive, and that they will continue to bear their traditional names and carry out their traditional functions—to select, organize, preserve, and provide access to the records of human knowledge *in whatever form they take.* And increasingly, the form of those records will be electronic as will the means for performing library functions.

It is important that librarians keep their balance and their maps of reality up to date. If we have learned anything about technology in the last thirty years, we have learned that technological revolutions usually take longer than we think they will, some are less revolutionary than we expect, and some happen in ways that no one can anticipate. We have also learned that no one can predict the future, no matter how renowned a person may be in other areas of life. Each new technological development is hyped by a chorus of prophets as the basis for revolutionary change in libraries, society, or whatever. Revolution is one of those strong words that has lost its impact in the field of technology because of overuse.

The computer revolution has been surprising and amazing librarians for over forty years and there is no end in sight. On the other hand, the much-heralded microfilm and ultra-microfiche revolutions of the 1950s and 1960s failed to deliver as promised. The Xerox revolution of the 1960s came unheralded and gave us a whole new technology for reproducing and disseminating information. The teaching machine and audiovisual revolutions of the 1960s and 1970s never got off the ground. Now the experts are telling us that electronic publishing will soon create the library without walls where everything will be accessible from any personal computer. That may be so, but I am skeptical.

We have to keep all these "revolutions" in perspective. The reality is that librarians cannot implement revolutionary changes in libraries. We have to introduce technological change in a way and at a pace that is acceptable to the communities we serve, and most communities will not tolerate revolutionary initiatives. They can be "educated" and led in new directions, but those directions have to be reasonable in reality as well as in perception. Universities are conservative places, and librarians cannot afford to get too far ahead of their constituents. They will not permit us to take undue risks with the libraries they have entrusted us to manage for them.

In the end, the future of academic libraries depends on the future of the institutions they serve. The wiring of universities and the way and rate at which they embrace and use technology will largely determine how libraries are wired and use technology. Libraries cannot set courses that are not in tune with the felt needs of the people and institutions they serve. Libraries serve teaching and research. As these functions change, libraries will change with them.

In song and story over the last two or three decades there has been a constant refrain from a parade of futurists, technologists, and assorted experts and library leaders exhorting librarians to embrace the new technology or be left behind on the ash heap of the technological revolution. They warn us that if we don't get with it and use the technology, other, more aggressive players will take over the library function and we will be left without a role. They are saying that technology exists to do things that need doing in libraries, but that librarians are too uninformed, too conservative or otherwise unwilling and unable to use it. This is nonsense.

My experience tells me that librarians have not only been eager (frequently too eager) to use new technology, but have actually been leaders in its development and use in the information field. Let me cite some examples. The National Library of Medicine led the way in computerizing the production of the Index Medicus and then developed Medline, the first major online bibliographic information service and the model for Dialog, Orbit, and BRS. Librarians developed the OCLC, Utlas, RLG, and WLN shared cataloging and network systems with their enormous databases. The Library of Congress paved the way for two decades of advances with its development of the MARC formats and database, and is now pioneering optical video and digital disk applications for library and information work.

The fact is that librarians are running as fast as they can to implement technology just as soon as it is technically feasible and financially possible. Libraries are not lagging behind in the use of appropriate technology. Automating libraries and building library networks has turned out to be more difficult and more complex than anyone imagined twenty years ago. And the technology required to do the job simply was not there at that time.

I can still remember how excited I was as a young librarian at Harvard in the 1960s about using computers and reprography to transform the library. My goal was to combine the library's computer systems and photographic services units into a single new department that would be the library's principal vehicle for change. I was convinced that the marriage of these two technologies would give us the tools we needed to bring about a revolution in library operations and services to users. It is twenty years later and that promise is only now being fulfilled with the symbiotic melding of computing, telecommunications, reprography, and several new generations of software. In retrospect, the revolution happened very quickly, but it took far longer than any of us thought it would.

TECHNOLOGY AND ACCESS

Thirty years ago, a library's stock in trade consisted of books, journals, newspapers, and manuscript materials, and the only means of access was the library's card catalog. The only machines in use were typewriters, photostat machines, and some microcards and microfilm containing early printed books, newspapers, and doctoral dissertations. Those who wanted access to library materials had to come to the library and either use them in the building or borrow them for home use. If a library did not have what the patron wanted, he either had to send for it on interlibrary loan, which took up to three months, or he had to find out where it was and go to that library. Copying was done by the user in longhand or on a typewriter. Libraries were the only source for back files of books and journals and other research materials. This is why it was so important for them to have large local collections and why the value of a library was measured by the number of books in its collections.

New technology was first introduced into libraries in the 1950s. One of the first and most important advances was the introduction and widespread use of microfilm as a means of expanding the resources of libraries. Microfilm had been used in libraries since the 1930s, but it came into its own in the 1950s with the development of a variety of new and improved automatic cameras, processors, and printers. Microfilm was a form of republication that made available to libraries materials they could not otherwise acquire. It also enabled—for the first time—such large collections as an entire run of a newspaper or a manuscript archive to be lent from one library to another.

A combination of microfilm and the Xerox Copyflow

process came into use in the early 1960s and provided a means for the economical reproduction and publication of card catalogs by photographing them twenty-one cards to a page and producing them in book form. G. K. Hall and Co., KTO Press, and a number of other companies specialized in making book form catalogs out of card catalogs. This made possible the wide dissemination of catalogs of the holdings of various special collections, which, in turn, helped to make them accessible to scholars at a distance. The next best thing to having one of these special collections in one's library was to have a printed book catalog of that collection. The purchase of these catalogs by aspiring research libraries became quite commonplace in the 1960s. All of this came about as the result of the rapid advances in photographic and graphic arts technology.

The next step was for publishers not only to produce the catalog of the materials but also to reproduce and republish the text of the materials themselves. Thus we had collections of Spanish plays, collections of French revolutionary documents, the Kress collection of the history of economics, and the Short Title Catalog. This new technology allowed libraries for the first time to acquire entire collections of fully cataloged materials. Scores of instant research libraries came into existence as colleges for teachers and other small colleges and universities were transformed into full-scale state universities during the expansion of higher education in the post-Sputnik late 1950s and 1960s. The growing use of reprographic technology for republication of library materials was an important step in the process of using technology to facilitate and equalize access to library resources.

Another major development in the mid-1960s was the introduction of the Xerox 914 machine. The Xerox machine, more than any technological advance to date, revolutionized the way libraries were used and made it possible for users to use library materials off the premises. It enabled users to make a copy of a document in a library and take it home and own it. The Xerox machine also made it possible to write to a library and receive a copy of a document that a library owned and use that document at a distance. It was no longer necessary for scholars to go to distant cities to consult documents or publications that their library did not own. With this development a collection could be viewed as a source for making copies of publications rather than as a place where one read the documents.

During this same decade a number of commercial vendors, most notably University Microfilms, Inc. (UMI), made a thriving business of producing and selling microfilm copies of research materials to libraries. This type of firm borrowed originals from one library, made and kept a master archival film, and sold copies to other libraries. UMI started with dissertations, expanded into newspapers and journals, and finally got into individual monograph titles. It now has one of the largest and most comprehensive collection of research materials on microfilm and is a major player in the document delivery business, not only selling to libraries but also competing with them. The clear advantage that vendors such as UMI possess is the ability to concentrate on the profitable part of the document supply business and use libraries of record as their source of supply.

Another significant advance in the 1960s was the introduction of the computer into library and information activities. By the early 1970s, the National Library of Medicine, System Development Corp., and Lockheed were all squarely into the online bibliographic search business. These online database services made vast quantities of up-to-date information about new publications readily available to libraries and users at reasonable prices. Availability of online searching and access was another major step in the process of making those collections and information about library collections widely available. It was a logical continuation of the same trend that the published book catalog started a decade earlier.

Further information about the contents of library collections was made widely available in the late 1960s and early 1970s with the emergence of such major bibliographic utilities as OCLC, RLG, WLN, and Utlas in Canada. As part of their bibliographic systems, these utilities began providing electronic mail services for ordering and communicating information about interlibrary loans online. This greatly facilitated and increased the volume of interlibrary loan and made effective resource sharing a practical reality. Interlibrary loan offices are now being equipped with telefacsimile transmission and receiving devices, adding another capability to what is now one of the most electronically sophisticated units of a library.

The next major advance in this march of technology promises to be the widespread use of CD ROM and other forms of optical and video disk systems in combination with powerful microcomputer systems. This new optical disk technology will not supersede the existing archives of microforms, but it will probably supersede film as the medium for making and distributing new comprehensive collections of research materials.

The new optical disk technology will make possible the storage, retrieval, communication, and manipulation of vast quantities of research resources in electronic form. And the availability of information in this form, along with the availability of information in distant online databases, will transform the way libraries operate and provide resources to their users in the next decade. In the future, the size of a library's collection of conventional materials will matter far less than it does now or than it did in the past. The question is no longer how many volumes a library has or how large it is, but how effectively the library can deliver needed resources to users via the new technology. The new technology will not make existing collections of books and journals obsolete and unnecessary, but the collections will no longer be the only or even the primary resources of the library of the future. In this world of electronic resources, the relative advantage that a scholar now has at one of the large established research libraries is lessened.

New technology is democratizing the availability of research resources. I am not suggesting that the libraries that were rich in the past will be poor in the future. For the same reasons that the major research universities were willing and able to amass and maintain enormous libraries, so in the future they will have the resources and the incentive to provide access to vast quantities of information in electronic form. Nevertheless, the new information technologies provide a new beginning and a new opportunity for all libraries to compete.

The vast retrospective collections of printed materials in the old libraries will be both an asset and a liability in the electronic future. They will be an asset because they will become increasingly rare and important and will constitute the source for the compilation of collections on optical disks. But they could also be a liability because those institutions will have a heavy responsibility for housing, preserving, and providing access to those important archival collections.

In sum, the major development of the 1950s was the use of microphotography, that of the 1960s was the use of Xerography and computers, that of the 1970s was online computer systems, telecommunications and networking, and that of the 1980s microcomputers and optical disk systems.

The principal effect of technology on libraries over these four decades has been to bring about a revolution in access to library resources by users. Technology is making the resources within a library available beyond its walls, and the resources beyond its walls available within the library.

LIBRARIES IN THE MARKETPLACE

In the preface to the 1983 reprint edition of his classic, *Automation,* John Diebold outlines three stages of automation. In the first stage you automate what you did yesterday; in the second stage you find that what you do changes; and in the third stage you find that as a result of these changes, the greatest change of all occurs, and that is a transformation of society.

Putting this into a library context, we could say that in the first stage of library automation we automate the library's operations, procedures, and functions through local efforts and by forming cooperatives and utilities to share technology and bibliographic resources; in the second stage libraries take on new and different functions; and in the third stage the changes brought about by the first two stages transform the library's environment and redefine its function.

Diebold's three stages can also provide a frame of reference for the development of the information industry. For example, in the first stage existing information vendors such as Chemical Abstracts Service, BIOSIS, and Engineering Index, automate their data collection and publishing operations, in the second stage they and a growing number of new vendors begin offering new online and full text services, and in the third stage the way in which information is produced, marketed, and used in our society is totally transformed. Of course, these stages do not happen in a neat progression; they overlap, and it is difficult to distinguish clearly the boundaries between them.

An important aspect of the transformation is a blurring of distinctions between commercial and not-for-profit information suppliers, between vendors and libraries. The pressures of the technology-based information marketplace give rise to a growing competition between and among the various information suppliers. Library cooperatives create computer networks and utilities to take advantage of technology, and in response to financial pressures these not-for-profit organizations begin to compete with each other and with commercial vendors in the market place. OCLC, RLG, WLN, Utlas, and other library cooperatives are compelled by economic realities to compete with each other for business and customers. OCLC has effectively put the Library of Congress out of the card distribution business. It is now marketing an integrated library system, the LS/2000, in competition with other vendors of turnkey library systems. WLN licensed a commercial firm, Biblio-Techniques, Inc., to market a version of its software (BLIS) to other libraries and networks. In addition to the commercial vendors of library systems, several universities, including Northwestern, Virginia Polytechnic Institute, and Penn State, and a number of public libraries are marketing systems that they developed for their own use. Other libraries, such as New York University and Guelph University, entered into joint development agreements with a commercial vendor (GEAC) and have a stake in the success of the resulting product.

Two systems developers employed by National Institutes of Health (NIH) to develop an integrated library system leave NIH to form their own separate firms to further develop and market versions of the system that was in the public domain. These firms are in turn bought by OCLC to eliminate competition and to facilitate the development of its own version of the same system. Similarly, the systems developers at major universities take versions of the systems they have developed and form their own commercial firms to market them. It has become commonplace for libraries to exhibit their own systems at conferences to publicize their accomplishments as much as to seek possible buyers.

RLG is trying to recruit members from OCLC, which sees itself as the national library network and is determined to permit no further defections by its members. For similar reasons, CLSI once felt that it owned the library circulation system market and viewed would-be competitors as trespassers. Cooperatives are in competition with other cooperatives, not only for members, but also in selling particular services such as cataloging, interlibrary loan, and searching. Vendors compete with the utilities and the utilities compete with vendors. The regional networks that broker OCLC services are in a life-and-death competitive struggle with OCLC over who will control what products and services. CLASS, once a California state agency, is freed to offer services to libraries nationwide in competition with other regional networks. And other regional networks are expanding beyond their original boundaries and missions.

The growing use of high technology is also beginning to erode the free library ethic. Libraries have been compelled to begin selling certain high-tech services to their users beginning with Xerox copies in the 1960s and online search services in the 1970s. In the 1980s they will be selling access to online information and a growing number of other expensive high tech services. Some libraries have established semiautonomous reference and information services to facilitate the sale of services to commercial and other users.

Libraries are being forced to compete with each other and with commercial information brokers for a variety of library and document delivery services. Chemical Abstracts Service and University Microfilms Inc. have entered the document supply business in a serious way. They are competing not only with similar services provided by the Institute for Scientific Information and the British Library Document Supply Centre, but also with the OCLC and RLG interlibrary loan networks based on the collections of conventional libraries. The role that conventional libraries played (with considerable reluctance) as the sole or primary source of ILL or document supply twenty years ago in the pre-electronic age is being taken over by a variety of other information vendors in the new competitive information marketplace. What was a burden to research libraries has become a commercial opportunity to the new vendors. The market demand for documents has increased enormously in the last twenty years, and while the number of library transactions is increasing so is the market share of the new vendors.

Technology is transforming the library and information scene and it is no longer possible to make clear distinctions between the commercial and the not-for-profit sectors. Moreover, a large proportion of the exhibitors at a major American Library Association convention today are high-tech companies that did not exist twenty years ago. In the pretechnology days, we could tell the good guys from the bad guys, that is, the virtuous not-for-profits from the greedy commercial vendors. But it is not so easy anymore. Under its not-for-profit cooperative guise, OCLC has emerged as one of the most aggressive and profitable competitors in the marketplace, with its monopolistic tendencies and tough stance on copyright and contract negotiations with its broker networks and member libraries. The librarians who created OCLC may want and expect it to be true to its cooperative origins, but OCLC has outgrown those origins and is aggressively forging a new role for itself as an international information company selling services to end-users in competition with libraries and other information companies. Utlas became Utlas International when it was bought by the International Thompson Organization in 1985 and is now competing with OCLC and other cataloging services in the U.S. and abroad.

If the libraries and the library utilities are beginning to behave like commercial vendors, the commercial vendors are, in turn, beginning to behave like cooperative not-for-profit organizations. In this interesting reversal of roles, we see companies forming user-groups and advisory boards and entering into joint development arrangements to elicit the ideas and cooperation of their valued customers. We see business people writing papers and contributing their time and expertise to serving on committees and boards without pay. And we see companies sponsoring a variety of useful functions and activities in the library and information arena. On another level, we see companies like IBM, AT&T, and DEC contributing millions of dollars worth of equipment to universities. And we see universities selling their research and development capabilities to the Fortune 500 corporations.

In another significant historic reversal, we see the once-dominant role of the federal government rapidly diminishing. In the late 1950s the federal government initiated a number of major programs in support of education and libraries. Those programs were thriving until the Reagan administration came in and targeted all of them for elimination.

In the 1970s there was a major effort by the leaders of the research library community to establish a federally funded National Periodicals Center modeled after the British Library Lending Division. It was defeated in 1978 largely by the efforts of the Information Industry Association and the lukewarm support and outright opposition by some segments of the library community.

Since then there have been some half-hearted attempts to revive the idea, but it is clearly a dead issue for the foreseeable future.

All this commercial and competitive activity on the library scene started with the use of new technology in the 1960s. The way libraries reacted to these forces over the last three decades can be summarized in three words: *autonomy, cooperation,* and *competition.* Diebold is right. Technology is transforming not only our library and information environment, but our entire society.

The trends I am describing in the library and information field are parallel to and part of the major economic, social, and political trends of the last two or three decades. We have seen the relative stability of the 1960s give way to the volatile changes of the 1970s and 1980s. We are experiencing a number of historic swings in our society. Democrats are out, Republicans are in; government is out, business is in; welfare is out, self-reliance is in; regulation is out, competition is in; public is out, private is in; central is out, local is in; free is out, fee is in; cooperation is out, competition is in. I am not saying all these changes are desirable, but they are happening, and the reason they are happening is attributable in large part to the high-tech revolution that began in the 1960s.

The technologists and prophets of the information age are predicting that information technology will put libraries out of business. But the evidence is that technology is, in fact, putting libraries into business, for better or for worse. Technology is bringing a profusion of new players into the library and information marketplace. Before technology, libraries were the major, sometimes the only, sources of scholarly information. They continue to grow in importance and to serve a vital function, but their relative share of the expanding information market is diminishing.

ONLINE CATALOGS AND INTEGRATED SYSTEMS

One of the most significant turning points in library automation was the acceptance by librarians of the online catalog around 1982. For a number of reasons, that was the year when it suddenly became clear that the time of the online catalog had finally arrived. A stream of articles, seminars, and conferences on that subject began to gush forth and librarians began to survey the marketplace for systems suited to their needs.

There is no more debate on whether online catalogs are technically possible, desirable, economically viable, or acceptable to users. Nor is there any further discussion about the relative advantages and disadvantages of computer output microform (COM) catalogs and book catalogs. It is simply accepted that library catalogs must and will go online—and it is accepted by librarians, users, and governing bodies.

This rather sudden acceptance of online catalogs came as a result of several libraries' successful experience with them. These pioneer installations showed that online catalogs really worked and that users liked them. The proliferation and acceptance of personal computers on campus and in our society during the last several years also paved the way for the easy acceptance of online catalogs. Librarians used to fear faculty resistance to closing card catalogs and relying on online catalogs, but since faculty members have gained experience using microcomputers they are much better prepared to accept computerized catalogs. Now the concern of faculty and university administrators is that the library is not automating rapidly enough.

In the past, a library's automated circulation or acquisition system could stand alone because its purpose was to help librarians manage their internal operations. The users of the library were only involved indirectly. With the online catalog it is different. While the online catalog provides the staff with the means for managing the catalog, its ultimate purpose is to give users a means of access, not only to the library's collections, but also to a variety of other local and remote information resources. Thus, the online catalog must be an integral part of the integrated library system (ILS) and the ILS in turn must have effective interfaces with the parent institution's local area network (LAN) as well as with the growing variety of external library and commercial information networks.

Librarians used to be the sole driving force behind online catalogs, but now they are being joined by library users. In universities, acceptance of online catalogs has come about as a byproduct of the current movement to wire campuses and to make information processing technology available to all. In the last several years many universities have launched multimillion-dollar projects to connect all the key buildings on campus into a LAN. Although the initial case made for these campus networks sometimes made little or no mention of libraries, providing access to online library catalogs on the LAN has emerged as a high-priority goal. This is because many of the other uses that were projected for these university networks in the initial euphoric planning stages have been slow in coming and there is a pressing need to justify the large sums of money being spent to wire the campuses.

The current concern with online catalogs centers on which system to select and where to obtain the money required to buy, install, and operate it. A rapidly growing number of libraries is finding the financial resources they need to purchase systems. One prominent U.S. foundation has been the largest single source of grant funds for library systems and for catalog conversion. In the last three or four years it has made grants of up to $1.5 million to each of more than a dozen private universities and colleges to fund the purchase of library systems and the conversion of catalogs. The effect of these grants on library automation has been dramatic. It has created a wave of interest and momentum that is allowing integrated systems to be developed and installed and catalogs to be converted, at a rate that exceeds anything anticipated five years ago.

When I surveyed the integrated library systems market in

1984, I found a vast gap between promise and reality. I concluded that there were no finished integrated online library systems on the market for any size library and that there would not be any for the next year or two, no matter what the vendors were promising.[1] Since then there has been much progress in both ILS and online catalog developments, but it is still not possible for a large library to purchase either an ILS or an online catalog with all the basic features fully developed and functioning.

A number of systems, however, have online catalogs that are sufficiently developed to warrant being considered ready for use and libraries have been rushing to purchase and install them. Although these systems may not have all the features needed or desired in an online catalog, they are the only game in town and they are being used gladly and effectively by eager users in a growing number of libraries. It seems likely that several more or less complete integrated systems with quality online catalogs will be available from vendors in the next few years.

RECON: Foundation for Online Catalogs

Along with the acceptance of online catalogs has come acceptance of the need to convert card catalogs to machine-readable form and to make their contents accessible online. The debates about whether retrospective conversion (RECON) is necessary, desirable, or economically and technically feasible have effectively ended—except in a few of the largest and oldest libraries. For most libraries the question is no longer whether, but when, how, and at what price.

We now recognize that there are two kinds of RECON: one is like copy cataloging and the other is like original cataloging. In the first case we search for and find our manual records in an existing machine readable database such as the Online Computer Library Center (OCLC) or the Research Libraries Information Network (RLIN). In the second case we convert the unconverted. This requires keying the catalog records that cannot be found in the existing machine readable databases.

OCLC, RLIN, Utlas, and a number of other commercial vendors offer effective online and offline retrospective conversion services to libraries. The Association of Research Libraries has recently taken an initiative to encourage a coordinated national strategy for RECON with the participation of the Research Libraries Group, Inc. (RLG), OCLC, and the Library of Congress (LC), among others. Hundreds of libraries have already converted their catalogs and hundreds of others are in the process of doing so.

The experience of libraries with online catalogs has shown that once an online catalog is available—even a partial one—most users will prefer it and avoid using the old card catalog.[2,3] The online catalog will be the first, perhaps the only, choice of many readers, and it must therefore be as complete as possible. A successful online catalog raises the level of expectation of users. After they obtain catalog records for the library's books and journals, they want citations for journal articles, manuscripts, and anything that may be available. And soon they will be asking for access to the full text online, and not just the catalog records. Thus, after RECON will come the augmented catalog. And as users learn to access the library's online catalog from their personal computers they will begin to use it in new and unforeseen ways. Special software packages are already being used to download records from library catalogs to create personal catalogs and bibliographies.

Interfaced Components vs. Integrated Systems

We used to debate whether it was better to purchase an integrated system from a single vendor or to select the best functional modules from several different vendors and then link them together into an "integrated" system. That question is still open, but I believe it will eventually be resolved in favor of the integrated system from a single source. We are finding that the online catalog database needs to be maintained on a regular basis as a by-product of acquisitions, cataloging, and serials control, and the best way to achieve this is with an integrated system. Experience has shown that it is no trivial matter to make the interfaces that are required to link different system components into a well coordinated system.

Among the most vocal advocates of linking components are vendors who are not yet ready to offer complete integrated systems. As those vendors develop additional components, their commitment to building interfaces to the components of other vendors will diminish. Indeed, there will soon be no place in the market for vendors of stand-alone components such as the online catalog, circulation, or serials control. The basic offering will be the integrated system with all the principal functions. Integration is escalating to a higher level and must be redefined. The thrust now is toward linking integrated systems to one another and to the bibliographic utilities rather than interfacing the functional components of different vendor's systems.

Authority Control in Online Catalogs

A burning question a few years ago was whether, or at what level, authority control should take place.[4] Should it be at the network level, the library level, or the user level, that is, not at all? And should it exist as a separate reference file or be linked to the bibliographic records? The networks took different approaches to this question. OCLC, given the time and the way in which its database was formed, could never consider implementing a linked authority control system. RLIN had initially planned to develop a linked authorities system, but dropped those plans in favor of further improving the capabilities of its existing unlinked authority file. In contrast to these two responses, Utlas International now offers a highly effective linked authority control capability to its customers.

Some librarians question both the need for, and the ability of, libraries to maintain linked authority control in their online catalogs. They argue that the powerful search capabilities available in sophisticated online catalogs make authority control unnecessary. The debate goes on, but the emerging consensus is that linked authority control must be provided in the local online catalog.

Interfacing Local Systems and Networks

Until recently, it was still an open question whether utilities such as OCLC and RLG should provide centralized systems for such local library functions as acquisitions, serials control, circulation, and even online catalogs for individual libraries. OCLC recently announced its intention to discontinue its network-based acquisitions and serials control systems in favor of microcomputer systems. RLG will continue to provide its acquisition system for libraries that wish to use it, but the current consensus is that these are local functions that are best performed at the local library level.

Cataloging and catalog maintenance are a special case. Cataloging is logically a local library function, but most U.S. libraries are now cataloging on either OCLC or RLIN in order to get the benefits of shared cataloging and access to a large database to facilitate interlibrary loan (ILL) and other forms of resource sharing. The networks are firmly grounded and totally dependent upon shared cataloging for their continued existence. Although OCLC reports in its 1984/85 Annual Report that only 34% of its total revenues came from shared cataloging (in contrast to 50% 10 years ago), most of the rest of its revenue comes from services and products that could not be offered without a database sustained by shared cataloging. This is true of other networks as well. Most of their current revenue derives directly or indirectly from shared cataloging and the future viability of the network databases depends on its continuation. If libraries cease contributing their cataloging data, the network structure that was built so painstakingly over the last decade will begin to disintegrate.

Before OCLC and RLG libraries had their own local online cataloging systems, they had no capability and no incentive for making cataloging a local function, and the role of the networks was assured. As libraries implement their local systems, however, they will acquire both the capability and the incentive to do cataloging and catalog maintenance on them. The heavy costs of maintaining local systems will put enormous pressure on libraries to maximize their use of those systems and to minimize their use of network services in order to reduce their payments.

Inexpensive CD ROM systems containing the entire MARC file (in some cases supplemented by other large databases) are already being marketed for use as local cataloging and retrospective conversion tools. Services such as Bibliofile, Inc., and Library Systems and Services, Inc., are providing libraries with what appears to be an attractive alternative to using the shared cataloging capabilities of the networks. Several hundred smaller libraries have switched to these less expensive cataloging alternatives. As this trend accelerates, it will have significant effects on the way the OCLC and RLIN databases are used, financed and maintained in the future. Both corporations are, of course, implementing strategies to compensate for this anticipated change.

In the coming years libraries will want to regain control over the building and maintenance of their online catalog databases and to optimize the use of their local systems. How can they accomplish these desirable objectives without undermining the financial and programmatic viability of the networks and the network databases that provide them with shared cataloging and other essential network services? This is the major problem that U.S. libraries and their two principal networks will have to resolve in the coming years.

RLIN and OCLC are facing difficult transitions in the next few years. Both are in the process of implementing expensive upgrades of their hardware, software and telecommunications networks. RLIN's problem is not as great as that of OCLC, but its capital resources are far more limited. OCLC's Oxford Project is far more extensive and expensive, but OCLC apparently has the resources and reserves required to implement it. The future of both organizations depends on how soon and how effectively they are able to implement their respective system upgrades and meet the growing competition from local systems and other vendors of cataloging services.

The Canadian Alternative

The preceding discussion pertains largely to U.S. libraries and utilities. The vast majority of Canadian libraries use the Utlas system as their cataloging, database management, and interlibrary loan utility. The International Thompson Organization, Ltd., purchased Utlas, Inc., from the University of Toronto in 1985 and changed its name to Utlas International.

Utlas successfully achieved in 1985 what OCLC and RLIN are now striving to achieve, that is, a complete restructuring and updating of its technical environments, its software, and its telecommunications networks. As a result, Utlas is an effective utility with a state-of-the-art technical system and network. Its database contains more than 30 million records, half of which are estimated to be unique. It will be considerably enriched when the nearly 5 million REMARC records are added to it in 1987.

The Utlas database architecture is unique among the utilities. Unlike OCLC, which is a union catalog of records and locations, or RLIN, which clusters the full records of its participating libraries into a single file, Utlas stores and maintains the catalog of each library in a separate file. This permits each library to retain ownership and control over its own records. All files, including the U.S., Canadian, and U.K. MARC files, are searchable through a single unified index. This makes it possible for Utlas to offer linked authority control as well as a large variety of online and offline products tailored to the specific needs of its users.

The Walls Come Down: Managing the Online Library

Operating in an online library environment breaks down the barriers that have traditionally divided libraries and forces a degree of communication and coordination among departments and branch libraries, which is as healthy as it is unprecedented. We are already beginning to see a blurring of the boundaries between public services and technical services, as well as between the various units within technical services.

Online systems routinely produce management information and statistics that could be had only with difficulty if at all from manual systems. Almost for the first time, library managers are being provided with hard data on productivity, expenditures, and use of the collections, services, and facilities. The online catalog makes what libraries are and are not doing much more visible, not only to library management, but also to library users. It is easier to display our assets and harder to conceal our deficiencies.

Our successful use of technology raises the expectations and whets the appetites of users for new and better services. We cannot provide a sophisticated online catalog search and access system without also upgrading the library's document delivery services.

One of the most exciting prospects of managing a library that has an integrated system with an online catalog of all the library's holdings is the opportunity it provides for rethinking the way we use space in our buildings and the way we provide library services. For example, the card catalog used to be the key to the library's collections and services and the entire building was planned around it. The circulation, reference, acquisitions, cataloging, and serials functions all had to be located within easy reach of the card catalog. In the online environment the need to maintain these rigid space arrangements will disappear and we will have the freedom and flexibility to rearrange and revise our spaces and services. The pros and cons of branch libraries and the question of centralization and decentralization of collections and services in large university library systems will have to be thoroughly reconsidered in the online environment. We can begin to unburden ourselves of the heavy load of received ideas and conventional wisdom that we all acquired during our professional careers. There will be fresh starts for everybody.

The Linked Systems Project: Foundation for Systems Integration

The online catalog in the context of an integrated local system provides the infrastructure for a transition to a new stage of development in library systems and services. The online catalog is not only the gateway to the library's existing collections, but it can be used to provide access to remote and locally held machine-readable bibliographic, textual, and numeric data files, and to the universe of information resources beyond the library. Thus, in planning the online catalog it is essential to provide for effective interfaces and linkages with the systems of the parent institution, the library utilities, and the commercial information services. We must develop computer-to-computer linkages to enable our now separate local systems and networks to communicate with each other. Systems integration is the next frontier. It will provide the infrastructure for a new wave of development in library and information services. The Linked Systems Project (LSP) is the library field's first and most promising integration initiative.

The Linked Systems Project is a joint effort of LC, RLG, OCLC, and the Western Library Network (WLN). It was initiated in 1981 with funding from the Council on Library Resources, Inc. The goal of LSP is to develop and implement a set of standard protocols for computer-to-computer communication of data between networks and local systems. Just as the development and acceptance of the MARC formats were the foundation for library systems and network development in the 1970s, so the protocols of LSP will provide the foundation for the network of networks that will be the major development of the coming decade. The LSP protocols are, specifically, the Open Systems Interconnection (OSI) protocols being developed by the International Standards Organization (ISO) with the support and participation of U.S. standards groups. The LSP protocols will be used by the participants not only to link their own networks but as the standard means of linking these networks with local integrated library systems.

LSP got off to a slow start, but the technical foundations appear to be in place for a series of useful applications in the next few years. The first regular exchange of authority records between LC and RLG began in November 1985; this exchange is demonstrating the effectiveness of the underlying layers of the LSP protocols. Beginning in late 1987, a limited capability for internetwork searching will be in place. About that same time, a record-transfer capability will be implemented that will facilitate transfer among the networks of sets or groups of records. The capability to exchange interlibrary loan messages in a standard form among the networks is also scheduled for early development.

The work of implementing LSP protocols between GEAC and RLG's RLIN is well underway. GEAC is testing the links it has developed between its New York University Library installation and RLIN. A number of other systems vendors have made commitments to use the LSP protocols as a standard for linking their systems.

The technical problems that must be overcome before LSP provides effective links between the networks and local systems are many and formidable, and they are matched or even exceeded by the political, economic, and emotional problems that remain to be addressed.[5]

Notes

1. Richard De Gennaro, "Integrated Online Systems: Perspectives, Perceptions, and Practicalities," *Library Journal,* 1 February 1985, 33–40 [reprinted in this volume].

2. Charles R. Hildreth, "Pursuing the Ideal: First and Second Generation Online Public Access Catalogs," ALA LITA/RTSD Preconference: Online Catalogs, Online Reference, 23–24 June 1983 (typescript).

3. Emily G. Fayen, *The Online Catalog: Improving Public Access to Library Materials* (White Plains, N.Y.: Knowledge Industry Publications, 1983.

4. Henriette D. Avram, "Authority and its Place," *Journal of Academic Librarianship* 9, no. 6 (1984):331–35.

5. For a recent and perceptive review and analysis of the Linked Sys-

tems Project and other facets of linking local and network systems, see Susan K. Martin, *Library Networks, 1986–87* (White Plains, N.Y.: Knowledge Industry Publications, 1986, 153–60.

ELECTRONIC DATA FILES: THE NEW FRONTIER

The frontier of library automation has already moved beyond online catalogs, integrated systems, and retrospective conversion to reorganizing the library and its new online infrastructure to provide effective access to the rapidly growing universe of information in electronic form. This is still largely uncharted territory. I do not mean to minimize the effort and expense that libraries face in installing integrated library systems and converting their catalogs to machine-readable form. The need to do these things has been established, however, and the means of doing them are known and available. It is what lies beyond the integrated library system that is now occupying the creative energies of leading library and information managers.

The new challenge for libraries is to develop ways of using a library's online catalog and integrated systems infrastructure, with its connections to other networks and systems, to provide access to resources in electronic form and other new kinds of technology-based library and information services.

The age-old mission of libraries is to select, organize, preserve, and provide access to recorded knowledge in whatever form it takes. With effective online catalogs and integrated systems in place or on the way, librarians must explore and develop the ways and means of making information in electronic form a regular part of the library's collections and services. Librarians have developed standard and accepted conventions and methods for performing these curatorial and service functions for books, journals, manuscripts, microforms, maps, music scores, and audio recordings. They are still a long way, however, from developing equivalent capabilities for dealing with recorded knowledge in the rapidly growing and changing variety of electronic formats such as magnetic tapes and magnetic, optical, and digital disks.

Providing access to electronic data files (EDF) includes, but goes far beyond, the now conventional online searching of bibliographic data files available from commercial vendors and abstracting and indexing services. Libraries have been offering these search services since they became available in the early 1970s. What is new is that it is now technically and economically feasible to capture large quantities of bibliographic, textual, and numeric data in machine-readable form and to manipulate it, replicate it, and make it easily accessible on personal computers. EDF can be made accessible remotely via telecommunications and locally via high density magnetic, optical, and digital laser disk technologies.

Electronic data files, like print on paper, come in two principal forms: published and unpublished. Published EDF are products of the marketplace and access to them may be purchased for a fee. Many of them are bibliographic files, but there are a growing number of full text and numeric files. Unpublished files, in this context, are working files created by scholars primarily for their own use. Access to or copies of them may be available on a cost recovery basis once their existence and location is known, but they are difficult to use because they come in a wide variety of nonstandard formats and require special programs.

The library's task in the coming years is to develop appropriate policies, strategies, and technologies for providing access to published as well as unpublished electronic files just as it now provides access to other (and frequently closely related) published and unpublished materials in paper formats. The primary emphasis, however, must of necessity be on providing access to a limited selection of published data files. For many lesser used published and unpublished EDF, it will probably be less costly and more efficient to access them remotely via telecommunications. For other more heavily used files and portions of files, it will be more cost-effective to make copies of them available on local mainframe computers or, alternatively, on personal computers with magnetic storage or in CD ROM and other disk formats. Such disk-based information services will become commonplace in the next few years. Libraries may also contract with vendors for special licenses to mount portions of certain heavily used published bibliographic files, along with the required access software, and make them accessible on their online catalogs. The library utilities could play an important role in providing shared access to certain kinds of specialized data files that would be too expensive for any one library to acquire and maintain as a local resource.

Ideally, libraries would absorb the costs and provide free access to users of these electronic files in the same way that they provide free and unlimited access to their book, journal, and manuscript collections. The question of who pays for these new services is still unresolved, but I believe a consensus will emerge in favor of free access to locally held databases.

Selectivity and sharing will be the keys to success in every library's efforts to provide access to electronic data files. Just as no library can afford to acquire more than a small fraction of all published books and journals (and an even smaller fraction of manuscripts and archives), so no library can aspire to acquire or provide access to more than a small fraction of the rapidly growing files of published and unpublished information in electronic form. Any attempt on the part of librarians or any other single group to take responsibility for providing access to all or even a significant portion of the growing universe of electronic data files is doomed to failure.

A MARC format for Machine Readable Data Files (MRDF) on magnetic tapes has been developed and is in use. Magnetic tapes have not been accepted by libraries, however, and with good reason. They are nonpermanent and must be refreshed periodically, and they do not lend themselves to being dealt with by library conventions and physical facilities designed to handle print on paper and film. In contrast, the new CD ROM and other nonerasable optical and digital disks are exceptionally library-friendly. They are permanent carriers of vast stores of easily accessible and reproducible information. In addition to the information they contain, they can also carry their own code books, their own cataloging or indexes, and analytics of their contents.

Many libraries are trying to decide what magnetic tape files to acquire and catalog and how to make that cataloging available on their networks and local online catalogs. I think these initiatives, though commendable, are misplaced. Magnetic tapes have no future as permanent library resources. Optical and digital disk formats do because they are a form of permanent publication and they share many of the characteristics of print on paper. Nevertheless, the enormous quantity of information they can contain and the ways in which they can be accessed and used make these disks so fundamentally different from other conventional library formats that we need to develop new and imaginative ways of integrating them into the library environment. We cannot use conventional library cataloging rules and procedures any more than we can use conventional stacks and reading rooms.

Since libraries can barely afford to continue full-scale cataloging of traditional books and journals according to the current Anglo-American Cataloging Rules (AACR2), it is simply out of the question to extend those rules to a variety of complex electronic formats. Whether and how electronic data files will be cataloged is still an open question. We may well see a repetition of the experience of a decade or two ago when publishers of large microform collections distributed them without adequate cataloging. Libraries bought them, but could not afford to catalog them.

The current generation of electronic data files is accessible only to specialists and at considerable expense and trouble with the assistance of librarians and other specialist-intermediaries. The use of electronic data files will soar when they are finally available in a form that is inexpensive and easy to use. Just as word processing and spreadsheet programs on personal computers brought computing to ordinary faculty and students, so we need an equivalent breakthrough in technology to make electronic information readily available to users. That breakthrough will come when a variety of useful data files are published and distributed on CD ROM and other disk formats that can be used on personal computers and workstations. The information will then be directly accessible to users with minimal help needed from librarians or other specialists and intermediaries.

At the 1985 Information Industry Association conference, a Philips executive described the CD ROM as the most significant advance in publishing technology in the last 400 years. Such statements typify the euphoric reception that CD ROM has received since it appeared a few years ago. I would be more cautious in my assessment at this stage, but it is clear that the various optical and digital disk formats offer an incredibly powerful publishing and distribution capability that parallels print on paper with all its advantages of portability and permanence. By giving us direct local access to vast quantities of data, it eliminates many of the complexities and expenses associated with using remote online databases in a metered mode.

The CD ROM is an information package that has many of the desirable characteristics of the printed book and journal, and it can be acquired by libraries and made available to users in familiar ways. It promises to make more information available to more people at lower prices than ever before. The fixed-cost off-line environment will permit and encourage unlimited browsing. Users will have the opportunity to familiarize themselves with the contents of a database in a way that is not possible with online remote systems with the meter running. And with local databases users can easily download information and manipulate it with word processing software on their own workstations.

Although the future of optical and digital disk technology is obscured by hype and hyperbole, there is no question that, coupled with increasingly powerful personal computers and workstations, it will give us an extraordinary capability for storing, retrieving, and manipulating information.

LIBRARIES AND COMPUTING CENTERS IN THE WIRED UNIVERSITY

In the 1956 Hollywood comedy hit, *Desk Set,* Katharine Hepburn is the brainy head of a large TV network's reference library. Together with her capable staff she can answer practically any question. Along comes a computer engineer (Spencer Tracy) with a new electronic brain that the librarians fear will ultimately replace them and their library. After much amusing interplay, the librarian and the engineer fall in love and join forces and the computer is accepted by the librarians as a useful tool to help them do their jobs even better. In the end, the machine doesn't take over the library, the librarians take over the machine. And that is the way it has been happening ever since.

Librarians should have been reassured by the happy ending of the *Desk Set* story, but they weren't. For three decades they have been haunted by the specter of computer experts invading their turf and taking over the new and glamorous electronic information services and leaving them to take care of the library's traditional collections and services. In the last few years that specter has loomed larger than ever as universities finally discovered information technology and began wiring their campuses and hiring computer and information czars.

Those fears were and are largely unjustified. Computing center directors were too absorbed in their own technical and budgetary concerns to give much thought to automating library functions or to providing text-based electronic information services. Some tried and gave up when they learned how difficult it was. Others succeeded and were absorbed into the library profession. Moreover, there was not much electronic information available (other than bibliographic files), the technology for delivering it to users was complex and expensive, and the market for it was limited.

All that is changing now. The state of the art and economics of information technology have made enormous advances. A mass market for information in electronic form is in the making. There is a synergistic relationship between the number and usefulness of the electronic data files available and the cost, ease of use, and effectiveness of the means of accessing them. The range and quality of the electronic data files offered by commercial vendors are growing rapidly as is the demand for access to them. As the technology for satisfying that demand becomes commonplace—as it must for a mass market to develop—attention will shift from the technology for handling information to the quality and usefulness of the information itself.

Providing Access to Electronic Information

As information in electronic form becomes an important resource, responsibility for providing access to it is becoming a critical policy issue on university campuses. To librarians the issue is clear. They see electronic information as merely an additional dimension to their traditional library function. Information in electronic form, no less than information in print form, must be selected, organized, preserved, and made accessible to users—all traditional library functions. The collection and preservation functions apply as much to electronic information resources as they do to print resources, although they may be performed in new ways by a new kind of central electronic library. Moreover, electronic data files are usually used in conjunction with, or as a means of gaining access to, other library resources in print form. For example, a user who searches an online bibliographic file retrieves a list of citations to journal articles that must be obtained for the most part in or through a library.

The most important issue facing librarians is how to provide access to the growing volume of information in electronic form while at the same time maintaining traditional book and journal collections and services and providing appropriate links between the two. Librarians are alone in their attempt to bridge these two worlds.

New Players

There are other contenders on university campuses for a role in providing electronic information services. Among them are computing centers, computer resource centers, social science and humanities data centers, vice provosts for information and computing, and an assortment of newly created information technology officers in professional schools and academic departments. All of a sudden it seems that information is too important to be left solely in the hands of librarians and that everybody wants to get into the information business.

Just as we have seen many new commercial information providers enter the field and prosper in the last decade, so we can expect to see many new information providers in universities in the coming decade. Some of these newcomers will persevere and succeed in carving out important roles for themselves, and others will lose interest and withdraw when the glamor and hype of electronic information subsides. But those who succeed will not put the library out of business any more than the successful commercial information providers did.

The commercial information brokers did not replace libraries or even library reference departments. The document delivery services provided by the Institute for Scientific Information and University Microfilms, Inc., did not replace interlibrary loan (ILL) departments—in fact, ILL departments are among their best customers. On the other hand, the concept of the commercial "information supermarket," which was supposed to put libraries out of business in the 1970s, was never tried. And no one has yet succeeded fulfilling the ultimate dream of the technologists—putting the contents of the Library of Congress in a shoe box.

There is no reason for librarians to feel threatened by such niche players as computing resource centers, social science data archives, and centers for texts in the humanities. And the idea that the computing centers will take over the library and information function on university campuses is as unlikely today as it was at the time of *Desk Set.*

Cooperative Efforts amid Changing Environment

There are clear signs that the interests of libraries and computing centers are converging and that they need to develop an integrated approach to delivering electronic information to the university community. During the last ten years librarians have acquired considerable knowledge and experience in providing electronic information services to users, but they are beginning to look to computing centers to supply them with the computing power and technical expertise needed to support the acquisition and operation of local online electronic data files. Many of the larger libraries that are implementing online catalogs are contracting with their university computing centers to house and operate the necessary computer and communications equipment. This goes counter to the conventional wisdom of the 1970s that held, and with good reason, that libraries could not rely on computing centers to provide computing power unless the library owned the equipment. Computing centers have become more reliable and responsive in recent years and librarians more knowledgeable and assertive about their needs.

Computing centers are under considerable pressure to redefine and expand their role beyond that of supplying raw computing power from large mainframes. Cheap decentralized computing power in the form of super mini- and microcomputers is now available to users in their offices and laboratories and through connections to local area networks. This increased access means that many computing center directors must reach out for a role in providing electronic information services to users, either independently or through the library.

Articles advocating and predicting the merger of libraries and computing centers are becoming a regular feature in library and information journals.[1,2,3] Merger is beginning to be accepted uncritically as an idea whose time has come. I am not at all convinced of either the necessity or desirability of such mergers, and I do not think we are going to see many true mergers of libraries and computing centers in the next ten years. There is certainly a growing need for mutual support and collaboration, but whether that need justifies, or can be best accomplished by a full-scale merger of these two separate but related functions is still very much an open question on most campuses. Large universities have many libraries and many computing centers, each serving different needs and users. Moreover, some large libraries have their own computing centers. Which computing centers would merge with which libraries, and to what end and effect?

Columbia University set a precedent in 1986 when it moved

to merge its academic computing center with its university library under the leadership of Vice President Patricia Battin, the former university librarian. A number of other universities are trying to achieve more and better coordination by having their libraries and computing centers report to a senior officer with a title of vice president or vice provost for information technology. It remains to be seen how effective and lasting these organizational changes will be.

Bill Arms, one of the truly wise men of computing, concludes an article on scholarly information with this balanced view:

> "Scholarly information is too big a topic for universities to ignore. Moreover it has so many ramifications that leaving its planning to the library, or worse still to the computing center, is unlikely to provide good balance. The only sensible solution is a coordinated plan in which many parts of the university work toward the common goal of providing faculty and students with the information they need for study and research."[4]

The question is how to achieve that coordination. There will be no one best way for all universities. Some will achieve it through administrative reorganization, others through voluntary collaboration.

The Place of the Library in the University

Librarians have a tendency to think in simplistic either-or terms, that is, that the library has to be the sole information provider on campus or in society or it is out of business. Libraries have never had a monopoly on information in print form and they will not have one on information in electronic form. They were niche players in the print world—their niche was a selection of books, journals, and manuscripts—and they will be niche players in the electronic world.

It is still too early to define precisely what that niche will be, but libraries, unlike the other contenders, enjoy the advantage of having a well-defined and accepted mission as collector, organizer, preserver, and provider of information resources to the university community. They have buildings, budgets, staff, collections, years of experience, and a tradition of serving the needs of users.

Libraries are venerable, vital, and resilient institutions that have been around for 4000 years. Computing centers are less than 40 years old. Each university created a library early in its existence and continues to support it. A university's purpose is to create and transfer knowledge and the library supports that purpose with its array of collections and services. The library is the memory of human knowledge and achievement. Every university needs such a memory because it is central to its purpose and spirit. The library, in addition to its practical functions, also symbolizes the mission of the university. That is why it is frequently the largest and most impressive architectural monument on campus. Harvard's Widener Library, Yale's Sterling, Princeton's Firestone, Penn's Van Pelt—these are among the most imposing and important structures on their campuses, and they are visited and used for a variety of purposes by thousands of students and scholars each day. The concept of the library without walls is a pipe dream like workers "telecommuting" from their "electronic cottages" or the paperless society. The library is a place where people come to find research materials, to read and study, and to seek knowledge and inspiration.

The place of the library in the university's academic, administrative and budget structure is firmly established, well understood, and generally accepted by all members of a university community. There is no other function or organization that could mobilize or command an equivalent acceptance. The university library is flexible and adaptable and I believe it will continue to function as the university's primary information resource in the electronic age, just as it has in the print age.

References

1. Pat Moholt, "On Converging Paths: the Computing Center and the Library," *Journal of Academic Librarianship,* November 1985, 284–88.

2. Raymond K. Neff, "Merging Libraries and Computing Centers: Manifest Destiny or Manifestly Absurd?" *EDUCOM Bulletin,* Winter 1985, 8–12, 16.

3. C. Lee Jones, "Academic Libraries and Computing: A Time of Change," *EDUCOM Bulletin,* Spring 1985, 9–12. Jones advocates collaboration between libraries and computing centers, not merger.

4. William Y. Arms, "Scholarly Information," *EDUCOM Bulletin,* Fall/Winter 1983, 23.

PART TWO

ESSAYS AND PAPERS

LIBRARIES AND THE INFORMATION MARKETPLACE

LIBRARIES, TECHNOLOGY, AND THE INFORMATION MARKETPLACE

This article was written during a residency at the Villa Serboloni, the Rockefeller Foundation's Study Center in Bellagio, Italy, in the Spring of 1981. It was presented at Wesleyan University's Sesquicentennial Symposium, "Knowledge in an Information Era," on 12 February 1982. It was published in *Library Journal,* 1 June 1982, and reprinted in *Library Lit. 13—The Best of 1982,* edited by Bill Katz (Metuchen, N.J.: Scarecrow Press, 1983). It was also published in Danish in: *Bibliotek 70,* Bibliotekarforbundets blad 1982-15. It was reprinted in *National Forum: Phi Beta Kappa Journal,* summer 1983.

"Reports of my death are greatly exaggerated." With that brief rejoinder Mark Twain squelched the stories of his death that appeared in the New York papers when he was living in London in 1897. Unfortunately, it is not so easy to squelch the equally false reports of the death of libraries that have been appearing in the press since the 1960's. The truth is that libraries are alive and well and adapting to a changing world. They continue to serve millions of grateful users in both old ways and new, despite the ravages of inflation and budget cuts. It is true that a variety of new and expensive commercial information services are mushrooming to serve the special needs of business and industry, but for most of us, libraries are, and will be for years to come, the only affordable information game in town or on campus.

Beware of Predictions

There is a growing consensus among a new wave of technologists and futurists that books and other forms of print on paper are on their way out, along with the libraries and librarians whose stock in trade they are. They are telling us that books and libraries are being made obsolete or irrelevant by new electronic technologies in the hands of an aggressive new breed of information entrepreneurs. If this sounds familiar, it is because similar predictions were being made during the early 1960's in the first flush of enthusiasm that greeted computers and electronic media.

The current wave of predictions that electronic technology will soon replace books and libraries is inspired by a rapidly accelerating series of developments in that technology which multiplies its power while drastically reducing its costs. Among these developments are communications satellites, cable TV, inexpensive mass-storage in the form of optical and digital videodiscs, and powerful microcomputers on chips. With them we are acquiring a level of technology which fires the imagination and gives credence to even the most fanciful forecasts. In this heady environment, there is a danger that those responsible for the financial support of libraries will neglect or prematurely abandon traditional libraries in favor of more glamorous alternatives in promising, but as yet untested or even nonexistent, technologies.

We have seen many advances in information technology and we will see many more, but our experience in the last 20 years should teach us that they frequently take longer, cost more, or come in ways that we do not expect and cannot foresee. Meanwhile, we need to continue to develop and support libraries because they work, and because they contain the knowledge resources upon which our information society is based.

The experts who are predicting the early demise of books and libraries have impressive credentials. They include management consultants, information entrepreneurs, government officials, university professors, and popular futurists. Their forecasts of things to come are based on insights that come from solid knowledge and years of experience. They can neither be ignored nor accepted uncritically. There were two recent essays that put forecasting into perspective: "Why Forecasters Flubbed the 70's" (*Time,* January 21, 1980, p. 91–92) and "For the 1980's Beware All Expert Predictions" (*Science,* January 18, 1980, p. 287–88).

They remind us that no one, no matter how impressive his or her credentials, can predict the future with any degree of accuracy—and those who try are more frequently wrong than right. Life is full of surprises, and as a Chinese philosopher said: "Prediction very difficult, particularly of future."

These are the same kind of experts who, in the 1960's, were predicting the end of books and libraries along with a revolution in education based on teaching machines and new media. Important advances were made, but the extravagant forecasts failed to materialize. The publishing industry in the U.S. is thriving (it published about 15,000 titles in 1960 and 45,000 last year) and libraries have grown proportionately. The use of media in education is still a promise unfulfilled. And no one predicted the hand-held calculator or the energy crisis. Librarians will remember the bad timing of the predictions made by Florida Atlantic University, MIT's Project INTREX, the King Report on Technology in the Library of Congress, and countless others. We can all recall the predictions that were made about picture phones and flying family cars. Nothing dates faster than our fantasies about the future. It is also worth noting that during the 1960's, there was another, equally impressive and much larger body of experts, who thought that electronic and print media would coexist and complement each other, that books would survive, and that technology would reinforce and revitalize libraries. Those more conservative experts were closer to the mark, but moderate forecasts are never as newsworthy as the dramatic ones. There is a similar silent majority of experts at work today.

The most dramatic predictions about the future of books, libraries, and information technology tend to be made by men of thought rather than men of action—by writers, professors, and committees that do not have to implement their ideas in the marketplace and take personal responsibility for the results. Nothing is impossible to the man who does not have to do it. The practitioners who are charged with managing libraries and information businesses tend to be more realistic and focused in their views. Theoreticians who are not responsible and accountable for implementing change can afford to be a few years or even decades off in their predictions of the replacement of one technology, product, or service by another. They get credit for hitting close to the mark and even for trying. However, those in operating positions must have the right timing as well as the right idea and approach.

The right idea at the wrong time spells failure; they get no credit for near misses and no A's for effort. Entrepreneurs and managers have a limited number of options and opportunities. Resources committed to a course of action today are no longer available for tomorrow's more promising course. The stakes are higher; they bet their money, jobs, and sometimes even the future of their organizations on their decisions. And timing is everything. Here are some examples:

- One major science library building was planned and built in the late 1960's on the assumption that books and journals would soon be replaced by microforms and electronic media. No provision was made for normal growth of the collections beyond five years. The planners were wrong in their assumption and the building was inadequate.
- Another library was planned at that time with similar assumptions. A large computer room was provided in the basement in lieu of stacks. The room never housed a computer, but no real harm was done because it was converted to much-needed stack space a few years after the building was opened.
- In several instances, colleges and universities delayed or decided against building new library space in the 1960's on the assumption that books and libraries would be replaced by electronic media.
- Numerous business ventures in the information field have failed because they were based on faulty assumptions about technologies and markets. Two well-known examples are the ill-fated attempts by National Cash Register and the Encyclopaedia Britannica, Inc. to market ultrafiche libraries in the early 1970's.

Anyone can enjoy the intellectual sport of speculating about the wonders of information technology in the year 2000 and beyond, but some of us—managers, trustees, entrepreneurs—must try to see and assess the near-term future of that technology and make plans to use it appropriately. I define near-term future as five to ten years ahead; trying to see and plan beyond that is largely guesswork.

The insights and perspectives of theoreticians and futurists are useful; they help us to see and understand the complex, social, economic, and technological forces that are at work in our larger environment, but only those with authority and responsibility can decide how and when those forces might affect any particular enterprise. Futurists can tell us what the future may be like, but they cannot tell us how to get there or when to make our moves. The really important long-term decisions about any organization or institution must in the end be made by those responsible for it, based on their best judgment and as much practical wisdom as they can muster.

Books already have many strong and articulate defenders and need no help from me. I will merely cite two recent defenses of the book and move on to discuss the future of libraries in our emerging information society. They are Herbert S. Bailey's Bowker Lecture, "The Traditional Book in the Electronic Age"[1] and John P. Dessauer's "Why Books Won't Die."[2]

The "Paperless Society"

Prominent among and representative of those who are predicting an early end to books and libraries are Dr. F. Wilfrid Lancaster, Professor of Library Science at the University of Illinois, and Dr. Vincent E. Giuliano, Senior Consultant with Arthur D. Little, Inc. in Cambridge, Massachusetts. Lancaster sums up his views as follows:

> We are moving rather rapidly and quite inevitably toward a paperless society. Advances in computer science and in communications technology allow us to conceive of a global system in which reports of research and development activities are composed, published, disseminated, and used in a completely electronic mode. Paper need never exist in this communication environment. We are now in an interim stage in the natural evolution from print on paper to electronics.[3]

Lancaster is one of the most thoughtful and articulate spokesmen for this point of view.[4] To the extent that he is concerned with electronic systems in support of research and communication in science and technology and other scholarly areas in the 20-year time frame, his views have considerable validity as a conceptual framework. However, when he predicts the coming of a paperless society by the year 2000 and the passing of books, journals, and libraries in that timeframe, his writings must be treated as mere speculation or a kind of science fiction.

In any event, if the paperless society comes on Lancaster's

schedule, it will be but a small part of a massive transformation of our society and our way of life. In that society not only libraries, but the institutions and scholars they serve, may also become obsolete. We cannot do much now to prepare for that kind of massive change. The best we can do, and this is difficult enough, is to try to cope with the changes that are coming now and in the next few years, and to try to plan for those that are coming in the next five, ten, or even 15 years when books and paper will surely coexist with electronic media.

Giuliano's Manifesto

Giuliano is a spokesman of a different kind. A mathematician and former dean of a library school, he has been a consultant for Arthur D. Little, Inc. (ADL) on information technology and organizations for many years. In his position, he advises government, business, and professional societies and associations. He is well-known and respected as a friendly and articulate critic of libraries. When Giuliano concludes, as he did as the senior author of a recent ADL report entitled *Into the Information Age, A Perspective for Federal Action on Information,*[5] that libraries are becoming irrelevant and are not information age institutions, his views carry considerable authority and demand a response. The gist of Appendix A on the ADL report, which dealt with the future of libraries, was summarized in a popular and provocative *LJ* article by Giuliano entitled: "Manifesto for Librarians."[6]

Ironically, the ADL Report itself is a good example of the hazards of scenario writing and forecasting. The report was sponsored by the National Science Foundation in 1978 when the economy was booming and the federal government seemed poised to take decisive action in the information arena. Three years and one presidential election later the report was made obsolete by a massive shift in government spending policy.

Giuliano begins his Manifesto by calling attention to the paradox that libraries everywhere are in decline while our economy is booming and our society is rushing into the Information Age. Library budgets are being cut, use is down, staff are being laid off, hours are being reduced, branches are being closed, and book and journal purchases are being severely curtailed. Libraries, he says, are in year five (i.e. 1979) of a retrenchment and the situation is desperate and hopeless.

To Giuliano we are seeing the beginning of the end of libraries and librarians as we know them. He says we cannot save traditional libraries, which have outlived their usefulness anyway, but it is not too late for librarians to save themselves. They can do it either by transforming their libraries into centers for contemporary information which serve their constituents by any and all appropriate means and media, or by abandoning libraries completely and setting themselves up as independent information professionals or moving into other Information Age jobs.

Yes, libraries have been retrenching for the last several years; their situation is grim now and will get worse in the years ahead, but it is by no means desperate or hopeless. The reason for the decline of library budgets in the last five years is not that society has in some mysterious way concluded that libraries are not Information Age institutions and is, therefore, withdrawing support, as Giuliano and others suggest. Libraries are not being singled out for extinction; they are just being squeezed like other educational, cultural, and civic institutions on campuses and in towns and cities all across America.

There is no evidence of a nationwide decline in the use of libraries. If the use of libraries is down in some cities and regions, it is not because people no longer need or want them. Where use is down, it is largely due to changing demographic trends and shifting populations in the cities. There is a well-documented migration from the old cities of the Northeast and Mid-West to the Sun Belt states. The postwar babies have grown up. Just as many schools are closing for a lack of children to fill the classes, so library use is declining in many places for the same reason. Young people and students are among the heaviest library users, and as their numbers diminish, library use falls.

Giuliano seems to include all libraries and not just public libraries in his doomsday scenario. It is an oversimplification to talk about libraries as though they were all alike and share a uniform fate. It may seem obvious, but it should be said that public, academic, and special libraries serve different purposes and user groups and are funded from a wide variety of sources. Some libraries or types of libraries may be more vulnerable than others to the effects of recession and new technology. Naturally, if one starts with the premise, as Lancaster and Giuliano do, that print on paper is passing, then libraries, to the extent that they deal with this medium, are threatened. But no convincing case for the end of print on paper has been made. In any event, libraries—and especially research libraries of record—are still the only practical means of access to the records of human achievement and therefore merit society's continued support until other means are developed. The fact that library support is faltering is not necessarily proof that society's need and appreciation for libraries is declining. On the contrary, the need for libraries has never been greater and it is our duty to make the case for libraries and to make them worthy of continued support.

Information Professionals

Libraries and librarians do have a future, but not as the overarching information agencies and managers of our society. Let's face it, they never have been that. Some librarians and other information professionals are in danger of being carried away by the current rhetoric about the postindustrial or information society. There seems to be a widely held view that the library profession has an opportunity to become the principal manager of information in the information society, and that if it fails to seize that opportunity, it will richly deserve the early demise that is in store for it. I don't believe this. I believe that librarians are going to survive and continue to play the same essential but limited role in the future that they have in the past, but there simply is no chance that they will become the principal handlers of information as it is defined in the context of the information society.

The information society was defined into existence in the 1960's and 1970's by a number of prominent sociologists, futurists, economists, and Department of Commerce statisticians. They took an array of economic activities which used to be classed in various categories and grouped them together into a single category called the Information Sector of our economy. Thus, what used to be called commerce, communications, postal services, banking, publishing, education, libraries, and practically all other activities based on information transfer are now defined as the information sector of our economy. By that definition, information work employs half the labor force and accounts for half the GNP.

This may be a valid way of viewing our economy in the 1980's. The problem is that librarians and other information handlers started calling themselves "information professionals" and "information scientists" in the 1960's before the information society was born. With the coming of the information society, many of these information professionals have come to believe that they somehow have a right or a responsibility to go forth and become the principal managers of information in this newly defined sense. It will not happen that way. A banker is still a banker, a publisher is still a publisher, and a librarian is still a librarian, even though they are now all classed together as "information workers" in the information society.

Abandon Libraries?

According to Giuliano, "Establishing libraries and the library profession as central in our current information-oriented society does not take a big change; it requires only a shift in perspective, a change in view." He continues: "My main message is that it is time now for librarians to shift context—to start looking at the situation from the other end of the telescope. The shift has to be away from libraries and their institutional structures as the main focal point, towards providing contemporary and needed information services to their constituents, using whatever means, media, or structures that are appropriate. For some, the shift in perspective may mean working outside a library; for many, it may mean transforming a library institution."[7]

Giuliano is saying, in other words, that librarians should stop being librarians and become something else. That is becoming the conventional view among a growing number of librarians and particularly library school deans who are deemphasizing or even dropping the word library from the names of their schools.[8] They believe that a growing number of interesting and well-paying jobs will be outside the library institution in the future and that many librarians would do well to go after them. They may be right about the jobs, and librarians and prospective librarians cannot be blamed if they take that advice because librarianship is a poorly paid, low status, and somewhat overcrowded field now.

Those who remain committed to libraries will continue to define librarians as persons who are responsible for libraries and to define libraries as institutions which, in the aggregate, contain and provide access to man's recorded knowledge. At the present time, this recorded knowledge is largely in the form of print on paper, film, and in electronic forms. As technology advances, new forms will appear and the proportion of books to film, tapes, disks, and other media will change but the function of the library will continue. Libraries cannot exist without librarians and librarians cannot exist without libraries. The names may change in the future, but their functions will continue as long as there are users who need to gain access to the record in whatever form it takes and wherever it is located.

The continuing role and importance of libraries as the repositories of society's records in various forms was reconfirmed in a dramatic way in 1980 by a gift to the University of South Carolina Library of 60 million feet of film from the old 20th Century Fox Movietone News. Along with the film are 1.87 million index cards used by Movietone News librarians and the logs of the shooting turned in by the cameramen. The process of cataloging the film on the computer for use by scholars and the public is in progress.

Other examples of libraries taking responsibility for preserving the history and creations of new media and technology are the Library of Congress's unique collection of early Hollywood films, Vanderbilt University's growing archives of CBS television news broadcasts, and the University of Pennsylvania's recent acquisition of papers and records of John W. Mauchley, the co-inventor of the first stored-program computer.

Giuliano says that "reading is not now, and never was, the way most people get the information that counts to them." He may be right, but the information that counts always comes to them in one way or other from people who do read and have information. The ultimate source of most of that information is in printed form in libraries. He says that "for those who do read, the library is of less and less importance as a place to get reading" and cites the proliferation of mass-market paperbacks, book clubs, and specialized magazines. This may be true, but the authors of these books and magazine articles are among the heaviest library users—the Barbara Tuchmans and the Arthur Haleys could not write their books without libraries. The library has always been the court of last resort, the place where serious researchers go to find collections of materials that are not available elsewhere or that they cannot afford to buy.

Are Libraries Obsolete?

Of all the statements that Giuliano makes about the declining role of libraries in our society the one that is potentially the most important, and therefore the most demanding of a careful response, is this one: "As far as information institutions in our society go, libraries are of minor importance. Technology has already evolved to a point where access to most of the world's literature can be obtained within a couple of days through a combination of the online bibliographic searching utilities and vendor-supplied, computerized order fulfillment systems for books, documents, and periodical articles."[9]

If Giuliano is right on that point then libraries have indeed served their purpose and can quietly fade away. But I believe his assertion is totally unfounded. It is one of those "big lies" that should be refuted before it gains wide acceptance through repetition. The truth is that most of the new technology-based information businesses are still largely dependent on the library market for survival and the new information brokers ultimately rely on libraries as the source for most of the documents they supply to their clients. Just as Willie Sutton robbed banks because that is where they kept the money, so information brokers use libraries because that's where we keep the information—in the form of print on paper.

It is still true that libraries—public, academic, governmental, and special—provide the only means of access in our society to any book, journal, or document that is out of print or more than a few years old. Bookstores, even in major cities, carry only a small selection of current English language in-print books; the rest have to be ordered from publishers or jobbers. Most books and journals go out of print within a few years or even months of their publication and are no longer available except in libraries. The time that books are in print is decreasing rapidly as the cost of warehousing books increases. The recent Thor Power Tool Decision will make that time even shorter.

Most foreign books and journals and most specialized documents are not obtainable at all through regular book-trade channels. Only a few score major research libraries in North America and Europe manage to acquire and preserve any more than a small fraction of the universe of materials that are currently published.

The rest of the recent materials, when they are available at all, are dispersed among thousands of smaller and more specialized libraries in every country of the world. Older publications, from recent out-of-print titles all the way back to Gutenberg, can be obtained from libraries or not at all.

Document Delivery

Several major nonlibrary information vendors have recently gone into the document supply business for selected research materials. One of the most frequently cited as the forerunner of things to come is ISI (Institute for Scientific Information) in Philadelphia. ISI is a very successful computer-based information company which indexes a selection of some 6500 of the world's principal and most cited research journals. It publishes the results in a variety of printed services which are sold to individual subscribers and libraries. As a by-product of that process, and as an additional service to subscribers, it undertakes to supply them on request with copies of articles from most of the journals it indexes.

ISI's OATS Service (Original Article Tearsheets), as it is called, is used by researchers in business, industry, and government as a convenient means of obtaining papers which are cited in ISI's current awareness services. Libraries also use OATS as a convenient source for articles in journals they do not receive. ISI's prices and delivery times are reasonable. The problem is that ISI only retains these journal files for the latest four years and 6500 titles are but a small fraction of a larger universe of useful journal titles which is estimated at upward of 50–75,000 titles. No books or parts of books are included in the service. OATS is a specialized service which serves only a small fraction of the total need and demand for journal articles and poses no threat to libraries. In 1980, it filled 156,000 requests.

Chemical Abstracts Service has begun offering its subscribers an attractive Document Delivery Service covering the 12,500 periodicals and other documents it abstracts. The cost for a photocopy or document loan is $10–20 including copyright fees. Orders can be placed via the online search services, OCLC, or by Telex/TWX. The service is good and payment is convenient. Like OATS, libraries will use CAS service to purchase articles on demand from journals to which they do not subscribe.

The BLLD (British Library Lending Division) offers a

similar service from some 50,000 journal titles and a lending service from its growing collection of approximately one million books. Since it is a library of record, it attempts to maintain complete historic files of its journals. The BLLD charges fees for this service, but it is a subsidized library as are most libraries. In 1980, BLLD's journal service filled over a million orders of which one third came from outside the United Kingdom.

The Center for Research Libraries (CRL) in Chicago provides its members with a Journal Access Service which is backed-up by the BLLD via an online computer ordering system. Libraries are the principal users of both the CRL and BLLD services. CRL and BLLD are examples of a new kind of libraries' library which complement and expand the collections and services of other libraries and enable them to better serve their users.

Another type of major commercial work that is frequently cited as offering the kind of information age document delivery service which will make libraries obsolete is University Microfilms, Inc. (UMI), a Xerox company in Ann Arbor, Michigan. UMI started by microfilming and selling copies of dissertations along with *Dissertation Abstracts*. It later expanded its scope and added a service to film and supply back runs of journals and out-of-print books on demand. It creates its master negative file by filming books and journals, some of which it borrows from libraries. UMI does most of its business selling copies to libraries. UMI, Bell & Howell, and other similar firms could not exist without their library suppliers and customers, and the libraries would be poorer without their vast collections and useful services.

Some may see these growing document delivery services as a serious threat to the continued existence and development of libraries. I believe, on the contrary, that these new services are essential to the continued well-being of libraries. They enable libraries to gain easy access to a range of resources which would be out of reach otherwise.

Despite the commendable efforts of ISI, CAS, UMI, and some others, there is simply no way "to gain access to most of the world's literature within a couple of days" or even a couple of months unless one turns to conventional libraries—public, academic, special, or government—all of them subsidized one way or another and none of them profitable or even self-supporting. Libraries have a near-monopoly on one of the most important but unprofitable pieces of the information business—that of selecting, acquiring, preserving, organizing, and providing free access to the retrospective records of our civilization. That is both their strength and weakness. For-profit information companies will be offering an increasing number and range of information services, but it is unlikely that any of them will ever find it profitable to acquire and maintain comprehensive retrospective collections. UMI, Bell & Howell, and similar suppliers of research materials in microform seem to be exceptions, but their business is to supply libraries. If they develop truly effective electronic storage, retrieval, and delivery systems to replace their cumbersome film files, they could become the forerunners of commercial libraries of record. The viability of commercial libraries is a technical and economic issue, but their desirability in our society is a serious political issue which will be hotly debated.

Online Services

What about the online bibliographic searching utilities with their computerized ordering systems? Are these helping to put libraries out of business as Giuliano and others suggest? Let's look at the evidence.

In the 1960's and 1970's, most of the major indexing and abstracting services such as Index Medicus, Chemical Abstracts, Physics Abstracts, BIOSIS, etc., computerized their data handling and publishing operations and created machine readable data tapes as a by-product. NLM provides its own online MEDLARS service, but most of the other A&I services sell or lease these tapes to commercial online bibliographic utilities such as Lockheed's DIALOG, SDC's ORBIT, and BRS. These firms are sometimes referred to as data base spinners because they maintain searchable online files containing hundreds of bibliographic records. Searching these online data bases from computer terminals in libraries, offices, and laboratories in technologically advanced countries began in the 1970's and is becoming an accepted way of doing literature searches in all subjects, including the humanities. The vast majority of searches, however, continue to be done from the printed indexes in libraries. The product of these computer searches is a printout of a bibliography (sometimes with abstracts) of retrieved records numbering from a few to hundreds of items. It is important to note that a search retrieves only the bibliographic descriptions of documents and not the full text. Carrying the full text of documents online is still too expensive for all but a few specialized systems covering law and current news.

When searchers have their computer-produced bibliographies in hand, they must then turn to the library or send someone else to the library to retrieve the documents. They must turn to the library because that is still the only place where most of the documents can be found. Recently the three principal online search services began to offer online document ordering services whereby searchers can order copies of many of the documents listed in the bibliographies they retrieve. The database spinners do not supply the documents because they do not have them in their computer files. They are middlemen. They forward the orders to other vendors, sometimes the publisher, but usually to information brokers who, in turn, use conventional libraries as the source for filling most of them.

The bibliographic search function is being successfully computerized, but the document delivery function is not. It is still largely dependent on libraries, copying machines, postal services, interlibrary loan, and other nonelectronic methods. The promise of computerized bibliographic searching (and library networking) cannot be fully realized until the full text of documents is accessible in electronic form, either directly online or in secondary storage, and text access is brought into line with bibliographic access. Affordable telefacsimile or videodisc systems for storing, transmitting, and receiving copies of existing documents would be a significant interim advance, but several years may pass before they are widely available and used.

Six of the largest commercial journals publishers recently launched the ADONIS project, an exploratory effort to make the contents of their journals available on videodisc. However, no significant results can be expected for three to five years in my opinion.

There are at least two important full-text online systems already commercially available—LEXIS and NEXIS, services by Mead Data Central. They may be forerunners of things to come.[10] LEXIS is putting a growing corpus of legal materials, including compilations of statutes and decisions, online in full text. Searching and retrieval of these specialized, high-use materials is very effective and very expensive. NEXIS has the *New York Times,* the *Washington Post,* and a selection of other important current news and business publications searchable and retrievable online in full text.

As the cost of full text services come down, they will become increasingly important for specialized fields and uses. The commercial providers of such services may well skim off certain parts of the library business. However, they will also create and satisfy a whole new market for those services, and libraries will be a part of that market. Their gain need not be the library's loss.

The main business of Abstracting and Indexing (A&I) services is to abstract or index the literature of a subject field or discipline and to publish printed volumes which are then sold almost entirely to libraries. Sale or lease of the data base for online searching provides them a secondary source of income, but the cost of creating and maintaining the data bases are still covered largely by the sale of printed volumes. A BIOSIS official said in 1979, "if the full cost of producing the data base were to be recovered from online use, we would have to charge about $700 a connect hour."[11]

Clearly, the financial viability of both the A&I and the online search services rests firmly, now and for some years to come, on the sale of printed volumes to libraries. Eventually, the printed volumes may be superseded by electronic forms, but the library market will continue to be a major support for these services. Why? Because libraries are and will continue to be the principal point of interface between researchers and the collections being indexed and abstracted.

The bulk of online searches are done in libraries, by librarians, for library users. Online searching is enhanced reference service using new tools. Just as few users had the necessary skills or the desire to do their own searching in printed indices, so few users have the skills or the desire to do their own computer searches. Those library users are the same scholars and researchers who do the research and write the books and papers that are being abstracted and indexed by the A&I services. They work in universities, in commercial firms, in industrial laboratories, and government agencies—the same institutions that create and maintain research libraries. It is unlikely that the principal market for A&I services (whether in printed or online form), and for scholarly and scientific information will move somewhere far from libraries and those who own and use them.

Online searching is not putting libraries out of business; libraries have helped put online searching into business and constitute its principal market. The online services will, in turn, generate new business for themselves and for libraries.

Information Brokers

Another interesting development of the information society is the appearance on the scene of a growing number of small, for-profit information firms which provide a wide variety of specialized information services to commercial and industrial customers.[12] Staffed largely by people with library backgrounds, they do online literature searches, retrieve and supply documents, compile bibliographies, prepare research reports, and serve as consultants on a variety of information problems. The firms range in size from a freelance librarian working at home, to well-established firms like FIND/SVP, Inc., Warner-Eddison, Inc., and Information-on-Demand, Inc. They came into existence during the last 10–15 years when both the need and the means for fulfilling the need for special information services to special clients developed.

Some people see these aggressive new firms as a threat to libraries and possibly as the beginning of either a deplorable or a desirable trend toward the displacement of free libraries by for-profit vendors or "information supermarkets." These firms, in my view, pose no threat to libraries. Like online services, they supplement them by filling needs and demands that publicly supported libraries cannot and should not try to meet—providing special and expensive services to business, professional, and other users who can afford them.

Some libraries already sell special services to corporate users. A few others have spun off for-profit service units physically and administratively separate from their regular free public service departments. As times get harder, more libraries will try to find acceptable ways of earning money by selling services. The danger, of course, is that they could jeopardize or alienate their main support base while trying to earn this extra income.

Most librarians, however, will continue to find it offensive in principle and difficult in practice to offer a range of services to users, some of which are free and some of which carry high charges. Inevitably, those who can afford to pay will get preference and those who cannot will feel discriminated against and object. With some few exceptions, libraries are not and cannot be staffed sufficiently to offer, at no charge, the kinds of services provided by the new information brokers. If they did offer these special services, demand for them would quickly soar to a level where the staff would be overwhelmed and costs would exceed the budget. In these times of retrenchment, it is naïve to think that additional staff will be added to meet the added demands. Libraries cannot cope with too much success in their labor-intensive free reference services, but they can absorb considerable increases in the self-service use of their collections and facilities without incurring significant additional costs.

Information brokers rely heavily on library collections as their ultimate source for documents and information. It is no accident that FIND/SVP, one of the leaders in the field, is located across the street from the central research collections of New York Public Library. A number of others are located near and make extensive use of large research libraries such as the University of California at Berkeley and at Los Angeles. The brokers are a new kind of library user. Libraries support the brokers and make it possible for them to skim off a profitable piece of the library and information business.

The existence of these new commercial information services and consultants could, however, make it attractive for many corporations which now maintain their own special libraries to reduce or eliminate them in favor of purchasing services as needed—to rent a librarian instead of buying one.

Business vs. Free Libraries

Back in 1974, when the Information Industry Association (IIA) was young and brash, a spokesman testified at a hearing of the National Commission on Library and Information Science that pay libraries were inevitable and would be forced on the nation by the information explosion and technological advances.[13] The IIA was registering its disapproval of libraries giving scientific and technical information free to the public in competition with some of its members. More mature now, the IIA appears to have softened its position on this issue or at least lowered its voice. In any case, there is little evidence of pay libraries displacing free libraries or of free libraries inhibiting the development of for-profit information services.

If we have an information or knowledge society today, it is because we have had for the last century a strong tradition and an effective system of free public education with free libraries as an integral component. Giuliano and other prophets of the information society are now telling us that free libraries are a creation of the passing industrial society and are no longer viable institutions in our postindustrial information age. They are urging librarians to abandon the "free" library ethic and either go into the information business themselves or transform their libraries into self-supporting information businesses by charging fees for services. This is bad advice. The "free" library ethic is what makes libraries worthy of society's support. It would be a blunder and a tragedy for librarians to turn their backs on free libraries and try to make them self-supporting by charging fees. Subscription libraries have never flourished. Libraries are subsidized because a basic premise of American society has been that an informed citizenry is essential to a free society.

I do not agree with those libraries who insist as a matter of principle that libraries should never charge fees. Many libraries do charge fees for a variety of special services including photocopies, online computer searches, certain interlibrary loan requests, and the fines for overdue books. Some libraries also impose special card fees for those who come from outside the jurisdiction or constituency that the library is mandated to serve. In nearly all cases, those fees are primarily administrative devices and serve to ration or regulate the use of a special service that is partially subsidized, particularly expensive, or of limited availability. I know of no libraries that charge fees with the intention of becoming fully or even substantially self-supporting. It is hard to see how a library could earn enough money through fees to support its operations and building, and to accumulate the capital needed to replace physical plant and purchase new technology.

Librarians should not try to transform their libraries into businesses, and businessmen should not try to get into the library business. Libraries are by their very nature unprofitable. The use of new technology will not change the basic functions of libraries: to acquire, preserve, organize, and make available the records of human achievement. They also serve as powerful and visible symbols of our culture—a function that is frequently overlooked or undervalued.

This is not to say that businessmen cannot or should not make profits assisting librarians to do their job better by creating and selling them useful products and services. Nor is it to say that it is improper for businessmen to make profits by identifying and meeting special information needs and demands that libraries cannot adequately satisfy for lack of resources. Librarians and businessmen both have essential roles to play in the information society as they did in the industrial society, and those roles are complementary and mutually supportive. Librarians, publishers, and the new information entrepreneurs are not adversaries, or even competitors; they are natural allies who need each other's services and products in order to prosper.

The information business is not a static, zero sum game where one player's gain is necessarily another player's loss. It is a rapidly expanding business where all the players can win if they recognize and accept that each one has a unique and important contribution to make. We need to lay to rest the simplistic idea that electronic technology in the hands of information entrepreneurs is going to put an end to libraries. Libraries are here to stay, but by no means are they going to stay the same. Their basic functions will remain, but the ways and means they use to perform those functions will change in varying degrees and at varying speeds for different kinds of libraries in different countries.

Every library has specific functions to perform for a particular institution or constituency. Academic libraries, for example, exist to serve the educational and research activities of their parent institutions. Whether they survive or not depends less on what their librarians do or do not do about new technology than on the fate of the institutions that support them. If academic libraries become obsolete in the information society, it will be because the institutions they serve have also become obsolete or have no further use for them. Libraries cannot exist apart from the needs and wants of their constituents and they should cease to exist when they are no longer needed or used.

Changing Libraries

The stereotype of libraries as static, unchanging institutions is no longer valid if it ever was. Libraries, and especially large libraries of record, are necessarily and by nature conservative institutions. However, in the last hundred years they have demonstrated a remarkable ability to grow, to adapt to changing conditions, to meet new demands, and to implement new technologies. American research libraries used to double in size every 16 years on the average during the past century. Growth at that rate means constant change. Most of this country's library physical plant was replaced or built during the last 30 years and the large bulk of library collections have been accumulated during that same period. It is this explosive rate of growth and change that keeps our libraries in what may seem like a state of chronic fiscal and managerial crisis.

In 1950, there were fewer than 20 research libraries in the U.S. and Canada with more than one million volumes. In 1980, there were nearly 100. Derek Price concluded, in his much cited *Little Science, Big Science,* that most of the scientists who ever lived are alive and working.[14] The same can be said of librarians. And it may well be that most of the libraries in existence today were established or revitalized in the last 30 years and most of the books and journals in those libraries were published or acquired in the same period. Libraries and librarians as we know them are relatively new phenomena.

Far from being conservative, librarians are eager, sometimes too eager, to change and to embrace new technology. They are frequently dangerously ahead of their governing boards and users in that regard. If libraries were inflexible and slow to change, they would have been overwhelmed by the enormous increases in the number and variety of new publications and in the demands made on them for new and expanded services in the last 30 years. If libraries have been able to cope with this flood of publications and demands, which were largely created by new technology and a growing and more affluent population, it is because they have begun to make effective use of that same technology.

Partners for Progress

The relationship between librarians and the vendors who serve them has been badly strained in recent years. Two divisive issues were the "fair use" copying provisions of the Copyright Act of 1978 and the proposal by librarians for a federally-sponsored National Periodicals Center. These conflicts, now fortunately subsiding, have made it difficult for both camps to see how mutually dependent they are, and how effective their collaboration has been in the past and could be in the future. A brief look at some notable examples of past collaborations will help make this point.

In the 1950's, American research libraries were being overwhelmed by a flood of doctoral dissertations and the problems involved with acquiring and cataloging them. They helped and encouraged a small commercial firm, University Microfilms, Inc. to design and implement a systematic program to regain control of this valuable but difficult form of research material. UMI now systematically collects and microfilms the dissertations and provides full bibliographic control over them in its published and computerized version of *Dissertation Abstracts*. It also supplies films or paper copies on demand and this makes it unnecessary for individual libraries to acquire, organize, and preserve these numerous and elusive materials. Libraries save money while access to dissertations is now greatly facilitated.

Librarians pioneered the use of microfilm for document reproduction, preservation, and storage, and created a market for library materials in that form. Newspapers were a troublesome problem for libraries—expensive to acquire and service, space-consuming, and impermanent. They were a prime candidate for the new medium of microfilm. Libraries collaborated with other libraries and then with commercial vendors to film and make available copies of back files of thousands of newspaper titles which would otherwise have been lost. Current files of major newspapers, foreign and domestic, are now available through commercial vendors and the newspaper problem has been brought under control.

To provide the retrospective materials needed to strengthen the collections of existing libraries and to stock the thousands of new libraries that have come into existence in the last 30 years, a number of commercial vendors went into the business of reprinting and republishing out-of-print books and journals on a massive scale. Several of them made significant contributions to research by assembling, organizing, and publishing comprehensive collection of research materials that were heretofore practically inaccessible to scholars. The *Kress-Goldsmith Collection of Economic History*, *The Court of Arches Archives*, the collections contained in the *Short Title Catalogue of Books Published in English to 1600*, the *American*

Periodical Series, and the *Landmarks of Science* are but a few examples of the genre.

Other companies have greatly expanded the resources available to scholars through libraries by assembling and publishing in book form a whole array of library catalogs. The many catalogs of firms such as G. K. Hall, Edwards Brothers, Mansell, Kraus-Thompson, and others come to mind.

The commercial publishers of abstracting and indexing services make an incalculable contribution to the use of library collections by providing efficient access to materials that would be inaccessible without the existence of these services.

The rapidly growing mass of local, state, federal, and foreign government publications, which were threatening to inundate libraries, are being brought under control and made accessible to users through libraries by a number of imaginative commercial entrepreneurs who organize, index, and publish collections of them and guides in various paper, micro, electronic, and other formats.

There are other firms that expand the resources and service capabilities of libraries by providing and marketing a variety of specialized catalogs and collections of materials for specialized groups of users. These include art exhibition catalogs, photograph collections, annual reports of companies, college and university catalogs, and countless others.

Still other firms design and provide libraries with a variety of computer-based systems and services to perform a number of functions ranging from circulation control to searching online bibliographic data bases.

These are examples of the kind of collaboration that take place between libraries and vendors and the kinds of products and services that some of the new information industry firms are bringing to libraries and those who use them. Not to be overlooked, of course, are the thousands of traditional publishers of books and journals and the hundreds of library suppliers that have been serving libraries for decades.

In sum, commercial firms invest millions of dollars every year in developing and supplying new products and services to libraries and library users. Without that capital investment, and that investment of entrepreneurial know-how, libraries would, in fact, be the static and unchanging institutions that the conventional wisdom believes them to be.

With Andrew Carnegie as the all-time champion, American business and the philanthropic foundations it spawns and nurtures have been among the most generous and faithful supporters of libraries. Librarians could do more to recognize these friends and strengthen the special relationship that exists between libraries and business—a relationship that is unique to this country.

I have stressed the importance of the contributions that business makes in keeping libraries dynamic and responsive by expanding and improving library resources and services, but the flow of benefits is not one way. In 1980, 104,000 libraries spent $5.6 billion on staff, materials, and services.[15] The library market may not be large by some measures, but it is critically important for many of the businesses that serve it, and virtually the sole support of many others.

Libraries provide many of the new ideas and resources that make this business contribution possible. For example, librarians first started indexing and abstracting journal literature and parts of books (making "analytics" for card catalogs) on a cooperative basis in the 19th century. This approach proved to be impractical and the function was taken over and perfected by commercial firms and professional societies. A number of firms that provide computerized bibliographic services to libraries are dependent for their machine readable data on the Library of Congress's MARC tapes. Nearly all the applications of computer technology to library operations such as circulation, serials control, acquisitions, online cataloging, etc. have been (and continue to be) developed by libraries and library networks. When the systems prove their potential and create a market, commercial vendors develop and offer their own improved systems and services based on the best available designs and experience. Specialized reference services, book-form catalogs, and many forms of library equipment are among the other products and services that were pioneered by librarians and picked up by vendors.

In general, whenever a sufficient market is created to make a particular library service profitable, it will be skimmed off and provided by commercial vendors—usually, but not always, to the ultimate benefit of all concerned. Libraries can develop prototype products and services for local use, but they usually lack the capital, the organizational capability, and the legal mandate to complete the development and market them successfully.

The emergence in the last decade of not-for-profit library

corporations in the form of consortia and networks such as OCLC, Inc., the Research Libraries Group (RLG), and the Washington Library Network (WLN) has opened new possibilities for libraries to create and satisfy their own market for certain services without the intervention of commercial vendors. It is becoming increasingly clear, however, that in order to succeed, these library networks or utilities will have to adopt the same sound business practices and marketing skills that characterize successful vendors.[16]

The Library Future

Is information technology in the hands of commercial vendors making libraries obsolete? I conclude that libraries are and will continue to be a critical link in the chain that produces, preserves, and disseminates the knowledge that has created and sustains our information society. The information industry is not making libraries obsolete. Rather, it is revitalizing them with new technology and services. Libraries, in turn, nourish that industry with the knowledge resources it needs while providing a vital and ready initial market and distribution system for its new services and products. Libraries are becoming more, not less, important in our information society even though their relative share of the total information market is declining.

Technology in the hands of businessmen and librarians has been responsible for the enormous growth and expansion of libraries that has occurred since Gutenberg invented movable type and started mass-producing printed books in 1452. The coming of computer and related electronic technologies in the last two decades represents a development of similar magnitude and significance. The difference is that the development and effects of printing technology took centuries to unfold while the development and effects of electronic technology are compressed into decades and are transforming our entire technological society.

Gutenberg's invention made libraries as we know them necessary and possible. It is already a fact that our electronic computer technology is making new kinds of electronic "libraries" or data banks necessary and possible, but whether or when it will make Gutenberg-type libraries obsolete, nobody really knows. In the meantime, those charged with the stewardship of libraries should be assured that librarians and businessmen are using electronic technology to give libraries the enhanced capabilities they need to continue to function effectively in the present mode and to make the transition to new and as yet unknown future modes.

Notes

1. Bailey, Herbert S. "The Traditional Book in the Electronic Age," *Publishers Weekly,* December 5, 1977, p. 24–29.

2. Dessauer, John P. "Why Books Won't Die," *Publishers Weekly,* November 26, 1979, p. 23–25.

3. Lancaster, F. W., "Whither Libraries? or, Wither Libraries," *College and Research Libraries,* September 1978, p. 356.

4. See especially: Lancaster, F. W., *Toward Paperless Information Systems,* Academic Pr., 1978.

5. *Into the Information Age, A Perspective for Federal Action on Information.* Vincent Giuliano and others. Arthur D. Little, Inc. American Library Assn., 1978. (A Report prepared by Arthur D. Little, Inc. for the National Science Foundation).

6. Giuliano, Vincent E. "A Manifesto for Librarians," *LJ,* September 15, 1979, p. 1837–42.

7. Giuliano, "Manifesto," p. 1838.

8. See, for example, Pauline Wilson, "Taking the Library out of Library Education," *American Libraries,* June 1981, p. 321–25.

9. Giuliano, "Manifesto," p. 1840.

10. For a more conservative view see: Richard Kollin and Brett Butler, "Beyond full text: Indexing and Abstracting in Legal and other information services," a presentation at the 89th Cranfield Conference on Mechanized Information Transfer, 21–24 July 1981. Cranfield Institute of Technology, Cranfield, Bedford, UK.

11. Elias, A. W. "The Economics of Online Data Base Creation," Text of a presentation at the ASIS Annual Meeting in Minneapolis, Minnesota, October 16, 1979.

12. See Lorig Marangian and Richard W. Boss. *Fee-Based Information Services,* Bowker, 1980.

13. For a more complete discussion of this subject see: R. De Gennaro, "Pay Libraries and User Charges," *LJ,* February 15, 1975, p. 263–67 [reprinted in this volume].

14. Derek De Sola Price. *Little Science, Big Science.* Columbia Univ. Pr., 1963, p. 14.

15. Quirk, Dantia and Patricia Whitestone. *The Shrinking Library Dollar*. Knowledge Industry Pub., 1982. (Source: KIP Estimates based on data from US National Center for Education Statistics, Bureau of the Census, Department of Labor, and Association of Research Libraries).

16. See R. De Gennaro, "Libraries and Networks in Transition," *LJ*, May 15, 1981, p. 1045–49 [reprinted in this volume].

RESEARCH LIBRARIES ENTER THE INFORMATION AGE

This was the 1979 R.R. Bowker Memorial Lecture. It was published initially in *Library Journal,* 15 November 1979 and then published in the R.R. Bowker Lecture series in 1980. It was reprinted in *Library Lit. 10—The Best of 1979.*

Librarians have been engaged for a century in an unending and unequal struggle to keep up with the ever-increasing output of the world's publishing industry. However, it was not until the post-World War II period, when the problem became acute, that any real progress was made. Two major approaches to the problem of the growth of libraries and information began to emerge at that time. One was to use new technology to reproduce and make available the contents of publications in new ways—either by miniaturization through photography or by the use of electronics, or by a combination of the two. The other was to develop new or improved organizational mechanisms for sharing existing resources and thus make it possible for libraries to increase their effectiveness while limiting their rate of growth and expenditure. These mechanisms include interlibrary lending, cooperative collection development, and centralized pools of resources. A third and critical element has recently been added and that is the use of powerful new online computer and communications capabilities which have made possible the marriage of the first two approaches and the creation of effective library and information networks. It is through these networks that libraries will play their role in the information age that we are entering.

A Historical Perspective

In 1944, the true nature and dimensions of the library growth problem were dramatically and graphically set forth by Freemont Rider in a landmark work entitled *The Scholar and the Future of the Research Library*.[1] Rider was an author, publisher, inventor, and at that time librarian of Wesleyan University. By analyzing historical growth statistics, he was able to demonstrate that research libraries tended to grow at an exponential rate, causing them to double in size every sixteen years on the average. He drove that message home by calculating that at that rate of growth the Yale Library would contain 200 million volumes by the year 2040 and that its catalog would occupy eight acres of floor space.[2] But Rider not only defined the central problem of research libraries—exponential growth—he had a technical solution to offer. He visualized a research library of the future which would consist entirely of Microcards, which he had just invented. Rider's Microcards would have the catalog entry on one side and the text of the book on the other. It was an ingenious idea, but it proved to be impractical. Since then, other kinds of microcards and microfiche have found a useful place in libraries; they mitigated, but did not solve, the growth problem. Devising solutions to the problem of the growth of libraries and information has been a prime concern of librarians, scientists, engineers, inventors, and entrepreneurs ever since Rider called attention to it.

In 1945, a year after Rider's book appeared, the distinguished scientist Vannevar Bush published his now famous "As We May Think" article in *Atlantic Monthly*[3] in which he called attention to our desperate need to make more accessible the bewildering store of knowledge that we were so rapidly accumulating. His conceptual solution was a desk-size device called the "memex" in which a scientist or scholar could store and have instant access to the equivalent of a million volumes. The article had an immediate and lasting impact, and it has been cited as a seminal piece ever since. Rider and Bush dramatized the library and information problem in the postwar period and set the stage for the technical developments that followed.

Ralph Shaw, distinguished librarian and dean, used Bush's concept of the memex to develop an information retrieval device in the 1950's called the "Rapid Selector,"[4] It was a machine which tried to combine electronic search and selection from a large store of research material on reels of high-reduction film. It, too, was ahead of its time. Around 1970, MIT's Project INTREX tried, among other things, to develop a workable version of the Memex-Rapid Selector idea using computer searching to access a microform store.[5]

Freemont Rider's Microcard idea surfaced again in a Rand Corporation Memorandum in 1968[6] which outlined a proposal for an inexpensive one million volume research library on high-reduction microfiche (ultrafiche) and a special catalog to go with it. Library Resources, Inc. (a subsidiary of Encyclopædia Britannica), and the National Cash Register Company each developed and marketed ultrafiche libraries. Both ventures failed—probably because micro reading technology continues to lag behind micro storage technology.

While the technologists and entrepreneurs were seeking, with limited results, the solution to the growth and access problem through miniaturization of print and mechanization of the bibliographic access to it, library administrators were seeking cooperative resource-sharing solutions to the same intractable problem.

The origins of these efforts go back to the beginnings of American librarianship in 1876. Basil Stuart-Stubbs, the librarian of the University of British Columbia, recently surveyed the largely futile efforts of American library leaders to create a viable system of interlibrary loan and a national lending library.[7] Stubbs found that the idea of interlibrary loan was first proposed by Samuel S. Green of Worcester in 1876, and that of a national lending library by Ernest C. Richardson, the librarian of Princeton University, in 1899. Richardson said a lending library for libraries would lead to the "direct encouragement of scientific research, a very large national economy in removing unnecessary duplication of purchases, and an improvement of existing libraries by removing the strain of competition and of effort to cover the whole ground."[8] Stubbs remarked wryly that the idea of a lending library for libraries was such a good one that it is still being discussed seventy-five years later. (It is still being discussed in the United States, but it has been successfully implemented in Britain, and it works—just as Richardson said it would. It is called The British Library Lending Division [BLLD].)

Actually, just as there has been considerable progress in the photographic miniaturization of some categories of library resources such as newspapers, journals, manuscripts, etc., so there has been considerable improvement in the interlibrary lending system through computerized networks in recent years. The continued growth of the Center for Research Libraries (CRL), a libraries' library for little-used research materials in Chicago, attests to the progress that has been made in centralized resource-sharing. Founded in 1949, the CRL now has a collection of over three million volumes which it makes available to over one hundred dues-paying member libraries. But these are limited successes, and the problem of the growth of research libraries and information remains as intractable as ever. As a matter of fact, while these improvements were being made during the last thirty-five years, scholarly publishing increased to a flood, and many research libraries experienced two or more doubling cycles.

Everyone knows that the exponential growth in libraries—doubling every fifteen to twenty years—cannot be sustained indefinitely, but the problem is to predict accurately when and how the pattern will change. Freemont Rider and other library leaders of the 1940's thought that the turndown would come in a decade or two. They had been projecting forward to the future their experience in libraries in the depression years, but the war came and created a new environment. They, like the rest of us, had no way of foreseeing that the postwar education boom and the expansionary effects of "Sputnik" would not only postpone the day of reckoning for the growth of existing research libraries, but would also lead to the birth of scores of new academic libraries with research missions.

But the boom ended in the 1970's, and escalating inflation, declining support for libraries, and declining student enrollment are setting the stage for a new depression in higher education in the 1980's and with it an absolute necessity for research libraries to develop new and more effective ways of fulfilling their mission. However, another and even more significant trend of the 1970's will provide the means for libraries to face that future with optimism. In the 1970's, we witnessed an almost explosive development of new computer, communications, and micrographic technologies. As the growth accelerates in the 1980's, it will provide at affordable costs the advanced electronic technologies needed to implement successfully the several approaches for controlling growth and sharing resources that were marginal or unsuccessful in the past.

The coincidence of this fiscal crisis, increasing demands, and the availability of these new and powerful technical capabilities promise new approaches to the problems of growth and information overload, a redefinition of the function of research libraries, and a wide-ranging restructuring and realignment of their traditional relationships.

This upheaval in the library world began in earnest eight years ago when OCLC, Inc., established the first successful online computer utility. Organizations that are already in place and others yet to come will play a vital role in the transition of libraries from the 3 × 5 card technology of the nineteenth century to the online computer catalog and network technology of our emerging information age.

My purpose is not to review the history of library technology and resource sharing, nor is it to try to forecast the distant future. Librarianship is a practical art, and being a library director forces me to deal with realities and to focus on visible and achievable goals. I am concerned here with technology and resource sharing and how they will be used to help solve the chronic growth problem of research libraries in the next decade. I use the term "growth problem" as a kind of shorthand to indicate the entire range of problems caused by the exponential growth of research libraries and the recorded knowledge they are attempting to control and make accessible to their users. Seen from another perspective, the problem is that research libraries can no longer continue to grow rapidly enough to keep pace with the flood of new publications and the expanding needs of researchers. They can no longer even hope to fulfill their traditional promise of providing convenient and free access to all the publications their users need and demand.

Although the problem of growth and access is most acute and most pressing in large research libraries, it is by no means theirs exclusively. Other libraries have similar problems, but they have managed to cope better because they have been willing and able to depend on the collections of the research libraries to back up their own resources. Having these collections to rely on permits them to be more selective in acquisitions and in the services they offer. But now their back-up research libraries are suffering from overly ambitious collection policies, over-promising services, diminishing support, increasing use, and all the various problems of growth. The research libraries need to develop their own back-up libraries or central-resource pools and other resource-sharing mechanisms, not only for their own benefit, but also for the benefit of the thousands of other libraries that depend on them. What is needed, and what is being developed and implemented, is a new library technology based on electronics as well as fundamental restructuring of traditional library goals, relationships, and dependencies; this restructuring will force all libraries to undergo a major transformation in the coming decade.

Strategies for Resource Sharing

There is now a clear consensus among librarians that no library, however large or rich, can afford to strive for or hope to achieve self-sufficiency, and therefore increasingly effective means of resource sharing must be developed to meet the needs of users. The objective of resource sharing is to control the growth of library collections and expenditures while at the same time meeeting a growing demand for access to an ever-expanding universe of resources. The urgent questions now before the library community are: What kind of resource sharing should we have, and who will pay for it? Some librarians argue that the best and most cost-effective resource-sharing strategy is to develop one or more libraries or central pools of resources modelled after the membership-supported Center for Research Libraries (CRL) or the government-subsidized British Library Lending Division (BLLD). The proposed National Periodicals Center (NPC) introduced as Title II-D of the Higher Education Act is an example of a central pool which would be available directly to all libraries on equal terms.

Other librarians argue for a more decentralized approach which would involve substantial improvement, through electronic networking, of the traditional hierarchical interlibrary loan system and other forms of library cooperation such as shared collection-development and the establishment of centers of specialization in existing libraries.

The Central Pool Approach

Professor Herman H. Fussler of the University of Chicago, whose work is informed by a rare combination of research and years of experience as a library director, has made an extraordinary contribution to the literature of resource sharing and technology in his excellent 1973 report to the Sloan Foundation entitled *Research Libraries and Technology*.[9] Fussler was among the first to comprehend the complexity of resource sharing, to categorize and describe the various approaches to it, and to analyze the advantages and disadvantages of each approach. His view is that the most cost-effective solution of the growth problem would be the establishment of "one (or a very few) national pools for the acquisition of current serial and monographic resources on as comprehensive basis as possible. . . ." Such a facility, he argues, would (1) extend the resource base of all libraries, (2) enable individual libraries to be more selective in acquisitions, (3) enable local libraries to increase duplication of high-demand material, and (4) limit space and processing costs to important and high-demand materials. Access to the pool would be by loan or photocopying as appropriate and in conformity with the law.[10]

He goes on to say that "there is a professional library view that a superior alternative to the central 'pool' concept for back-up resources would be based upon a division of acquisition responsibilities among existing libraries by designated subject fields or other categories and a reliance upon an improved system of interlibrary loan for access. This seems likely to be more costly in aggregate expenditures, less stable, less reliable, less comprehensive, and a slower system of access for contemporary and future acquisitions than a centralized pool approach."[11]

Fussler concedes that it is not feasible to duplicate the present resources of the major research libraries for a central pool and that access to those retrospective materials will need to be provided by improved systems of interlibrary loan and photocopying. Since 1973, when Fussler wrote this, there have been substantial improvements in interlibrary location and communication systems through online networks. Interestingly, the initial effects of these improvements have been to increase access to current materials, but in time and as more and more retrospective records are added to the network data bases, access to retrospective materials will also be enhanced.

Fussler's logic was basically sound. The central pool approach—if it could have been implemented at the time he proposed it—would certainly have been more cost effective for sharing current research material (which in time becomes retrospective) than the traditional interlibrary loan system. But interlibrary loan is being improved through the use of computerized data bases and communication systems, and new text transmission systems at affordable costs are in the offing. Moreover, the idea of a central pool or a library for libraries was first proposed eighty years ago, and it is still not a reality. Some Association of Research Library leaders were advocating a comprehensive National Libraries Resources Center[12] in the 1970's, but it was deemed to be too ambitious and controversial, and the proposal that emerged was for a more limited National Periodicals Center.

The proposed NPC would acquire, preserve, and make available through loan and photocopying some 50,000 periodicals. The NPC would be merely one important component in our complex system of resource sharing. It will not handle all or even a majority of this country's interlibrary loan demand for periodicals. Local, state, regional, and national library networks for resource sharing will be needed and will flourish as other important components of the system. It is important to keep the NPC in perspective. It is not something that will replace libraries and networks, end copyright, and destroy the publishing and information industries. It is just another library; only instead of serving users who walk in off the street, it will function like a mail-order house for other libraries.

Finally, it seems likely that the central pool approach as advocated by Fussler would probably have to be funded and administered by the federal government. I am becoming increasingly pessimistic about the ability of the library community to come to a consensus on any major program and line up the political support needed to get it through Congress. Moreover, the more I observe the workings of the federal government, the more convinced I become that the solutions to our research library problems are not to be found primarily in Washington, but in the voluntary and concerted actions of a peer group of research libraries with a common need and a common interest in solving those problems.

The Cooperative Network Approach

The network approach to resource sharing is based largely on traditional interlibrary lending. Before the advent of online networks in the 1970's, interlibrary loan was in theory oriented in a hierarchical system extending from locality to state and region, with the largest research libraries at the apex serving as collections of last resort. In practice, however, borrowing libraries would routinely send their requests directly to the larger libraries which were most likely to have the needed titles. This process created an imbalance in load distribution, and the larger libraries became large net lenders. Since these major resource libraries were (and still are) expected to provide this expensive service without compensation of any kind, they lacked the means and the incentive to give it a high priority. Filling free interlibrary loan requests has always been a burdensome extra for the large net lenders, and this, along with slow request and delivery systems, and cumbersome record-keeping procedures, accounts for the low esteem in which traditional interlibrary loan has always been held.

But interlibrary loan is making a major advance thanks to the development of online networks like OCLC, Inc., The Research Libraries Group (RLG), the Washington Library Network (WLN), and others. The networks are creating online union catalogs of the recently acquired holdings of their members. Borrowing libraries on the OCLC network can now look up book locations in the data base and transmit their requests by computer. The online network systems are beginning to equalize the load somewhat between the large and small libraries, speed up communications, and simplify procedures and record keeping. In time, the online systems will be further improved, the data bases will increase in size and richness, and interlibrary loan traffic will increase.

A parallel development of great significance began in 1975 when commercial vendors started offering online bibliographic search services. As online searching becomes a way of life in libraries, the expectations and demands of library users for publications will increase. The online searches are bringing to the attention of users quantities of citations to a variety of publications that their libraries—even the largest of them—will simply not have and which they will routinely try to obtain through the interlibrary loan system.

When interlibrary loan becomes a high-volume activity in the online searching and network environment of the 1980's, librarians will finally have to put a realistic price on it. Interlibrary loan is based on the moral obligation that librarians have to share their resources. It could be "free" as long as the requests were few in number and the costs to the lending libraries were trivial.

But this is no longer the case. Libraries still have a moral obligation to share their resources, but borrowing libraries will have to assume a moral obligation to pay the costs involved. Putting a price on interlibrary loan will put some necessary limits on the traffic and force borrowing libraries to compare the cost of borrowing an in-print book with the cost of buying it. This would be no bad thing for authors, publishers, and net lenders.

I doubt that even the improved network-based interlibrary loan system will be capable of handling the volume of traffic that will be generated by the online search services. I also doubt that research-library collections will be able to keep pace with the rapidly expanding growth and scope of the online data bases. The end product of many online searches is, and will continue to be, lists of citations that include many documents that conventional libraries do not have and cannot easily obtain. This need will probably be met when online bibliographic searching combines with online ordering and eventually with online electronic delivery of the documents cited. This service, when it comes, will most likely be provided to libraries and users by commercial vendors.[13]

OCLC, Inc. OCLC, Inc., started life in 1968 as a statewide consortium of college and university libraries in Ohio, and brought up the first online shared-cataloging system in 1971. The glamour and value of being "online" was irresistible, and after some cautious hesitation libraries outside Ohio flocked to join, and OCLC became an instant technical and financial success.

In the early 1970's, a number of existing consortia as well as several newly formed ones adopted as their purpose the replication of the successful OCLC online system. Among the early ones were NELINET, PALINET, PRLC, SOLINET, AMIGOS, and SUNY-OCLC. When OCLC demonstrated a willingness and a capacity to serve, in utility-like fashion, the needs of the members of these consortia, they set aside the idea of replication and became instead regional service centers devoted mainly to brokering OCLC services. There are some twenty such networks.

When OCLC went online in 1971, it started building a comprehensive bibliographic data base—a central computerized national union catalog—as a by-product of its shared cataloging system. The interlibrary loan communications subsystem, mentioned earlier, was implemented in 1979 and is beginning to alter existing borrowing patterns. The traditional spirit of cooperation among librarians will be sorely taxed as they start receiving an increasing number of computerized interlibrary loan requests from distant libraries with which they have no ties or affinity. The question of who pays—heretofore muted because of low volume and pride of ownership—will become urgent and divisive among idealistic librarians as the volume and cost of interlibrary lending increase.

With OCLC's remarkable achievements in recent years, many librarians have come to believe that it is capable of serving all the needs of all types of libraries, and that it should be given a clear track to become *the* national library network. They hold that the parallel development of other special purpose or regional networks is wasteful and unnecessary. While I have great admiration for OCLC's extraordinary technical, organization, and business achievements, I do not believe that it, or any other single utility or network, can meet all the varied needs of multitype libraries in our rapidly changing information world.

I said recently in an article on current developments on the library network scene that ". . . there is a role and a market for a number of general, special, and regional networks. A single monolithic national network embracing all libraries and providing all types of services is neither a realistic expectation nor a desirable goal in this country with its traditions of diversity and free enterprise."[14] I continue to think that diversity and friendly competition will be beneficial rather than wasteful or destructive.

In spite of its deserved popularity and success, the OCLC system and organization have certain limitations which many of its customers have tolerated only because there was no alternative available. OCLC is still the "only game in town" for most libraries. The principal limitation of the OCLC organization, in my opinion, is precisely that quality that has contributed so greatly to its rapid growth and financial success, namely, that it functions as a general library computer utility which provides services to any library that agrees to do all its cataloging on the system. Thus, it must try to be all things to all libraries, and this will become increasingly difficult as users become more sophisticated and demanding, and the variety and complexity of their needs outpace OCLC's ability to respond to them.

A few of the regional networks that broker OCLC services are already becoming dissatisfied and are exploring the feasibility of mounting their own online systems to support their regional programs and activities. Some large research libraries have long felt the need for a specialized research libraries consortium and an online network system to support its programs. They are joining the expanding Research Libraries Group (RLG) and using its Research Libraries Information Network (RLIN) to meet their needs. Because of their size, complexity, and special mission, these libraries feel that they need the more sophisticated capabilities of the RLIN system including a high-quality data base with authority control, the ability to build and maintain online catalogs of their own holdings with copy-specific and other local information, and powerful subject search capabilities.

Although the OCLC data base has some 5 million unique bibliographic records and over 45 million locations, limitations in the structure of the system and data base preclude the contributed records of a particular library from being linked or kept together as an accessible file. In other words, OCLC functions well as a shared cataloging and card and tape production system, and as a national union catalog, but it cannot provide an online catalog of the holdings of each of the contributing libraries. OCLC has announced its intention to develop this and other improved capabilities in the future.

Despite its limitations, OCLC is providing some 2,000 user libraries with an increasing variety of extremely valuable online services at reasonable costs. With gross sales over $25 million a year, a staff of 400, and a new building under construction, OCLC's future seems assured.

The Research Libraries Group, Inc. RLG is a rapidly expanding nationwide partnership of research universities and major independent research libraries dedicated to providing its owner-members with the capacity to work together to solve common problems and to support the needs of scholars, researchers, and students in the decades ahead.[15] In its present form, it is the result of the merger in 1978 of the original Research Libraries Group and the Stanford BALLOTS system into a single organization. Its central offices and computer facilities are located at Stanford University, and its Bibliographic Center is at Yale.

RLG already has twelve institutional members (Yale, Columbia, New York Public Library, Stanford, Michigan, Pennsylvania, Princeton, Dartmouth, Rutgers, Iowa, Brigham Young, and Colorado State) and is actively seeking to expand its membership in the next few years to include a majority of the nation's research universities and their libraries. Although start-up funds in the form of grants and loans were provided by a consortium of leading foundations, RLG plans to become self-supporting within the next several years. RLG has four active programs:

1. Cooperative collection development and management;
2. Shared access to collections;
3. Preservation of research materials;
4. Creation and implementation of new bibliographic tools.

The Research Libraries Information Network (RLIN), which is RLG's online network system, is the first product of the bibliographic tools program, and it serves as the means of linking the members together and facilitating the accomplishment of the other programs. The RLIN system exists to serve the present and future goals of RLG. Is it the means to an end as well as an end in itself. As new approaches to information access are developed, RLG will incorporate the best of them into its programs and technological support systems.

RLG has a powerful organizational capability. It seeks to meld the collections and staffs of its owner-members into a single voluntary coordinated library system in which their collective strengths and resources can be mobilized to serve the needs of researchers. Eventually the separate collections of the member libraries will be viewed by users in the various libraries as a single large distributed collection to which they can gain efficient access via online searching and the rapid delivery of requested items as well as by personal visits.

Libraries that join RLG are not turning away from regional or multitype library cooperation and resource sharing. Although the primary obligation of RLG members must be to their own constituencies and to one another, participation in RLG's programs will improve their ability to respond more effectively to the special research needs of other libraries and users. To this end, RLG is seeking to negotiate appropriate interfaces with OCLC and other networks so that RLG libraries can continue to add their holdings to the OCLC data base and thereby make their resources known and available to OCLC libraries, and serve as links between the networks.

Agreements to cooperate and share data have already been concluded between RLG, The Washington Library Network (WLN), and the California Authority for Systems and Services (CLASS), but OCLC has certain policies that discourage or even preclude sharing data or developing computer linkages with other networks. But in my opinion, such linkages between the networks are not only necessary and inevitable, but also in the best interests of all concerned; it, therefore, seems likely that OCLC will in time soften its position on this critical issue.

Publishers and Information Entrepreneurs vs. Librarians

While librarians have been struggling mightily during the last fifteen years to create new organizations and to use advanced technologies to improve their ability to serve users and share resources in a time of rampant inflation and diminishing support, it seems that the leaders of the publishing and information industries have been struggling almost as mightily to keep them from succeeding. What is going on? What is behind this war between librarians and their former friends, the publishers?

Until the early 1960's, librarians and publishers were allies in the relatively stable world of books and publishing. Book people still owned and managed the publishing houses, and they treated librarians as valued customers; librarians in turn viewed publishers as the indispensable suppliers of their main stock in trade—books and journals. Librarians were conservative people and libraries were traditional places. There was no "information industry" and no Information Industry Association (ILA).

A decade later, in the 1970's, the scene had changed completely. Librarians were using copying machines and online networks for resource sharing and improved interlibrary lending. They were lobbying the Congress to fund the creation of an NPC in response to the proliferation of new journal titles, escalating prices, and diminishing support. Meanwhile, publishers and librarians were fighting fiercely over the copyright issue. The ILA was attacking librarians for giving away services that its members were now trying to sell and was lobbying Congress in opposition to the NPC.

What happened in the decade of the 1960's to cause this schism and subsequent guerilla warfare between publishers and ILA people on the one hand and librarians on the other?

The 1960's was the decade during which it became both necessary and possible to create, produce, manipulate, and sell vast quantities of information with the aid of new technologies based on advances in reprography, electronic computers, and telecommunications. The Xerox machine was the first wave, the computer was the second, and telecommunications was the third. Now they are all combining to produce powerful new and heretofore unimagined capabilities for information handling. Our information world, of which libraries are a diminishing part, is expanding and undergoing a series of revolutionary changes and developments that are beyond our ability to comprehend and control.

Each of the three main groups of players in this drama is trying to take maximum advantage of the opportunities offered by these new and rapidly developing technologies. As a matter of fact, the divisions and skirmishing between subgroups of the main participants, such as research librarians and public librarians, and between one kind of publisher and another, and between competing groups of commercial vendors of information products and services are part of the same picture. It is a struggle for position, profits, and survival in the emerging information world of the 1980's. For librarians particularly, it is a struggle to come to terms with new technology and expanding opportunities and needs in the face of shrinking support. But there are no real villains in this drama.

Librarians have perhaps not yet fully grasped the extent to which advanced technology and expanding needs and markets are changing that part of the information world they once dominated but which they now have to share with an increasing number and variety of information vendors. As the information world grows, the relative influence of traditional libraries diminishes. It is hard for librarians to accept this. It is hard for them to see that it may no longer be possible or justifiable to continue with free interlibrary loan or to equate traditional interlibrary lending with sophisticated online network systems and eventually with the transmission of textual data by telefacsimile or other electronic means. Electrostatic copying at a nickel a page is no longer merely a substitute for manual note-taking; it is a new means of disseminating and communicating information. An NPC in the online information environment of the 1980's cannot be equated completely with the Center for Research Libraries of the 1950's or even the British Library Lending Division of the 1970's. Librarians need to re-examine and re-assess their traditional attitudes and conventional thinking on these issues and adopt positions that are more in tune with the economic and technical realities of our emerging electronic information age.

On the other hand, publishers and the information industry must face up to and accept the reality that subsidized libraries and information services are and will remain an integral part of the information world, and that libraries have every right and obligation to develop and use new organizations and new technologies for resource sharing in the service of their users. It is unrealistic and unreasonable for the commercial vendors to call for an end to subsidized libraries and library services in favor of "pay libraries." The new commercial information industry has grown and prospered alongside subsidized libraries and there is no reason why both cannot continue to coexist and expand in a world in which the quantity and market for information are increasing at a prodigious rate.

Publishers have little to fear from improved library resource-sharing systems. Human nature being what it is, librarians are going to continue to ask for and spend as much money as they can get from their funding authorities for books and journals and other materials with or without an NPC or other new and improved resource-sharing capabilities. However, as Fussler so succinctly puts it, "Scholarly and trade publishers simply cannot expect libraries to provide access in traditional ways to an unlimited number of traditionally generated publications at steadily increasing prices. Furthermore, the costs of collecting and distributing reasonable royalties for the photocopying of serial articles or short extracts from monographs seem likely to approximate or exceed the probable revenue."[16]

The considerable benefits that libraries bring to the commercial sector as purchasers and disseminators of their products and services must surely outweigh any minor damages they may do as competitors. Libraries spent more than a billion dollars on books, journals, and other materials and services last year. The publishing and information industries stand to lose more in the long run by alienating and weakening their good customers, the libraries, than they will gain by trying to collect trivial sums from copyright fees or discouraging resource sharing. To put the matter more plainly, it must surely be better for business to cultivate the library market than to kill it.

The debate that has raged between librarians and their new adversaries, the publishers and the information entrepreneurs, during the last decade has been harmful and distracting; but it has also served to inform and educate the participants about the interrelatedness of their interests and the problems they face as they try to find a secure place in a rapidly changing and expanding information environment. There is no point in trying to gloss over the real issues that still divide us, but we may be ready to begin a dialogue that would lead first to a better understanding of our mutual concerns and interests and then perhaps to a new and less adversarial working relationship.

Conclusion

It has been said that for every complex problem there is always a simple solution—and it is always wrong. But I think we have finally learned from the efforts of Rider, Bush, Shaw, INTREX, and other pioneers that the library problem is complex and changing and there is no simple or final solution to it. The solution is not in miniaturization, or in a new black box like memex, or in any one new technical capability like telefacsimile or video disk; nor is it in a new central library like the NPC, or in any one network like OCLC or RLG; and neither will it come by simply unleashing the for-profit sector. The solutions will come through the optimal use of all of these various technologies and capabilities, and librarians are well on their way to adopting, developing, and successfully implementing a number of them. We have begun our painful and exciting transition to the new information age of the 1980's and beyond.

Notes

1. Freemont Rider, *The Scholar and the Future of the Research Library: A Problem and Its Solution,* New York, Hadham Press, 1944.

2. Rider, p. 12.

3. Vannevar Bush, "As We May Think." *Atlantic Monthly,* July 1945, p. 101–108.

4. Ralph R. Shaw, "Machines and the Bibliographical Problems of the Twentieth Century." In: L. N. Ridenour, R. R. Shaw, and A. G. Hill, *Bibliography in an Age of Science,* Urbana, University of Illinois Press, 1951.

5. *INTREX: Report of a Planning Conference on Information Transfer Experiments,* September 3, 1965, edited by Carl F. J. Overhage and R. Joyce Harman, Cambridge, M.I.T. Press, 1965, p. 61–91.

6. David G. Hays, *A Billion Books for Education in America and the World: A Proposal.* Memorandum RM 5574-RC. Santa Monica, California, Rand Corporation, April 1968.

7. Basil Stuart-Stubbs, "An Historical Look at Resource Sharing," *Library Trends,* April 1975, p. 649–663.

8. Stubbs, p. 652–3.

9. Herman H. Fussler, *Research Libraries and Technology: A Report to the Sloan Foundation.* Chicago, University of Chicago Press, 1973.

10. Fussler, p. 76.

11. Fussler, p. 77–78.

12. Richard De Gennaro, "Austerity, Technology, and Resource Sharing: Research Libraries Face the Future," *Library Journal,* May 15, 1975, p. 922 [reprinted in this volume].

13. For a current and comprehensive overview of networks see: Susan K. Martin, *Library Networks 1978–79,* White Plains, New York, Knowledge Industry Publications, 1978.

14. Richard De Gennaro, "From Monopoly to Competition: The Changing Library Network Scene," *Library Journal,* June 1, 1979, p. 1217 [reprinted in this volume].

15. For a more detailed account of RLG and its current status see: *The Research Libraries Group, Inc.: Progress Report, June 1979.* Encina Commons, Stanford University, Stanford, California.

16. Herman H. Fussler, "Current Research Library Issues." In: Herman H. Fussler and Harrison Bryan, *Reflections on the Future of Research Libraries: Two Essays.* Monash University, Australia, 1978.

COPYRIGHT, RESOURCE SHARING, AND HARD TIMES: A VIEW FROM THE FIELD

This article was first published in *American Libraries,* September 1977, and was the first place winner in round 2 of the *American Libraries'* Prize Article Competition. It was subsequently reprinted in *Technology and Copyright,* edited by G. P. Bush and R. H. Dreyfuss (Mt. Airy, Md.: Lomond Books, 1979), and in *The Copyright Dilemma,* edited by H. S. White (Chicago: ALA, 1978).

As the effective date (1 January 1978) of the new copyright law approached, there was widespread fear that it would drastically limit the ability of librarians to provide copying facilities to users and to engage in interlibrary resource sharing of journal articles. The purpose of this article, which was written in 1977, was to allay those fears and to reassure librarians that they would be able to continue doing business as usual under the new law's "fair use" provision. This turned out to be the case.

Remember the bumper stickers from the Vietnam peace movement that read: SUPPOSE THEY GAVE A WAR AND NOBODY CAME? We could use a slogan like that to help end the long and tedious war of words between publishers and librarians over the fair use and photocopying provisions of the new copyright act scheduled to take effect Jan. 1, 1978. Our line might read: SUPPOSE THEY GAVE A NEW COPYRIGHT ACT AND NOBODY CARED?

That is what may happen once the unfounded fears of publishers and librarians are allayed, after they live with the new law for a time and discover that it changes virtually nothing for the vast majority of them. But right now, many librarians are worried sick about complying with the new act. It is complex and unfamiliar and they are afraid of the adverse effects that its provisions, particularly sections 107 and 108(g), may have on their capacity to continue to serve their users in the usual ways. These fears stem in part from the publicity given to early proposed versions of these sections which threatened to seriously limit or even put an end to "fair use" and photocopying in interlibrary loan operations.

But that is behind us now. I believe the final versions of Sections 107 and 108 and the CONTU (National Commission on New Technological Uses of Copyrighted Works) guidelines are fair to authors, publishers, and librarians. I can foresee no real difficulties in complying with them, and I do not believe they will significantly affect the way most libraries serve their readers. Most librarians in public and academic libraries need not try to master the legal intricacies of the new law or make elaborate preparations to implement it. The leaders of library associations and their legal counsel should and will continue to monitor and influence the implementation and administration of the new law; the rest of us should set the copyright issue aside and turn our attention and energies to other more critical matters.

The continued preoccupation of the entire profession with the copyright issue will keep us from coming to grips with such pressing problems as escalating book and journal prices, mounting losses from theft and mutilation, rising personnel costs, and steadily declining budgetary support. In comparison to these and other problems facing us, the impact of the new copyright law on libraries will be relatively slight.

This article has three aims. One is to put the matter of copyright and its possible effects on libraries and publishers into better perspective by offering some data and insights based on practical experience. Another is to urge librarians to exercise freely all the considerable rights the new law grants them. They should not permit themselves to be bullied or bluffed by hard-sell publishers into buying copyright privileges they have always had and which the new law reinforces.

The third is to dispel some of the exaggerated fears and hopes that many publishers and librarians have about the harmful or beneficial effects that increasingly effective interlibrary loan, networking, and other resource sharing mechanisms will have on their finances and operations. Some publishers fear that library resource sharing will seriously diminish their sales, and some librarians hope it will save them from the crunch that is coming. Both views are quite unrealistic.

A special issue of the ALA *Washington Newsletter* on the new copyright law is a readily available and indispensable guide through the complexities of the law.[1] It contains brief highlights of the new law, a librarian's guide to it, recommended preparations for compliance, and excerpts from the law and the Congressional Reports, including the CONTU guidelines. (Also of interest is the May 1977 issue of *American Libraries,* which has two excellent articles—one by librarian Edward G. Holley and the other by attorney Lewis I. Flacks).

Our interest here is not the entire copyright law but the Fair Use provisions and CONTU guidelines.

In Section 107 of the new law, the Fair Use doctrine is given statutory recognition for the first time. Section 108 defines the conditions and limitations under which libraries can make copies for their internal use and for interlibrary loan. Nothing in Section 108 limits a library's right to fair use of copyrighted works; the new law reconfirms most of the rights librarians had before and even extends some. It prohibits "systematic copying," but this is no problem since few academic or public libraries engage in systematic copying as defined in Section 108(g)(2) and the CONTU guidelines. Librarians are not liable for the unsupervised use of photocopying machines by the public provided certain conditions are observed. This is no change from the existing situation.

The most serious limitation appears not in the law itself but in the CONTU guidelines. They recommend that libraries refrain from copying for interlibrary loan purposes more than five articles a year from the last five years of a periodical title. They also stipulate that libraries must maintain records to document this use, placing responsibility for monitoring it on the requesting library.

What do these limitations really mean in practical terms? If the University of Pennsylvania Library's experience is in any way typical, then the five-copy limitation will not seriously interfere with present interlibrary loan operations and services to users. Why not? Because interlibrary loan photocopying constitutes a relatively insignificant portion of our total library use to begin with. Once we exclude from our total interlibrary loan photocopying requests those that are from monographs, from journals more than five years old, and from journals to which we subscribe, those that are left will be a fraction of the total—probably on the order of 20 percent. As much as 90–95 percent of this remaining 20 percent will be requests for less than six articles from the same title in a year. Of the 5–10 percent that may exceed the guideline limitation, some will be for articles from journals whose authors and publishers have no interest in collecting royalties and from foreign journals which may not be part of the copy payment system. In the end, a library could simply decline to request more than five copies from any journal which required the payment of royalties.

The record keeping required by the guidelines is a trivial matter and involves only maintaining and analyzing a file of the third copy of a new three-part interlibrary loan form being developed. It could produce some interesting and unexpected consequences by reminding librarians that their subscription decisions should be based more heavily on actual rather than potential use. Librarians may identify some journals whose use will justify a subscription and a great many others whose lack of use will invite cancellation.[2]

These conclusions are based on statistics gathered at the University of Pennsylvania and on a report of a sampling of photocopy statistics from Cornell.

Applying the CONTU guidelines (no more than five copies in a year from the last five years of any title), the Penn Interlibrary Loan Office (excluding law and medicine) reported the following experience during the year from July 1976 through June 1977.

Articles were requested from 247 different journal titles. Of these, 173, or 70 percent, of the journals had requests for only one article. Five had five requests, two had six requests, and one had seven requests.[3]

In every case where five or more articles were requested from a single journal, all were requested by one person working on a specific project or an annual review article. A total of four scholars were responsible for all these requests; two of them were working on annual review articles. The authors and publishers of the papers requested for mention in annual review articles should be grateful to have their works cited and not ask for royalties. Indeed, there were only two commercial journals listed which might qualify for royalty payments. The rest were nonprofit, scholarly journals. In any event, this type of occasional use hardly justifies a library subscription.

Last year Penn circulated nearly a half million volumes from its libraries, not including periodical volumes, which do not circulate. The total of home loans and in-building use is estimated at well over 2 million. During that year, we borrowed 2,941 volumes and received 3,726 photocopies from other libraries for a total of 6,667 items (less than one half of one percent of our total use). We lent 7,748 volumes to other libraries and filled 7,682 photocopy requests—a total of 15,430 items. The sum of all such extramural transactions—borrowings as well as loans—was 22,000, or about one percent of our intramural use.

Penn is not unusual in this regard. The median for all university members of the Association of Research Libraries in 1975–76 was 11,053 loans and 4,505 borrowings for a total of 15,558 transactions. All these libraries together borrowed a half million originals and photocopies in 1975–76 and lent about two million.[4] Even if this traffic doubled or tripled in the next few years, it would still be relatively insignificant.

What can we conclude from these gross statistics? Simply that the total amount of interlibrary loan and photocopying in lieu of interlibrary loan is and will always remain a relatively small fraction of total library use. The point is not to denigrate the value of interlibrary loan or resource sharing but to emphasize the overriding importance of the local use of local collections. Publishers, librarians, and particularly network planners should keep this basic truth in mind.

Last year Penn spent $1.3 million on books and journals, and we would spend considerably more if we had it. We *saved* virtually nothing by using interlibrary loan and photocopying; in fact, we incurred substantial additional costs using interlibrary loan channels to obtain some important little used materials for a small number of users who might otherwise have done without.

The Cornell experience with the five-copy limit is similar to Penn's. Madeline Cohen Oakley, Cornell interlibrary loan librarian, reports it as follows:

> The new restrictions on photocopying pose a number of questions of policy and procedure for Cornell interlibrary loan operations. Although the five article per journal photocopy limit may seem low, our experience in interlibrary borrowing (the term covers both requests for loans and for photocopy) at Olin Library has not, for the most, borne this out. We consider a journal for which we have four or more photocopy requests to be "frequently ordered," and all such journals are considered for purchase. To give an example, in the 1975–76 fiscal year, out of a total of 188 different journal titles represented in one group of requests, only 15 involved multiple copies of four or more from one journal. (Of those 15, nine were for more than five articles.)[5]

She remarks that the five-copy limit is likely to be a problem when a single individual or research project requires a number of articles from one journal. This is Penn's view as well. In such cases some restrictions will have to be worked out, and our users will have to be more selective in what they request. In those few cases for which we need to exceed the five-copy limit, we can presumably choose to pay a reasonable royalty to a payments center or do without. The mechanism for paying such fees may be in place by next year.

Ben H. Weil of Exxon has been appointed to serve as program director of the Association of American Publishers/Technical-Scientific-Medical Copy Payments Center Task Force, which is expected to design and implement a payments system by Jan. 1, 1978. The center would periodically invoice the users and allocate the payment, less a processing charge, to the appropriate publisher. I wish the center luck, but my guess is that the processing charges will far exceed the royalty payments, making it a financially precarious service.

It is important that librarians exercise all the rights and privileges the new law gives them, uninhibited by the fear of lawsuits or by an exaggerated or misplaced sense of fair play and justice. Section 504(c)2 relieves employees of nonprofit libraries from personal liability in case of infringement if they had reasonable grounds for believing their use of the work was a fair use under section 107. Librarians must comply with the law as best they understand it, but they are not obliged to do more. Even the Internal Revenue Service encourages taxpayers to take all the deductions to which they are legally entitled and to pay no more taxes than the law requires.

Some librarians are already going to great lengths to establish elaborate and far more restrictive procedures than the law or the guidelines require in order to demonstrate their intent to comply with the spirit as well as the letter of the law and to show their good faith. By so doing, they appear defensive and guilty and run the risk of losing the rights they are too cautious to exercise. It is a time for boldness and courage.

Based on past performances, we can be sure that the publishers will not be cautious or diffident about exercising all the rights the law allows them—and even a bit more on occasion. Last fall, for example, one publisher misrepresented the provisions of the new law in a letter to his library customers offering to sell copying privileges that the law already gives them as a right.

Libraries that buy subscriptions with strings attached may forfeit their rights under the law. "Section 108(f)(4) states that the rights of reproduction granted libraries by Section 108 do not override any contractual obligations assumed by the library at the time it obtained a work for its collections. In view of this provision, libraries must be especially sensitive to the conditions under which they purchase materials, and before executing an agreement which would limit their rights under the copyright law, should consult with their legal counsel." (ALA *Washington Newsletter,* Nov. 15, 1976, p. 5)

Actually, urging librarians to consult legal counsel in copyright matters may not be very helpful advice. Because of its vagueness and complexity, the new copyright law is already being called the "full employment act" of the legal profession. The typical general counsel that the typical librarian can turn to will know little about copyright law and will, as lawyers customarily do when asked for advice by cautious clients on unfamiliar matters, give the most conservative opinion possible in order to be on the safe side. Librarians might be better advised in general to study the appropriate sections of the law and have the courage to make their own interpretations and decisions.

The vast majority of academic and public librarians have nothing to fear from the new copyright law. The amount and kind of copying that is done in their libraries will not require the payment of any significant amount of royalties, and the dollar amounts involved will be trivial to publishers and library users alike. I think that time and experience will show that the whole publisher-librarian controversy over copyright, interlibrary loan, and photocopying was the result of fear and misunderstanding—largely on the part of the publishers.

Resource sharing and networking give publishers nightmares and librarians hope, but both groups are seriously overestimating the impact these developments will have on their financial status and operations. Inflationary trends and market forces at work will soon change much of our current thinking about these matters.

Libraries are cutting their expenditures for books and journals because they do not have the acquisition funds, not because they are able to get them on interlibrary loan or from the Center for Research Libraries or the British Library Lending Division. Publishers still have the idea that if they can discourage interlibrary loan and photocopying, libraries will be forced to spend more money to buy books and journals. This is bunk. Libraries can't spend money they don't have. The fact is that with or without effective sharing mechanisms, with rising prices and declining support, libraries simply do not have the funds to maintain their previous acquisitions levels. If we cannot afford to buy the materials our users need, and if the law prohibits us from borrowing or photocopying what we do not own, our users will simply have to do without. Moreover, there is an increasing recognition that librarians and faculty members alike have developed highly exaggerated notions of the size, range, and depth of the library collections that are actually needed by most library users.

Studies have repeatedly shown that in general roughly 80 percent of the demands on a library can be satisfied by 20 percent of the collection. Journal use is a Bradford type distribution where a small number of journal titles account for a large percentage of the use. Eugene Garfield's numerous studies using citation analysis and the Institute for Scientific Information's *Journal Citation Reports* also corroborate it. A recent University of Pittsburgh Library School study showed that 44 percent of the books acquired by one major research library in 1969 were never used in the succeeding five-year period.[6] A recent study at Penn produced a comparable finding. Earlier studies on library use by Fussler,[7] Trueswell,[8] and Buckland[9] showed similar use patterns.

Large collections confer status and prestige on librarians and faculty members alike, but when the budget crunch comes to a library, many of these status purchases will be foregone or dropped and the essentials will be maintained. Although we will rely on interlibrary loan or a National Lending Library to obtain these missing items when needed, they will rarely be called for, for they are rarely, if ever, used.[10] Libraries will continue to buy and stock as many of the high use books and journals as they can possibly afford.

It is also worth noting here that the word "research" is much overused to describe what professors do and what libraries support. This is another legacy of the affluent 1960s when there was seemingly no end to the increase in the numbers of Ph.D. candidates and professors in our universities and the wide variety of their research needs and interests. The economic decline in the 1970s is changing this attitude. Apart from those located at the major research-oriented universities, the primary mission of most academic libraries is or should be to support the instructional needs of their students and faculty. This function can be documented by a quote from the 1975 Ladd-Lipset survey of U.S. faculty members reported by the authors in an article entitled "How Professors Spend Their Time," which appeared in the *Chronicle of Higher Education* (Oct. 14, 1975, p. 2).

> The popular assumption has been that American academics are a body of scholars who do their research and then report their findings to the intellectual or scientific communities. Many faculty members behave in this fashion, but that overall description of the profession is seriously flawed.
>
> Most academics think of themselves as "teachers" and "intellectuals"—and they perform accordingly.
>
> Although data on the number of scholarly articles and academic books published each year testify that faculty members are producing a prodigious volume of printed words, this torrent is gushing forth from relatively few pens:
>
> —Over half of all full-time faculty members have never written or edited any sort of book alone or in collaboration with others.

—More than one third have never published an article.

—Half of the professoriate have not published anything, or had anything accepted for publication in the last two years.

—More than one quarter of all full-time academics have never published a scholarly word.

They summarize as follows:

American academics constitute a teaching profession, not a scholarly one. There is a small scholarly subgroup located disproportionately at a small number of research-oriented universities.

These conclusions about how faculty members spend their time correlate well with what library statistics show about faculty use of libraries—namely, that it is on the order of ten percent of the total and that much of it is for instructional purposes rather than research.

As for the publishers, they may make themselves feel better by blaming journal cancellations and shrinking book orders on increasingly effective library resource sharing via systematic photocopying and interlibrary loan rather than on inflation and declining library budgets, but they will be deceiving themselves.

Resource sharing will not seriously erode publishers' profits, nor will it help libraries as much as they think. Interlibrary loan will increase, but it will still continue to be a very small percentage of total library use. The high cost of interlibrary loan and the needs and demands of library users will not permit it to grow into something major. Its importance will always be as much in the capability for delivery as in the actual use of that capability. Like the Center for Research Libraries, it serves as an insurance policy. We do not justify our annual membership fee in the center by the number of items we borrow every year but by the fact that our membership gives us access—if and when we need it—to several million research items which might otherwise not be available to us.

In the long run, librarians cannot count on interlibrary loan or their regional consortia or networks for the major economies they will need to make to weather the hard times that are ahead. This is as true for the many small college library consortia as it is for the prestigious Research Libraries Group and the now defunct Five Associated University Libraries cooperative. All too frequently, cooperation is merely a pooling of poverty. Many consortia members are vulnerable because the magnitude of the cuts they will have to make to counter inflation and declining support will far outweigh the relatively minor savings regional cooperation will yield in the end. In fact, like many automation projects, regional consortia may actually be costing their members far more than the benefits they derive if one includes the very substantial cost of staff time needed to make them work. This cost will become more apparent when the grant money that supports many consortia runs out.

Why can't consortia and resource sharing fulfill their promise? Because they focus almost exclusively on reducing expenditures for books and journals and only incidentally on reducing expenditures for personnel. But in the end, any significant savings in library expenditures must come from eliminating positions, because that is where the money goes.

A typical large academic or public library spends 70–75 percent of its budget for personnel and benefits, 20–25 percent for books and journals, and only 5 percent for other purposes. Thus, the amount of cost savings that can be made through resource sharing in any one year is necessarily only a small percentage of the book and journal budget. With these costs rising at the rate of 15 percent a year, the savings will be largely absorbed by inflation.

The unpleasant fact is that we must eliminate positions if we are to make significant cost reductions to cope with inflation and no-growth budgets. To reduce staff will require a drastic curtailment of the intake of materials, reduced services, and increased productivity. There is no other way. Resource sharing is essential but it is not a panacea.

The cheap and easy victories come early in library cooperation, but what do we do that is cost effective after we have agreed to reciprocal borrowing privileges with our neighbors and saved a few positions by joining OCLC? What do we do for an encore after we have reduced our staff, journal subscriptions, and book acquisitions by five or ten percent through cooperation, resource sharing, automation, and improved management? In the year 1975–76 inflation and declining support caused a 10 percent decrease in the median number of volumes added to ARL libraries and a 5 percent decrease in the number of staff employed.

Academic libraries are sharing the financial troubles of their parent institutions, and public libraries those of the local governments that support them. These troubles come from long-term economic, social, and demographic trends; they will probably get worse in the decade ahead. The troubles that publishers have are caused by rising costs and changing market conditions and not by library photocopying or deficiencies in the copyright law. These troubles will not be resolved by the collection of royalties on a few journal articles or the sale of a few more library subscriptions.

The library market is shrinking and hardening, and publishers—both commercial and scholarly—will have to accept that fact and make adjustments. Librarians will have to accept that the savings they make through networking, cooperation, and resource sharing in the next several years will be quickly absorbed by the continuing inflation in book and journal prices and rising personnel costs. Moreover, library budgetary support will continue to decline and the pressures to reduce expenditures will increase.

The fact is, libraries can no longer afford to maintain the collections, staffs, and service levels that librarians and users have come to expect in the last two decades. Libraries are experiencing a substantial loss in their standard of living as a result of inflation, increasing energy costs, and changing priorities in our society. We can rail against it and search for scapegoats, but it would be better if we came to terms with this painful reality and began to reduce our excessive commitments and expectations to match our declining resources.

The importance of resource sharing mechanisms, and particularly the most cost-effective ones—the centralized libraries' libraries, such as the Center for Research Libraries and the British Library Lending Division—is not so much that they will save us funds we can reallocate to other purposes, but that they will permit us to continue to have access to a large universe of materials we can no longer afford, spending our diminishing funds on the materials we need and use most. In sum, effective resource sharing will help ease the pain that will accompany the scaling-down of commitments and expectations we face in the years ahead.

Notes

1. Special Issue *ALA Washington Newsletter* on the New Copyright Law, Nov. 15, 1976.

2. For more on the need for a new attitude towards journals in libraries see: Richard De Gennaro, "Escalating Journal Prices: Time to Fight Back," *American Libraries,* February 1977, p. 68–74 [reprinted in this volume].

3. The eight titles which had five or more requests are *American Orchid Society Bulletin,* Harvard University, Botanical Museum, Cambridge; *Fizika,* Yugoslavia; *Journal of Electroanalytical Chemistry,* Elsevier Sequoia, Lausanne; *Nukleonika,* Polska Akad. Nauk, Ars Polona Ruch, Warsaw; *Pramana,* Indian Academy of Science, Bangalore; *Revue Roumaine de Physique,* Bucharest; *Synthesis,* George Thiene Verlag & Academic Press; and *Worldview,* Council on Religion and International Affairs, New York.

4. ARL Statistics, 1975–76. Washington, D.C., Association of Research Libraries, 1976, p. 14.

5. Madeline Cohen Oakley, "The New Copyright Law: Implications for Libraries," Cornell University Libraries *Bulletin,* No. 202, October-December 1976, p. 5.

6. Stephen Bulick, and others, "Use of Library Materials in Terms of Age," *Journal of the American Society for Information Science,* May-June 1976, pp. 175–8.

7. Herman H. Fussler, *Patterns in the Use of Books in Large Research Libraries,* Chicago, Univ. of Chicago Press, 1969.

8. Richard W. Trueswell, "User Circulation Satisfaction vs. Size of Holdings at Three Academic Libraries," *College & Research Libraries,* May 1969, pp. 204–13.

9. Michael H. Buckland, *Book Availability and the Library User.* New York, Pergamon Press, 1975.

10. For a more extended discussion of these points see: Richard De Gennaro, "Austerity, Technology, and Resource Sharing: Research Libraries Face the Future," *Library Journal,* May 15, 1975, pp. 917–23 [reprinted in this volume].

ESCALATING JOURNAL PRICES: TIME TO FIGHT BACK

This article was first published in *American Libraries* February 1977 and reprinted in *Library Lit. 8—The Best of 1977.* It called attention to the fact that publishers were raising journal prices at rates that far exceeded inflation and were engaging in pricing policies and strategies that discriminated against libraries and put the burden for supporting scholarly journals almost entirely on library acquisitions budgets. The article called on librarians to make concerted efforts to stem the tide of rising prices and discriminatory pricing policies. The librarians' response to the article was wildly enthusiastic, but prices continued to spiral.

In recent years the rate of rise of journal prices had begun to moderate somewhat, but in 1985 some British and European scholarly journal publishers adopted a policy of charging significantly higher subscription prices for journals going to U.S. libraries. The American price is frequently more than double the European price. American publishers will probably adopt similar increases under one pretext or another. American librarians are crying foul, but it is doubtful that they will be able to resist this new wave of price increases any more than they were able to resist the previous ones. Experience shows that scholars will not support efforts by librarians to counter inordinate price increases by canceling subscriptions from the offending publishers, and that is the only effective counter measure available.

Given the current harsh financial climate in higher education, however, it is unlikely that library journal budgets will be increased to keep pace with this new round of price increases. Thus, we can look forward to another wave of journal subscription cancellations and a further contraction of the library market for scholarly journals. The cycle will continue until the library market, which is the only remaining market for scholarly journals, is so diminished as to force the publishing industry to develop other and more efficient means of disseminating scientific literature.

Librarians have a weakness for journals and numbered series of all kinds. Once they get volume 1, number 1 of a series, they are hooked until the end. They love neat and orderly serials records and complete runs of periodicals on their shelves. They all know that scholarly journals, especially scientific research journals, are the medium for communicating all the latest advances, and that by the time new knowledge appears in monographs it is old hat. Shameful stories of how some unfortunate libraries were forced to cancel certain journals during the depression of the '30s and could never fill the gaps have become part of the folklore of academia. Journals, in short, are the sacred cows of libraries.

Faculty members have a similar weakness for journal subscriptions and numbered series. They don't care about serials records, but they don't like to see broken runs on library shelves. Most of all, they hate to see one of *their* subscriptions canceled once it has been entered. Because their careers depend on publication in these journals, they understandably have a strong interest in seeing them prosper and proliferate. The function of the scientific journal as a vehicle for the promotion and recognition concerns of authors has begun to eclipse its function as a vehicle for communicating scholarly knowledge. "The fact is," say economists William J. Baumol and Junusz A. Ordover, "that a growing proportion of scientific journals have virtually no individual subscribers, but are sold almost exclusively to libraries, and that a very high proportion of those journals are rarely, if ever, requested by readers. *This suggests that many journals provide services primarily not to readers but to the authors of the articles for whom publication brings professional certification, career advancement and personal gratification.*"[1]

A third group with a weakness for journals and numbered series is the publishers, both foreign and domestic. Publishers love journals not because they have the collector's instinct, but because the library market is so easy to expand and exploit. Long ago, publishers discovered that librarians could not resist subscribing to new journals and could only with great difficulty bring themselves to reevaluate and cancel a subscription once it was entered. Moreover, publishers know that library serials records and accounting systems are overburdened and inflexible and that librarians are reluctant therefore to tamper unnecessarily with their subscription lists and standing orders. In the old days, before the affluent '60s, the situation remained in equilibrium because libraries were poor and publishers (who were considered to be part of the scholarly enterprise) knew it. Publishers kept both the prices and the number of journals in line with the demand and the financial resources of libraries and personal subscribers. At that time, scholars could still afford to build their own personal working libraries despite their low salaries; they constituted an important market for learned publications.

Well, along came the affluent '60s and higher education came into its own. Library budgets expanded, and publishing—particularly scientific journal publishing—shook off its old ways and became big and efficient business. Everyone prospered and was happy—but not for long. The austere '70s came, higher education went into a depression, professors and Ph.D. candidates became fewer and poorer and could no longer afford personal libraries, and library budgets began to decline.

By this time, the publishers had developed higher expectations for their industry; they cared less about the usefulness of their publications and more about their profitability. But publishers are people, and like the rest of us, they are motivated largely by self-interest and cannot be blamed for making the best of their opportunities. Even some of the learned societies have come to view their publishing operations as a means of generating income from library subscriptions in order to subsidize low-cost member subscriptions and other desirable activities rather than simply as a means of disseminating the scholarly knowledge of their field.

With tighter budgets, librarians became more selective in their purchases—first of monographs and then of serials. They find it easier to resist buying monographs because there is less pressure from the faculty, and no effort is required to forego placing orders. The publishers responded to this sluggishness in sales by raising prices. These increases caused a further drop in sales, and the cycle was repeated. Book publishers were at a disadvantage because books are more price-sensitive and apparently less essential to library users. Large libraries shifted an increasing

Table 1: Five Years of Inflation, 1970–1975

Library Inflation Indicators	**1970**	**1975**	**% Increase**
U.S. Consumer Price Index	116.3	161.2	38.6
Average price of U.S. periodicals	$10.41	$19.94	92
Total materials expenditures in 79 ARL academic libraries as of 1970–71 (in millions of dollars)	$77.9	$106.3	36.5
Gross volumes added to 79 ARL academic libraries (in millions of volumes	7.9	6.9	(−14.3)
Examples of Escalating Journal Prices*	**1970**	**1975**	**% Increase**
Sciences			
Biochemica et Biophysica Acta (Springer)	$495	$1,551	213
Coordination Chemistry Reviews (Elsevier)	25	136	444
Inorganica Chemica Acta (Elsevier Sequoia)	26	235	804
International Journal of Theoretical Physics (Plenum)	26	135	419
Journal of Theoretical Biology (Academic)	80	234	193
Humanities and Social Sciences			
Accounting Review (American Accounting Assoc.)	9	25	178
Architectural Review (Architectural Press)	14.40	37.50	160
Historical Abstracts (ABC Clio)	151	495	228
Journal of Industrial Economics (B. Blackwell)	5	20	300
Survey of Current Business (U.S. Office of Business Economics)	9	48	433

*Annual subscription prices paid by the University of Pennsylvania Library percentage of their book budgets to maintain journal subscriptions. Commercial journal publishers, on the other hand, began to realize how addicted librarians were to journals and, therefore, how insensitive to price increases their product was. No matter how much journal subscriptions went up, enough libraries would continue to subscribe and pay the higher rate.

Some of the more efficient and aggressive publishers began to make annual price increases of remarkable proportions—20 to 30 and even 40%—or whatever they thought the traffic would bear. Many scientific journals and monograph series are now priced at several hundred dollars a year and some exceed a thousand (see chart). More and more, the titles are not really journals but numbered series with an unspecified quantity of volumes per year at an unstated price. In effect, a subscribing library agrees in advance to take whatever is published at whatever price the publisher sets. Large libraries are now spending nearly 50% of their periodical funds to acquire 10% of their titles. In the last few years, the rate of increase of scientific journal prices far exceeds the rate of increase of the U.S. consumer price index. Foreign commercial journals are among the most expensive.

Many book and journal budgets in departmental science and engineering libraries are now devoted almost entirely to maintaining long-standing journal subscriptions with little or nothing for monographs or new journals. Not to decide is to decide. The decision their librarians make every day is that their existing journal subscriptions are more valuable than any new monograph or even any new journal title. Periodic infusions of special appropriations from the central library or from departmental budgets merely stave off the day of default and permit publishers to continue raising prices. But now, prices are out of control, and soon decisions will have to be made as to which journals to keep, which to cancel, and which to add.

The larger scientific publishers—both here and abroad—have developed highly efficient editorial, production, and distribution capabilities which allow them to publish many additional journal titles at a relatively small incremental cost. Naturally, publishers have used that excess capacity to proliferate new journals in ever more specialized fields (the so-called "twigging effect") as long as libraries have continued to buy them at the inflated institutional rates. By now many commercial publishers have lost interest in personal subscribers and no longer quote rates for them in their advertising copy.

Librarians Fight Back

Some new trends are perceivable. Under increasingly severe budgetary pressures, librarians have begun to limit new subscriptions and cancel many old ones. At the same time they are organizing resource-sharing cooperatives and calling for the creation of a National Periodicals Library to backstop their diminishing collections. The publishers feel aggrieved; they accuse librarians of trying to beggar them by subscribing to fewer journals and sharing their use through interlibrary lending and photocopying. It is like the oil companies raising the price of gasoline to a point where motorists are forced to form car pools and then crying "foul" when they do.

Commercial, society, and university press publishers now rely to a very large and dangerous extent on library subscriptions to support their publications. The differential subscription rate, where libraries pay a substantially higher rate than individual subscribers, has become widespread, and publishers have come to view libraries as a captive market. Library subscriptions now constitute a subsidy for the dissemination of scholarly literature.

This unhealthy system is going to end. Why? Not because librarians will suddenly lose their love for journals, but because the relative decline in library budgets and purchasing power has reached crisis proportions. In my library, as in many others, despite a 20% increase in total book and journal expenditures in the last five years, the purchasing power of those funds has declined by approximately 50%, and the outlook for the future is even more bleak. The total spent on library materials by 79 academic library members of the Association of Research Libraries increased by 36.5% in the five-year period from 1970–71 to 1975–76 while the aggregate number of volumes added dropped by 14.3%. Obviously, periodical expenditures are taking an increasing percentage of the total library materials budget. Libraries are spending more to buy less.

During the last five years, most libraries have been steadily trimming the fat that swelled their budgets in the '60s—both in personnel commitments and in book and journal allocations. But further economies will surely be called for in the next few years;

to make them, librarians are going to have to sacrifice some of their most sacred cows, including many important, even essential, journal subscriptions which are now priced beyond their ability to pay.

It was difficult for librarians to make the hard and unpopular decisions to cancel journals as long as book funds could be diverted to sustain subscriptions, but such diversion is no longer possible in many libraries. As the money runs out, even the meekest of librarians will acquire the courage to say no to the most powerful and vocal faculty members, library committee chairpersons, and department heads.

That is where we are now in college and university libraries; the large public libraries arrived there some time ago. The competition for the diminishing library dollar will intensify and become increasingly bitter in the next few years. Librarians need to adopt tougher attitudes and more aggressive tactics to defend their budgets. It is time to fight back, but it is also time to adopt more realistic expectations and to improve collection management techniques.

Up to now, our standard response to the problem of escalating journal prices has been to plead and beg for higher budgets from our funding authorities, for subsidies from the government, and for grants from foundations. All these and more are desperately needed, but this kind of help is certain to be too little and too late. And when such help comes, it will only encourage publishers to raise the institutional subscription rates even higher and to publish more unnecessary, largely unread journals. Something more is needed.

The real problem is that scholarly and research journals, particularly in the sciences, are in serious trouble, and the system for supporting them is breaking down. The practice of charging authors a page rate for publishing their articles is under attack from the U.S. Postal Service and other quarters, and libraries—the last market—can no longer afford to buy the product. Libraries have no responsibility to continue to support the scholarly journal in the manner to which it has become accustomed of late. I think it is time that we let the forces of the marketplace take over and create a new environment for the journal and whatever forms will evolve in competition with it.

Librarians can stimulate the process by challenging and

testing the ethics and legality of differential subscription rates that allow publishers, and especially learned societies, to charge libraries substantially more than individual subscribers. Up to now librarians have voluntarily accepted the higher library rate because the differential was not large enough to justify the administrative difficulties that would result. This response was appropriate to an earlier time when the differential was smaller and when publishing was still considered a partner in the scholarly enterprise. But now that the differential is significant and publishing has become a business that treats libraries as a captive market to be exploited, the only appropriate response for librarians is to make decisions on practical and legal rather than on ethical grounds. With a little ingenuity, libraries can probably find legal ways of obtaining some of their most expensive journals at the lowest available market price. One way may be to get copies through personal subscribers.

Now that consumerism has achieved recognition in the federal government, librarians should begin making organized efforts to resist rising journal prices and twigging. As long as librarians continue to buy at ever-increasing prices without protest, the publishers will continue to raise prices and multiply titles. Librarians have a powerful deterrent on hand if they learn to use it effectively: They can simply refuse to buy at inflated institutional rates and refuse to enter or continue subscriptions to overpriced and under-used journals.

Obviously, librarians will only weaken their collections and deprive their users if they act arbitrarily or capriciously. First, they need to do a good deal of consciousness-raising to call the attention of library decision makers, users, academics, and government officials to the crisis-proportions of the price escalation problem and the questionable practice of differential pricing. One way of doing this is to assemble and publicize specific and detailed information about the pricing policies of certain U.S. and foreign publishers and the recent increases of specific journal titles. *Library Journal*'s annual survey of periodical prices is very helpful in many ways, but it deals only in average subscription costs by category. What we need, in addition, is to put the spotlight on specific examples that significantly surpass the averages. (One is reminded of the story of the statistician who drowned in a river with an average depth of two feet.) Perhaps the source data upon which the annual averages are based could be mined to obtain the needed examples and documentation.

These measures will help, but in the long run the most effective remedy is for librarians to become more skillful at identifying low-use journals and far more ruthless in weeding them from their collections. The library's diminishing resources must be devoted to maintaining subscriptions to the few key journals used most frequently in each field.

The Institute of Scientific Information's *Journal Citation Reports,* published annually as part of *Science Citation Index,* ranks the indexed journals by the frequency with which they are cited and can, according to Garfield,[2] serve as a useful tool for managing journal collections in libraries. The least-cited journals can be viewed as prime candidates for cancellation after other important factors have been considered. However, research by Scales[3] questions the validity of using ranked lists produced by citation analyses as selection tools for journals, and caution is advised.

Other systems for ranking journals by article productivity in relation to cost factors are moving from the theoretical and experimental stage to the point where they are now ready for development as useful tools for optimizing expenditures on journals. Productivity/cost rankings take into account subscription and other ancillary costs and relate them to the number of significant articles contained in the journals of a particular field as measured through available indexing and abstracting services. Because most of the important articles in any given field appear in relatively few journals (the Bradford distribution),[4] these ranking schemes can help us determine which journals provide the most articles at the best prices and, therefore, which should be acquired, retained, or canceled. Acceptable methodologies for such ranking schemes have already been developed,[5,6,7] but the task of actually compiling and publishing usable rank listings in various fields remains to be done.

Although the development of these and other new quantitative techniques for managing journal collections is to be encouraged, the problems created by escalating journal prices will not wait; reasonably cost-effective decisions can be made using traditional common-sense methods based on experience with actual use of particular collections supplemented by expert advice from scholars.

The fiscal crisis in libraries is generating a new and lively interest in methods of weeding and increasing the selectivity of collections as well as in resource sharing. A quarterly depressingly entitled *The De-Acquisitions Librarian Newsletter* was started in 1975. The editors are betting, correctly in my opinion, that de-acquisitions and increasing selectivity will be an important library growth industry during the next decade or two. "Touching Bottom in the Bottomless Pit" was the catchy title of the first (1975) major library conference on the subject of no-growth libraries.[8] Last September the conference on Resources Sharing in Libraries at the University of Pittsburgh drew record attendance. I have given my own views on the changing library environment in an article entitled "Austerity, Technology, and Resource Sharing: Research Librarians Face the Future" (*Library Journal,* May 15, 1975, pp. 917–23).

Librarians need to make a variety of collective as well as individual efforts to resist escalating journal prices and increase the skills with which they administer their declining book and journal budgets. To the extent that these efforts are successful, they will cause pain and concern, not only among commercial, society, and university press publishers, but also throughout the academic research establishment and in the government agencies that fund it. So be it. A most desirable outcome would be a general agreement that research library book budgets are no longer an appropriate means of subsidizing the scholarly publishing enterprise. Other sources of subsidy will doubtless be found if subsidies are warranted, and if not, the laws of supply and demand will eventually create a new market environment more in tune with present and future economic realities. In any case, it is becoming clear that research libraries have reached the end of an era. They can no longer continue to provide '60s-level services and collections with present-day costs and budgets.[9]

Notes

1. William J. Baumol and Junusz A. Ordover, "Public good properties in reality: The case of scientific journals." (Typescript of a paper read and distributed at the ASIS Annual Conference, San Francisco, October 1976) p. 19.

2. Eugene Garfield, "Citation analysis as a tool in journal evaluation," *Science,* November 3, 1972, pp. 471–79.

3. Pauline A. Scales, "Citation analysis as indicators of the use of serials: A comparison of ranked title lists produced by citation counting

and from use data," *Journal of Documentation,* vol. 32, no. 1, March 1976, pp. 17–25.

4. Michael K. Buckland, *Book Availability and The Library User,* (New York, Pergamon, 1975) p. 15ff. (This outstanding work is an essential tool for managers of library book and journal collections.)

5. Donald A. Windsor, "De-acquisitioning journals using productivity/cost rankings," *De-Acquisitions Librarian Newsletter,* vol. 1, no. 1, Spring 1976, pp. 1, 8–10.

6. Maurice B. Line, "Optimization of library expenditures on biochemical journals," *Journal of Documentation,* vol. 31, no. 1, 1975, pp. 33–37.

7. S. E. Robertson and Sandy Hensman, "Journal acquisition by libraries: Scatter and cost-effectiveness," *Journal of Documentation,* vol. 31, no. 4, 1975, pp. 273–82.

8. Daniel Gore (ed.), *Farewell to Alexandria; Solutions to space, growth, and performance problems of libraries.* (Westport, Conn., Greenwood Press, 1976) 180 p.

9. The comprehensive and authoritative paper by Herbert S. White entitled "Publishers, libraries, and costs of journal subscriptions in times of funding retrenchment" (*Library Quarterly,* vol. 46, no. 4, October 1976, pp. 359–77) is an important contribution on this subject. Dr. White's paper on the economic interaction between libraries and journal publishers was based on a survey (directed by Bernard M. Fry and sponsored by NSF) of 1969–73 data predating the current period, during which prices have shown their greatest increases and library budgets their worst losses. However, he attempts to look forward in his perceptive analysis and conclusions. See also Bernard M. Fry and Herbert S. White, *Publishers and Libraries: A Study of Scholarly and Research Journals.* (Lexington, Mass., Lexington Books, 1976.)

PAY LIBRARIES AND USER CHARGES

Reprinted from *Library Journal,* 15 February 1975, 263–67.

In 1968 the medical publisher Williams & Wilkins filed suit against the U.S. Government and the National Library of Medicine in an effort to eliminate the "fair use" doctrine, which permitted making single copies of copyrighted materials. That suit marked the beginning of the increasingly bitter adversary relationship between the publishing and library communities that characterized the 1970s and 1980s. The Information Industry Association (IIA), also founded in 1968, became the principal advocate of fees for service and a formidable adversary of libraries giving away services that the information industry was trying to sell. The IIA introduced the concept of the for-profit library or the "information supermarket" with membership fees and metered use of the reading rooms and services as an alternative to free libraries.

The debates that ensued between librarians and their new adversaries were emotionally and politically charged. This article was part of that debate. The principal issue that was addressed, how library and information services are to be funded in the future are, is still largely unresolved today.

The battle lines are being drawn for a great debate over the emotionally and politically charged issue of how library and information services are to be funded in the coming decades. Most librarians will be on the side of "conservatism" and "democracy," favoring the continuation of traditional modes of tax-supported public library service with information freely available to all as a matter of right. Information industry people, publishers, government officials, engineers, and even, perhaps, authors will be on the side of "progress" and "profits," advocating a new concept of for-profit or pay libraries, user charges, and information as a salable commodity.

A similar debate took place in the decade of the 60's between the librarians and the technologists over the issue of the future of libraries and the printed book. The technologists were advocating and predicting the imminent demise of traditional libraries and the printed book and their replacement by computerized information centers providing instant access to vast stores of information from giant memory banks. The librarians, very much on the defensive because they appeared to be opposed to progress and the wave of the future, insisted that it could not happen, or at any rate that it would not happen soon. Now, after a decade and a half of technological development, books and libraries are—and promise to remain—very much with us, while computers, communications, and micrographic technology have already had an important impact on the library and information field and continue to develop at a rapidly accelerating pace.

The current debate over pay libraries and user charges appears in some ways to be a continuation of the debate of the 60's. In both cases much of the heat and misunderstanding that is generated comes from the very different images that the words "libraries" and "information" invoke in the various protagonists and the context or frame of reference in which they use them. Different kinds of librarians attach different meanings to these words, and the same is true for government officials, businessmen, scientists, and engineers. Thus, when an information industry spokesman or a government official calls for libraries to become self-supporting by selling their services, he is or probably should be thinking of large or specialized research libraries or information centers which are or will be using new technology to serve the special needs of scientific, commercial, industrial and other users, and not the mass of small public and college libraries scattered throughout the country. Again, when the technologists were predicting the demise of traditional libraries and books in the 60's we must assume that they were not thinking about these small general libraries or about all books.

On the other hand, when some librarians dogmatically insist that all library and information services must be available on a free and equal basis to all citizens as a matter of right, we should probably assume that they do not mean to exclude the possibility that new kinds of for-profit libraries could be created (indeed, some already exist) to serve the special and legitimate needs of industrial, commercial, and other users who are willing and able to pay for special computerized information services, or even that existing tax-supported libraries could not charge such users for providing these special services. In short, it could be that these debates are fueled by the careless use and misunderstanding of certain words and concepts and that there are no real villains in the drama.

Just as the debate of the 60's over the future of the library and the book is being resolved by librarians and technologists working together to achieve a new reality, so the current debate between the librarians and the business and government men over the issue of for-profit libraries and user fees will probably also be resolved in time by a new synthesis of views and interests leading to the further enrichment of the already mixed economy of "free" and for-profit libraries and information services.

The purpose of this paper is to contribute to that resolution and synthesis in two ways, and it is accordingly divided into two parts. The first part will attempt to identify the trends, the issues, and the political nature of the debate and will search for the middle ground between the extreme positions being advocated by partisan spokesmen for both groups. The second part will discuss some of the precedents and practical aspects of pay libraries and user charges in an effort to offer some guidance to librarians who are faced with the immediate decision of whether or not to impose charges for certain new computer-based information services. The author is neither an economist nor an information scientist and does not pretend to expertise in the theoretical aspects of pricing policy or cost analysis; he approaches these matters from the pragmatic point of view of an administrator who must make a reasonable decision based on the best available information.

Trends, Issues and Politics

In the last several years a whole series of events have occurred which, whatever else they mean, unmistakably signal a new and growing adversary relationship between the publishing and information industries (and possibly even government information policy makers) on the one hand, and librarians on the other. Following is a sampling of these disturbing events.

- The Williams & Wilkins Co., a medical publisher, launched this new trend in 1968 when it filed suit against the United States government in an effort to end the long-standing "fair use" doctrine which permitted users to make single copies from copyrighted library materials.
- The Information Industry Association (IIA) was also founded in 1968 and quickly became an important influence on the national scene under the capable and aggressive leadership of its executive director, Paul Zurkowski.
- The Association of American Publishers recently launched a press attack on the formation of the Research Libraries Group (RLG) and other library cooperative ventures and charged, without basis, that the RLG would resort to unlimited copying of copyrighted materials to achieve its economies at the expense of publishers' profits. (The publishers have apparently adopted the idea that if they can only stop library users from copying from books and journals they can force the libraries to spend more money on acquisitions. They seem not to believe that libraries simply do not have the money.)
- Last year, Rep. Ogden Reid of New York introduced a bill (HR 4850) calling for the establishment of a commission to study methods for compensating authors for the use of their books by libraries (*American Libraries,* May 1973, p. 255).
- William Knox, director of the National Technical Information Service, wants to turn this federal agency into a profit-making corporation to market government produced information (*American Libraries,* June 1974, p. 285).
- A spokesman for the Department of Health, Education, and Welfare, Bill Dungledine, said last year, "Obviously, libraries now have to reconsider how they're going to be financed; either more funds from the local government, or some form of private financing or user charges" (*American Libraries,* May 1973, p. 267).
- Eugene Garfield, president of the Institute for Scientific Information and chairman of the board of the Information Industry Association, testified at a National Commission on Libraries and Information Science (NCLIS) hearing on April 19, 1974 that pay

libraries were inevitable and would be forced on the nation by the information explosion and technological advances (*American Libraries,* June 1973, p. 335). Garfield said that the IIA disapproved of libraries furnishing scientific and technical information free to the public in competition with the for-profit companies such as ISI. He recommended that NCLIS create a National Information Funding Authority to "encourage the investment of risk and public capital" and to "develop an awareness of and an expertise in the use of these new information technologies." The products and services of IIA members are prominent among these new technologies.

• In an earlier draft of their statement to NCLIS, which was circulated internally to stimulate thought and discussion but which was not used, the IIA predicted that public support could no longer supply the economy's information needs and introduced the concept of a for-profit library, called an "information supermarket," complete with membership fees, parking meter rates for time spent in the reading room, sales areas, and mini-computer cash registers which would automatically total up royalties along with the price (*American Libraries,* February 1973, p. 79). In an effort to mitigate the alarm and the misunderstanding that the first statement created, Zurkowski denied that the draft proposed that all public support for libraries should be discontinued and that user charges should be substituted in its place. He said, "Such a suggestion is incredible. The draft statement sought, rather, to suggest that in certain specialized areas where available information services are very specialized and expensive, a for-profit library might well develop, thereby relieving some competition for the ever-diminishing public resources available for libraries" (*American Libraries,* May 1973, p. 258).

What do these events and statements mean? What is going on and how come we suddenly have all this talk of user charges, fees, and profits in connection with libraries and information?

Libraries Respond

Fay Blake and Edith Perlmutter, in an emotionally charged article which appeared under the title "Libraries in the Marketplace" (*LJ,* January 15, 1974, p. 108–11), sum up their interpretation with this statement: "Several recent developments in the world of

American libraries seem to foreshadow an ominous trend toward a new concept of library service. The concept is translated into a variety of proposals—the 'information supermarket,' 'libraries for profit,' 'user fees,' 'user-based charges'—but what's really being proposed is an elimination of tax-supported library service." The authors review and rebut the various arguments that have been put forward recently by librarians and information industry spokesmen advocating and predicting the demise of tax-supported libraries and the rise of a new concept of support for libraries and information services based on user charges. The principal arguments in favor of for-profit libraries are that they would increase library productivity and efficiency, make the user aware of the value of information, and relieve competition for public resources. The authors maintain that none of these claims are true, that they do the library users a disservice, and that what is needed is more public support, not less.

Most librarians will sympathize with the position taken by Blake and Perlmutter in opposition to the concept of supporting libraries by means of user charges rather than through public funds. However, another interpretation of what we see happening is that it is not so much an assault on the concept of tax-supported libraries as a concerted effort by the publishing and information industries to win some measure of federal support and assistance to assure the continued growth and development of for-profit library and information activities. Librarians fear, not without some justification, that such support can only be given at the expense of existing libraries and that both groups are in competition for the same diminishing fund of dollars.

It is no accident that this cycle of events started in 1968 when Vietnam, declining school enrollments, rising costs, shortages, and the beginning of the withdrawal of federal funds for education signaled trouble ahead for libraries, publishing, and the information industry.

In response to Sputnik in 1957, the federal government started pouring money into education and libraries, and "information explosion" became a cliché. Before this decade of affluence for libraries and information, interest in the field by the business community was limited to some publishers, book and periodical dealers, and a number of library furniture and equipment suppliers.

After Sputnik the scene changed. Imbued with the optimism that characterized this decade, business entrepreneurs sensed that there were large profits to be made from the information explosion, and there was a scramble to get in and get a piece of the action and government money. By the end of the decade, many of the old companies that had been serving libraries and education had been bought up by corporate giants who hoped to marry the electronics industry to publishing and education. In addition to this rash of acquisitions and mergers, a host of new companies came into existence to meet the growing needs for reprints, microforms, equipment, computer software, and a wide variety of other new and useful products and services.

Just about the time the optimism hit its peak, the affluent world of the 60's came to an end; education went into a recession, the government money was diverted to other uses, and hard times came to the information industry. The marriages between the conglomerates and the publishers went sour, and many of them were dissolved. It became evident again that the library and information field was still a relatively modest market and could not possibly support the number and variety of business enterprises that came in to serve it.

What happened? Government policies after Sputnik had created a boom in publishing as well as a whole new industry—the information industry. Government policies and priorities changed with the Nixon administration, and the diversion of federal money into other areas is causing those industries to try to protect their threatened economic interests. Like other industries, labor unions, educational institutions, and special interest groups feeling an economic pinch, they are lobbying in Washington to obtain protection from the workings of the economy, relief from the effects of poor business decisions and changes in federal political priorities. This is a normal and legitimate response in our society. Business people, in spite of their public rhetoric about free enterprise, the free market, and unfettered competition, are just as prone as other citizens to turn to the government for help when things get bad or to gain an edge over a competitor.

Lewis Engman, chairman of the Federal Trade Commission, in a speech to the Financial Analysts Federation said, "Most regulated industries have become Federal Protectorates, living in a crazy world of cost-plus, safely protected from the ugly specters of competition, efficiency, and innovation. Our airlines, railroads, our electronic media, and countless others are on the dole. We get irate about welfare fraud. But our complex systems of hidden subsidies make welfare fraud look like petty larceny" (*New York Times*, October 8, 1974, p. 1).

Although it would be absurd to suggest that the information and publishing industries aspire to achieve the status of regulated industries, it is unfortunate but understandable if in these recessionary times they turn to the government for a measure of support and assistance. What is really distressing to librarians is that they appear to be adopting the short-sighted strategy of trying to further their own interests at the expense of libraries and their users instead of uniting in a common effort to promote the use of books, libraries, and other information services for the benefit of all concerned. We should not view this as a zero sum game where one player can win only at the expense of another; we can all win, or, as appears to be more likely if the present trend continues, we can all lose.

Garfield asks how anyone can make money selling information if libraries are permitted to continue to give it away free. Well, libraries were here first giving away information before there was any question that it might be profitable to sell it. No one disputes Garfield's right to sell information, but it is hard for librarians to understand why they should not be permitted to "compete" with him, and why tax support for libraries should be withdrawn in favor, perhaps, of subsidies for the private sector. Surely there must be ample demand and opportunity for both public and private information services which serve real needs to survive and prosper in the long run.

Pay Libraries in the Past

Librarians may be tempted to dismiss the concept of the pay library as unworkable on the grounds that it was tried repeatedly during the last hundred years under the name of subscriptions or proprietary libraries and found wanting. They can cite several examples of medical society libraries which have died or are dying and conclude that if the affluent medical profession will not support libraries, then who will? But this may be a superficial interpretation of what is really being proposed.

The subscription library went out of existence because it

tried to rely on user subscriptions, fees, and gifts for its financial support, and sufficient paying users and other support could not be found. The contemporary advocates of pay libraries are probably not really suggesting, despite the rhetoric of the "free market," that these information supermarkets would actually be supported from profits. This would be too naive. Most of the new information products and services are based on high technology and were created by or for the federal government with public funds. This includes, for example, both the machine-readable data bases and the computer software that is used in most of the major bibliographical search services and statistical data banks that are available today, and many of the present and potential users of these services are or will be funded directly or indirectly from public funds. Even so, it is unlikely that pay libraries or for-profit information centers could survive and prosper solely on user charges. Substantial federal grants would probably be required to establish them, and once established, additional subsidies would probably be required to supplement the income from fees. This is the model that is really being proposed, or at any rate a reasonable forecast of what would happen if the pay library concept as advocated by the IIA were actually tried.

The arguments for pay libraries may be made in the name of economic theory, efficiency, or inevitable economic trends, but in essence it is a political idea just as the concepts of free public library service or free public education are political ideas. Whether or how strongly one embraces any of these ideas depends on one's point of view or one's politics, and frequently it boils down to a simple question of economic self-interest.

We make a serious mistake when we accept the premises of the information industry and argue the merits of the case for pay libraries on their terms. There are no valid economic trends, laws, or principles leading "inevitably" toward the demise of tax-supported libraries in favor of the so-called information supermarket. The idea of free public libraries is firmly embedded in the American tradition, and anyone who tries to undermine it will encounter fierce opposition. On the other hand, the idea of selling services for profit to those who will pay for them is also an old and honored American tradition, and it is likely that the two traditions will continue to flourish side by side and even complement each other.

The Case for User Charges

While most librarians can be expected to be opposed to the concept of pay libraries or user charges because of the traditions of the profession and as a matter of principle or political ideology, they should avoid locking themselves into dogmatic or inflexible positions on these issues. A strong case can be made for adopting user fees for certain special services—particularly those based on expensive new computer technology—not to support libraries or make profits, but simply to enable libraries to introduce, develop, and support these new services for the benefit of their users.

The remainder of this article will be devoted to a discussion of the question of user fees from the point of view of the practical working world, where principle must frequently be tempered by expediency, where funds are always limited, and where the librarian may be faced with the simple choice of either charging for special services or not offering them at all.

It is worth noting at the outset that although we use the term "free" library service, we are well aware of the fact that libraries are not free. They have been established and maintained by generations of taxpayers, or tuition payers, philanthropists, and assorted benefactors. It is extremely unlikely, however, that the current users of most libraries are paying anything more than a small fraction of the costs that they would have to be assessed if the library were to be totally supported from user fees.

Although there have been many private subscription libraries, most of them were initially created by philanthropy. It is doubtful that there have been any successful libraries founded and operated on the principle of a retail store where the users paid fees only for particular services such as borrowing books or using reading rooms. Why? Because a library requires a substantial initial capital investment and a stable or increasing level of funding year after year. It cannot thrive or even survive if its annual budget varies erratically or is unassured. Moreover, the level of expenditures in a traditional library is somewhat independent of the amount of use that is made of it. Using the books and facilities does not consume them. There is a natural limitation on the number of books a person can reasonably use at any time, and it is neither difficult, nor in most cases necessary, to limit or ration use—particularly of research materials.

Libraries ration or limit certain expensive services by making rules or policies rather than by charging fees. Reference service is an example. The amount of service given depends on staffing levels, time available, and the status of the requestor. Most libraries decline to do time-consuming literature searches, report writing, or translation, and refer these requests to other persons or agencies who will perform the service for a fee. Indeed, a whole new for-profit reference service industry has come into existence in recent years to fill the in-depth information needs of commercial and industrial firms. The largest and best known is the European SVP and its American affiliate FIND. They are not burdened by the overhead of maintaining their own libraries, but make legitimate and effective use of appropriate existing collections.

These observations give some indication of the complexity of the problems surrounding the idea of charging to use libraries and perhaps explain why librarians are so reluctant to travel that road. Nevertheless, there are certain instances where libraries do charge users fees for one reason or another. A number of private academic and independent research libraries have instituted fees in the last 20 years for unaffiliated users. Fees vary from $10 to $300 a year and are imposed mainly to recover overhead costs and to prevent an undesirable overload on the service and facilities. An increasing number of libraries, including the British Library Lending Division, charge fees to help defray the cost of interlibrary loans.

The Copying Precedent

When photocopying was introduced into libraries in the 1930's, many of them set up laboratories and charged the users the rather substantial costs involved. As electrostatic copying machines were introduced, they lowered the prices, turned it into a self-service operation, and finally many of them turned the whole activity over to concessionaires who could provide the service at lower prices. The service and pricing policy varies from one library to another, but both the librarians and the users have accepted the idea that copying service should be paid for by the person who uses it. It is true that some academic institutions have begun to subsidize free copying for faculty members as prices have declined, but this is still the exception. Most libraries feel compelled to charge in order to recover costs and as a form of rationing to keep the service from being abused. Unlike the use of the reading room or the book collection, the copying service is a limited, measurable, and consumable resource. Each user can pay for what he uses, the use is optional, and those who do not use it need not pay. It is possible that more libraries will offer free copying if and when the price is reduced to the point where the cost of monitoring the use of collecting the money begins to equal the fee. However, this is not likely, and copying fees may continue to offer the best precedent for charging users for special services.

Computer Service Fees

In the last few years, a growing number of research libraries have begun to offer relatively expensive computer-based bibliographic services to their users, and the question of whether they should be subsidized by the library as are traditional services or paid for by the user is a very live issue. Indeed, it is the advent of these services and the prospect of other new ones based on high technology that has generated the current interest in pay libraries and user charges. (For an excellent review of this subject see: J. Gardner, D. Wax, & R. D. Morrison, Jr., "The delivery of computer-based bibliographical search services by academic and research libraries," *ARL Management Supplement,* September 1974.)

There are two categories of computerized bibliographic services, off-line and on-line. The off-line batch-processed current awareness and retrospective search services are being offered mainly by a dozen university-based centers which are funded by either the National Science Foundation or the National Aeronautics and Space Administration. The on-line interactive search services using CRT terminals and long-distance telephone lines are being offered mainly by commercial vendors such as Systems Development Corporation, the Lockheed Information Retrieval Services, and the New York Times Information Bank. In addition, the National Library of Medicine offers the much used and heavily subsidized MEDLINE service.

The off-line university centers have been supplying subsidized or free services to an impressive number of local users and for-fee services to a much smaller number of nonaffiliated users, but the government support for these centers is running out and they must face the issue of charging users to recover costs or finding institutional or other funding to support their continued existence. Experience shows that when users are asked to pay for these services many decide to forego them or severely limit their use. With the current recession and the growing number, variety, and popularity of the on-line commercial services, the long-term viability of these off-line university centers would appear to be uncertain.

The on-line commercial services are gaining a rapidly increasing number of library subscribers, and here the issue must be faced right from the start. Will the library subsidize the service or will the user be required to pay all or part of the cost of his search? What about overhead costs? The same question is being faced for the National Library of Medicine services which were formerly offered free and are now carrying a nominal service charge.

When the direct charges of an off-line search can cost well over $100 and an average on-line search up to $30 or $40, and if a substantial overhead cost is added, the question of who pays becomes extremely critical. If the library begins by offering these expensive services free like its traditional services, the demand will expand and eventually create an overload situation requiring some form of rationing based on rules or by the imposition of charges. The latter alternative appears most likely. It should be understood that these services will require a net addition to budgets rather than transfer from another category, and this at a time when library budgets are being severely reduced.

If the user is required to pay both the direct and indirect costs, then the use of these services will be confined largely to those who can pay from grant, departmental, or company funds. It is unlikely that many individuals will be willing to spend their own personal funds to purchase computer-based search services at current prices of up to a dollar a minute. A combination of institutional subsidy and individual charges appears to be evolving as the dominant method of paying for the new computer-based information services. A common pattern is that the library absorbs the indirect costs such as the cost of the terminal and staff operators' time, but asks the user to pay the direct costs including computer time, printing, and communication charges. In this way, the direct costs, which are recorded by the computer and therefore easily justifiable to the user, can be recovered while the less obvious and harder to justify indirect costs are absorbed. This may permit the orderly implementation and growth of the new services and provide an acceptable rationale for imposing essential user charges. Libraries which refuse on principle to impose charges for these special services may have some difficulty implementing and administering them.

The picture may change in time as the cost of these services declines dramatically as it surely must if they are going to evolve from their current status as a glamorous luxury for the economically privileged to the practical working tools of the mass of ordinary library users. But even though the costs do come down as they did with copying technology, it seems likely that libraries will continue to ask the users to pay the direct costs as a form of control to prevent abuses.

In sum, different libraries can adopt different policies on the question of user charges for special services depending on their own local budgets and circumstances. There is no need for uniform or inflexible policies, and librarians can implement these peripheral charges on an *ad hoc* basis as a matter of practical necessity without embracing the concept of the user-supported library or the information supermarket as a matter of political faith or economic inevitability.

The aim of this article has been to identify and discuss openly and frankly some of the disturbing trends, issues, and attitudes that are emerging to divide librarians and the information and publishing industries into two opposing groups competing for the same diminishing dollars. It has been a plea for each group to try to moderate its positions and to diminish the emotional and partisan quality of a public debate which can only harm the interests of all concerned, including the users of books, libraries, and information services.

The potential royalties that publishers might receive from being reimbursed from library photocopying will not make a significant difference to the successful ones, nor will it save the marginal ones from whatever fate is in store for them. The potential profits that information vendors might receive if libraries refrained from offering certain free services based on technology will not be enough to sustain a firm with a marginal product or service. Libraries will not solve their budget problems by fighting to deprive users of the opportunity to benefit from new subsidized commercial information services. Such moves would only inhibit the use and development of libraries and information services and would benefit no one in the long run.

Perhaps we take ourselves and each other too seriously. We need some perspective. All signs indicate that our "industry" is being put through the economic wringer by forces that we did not create and that we cannot control. Library photocopying of copyrighted materials is not the cause of the publishers' economic woes; libraries giving away free services in competition with certain commercial vendors is not the true cause of their profit problems; and the diversion of some public money to subsidize certain for-profit information activities is not the cause of the acute budget crisis that libraries are experiencing. The information industry, of which libraries are also a part, does not exist in a vacuum; it is part of the national and international economies which are experiencing very serious dislocations. This is the true source of our problems. It does us no good to blame each other or to try to profit at each other's expense. We are allies, not adversaries; our interests are complementary, not competing.

PROVIDING BIBLIOGRAPHIC SERVICES FROM MACHINE-READABLE DATA BASES: THE LIBRARY'S ROLE

This paper was published in the *Journal of Library Automation*, 6, no. 4, 215–22, December 1973.

At a time when it was widely assumed that libraries would have to subscribe to tape services and establish local processing centers to provide bibliographic search services, this paper foresaw the coming of vendor-based online search services as the standard method of access. Thirteen years later, the appearance of large data bases in CD ROM form has reopened the question of how libraries will provide their users with access to data bases. Online access to remote data bases is losing its near monopoly and is beginning to share the field with a growing number and variety of separately published CD ROM bibliographic files.

This brief paper will attempt to counter the widely held view that the larger research libraries will soon need to begin subscribing to the growing number of data bases in machine-readable form and providing current awareness and other services from them for their local users. It will speculate on how this field might develop and will suggest a less expensive and more feasible strategy which libraries may use to gain access to these increasingly important bibliographic services. The key question of who will pay for these new services, the user or the institution, will also be discussed.

While it is clearly outside the scope of this paper to review the state-of-the-art of data base services, reference to a few key works and a brief introduction to the subject may be helpful.

The most comprehensive and authoritative review of the state-of-the-art of the field and its literature is the excellent chapter entitled "Machine-Readable Bibliographic Data Bases" by Marvin C. Gechman in the 1972 volume of the *Annual Review of Information Science and Technology.*[1] A useful selection of readings is *Key Papers on the Use of Computer-Based Bibliographic Services* edited by Stella Keenan and published jointly by the American Society for Information Science and the National Federation of Abstracting and Indexing Services in 1973.[2] *A Study of Six University-Based Information Systems* made by the National Bureau of Standards is essential and contains in convenient form comparative and descriptive information about these pioneering centers which are sponsored by the National Science Foundation.[3]

Some of the most useful and important data bases available are those that have been developed by the indexing and abstracting services as by-products of their efforts to automate the production of their regular printed publications. Like the publications, the tapes come in a wide variety of incompatible formats. Among the important producers are: Chemical Abstracts Service, Bio-Sciences Information Service, Engineering Index Inc., American Institute of Physics, and the American Geological Institute. CCM Information Corporation (PANDEX) and the Institute for Scientific Information are two examples of major commercial suppliers.

Several of the scientific societies received substantial grants from the National Science Foundation and other sources in the 1960s for this automation effort, and it was generally expected that an important new market for the by-product tapes would develop among researchers in universities and in industry. Imaginative and forward-looking librarians and computer people at various universities applied for and received grants to establish centers where these new data tapes could be used to provide current awareness and retrospective search services to users. The National Aeronautics and Space Administration established a network of Regional Dissemination Centers at six universities, including the Universities of Connecticut, Indiana, and New Mexico, the North Carolina Science and Technology Research Center, University of Pittsburgh, and the University of Southern California.

The National Science Foundation has been supporting centers at the University of Georgia, Lehigh University, University of California at Los Angeles, Ohio State University, and Stanford University. Other centers have been established at the Illinois Institute of Technology Research Institute and the University of Florida. It is worth noting that nearly all centers provide services free to their own institutional users and continue to be heavily subsidized. All seem eager to expand their markets to include paying customers from a larger region.

The latest entry into this field is the New England Board of Higher Education's Northeast Academic Science Information Center (NASIC) sponsored by NSF. NASIC's approach is basically different from the unitary centers that have been named. It will attempt to become a broker between the various existing centers and its own members, facilitating their access to existing services elsewhere. It will serve a ten-state region and is expected, perhaps somewhat optimistically, to become self-supporting after the three-year grant period ends.

The number of data bases available in the United States is now over a hundred and is growing rapidly, apparently without benefit of firm standards. A parallel development is taking place in Europe. As the number of available data bases increases, and as the activity at these centers expands, more and more librarians become interested in and concerned about how they are going to provide these new, important, and expensive services on their own campuses.

Interest among librarians in data base services is running high. A session at the Association of Research Libraries Conference in the spring of 1973 was devoted to it, and a program at the annual meeting of the American Library Association in Las Vegas on the subject was jointly sponsored by the COLA Discussion Group, the Information Science and Automation Division, and the Association of College and Research Libraries. While this interest is commendable and should be stimulated, it is also important that it be tempered and put into perspective by a realistic consideration of some of the costs and problems involved in providing these services. This is what the remainder of this paper will attempt to do.

The title of the ALA program was "Library Management of Machine-Readable Reference Data Bases." Implied in that title are two basic assumptions that are widely accepted: one is that libraries will play a key role in providing access to information in machine-readable data bases on their campuses. The other is that in order to provide this access they will have to acquire and maintain these data bases and develop the capability of searching and manipulating them for their local users.

The first assumption is valid; libraries will be responsible for assisting users in gaining access to information in this new form. The second assumption is highly questionable, if not invalid. It is extremely unlikely that many individual libraries will be able to afford to establish centers to acquire and process these machine-readable data bases. While it may appear that a straw man is being set up that can be easily demolished, the idea that academic libraries must and will begin acquiring and servicing many large and expensive data bases, and even statistical data banks, is still widely enough held that it ought to be put to rest.

How did this idea gain such currency? Perhaps it was because the first available data bases were from the indexing and abstracting services and contained machine-readable versions of their printed indexes. Since libraries subscribed to the printed editions, it followed that they should also subscribe to the tape editions. The same is true for the census tapes. Libraries were the chief repositories for printed census publications, so it was natural to assume that they would have to subscribe to and make available the machine-readable census data as well. We now know better about the census tapes; the problem was simply beyond our resources, and they are being made available from specialized centers. A similar solution may well emerge for the bibliographical data tapes of the indexing and abstracting services.

To help put matters into perspective, it might be useful to review a few other ideas we had in the last two decades on how certain technological developments would be implemented in the library. Take microfilm, for example. Back in the 1950s when microfilm came of age for library use, many librarians thought that every major library would require its own laboratory where large quantities of film could be produced and processed under the direction of a new breed of librarian called a documentalist. Several major libraries did establish such laboratories for a time, but the only remaining ones of any significance are at the Library of Congress and a few other large libraries. Most of the others were put out of business by the copying machine, the local service bureau, and commercial micropublishers—and the documentalists became information scientists.

Library automation provides other interesting examples. Many of us recall that in the 1960s it was a commonly held view that each major library would have to automate its operations, and that librarians would learn to master the computer that was soon to be installed in every library basement, or see themselves replaced by computer experts. As we all know, it did not happen that way. Librarians will probably end up with computer terminals or minicomputers, with software packages supplied by library cooperatives or commercial vendors.

When the MARC tapes were first made available, it was assumed (and that is what the MARC I experiment was all about) that each library would have to subscribe to the tapes and design, implement, and operate its own system to use the data in its cataloging operations. Again, it did not happen that way. MARC data are being used by libraries, but indirectly through cooperative centers such as OCLC, or through commercial vendors of card services such as Information Design or Josten's, Inc. Individual libraries are not subscribing to MARC tapes, as we had thought would be the case.

The point of citing these few examples is to suggest that it is extremely difficult in the early stage of a new technology to predict with any confidence how it will be introduced and implemented, and what effects it will have. We seem to have a natural tendency first to try to cope with each new technological development on a do-it-yourself individual library level, and when experience teaches us that implementing the particular technology is more difficult and more expensive than we thought, we regroup and try a broader-based approach. This is approximately where we are with data base services; it is time for a broader-based approach.

Again, it is unlikely that libraries will provide access to machine-readable data by setting up their own campus information centers to acquire and process data bases. Anyone who takes the time to look at a list of data bases available and their annual subscription rates will understand that research library book budgets will not be large enough to cover these additional subscription costs. In fact, the subscriptions are only a minor element in the total cost of providing these services. The data bases must be cumulated and maintained. Programs to manipulate and access them in their many nonstandard formats and contents must be written or adapted. The cost of administering and marketing the services and interfacing with the users will be high.

Perhaps the most critical question to be answered is: will the individual user be charged for the services he uses or will the costs be absorbed by the university? The answer to that question will determine how and to what extent the machine-based services will be used in the future. If they are offered free, as are traditional library services, then one can assume with some confidence that a substantial demand for them will materialize. This has in fact been the early experience of the centers at the University of Georgia and Ohio State and others where use has been totally subsidized by grant money.[3,4]

On the other hand, if the individual user is asked to pay for these services out of his own pocket or even out of departmental or grant funds, the market for them will be severely limited. It is extremely unlikely that large numbers of faculty and other researchers in universities will be seriously interested in becoming *paying* users of machine-based information services. The experience of C. C. Parker at the University of Southampton may prove to be typical.[5] He reported a drop from forty-seven to five users of an SDI service after charges were introduced. It was not that the users could not pay the charges, but that they preferred to use their resources for other more important needs. The National Library of Medicine recently instituted user charges in the MEDLINE system in order to effect a needed reduction in the number of users.

The case for giving these services to users free is theoretically sound in the traditional library context, but there are practical difficulties. First, these services will be expensive and they will require a net addition to library budgets rather than a transfer from one activity to another; the prospects for such budget increases seem dim in the next few years. Second, if the services are offered free, there will be no natural or automatic mechanism for controlling their use, and such control is essential to limit costs. Once users get on a free subscription list they will tend to stay on it whether they actually use the products or not. This happens in many libraries where current accessions lists are regularly sent to faculty, most of whom discard them unread. On the other hand, there is ample precedent for charging a modest fee for certain services in libraries. The best example is the almost universal charge for photocopies. In those instances where libraries offered free copies, the service was abused and charges had to be reinstated.

It seems likely that a combination of institutional subsidy and individual charges will evolve as the dominant method of paying for machine-readable services. In order to recover some costs and prevent abuses, an appropriate system of charges will have to be instituted in spite of the logic of the argument for free services. Incidentally, the case for free computer time in universities is perhaps equally valid, but it has never been accepted by the responsible budget officers.

Regardless of who pays, these services will have to be advertised and marketed aggressively to reach the limited number of potential users on each campus. It will not be enough to announce their availability and wait for customers. But even the best salesman on the most research-oriented campus will probably fail to find enough users to justify the high costs of providing the extensive and diverse subject coverage that every university will require. The solution, of course, lies in the establishment of a small number of comprehensive regional or even national information processing centers, possibly backed up by a much larger number of specialized centers or services for particular subject or mission-oriented fields such as physics, chemistry, medicine, pollution, urban studies, census data, etc.

Libraries will play a key role in facilitating access to data bases by functioning as the interface or broker between the users on campus and these regional and special processing and distribution centers. This means that they must develop a new kind of information or data services librarian on their reference staffs whose function it will be to publicize these services and maintain extensive files of information on their scope, contents, cost, and availability. These reference specialists will also guide users to the most appropriate services, help them to build and maintain their interest profiles, and provide assistance with the business aspects of dealing with vendors.[6] After an initial start-up period, this function should and doubtless will become a fully integrated part of the regular reference service, and the need for specialists will disappear as this knowledge becomes a part of every reference librarian's repertoire. The available data base services fall into two main categories: off-line batch and on-line interactive services. The most commonly available up to now have been regular off-line current awareness (SDI) services based on an interest profile; these have been supplemented by occasional requests for retrospective searches of the older files. The results of these off-line searches are delivered to the subscriber by conventional mail. On-line services permit the user or the reference specialist to access a portion of the data base directly via terminals and telephone lines and perform the search in an interactive mode. Some results are immediately displayed on the terminal and others are sent by mail.

The Lockheed Information Retrieval Service and Systems Development Corporation have recently begun offering interactive searching with on-line computer terminals of a large selection of the most useful bibliographic data bases. With this capability commercially available from leased terminals on a fee-per-use basis, it will be difficult for a university or even some existing centers to justify subscribing to and maintaining these data bases for their own limited use. If Lockheed, SDC, and other vendors can develop the market and operate these services at a profit, they may be able to satisfy a very substantial portion of the need for these new bibliographic services.

MEDLINE, TOXLINE, RECON, and the New York Times Information Bank provide other models for specialized and centralized interactive services. Some authorities assert that this trend toward on-line interactive searching will accelerate and eventually supersede tape searching.[7] Others argue that the cost of maintaining and searching on-line the really large data bases is prohibitive and will remain so for several years to come. It seems most likely to this author that the trend will be toward on-line systems covering a limited period of time, probably the latest three to five years, with supporting off-line services for retrospective searches. If this proves to be the case, libraries will find it practical and convenient to make terminals available at or near reference desks.

A close look at the several centers which now exist on individual campuses would probably show that they are heavily subsidized by grant or other outside funds, and that they are trying to expand to serve their states or even wider regions in order to achieve greater cost effectiveness. These centers deserve the credit that is always due pioneers. They are in the process of developing the patterns for providing these services in the future. One of the chief lessons they may have already taught us is that a single university, or even possibly a single state or region, is not a large enough market base upon which to build this activity. These centers will require a large volume of business to justify their high overhead and operating costs and they will seek and welcome additional paying customers.

To summarize and conclude, libraries will play a key role in providing access to machine-readable data bases, but they will generally not do it by acquiring and managing these data bases in local campus centers because of the high costs involved. These high costs and the limited market will restrict the number of processing centers to several regional or even national centers, supplemented by a larger number of specialized discipline and mission-oriented services. Many data bases and services will be available on a fee-for-service basis either through existing centers or directly from professional societies, government agencies, and commercial vendors with the library serving as facilitator or broker. It seems likely that a combination of institutional subsidies and individual charges will emerge as the pattern for paying for these new computer-based bibliographical services.

Notes

1. Marvin C. Gechman, "Machine-Readable Bibliographic Data Bases," in *Annual Review of Information Science and Technology,* v. 7 (Washington, D.C.: ASIS, 1972), p. 323–78.

2. Stella Keenan, ed., *Key Papers on the Use of Computer-Based Bibliographic Services* (Washington, D.C.: ASIS, 1973).

3. B. Marron, and others, *A Study of Six University-Based Information Systems* (Washington, D.C.: National Bureau of Standards, 1973 [NBS Technical Note 781]).

4. James L. Carmon, "A Campus-Based Information Center," *Special Libraries* 64:65–69 (Feb. 1973).

5. C. C. Parker, "The Use of External Current Awareness Services at Southampton University," *ASLIB Proceedings* 25:4–17 (Jan. 1973).

6. The University of Pennsylvania library . . . established a Data Services Office [in 1973] based on this concept with encouraging early results.

7. M. Cerville, L. D. Higgins, and Francis J. Smith, "Interactive Reference Retrieval in Large Files," *Information Storage and Retrieval* 7:205–10 (Dec. 1971).

MANAGING THE LIBRARY IN TRANSITION

SHIFTING GEARS: INFORMATION TECHNOLOGY AND THE ACADEMIC LIBRARY

This paper was presented at the School of Library and Information Science, University of Pittsburgh in 1983 as the Samuel Lazerow Memorial Lecture. It was first published in *Library Journal,* 15 June 1984, and subsequently reprinted in *Libraries and Information Science in the Electronic Age,* edited by Hendrik Edelman (Philadelphia: ISI Press, 1986), 23–35.

As everyone knows by now, there are a number of articulate spokesmen for a point of view which holds that information in electronic form will put an end to all but the most popular books, journals, and libraries by the year 2000. They urge librarians to save themselves either by abandoning their libraries and going into the information brokerage business or by transforming their libraries into electronic information services.[1]

Most librarians find that view simplistic and the advice impractical as a guide or strategy for coping with technology and change in their working environments. In a 1982 paper entitled "Libraries, Technology, and the Information Marketplace" (*Library Journal,* 1 June 1983, pp. 1045–1054), I offered a more practical and more optimistic view of the impact that information technology will have on libraries. I argued that the library function is essential and that libraries in one form or another will continue to be a critical link in the chain that produces, preserves, and disseminates the knowledge that has created and sustains our information society. I tried to show that technology is not making libraries obsolete; rather, it is revitalizing them and expanding their capabilities.

The Role of Libraries

It is obvious that information technology is already beginning to change publishing and libraries, and those changes will accelerate in the future, but no one can foretell yet whether or when technology will make books and libraries obsolete. The practical reality is that users continue to need libraries, and librarians must meet those needs with the resources and technologies that are now available. We have no choice but to assume that print materials will continue to coexist along with information in electronic form for at least another two decades—that is the rest of our working lives for most of us. The role of librarians, in the future as in the past, will be to carry out the library function, i.e., to decide what information to collect and preserve, how to organize it, and how to make it freely available to those who need it. The library function is vital to society, but it is not profitable and we cannot rely on the commercial sector to perform it.

Many, perhaps even most, librarians or information professionals will work outside libraries in the electronic future, but librarians who now work in libraries cannot and should not abandon their libraries to become information brokers or turn their libraries into information businesses. The job of librarians is to guide their libraries through a major transition from the collection-centered institutions that they are today to the access and service-oriented institutions that they must and, I believe, will become in the next two decades. The purpose of this paper is to assist librarians in making that transition, and to outline the major steps librarians must take to add a powerful new electronic dimension to the library's traditional collections and services.[2]

Economics and Technology

There is a quiet revolution going on in academic research libraries. It is a revolution that is being driven by powerful economic and technological forces. It started in the 1960s and is now accelerating at an extraordinary rate. By the end of this decade, libraries will be profoundly different from the libraries we have known and used in the past. To be sure, the buildings, book stacks, and the reading rooms will still be there, but the library will be fulfilling its mission in new ways, and it will be making extensive use of new information technologies.

Also in progress is a parallel revolution in the way universities fulfill their mission. The report of the Academic Computing Committee of the University of Pennsylvania begins with this statement:

> Information—its creation, transmission, and retrieval—is central to the function of a large research-oriented university such as the University of Pennsylvania. The changes in technology affecting the methods and economics of collecting, storing, retrieving, communicating, and displaying information will inevitably bring about large changes in the ways we teach, carry on research, and manage the institution. For Pennsylvania to maintain its position of excellence in instruction and research, the University must take advantage of the revolutionary changes occurring in computing.[3]

And for the library to maintain its position as the university's principal information resource and service, it will have to play a leading role in this technological revolution. In this electronic future, information will proliferate and become more ephemeral, and the task of bringing it under control will become more difficult and more vital. Thus, the new information-processing technologies will increase the importance and enlarge the role and capabilities of the academic library.

The challenge to librarians in the decade ahead is twofold: (1) to automate their public catalogs and internal operations and develop the capacity to deal with large quantities of information in a variety of new electronic forms, and (2) to continue to strengthen and provide for the growth of their traditional collections and services.

The challenge to those who fund libraries is to provide the financial resources that will be needed to accomplish this twofold task.

The famous line from Thomas Carlyle, "the true university is a collection of books," may have been true in his day, but it is not true today. This is an electronic age in which universities and the libraries that serve them must be much more than collections of books. Knowledge is being created and communicated at expanding rates, and this is causing profound changes in both the economics and technology of libraries. The way libraries are operated and funded must change if they are to continue to fulfill their mission of supporting instruction and research in this rapidly changing environment.

During the last decade, research libraries have been experiencing a significant erosion in their level of support and, therefore, in their ability to provide traditional levels of collections and services. Inflation in book and journal prices has far outpaced the annual increases in library book and journal budgets. U.S. periodical prices have quadrupled and hardcover book prices have tripled. The price of scholarly books and journals continues to rise at an average rate of 15 percent a year. Association of Research Libraries (ARL) statistics show a decline of 3 percent a year in the number of volumes added by its members in recent years. Meanwhile, the number of books and journals published in the United States and abroad continues to increase at record rates. Libraries are spending more money every year to buy an ever-decreasing percentage of the rapidly growing output of the world's publishers.

While the total number of budgeted positions in ARL libraries has remained stable during the last 10 years, staff reductions are becoming commonplace in a growing number of libraries. These personnel losses and the parallel erosion of book and journal budgets have created a management environment in which there are no slack resources which can be reallocated from one function to another or used to implement new programs and services. Thus, at the very time when libraries are struggling to maintain their traditional collections and services in the face of inflation and eroding support, they must computerize their manual operations, put their card catalogs online, and expand their capacity to deal with information in a variety of electronic forms. In sum, libraries are experiencing severe economic pressures at a time when the information explosion and the computer and communications revolution are increasing the number and variety of the demands that are being made upon them.

The combined effects of these long-term inflationary trends and the rapid growth of new information forms and technologies are causing a fundamental change in the way libraries support teaching and research and in the way library budgets are being allocated and spent. Until this decade, collection building and growth were the dominant driving forces in academic research libraries. Libraries were ranked by the size of their collections, and bigger was always better and more prestigious. The job of the library director was to get and spend as much money as possible for books and journals, and to provide the space in which to house them and the staff to acquire and service them. And as far as faculty and academic administrators were concerned, spending money to purchase books and journals was good, while spending money for any other purpose was bad or, at best, a regrettable necessity.

From Collections to Access

The emphasis in libraries is shifting from collections to access. Providing access to information will be the principal goal and activity, and coping with technology and change will be the principal driving forces of the emerging information age library. Those who use libraries, and those who provide their financial support, must recognize and accept this new reality. The explosion in the quantity, cost, and communicability of information is a new phenomenon which calls for new responses. Among those responses must be a willingness to embrace new technology and accept change. It should be clear to all by now that no research library can meet its users' needs solely, or even largely, from its own book, journal, and manuscript collections. Even the Library of Congress sees itself as part of a network of research libraries.

The economic and technical developments of the 1970s have convinced librarians of the need to restructure the university library to function as part of a national and international library network. However, we are far ahead of our faculties, administrators, and governing boards in that regard and we need to bring them up to speed. Librarians need to help develop within the academic community a new consensus about how the library should fulfill its mission, how it should be funded, and how its funds should be allocated in the changing environment of the 1980s and beyond. Faculty and administrators must accept and support the library's growing need to spend money, not only to purchase books and journals, but also to pay for computer systems, telecommunications, network participation, and the various other charges and fees that go with obtaining access to information in new ways and new forms.

Library and information services will cost more in the future than they do now, but they will be far more effective. The pattern of expenditures will change, and an increasing proportion of the library budget will go for new technology and access services. The acquisitions budget must be increased substantially and its function expanded to include acquiring and providing access to collections of information in electronic form. Libraries will have to rely increasingly on the collections and services of other libraries through library consortia, such as the Research Libraries Group (RLG) and OCLC, and commercial information vendors. To do this will require additional and more highly skilled staff in some areas.

Economic pressures are making it necessary, and technological advances are making it possible, for librarians to locate and deliver a wide range of books and journals that they do not own or cannot acquire. The multi-million record online databases and the powerful communications systems provided by RLG and OCLC are reducing interlibrary loan delivery times from weeks to days. The electronic text delivery systems that are being developed and tested promise to reduce document delivery times to a matter of hours and minutes before the end of this decade.

Penn's participation in the East Asian program of RLG provides a good example of technology-assisted resource sharing in action. This important program is based on RLIN's capability for processing Chinese, Japanese, and Korean (CJK) vernacular language records. The start-up costs for equipment and training are heavy. However, our participation in this program will, in time, give our East Asian scholars access to the combined resources of all the other CJK network participants. Included among them are the Library of Congress and 16 of the most important East Asian collections in the United States and Canada.

If, instead of investing in this program, my library spent an equivalent sum buying books for its own modest collection, our East Asian scholars should be less well served and the Penn Library would contribute nothing to building this important network. Moreover, I can make a more powerful case to my administration and to prospective donors for new technology than I can for a budget increase which will permit us to do a little more of what we have always done in the past. And what is true for RLG's East Asian Program is true for many of the other RLG programs and initiatives.

The hard lesson of the last decade is that the annual budget increases that libraries would need to carry on in the traditional mode will simply not be forthcoming. We have to invest in new technology and new ways of doing the library's business, and we must be prepared in some cases to wait several years before the investment begins to pay off. Just as we build library collections and space for future use, so must we build the library's technical infrastructure and networking capabilities for future use.

Finally, it must be said that resource sharing is a supplement to, and not a substitute for, strong, working collections in libraries. Librarians turn to resource sharing from necessity, not from preference. The reality is that most of the routine needs of most library users must continue to be met from a library's own collection in the future as they have been in the past. However, the interests of researchers are expanding, and a growing proportion of their occasional, special, and peripheral needs will have to be met from external sources. In addition, an increasing amount of information will be available only in electronic form. In the future, the excellence and usefulness of a library will be measured not only by the size and quality of its own collections, but also by the range of resources that its staff is able to deliver to users by conventional and electronic means from a growing variety of sources. Users will no longer be limited to what a library has, but to what it can provide.

Planning the Transition

Libraries are coming to terms with the new economic and technological realities of the 1980s. They are replacing their cumbersome manual procedures with more effective computer and telecommunications systems, and they are developing efficient resource-sharing capabilities by participating in networks. Some libraries have already laid the foundation and have taken a number of important and successful steps toward building an information-age library capability, but most of us still have a long way to go. It is time to shift gears and begin making comprehensive plans and a convincing case for adding a new electronic dimension to the library's traditional mode of operation. That new dimension involves using new organizational capabilities, such as RLG, and new information and telecommunications technologies to increase access to library collections and the means of making them and other electronic information resources available to users.

Determining the right goals and the best strategies and timing for achieving them is the central issue in directing libraries or any other enterprise. If a leader correctly assesses future trends and directions and adopts the right goals and strategies, then it matters much less if the means, the resources available, or the tactics used are deficient in various ways. Going part way toward the right goal is always better than going a long way toward the wrong one. Peter Drucker, as usual, says it best: "It is better to do the right thing than to do things right."

One Goal and Four Objectives

I believe the right goal for a research library in the next decade is to plan and implement a comprehensive program for using computer and communications technologies to add a powerful new electronic dimension to supplement and enhance its traditional collections and services. At the same time, it must also continue to strengthen its traditional collections and services and provide the necessary physical facilities to house them. The electronic dimension cannot be developed at the expense of the traditional; both must be given equal importance. And to achieve this twofold goal most effectively, it must be done within the context of a research libraries network, for no library can continue to function autonomously in this electronic information age. In the words of Patricia Battin, Director of Libraries at Columbia University, "We must change to survive . . . and we must reinvent the research library in the network environment."[4]

Identifying and stating that goal is easy. The hard part is to formulate a plan for achieving it that is appropriate to a particular library and institution, and then to sell that plan to the library's users and the officers and governing boards that make its policy decisions and provide its funds.

I believe there are four major tasks or objectives that need to be accomplished by any library that wants to shift gears and add this electronic dimension to supplement and enhance its traditional collections and services in the decade ahead: (1) to implement an integrated system with an online catalog and appropriate internal and external network interfaces; (2) to convert the library's card catalog records to machine-readable form and add them to the online catalog; (3) to continue to strengthen the library's own book and journal collections while also developing its capacity to provide access to scholarly resources elsewhere in both traditional and electronic forms; and (4) to provide for the library's growing and changing space needs during this time of transition.

I will further define and discuss each of these four objectives.

The First Objective

The first objective is to install an integrated system and online catalog with network interfaces. This comprehensive online system should link the separate units of a university library into a single coordinated library information network. This network must interface internally with the campus local area network of terminals and personal computers, and externally with one or more of the library networks, such as RLG or OCLC, and with the growing network of commercial and other information services.

The local library network has two principal functions. The first is to provide a comprehensive and integrated online system for handling all the library's internal operational needs, including acquisitions, cataloging, authority control, serials management, and circulation control. The second is to provide an online public access catalog of essentially all the holdings of the various units of a university library. The online catalog will replace the card catalogs and provide a system that will unify the physically separate libraries into a single comprehensive library and information network.

Separate systems capable of performing each of these library functions are available in the marketplace today, but despite the claims of vendors, it is not yet possible to purchase a fully integrated system that will perform effectively all the required functions for even a small library. It may be another two or three years before one or more integrated systems are available to meet the requirements of a medium-sized research library.

The Second Objective

The second objective is to convert all or a substantial part of the library's catalog records to machine-readable form and make them accessible on the online catalog. Once thought to be prohibitively expensive, the task of converting library catalogs to machine-readable form is now technically and economically feasible, thanks to the availability of the catalog conversion capabilities of OCLC, RLIN, and certain commercial vendors. A library that makes maximum use of these large databases and new conversion capabilities can avoid or minimize the costly task of keyboarding its own catalog records.

Libraries have made an enormous investment in acquiring, cataloging, and maintaining their older book and journal collections. Those collections are increasing in value and importance with the passage of time, and they continue to be used. It will be worth it for most libraries to invest the money and effort required to convert all, or a substantial portion, of the card catalog records of these older collections and make them available on the online catalog. If those books are represented in the online catalog, they will continue to be used; if they are not, they may be overlooked and the library's investment in them will be lost. Experience in libraries that have online catalogs shows that once an online catalog is available—even a partial one—most users will prefer it and avoid using the old card catalog. In other words, the online catalog will be the first, perhaps the only, choice of many readers, and it must therefore be made as complete as possible.

The Third Objective

The third objective is to continue to strengthen the library's book and journal collections, and, by using new technology, to enhance its ability to provide access to the resources of other libraries as well as to the growing universe of information in electronic form.

The library's traditional book, journal, and manuscript collections are and will continue to be the mainstay of libraries and their services to users for at least another decade or two. The new information technologies will increase greatly the quantity and range of research resources available to scholars, but they will not make it unnecessary for libraries to continue to strengthen their collections.

Strengthening local collections is essential, but a library cannot possibly acquire everything its users will want or need. Other approaches to making resources and information in other libraries accessible to users must be further developed and expanded. Computer assisted interlibrary loan through OCLC, RLG, and other networks is becoming increasingly important. The quantity of research information available in electronic form is growing rapidly. Since 1975, several hundred major databases have been made available online through commercial vendors, professional associations, and learned societies. Online searching of abstracting and indexing services is becoming the preferred way of doing literature searches. In addition, full text systems for searching and retrieving large stores of information in law, business, science, and current news are expanding rapidly.

In the next several years, a number of extremely powerful new technologies will come into use and will have an extraordinary impact on libraries and the research process. Prominent among these will be powerful workstations and new optical and video laser disk technologies which reduce dramatically the cost of storing and retrieving vast quantities of text in electronic form. The Library of Congress has taken the lead in developing and using these capabilities in libraries, both for more efficient access as well as for preservation purposes. Some commercial vendors are developing prototype systems which will contain the text of hundreds of journals stored on optical disks and linked to personal computers directly or by telephone lines.

Libraries must begin to develop the capacity to acquire and make available to users selected files and collections of research data and other information in electronic form. However, in many cases it will not be feasible to acquire the data, and we will have to provide access to it on demand. The question of who will pay the cost of accessing the data is an important policy issue which will have to be resolved.

The library staff will also have to keep users informed about new electronic information sources and teach them to do online searches on their own personal computers and terminals. New commercially available expert systems will make this possible for users with a serious interest.

The Fourth Objective

The fourth objective is to provide the physical facilities needed for the continued growth of the collections and the changing needs of users and staff in the next decade or two by making better and more intensive use of existing space and by building new space as needed.

It is difficult to generalize about library space needs and how to cope with them. Providing space for growth is a problem that nearly every library has, and each one must deal with it in its own way. Space is a compelling problem and one that librarians and university administrators are accustomed to dealing with on a high-priority basis. A library with a serious space problem may find it difficult to give a higher priority to the first three objectives that I have outlined unless it can demonstrate that retooling the library with new technology will help alleviate the space problem in the future.

The space needs of a central research library and each of the department and professional school libraries are usually distinctive and will be met in different ways. It is likely that new space for department and professional school libraries will continue to be constructed as needed. However, I believe that economic conditions in the next two decades will make it impossible, and technological developments will make it unnecessary, for many universities to build new central library buildings or major additions to them along conventional lines. The rate of growth of collections will continue to decline in the next decade as it has in the last, and emphasis on electronic access will grow. As the cost of constructing and maintaining new stack spaces continues to rise, libraries will turn increasingly to off-site storage and to the use of mobile compact shelving where floor capacities permit. Empty aisles are becoming an unaffordable luxury in large libraries. In the future, faced with the choice of moving books to off-site storage or installing mobile compact storage, many libraries will opt for the latter.

Funding the Transition

The cost of implementing these objectives and operating libraries with this added technological dimension will be high. We must face this fact openly and honestly. We must not try to justify this major investment in advanced technology on the grounds that it will reduce costs, because it will not. The reason for making this investment is not to save money, but to enable libraries to better serve the research and instructional needs of their parent universities in an information society and a high-technology world. If the library fails to make this transition, the tremendous investment that universities have made in their library collections and facilities will be seriously undermined. Libraries must keep pace with new information technology and the changing needs of users, or they will lose their support base and their role as the principal provider of information services to universities. If this happens, alternative means of meeting the universities' growing needs for information in electronic form will have to be developed outside the library—and probably at a much higher cost in the long run.

Our task as librarians is to convince our backers and funders to invest the large sums of money needed to add this electronic dimension to our libraries. We cannot bootstrap our libraries into the electronic age. When we first started using computers in libraries 20 years ago, we thought we would save money. Then we thought automation would at least reduce the rate of rise of library costs, but even this is proving to be illusory as the demand for new and more sophisticated systems and services increases. We are no longer merely automating our internal operations, we are providing new user services and access to a broader range of resources both traditional and electronic. As these new services become more efficient and more widely known, demand for them will increase, and while the unit cost of providing any given service will decline, the total cost of satisfying the increased demand will go up.

Online search capabilities such as those provided by RLG, OCLC, MEDLINE, ORBIT, BRS, and DIALOG are a good case in point. By using them effectively, reference librarians have expanded their capabilities along with the demand for their services. The net result is a rapid rise in the cost and quality of reference service. The same is true of interlibrary loan (ILL) service. The use of online search services increased the demand for ILL, and the use of the OCLC and RLG communications systems and dabatases increased its speed and effectiveness. Those and other factors are causing a dramatic increase in the use of ILL services. The cost per transaction is declining, but the total cost to the library of providing ILL services is rising. The trade-off is that improved ILL service compensates for reduced acquisitions rates and increases the range of available materials. These are good examples of how technology is changing the nature of library costs and benefits.

Convincing funding authorities to make multi-million dollar investments to add this electronic dimension to libraries during the years ahead in the face of falling enrollments, declining graduate programs, and chronic budget crises will be extremely difficult, at best. The ultimate decisions in these matters are made by laymen—trustees, foundation executives, academic officers, and faculty committees. The issues are complex and confusing, and there is no consensus yet about how libraries need to be retooled and linked in networks and the role that the Council on Library Resources, the Library of Congress, RLG, OCLC, ARL, and other organizations should play in the process.

At first glance, the prospects of finding the money for retooling libraries for the new mode of operation in the years ahead appear grim. However, there are a number of academic research libraries which, with local or foundation support, are in fact well along the road to making this transition. As those leaders succeed, they will serve as powerful examples, and gradually the necessary consensus will emerge and the financial resources will be found to fund library transitions in an increasing number of universities. The university library is a powerful symbol of what universities are all about, and when some libraries show the way, the others will soon follow. Universities must compete with each other for grants, students, and prestige, and they dare not be left behind.

A few years ago it was difficult to foresee the growing trend and the intense competition that now exist among leading universities to wire their campuses, install local area networks, and equip their students and faculty with personal computers. When those developments take place at universities whose libraries have accessible online catalogs and a full range of other electronic capabilities, the personal computers and terminals will be plugged into the library and a revolution in the way libraries are used, perceived, and funded will take place. And when those developments take place at universities whose libraries are not accessible electronically, the pressure will be on to make them accessible. In the past, the pressure to automate the library, to convert its catalog to machine-readable form, and to provide online access to it came almost entirely from the librarians themselves. In the future, it will come from computer-wise students and faculty. That pressure can be harnessed to produce the substantial capital investment needed to add an electronic dimension to the traditional library and make it an integral part of the university's information-processing network.

Where will universities turn for these capital funds? They

will turn to the same sources they turn to for capital funds to build new buildings and to finance other important new programs, including the wiring of their campuses and the creation of integrated personal computer networks. The funds required to retool the library will be seen as a necessary part of the much larger sums that will be needed to bring the rest of the university into the electronic age. Universities will mount fundraising campaigns among their alumni, foundations, and corporations, and they will also turn to state and Federal government.

Some state governments have special programs to encourage the growth of high-technology industries which tend to be located near and draw on the resources of research universities. The Federal government appears to be an unlikely source of support in view of its current efforts to eliminate all library programs. However, most of those programs belong to a passing era, and while some continue to be essential, most have either served their purpose or have lost their vitality and should be phased out. Academic and library leaders should join forces to make a fresh and compelling case for a new Federal program designed to retool libraries for an information society.

The question, in my opinion, is not whether, but when and how, libraries will get the money they need to retool for the electronic future. Universities generally find the money to do what they have to do. I believe they are going to have to invest heavily in information technology in the years ahead, not only to increase the effectiveness of teaching and research, but also of the libraries that support those functions. Thus, librarians, and particularly those who feel discouraged about the readiness or ability of their institutions to fund a major technological initiative, should take heart and begin planning ahead. And when they do so, they should be guided by the wise advice of Daniel Burnham, who said: "Make no small plans, they have no magic to stir men's blood. Make big plans and aim high."

Notes

1. See F. Wilfred Lancaster's *Libraries and Librarians in an Age of Electronics* (Arlington, Va.: Information Resources Press, 1982). Another useful recent book from a British point of view is James Thompson's *The End of Libraries* (London: Clive Bingley, 1982). See also *Into the*

Information Age: A Perspective for Federal Action on Information by Vincent E. Giuliano and others. This is a study by Arthur D. Little, Inc., published by ALA, 1978. A brief and popular presentation of some of the same material can be found in Giuliano's article, "A Manifesto for Librarians," *Library Journal,* 15 September 1979, pp. 1837–1842.

2. This paper draws heavily on the ideas and text of "A Five Year Plan for the Penn Libraries, 1985–1989" which appeared in *Into the Information Age: Report of the Director of Libraries, University of Pennsylvania, 1982–1983* by Richard De Gennaro, *ALMANAC* Insert, 17 January 1983, Philadelphia.

3. "Report of the Academic Computing Committee," University of Pennsylvania *ALMANAC,* 29 November 1983.

4. Battin, Patricia, "Research Libraries in the Network Environment: The Case for Cooperation," *EDUCOM Bulletin,* Summer 1980, pp. 26–31.

THEORY VS. PRACTICE IN LIBRARY MANAGEMENT

Reprinted from *Library Journal* July 1983, p. 1318–1321.

This article and "Library Administration and New Management Systems" (1978) were both written at a time when new management theories and systems were enjoying a tremendous vogue in the literature and at conferences. Most of the articles were being written by professors or staff people. My experience as a practitioner went counter to much of what was being said about management and I said so. I was taken to task by management professors who faulted me for undermining their teaching of management in library schools. My skepticism about efficacy of management theories and the teaching of management is now much more widely shared.

In a memorable scene in the movie *Little Big Man,* Dustin Hoffman, in the title role, plays the part of a Western gunfighter. Little Big Man has built a great reputation as the fastest draw and the straightest shooter in the territory. The camera shows him drawing his guns and blazing away with astonishing speed and accuracy at rows of bottles and tin cans behind the ranch house. His only problem is that he has acquired all his skills as a gunfighter on that makeshift target range. He has never actually killed a man or even faced one in a real gunfight. The first time he goes eyeball to eyeball in the old saloon with a real live, mean, ready-to-kill gunslinger, our hero loses his nerve, is paralyzed with fright, and is unable to draw his guns. Fortunately, Little Big Man's opponent spares him—but that is not what usually happens in real life.

Little Big Man knew the theory and technique of gunfighting, but he lacked courage and experience, and without those essential qualities, his knowledge and skills were useless. Well, they were useless in a gunfight, but they would be useful to him as a consultant or teacher. If he applied himself to studying and researching the history and techniques of gunfighting, he could become an authority on the subject. That is something, but it is not the same as being a successful gunfighter.

What is true of gunfighting is equally true of other fields. Military theorists don't necessarily make good field generals. Political scientists are not necessarily good politicians, and few economists are millionaires. Management professors and management consultants are not necessarily good managers. Without belaboring the point, we need to remind ourselves from time to time that there is a big difference between theory and practice, between thought and action. One is not better or more important than the other, but they are different.

In an essay entitled "Leaders of Men," Woodrow Wilson wrote:

> Those only are leaders of men, in the general eye, who lead in action. . . . The men who act stand nearer to the mass of men than do the men who write; and it is at their hands that new thought gets its translation into the crude language of deeds. . . . [1]

Wilson was discussing the nature of leadership and the differences between great literary and political figures, but he also gives us much insight into the nature of and differences between theorists and practitioners. He says theory is rational and elegant, but when practitioners apply it in the real world, it becomes crude and messy—and vital and effective. In Wilson's view, the true leader is the thinking person in action—and Wilson achieved that status himself, later in his life.

In a self-interview entitled "75 Years and Two Cents Worth" *American Libraries* editor, Art Plotnik, gives us another useful insight into the important differences between theory and practice and thought and action:

> If I've learned anything in 15 years of librarian watching, it's that the best judgements, the fairest policies, are made de facto by practicing librarians on the front lines. These are bright people; humanistic people. That's why they're in the field. They can handle such moral quandaries

as when and when not to charge user fees, and do so more realistically than those in secondary librarianship.

Secondary Librarianship?

Yes, those having no direct contact with day-to-day library services are part of what I call secondary librarianship. That includes library journalists, ALA staff, NCLIS, the Council on Library Resources, U.S. Education Department, network staff, library educators, and members of a hundred other bureaus, agencies, and services. I believe most of us are dedicated, necessary elements of the profession; but the day we start thinking we know more about librarianship than those in primary service will be the day our usefulness ends.[2]

That is a perceptive and courageous observation. It could only be made by a secondary librarian who is confident of his own valuable contribution to librarianship.

Forcing Theory into Practice

The practice of librarianship, like the practice of business, used to be a very practical and pragmatic activity. There was a time when there were no library schools and no business schools, and beginners learned by doing on the job. Then came the library and business schools and beginners were given formal courses laced with potentially useful theory and practical skills; and they were better prepared in a shorter time. Then in the last 15 to 20 years another change began to occur. The business schools, with library schools right behind them, began to put increasing stress on operations research, new management systems based on quantitative analysis, and acronyms like PPBS (Planning, Programming, and Budgeting System) and ZBB (Zero-Base Budgeting) became buzzwords.

Along with these new quantitative systems came a rash of new systems and theories from the behavioral sciences. We had Management by Objective, new systems for participative management, and a host of others. It was frequently said and widely believed that these new management systems and theories were going to change management from an art to a science and usher in a new era when management could cease to be full of risk and uncertainty and organizations would work with mechanical and electronic precision. Theory was going to merge with and become practice.

It didn't happen that way. In libraries, the practitioners

were either skeptical of the usefulness of these new systems and theories or they found them simply too complex and too costly to implement. Where they were implemented, they frequently did more harm than good. We librarians are a modest lot and we thought maybe the fault was in ourselves and not in the systems and theories. We were told and believed that these same systems and theories which came out of our most prestigious business schools, were working well in American business and industry, but they have not been working very well, as anyone knows who reads the papers these days. For example, the lead article in the Business section of the *New York Times* on May 30, 1982, "Management Gospel Gone Wrong," reported the new ideas of Robert Hayes and William Abernathy, two professors at the Harvard Business School, on the real causes of the decline of American business. Hayes and Abernathy wrote an all-time bestseller article in the *Harvard Business Review* entitled: "Managing Our Way to Economic Decline."[3]

Challenging the "B" Schools

These two scholars are challenging what is taught in the best business schools, passed on by the most prestigious consultants, and practiced in our leading corporations. They are saying that we shouldn't be blaming excessive government regulations, greedy labor unions, the declining work ethic, the Japanese, or the energy crisis for the ills of American industry. Instead, they put the blame squarely on American management doctrine as it is being promulgated by the elite business schools. They say that American managers have lost sight of the basics and are neglecting production—the factory floor and the assembly line—in favor of finance and marketing. That, plus excessive management concern for short-term profits, goes far to explain the current decline of American business. The business schools, they argue, have imbued a generation of business leaders with the wrong ideas.

This serious indictment is causing a lot of soul-searching and debate among business leaders and the faculties of business schools. Many of them agree, but others say that the Hayes-Abernathy view is too simplistic and is yet another false gospel coming from our most prestigious business school.

Hayes and Abernathy are not the first nor the only ones

questioning the "Gospel of Scientific Management" as preached by the business schools. In my own 1978 *LJ* article, "Library Administration and New Management Systems," I argued that management was an art, not a science, and that the new complex management systems were not working in business and would not work in libraries.[4]

Theodore Levitt, another Harvard Business School professor, published similar criticisms in a 1978 *Fortune* article, "A Heretical View of Management Science." The opening sentence reads: "There is only one way to manage anything, and that is to keep it simple." That sets the tone of the article and is, incidentally, the best piece of management advice around. If you add to that Bert Lance's dictum, "If it ain't broke, don't fix it" (which Levitt also cites), you have two commonsense rules of management that will carry you a long way.

The essence of Levitt's heretical view of management "science" is contained in this paragraph:

> Still, as a corporation gets better managed and more concerned with the quality and practice of management itself, its top people develop a powerful propensity to manage differently. They are encouraged in this by a rapidly expanding retinue of eager sycophants, equipped with new "scientific" tools and decision-making modes, who promise to free the manager from the inescapable uncertainties, risks, and traumas of running an enterprise. "Experts" trained to the teeth in the techniques (but not necessarily the practice) of management, are enlisted to do even better what people of native shrewdness, sound good sense, and abundant energy did quite beautifully before.[5]

Admiral Hyman G. Rickover is another articulate critic of the "management science" mystique. In a Columbia University address excerpted in the November 25, 1981 *New York Times,* (p. 23) he said:

> Our universities should emphasize the importance of a solid grounding in substantive learning and downgrade "management" science.
>
> What it takes to do a job will not be learned from management courses. It is principally a matter of experience, the proper attitude, and common sense—none of which can be taught in a classroom.
>
> I am not against business education. A knowledge of accounting,

finance, business law, and the like can be of value in a business environment. What I do believe is harmful is the impression often created by those who teach "management" that one will be able to manage any job simply by applying certain management techniques, together with some simple academic rules of how to manage people and situations.

Henry Minzberg is the author of *The Nature of Managerial Work* (Harper, 1973) and another all-time best selling article in the July-August 1975 issue of the *Harvard Business Review* entitled "The Manager's Job: Folklore and Fact." Like Rickover and Levitt, Minzberg concludes, from his studies of what managers actually do, that management, leadership, and entrepreneurship cannot be taught in the classroom any more than swimming can be learned by reading about it.

Library Managing

My own experience as a manager on the job and in the classroom, as both a teacher and student, has convinced me that business and library schools cannot really teach students how to be managers. What they can and do teach are a variety of theories and insights about management along with a range of useful techniques and skills that are used largely by management teachers, consultants, specialists, and staff people who work for or around managers. What they teach is what some critics call "a bag of tricks." On the quantitative side, they range from decision theory to statistical and systems analysis, and to complex systems like Zero-Base Budgeting. On the behavioral side, they range from Management by Objective to the many versions of McGregor's Theory Y.

Managers Are Generalists

In the library environment, these theories and systems are still only of marginal usefulness. When they are used at all, it is more by people in staff positions, such as personnel and financial officers, and systems people, than by line managers. Even among staff people, the knowledge of and ability to use those theories and techniques is almost always less important for success than good judgment and common sense. With some jobs, for example, computer programmers and technicians, technical skills are of overriding importance, but this is not the case in most library jobs. Most managers are generalists. They may have come from the ranks of the specialists, but to succeed as managers, they must become generalists.

In that 1978 *LJ* article I said that the new management systems contained many useful concepts, ideas, and techniques, but as comprehensive systems they are all too theoretical, complex, and simplistic, to be applied successfully by ordinary library managers in the day-to-day work world. Few managers have the time or the specialized knowledge and skills required to make these systems work, and those that do can probably manage as well or better without them.

In the hands of ordinary managers (most of us), the quantitative systems can produce misleading and wrong solutions, while the behavioral systems can be used to manipulate and exploit people. The real danger with both types of systems is that they offer mechanistic formulas for dealing with complex realities. They keep us from managing in practical, realistic, and common-sense ways.

Peter Drucker says that the most important qualities a manager must possess are integrity of character, courage, and vision. These are not qualities a manager can acquire. Managers bring them to the job, and if they don't bring them, it will not take long for their people to discover it and they will not forgive the manager for it.[6]

Drucker says somewhere else that it is better to do the right thing than to do things right. He also says that Management by Objective works if you know what the objectives are, but 90 percent of the time you don't. To identify the right objectives, to know what the right thing to do is, and then to have the courage to decide to do it in the face of uncertainty, and have the trust and confidence of your people so they will follow you—that is what management and leadership are about. They depend on character, courage, and commitment, not on techniques and tools. To be a leader is to have a vision, a goal, and a determination to reach it.

The success or failure of a manager is decided not in the normal day-to-day operations of an enterprise, but during those rare times of crisis when critical decisions have to be made. If a manager in a time of crisis, lacks the courage to stand up for principles, or to make or stand by the hard decision, he or she will lose the trust of the staff and the right and ability to lead them.

Entrepreneurs and Time Servers

Just as management specialists are different from managers, so managers are different from entrepreneurs. There are not many entrepreneurs in the library field, but there are some. I think of people like Fred Kilgour, the founder of OCLC, and Eugene Garfield, the founder of the Institute for Scientific Information, and some library and network directors who behave more like entrepreneurs than managers or administrators. Good entrepreneurs are usually poor managers and vice versa. The personal qualities required to found a new enterprise or chart a major new direction are very different from those required to manage a stable organization. Entrepreneurs are constantly experimenting and trying new ideas. They have healthy egos, enormous self-confidence, and a single-minded determination to succeed. They are risk takers, even gamblers.

Most truly good managers possess to some degree many of the qualities of successful entrepreneurs, but they are usually more practical and prudent. They know what can and cannot be done. Entrepreneurs don't recognize the traditional boundaries and limitations. They don't know that the thing they are trying to do can't be done, the way the conventional managers do, so they just go ahead. Sometimes they succeed. Entrepreneurs make the significant advances. If library and business schools have failed to teach practical management, they have not even tried to teach entrepreneurship.

At the other end of the management spectrum are the time servers. Their idea of success is to maintain a stable organization and survive until they retire. At their best, they keep the organizational machine oiled and running. At their worst, they create backlogs of problems and unfinished business.

The Need to Reexamine

If the management professors and business leaders who invented those dubious and sometimes troublesome scientific management theories and systems are beginning to question their validity and applicability in the practical world of business, then we librarians ought to begin questioning their use in the world of libraries. It is time for a thorough reexamination of all the theories, assumptions, and received ideas that have shaped the way we have thought about and managed libraries in the last several decades.

We need to reexamine our ideas about what the real needs of our users are and what it takes to satisfy them. Contrary to the folklore of our profession, the real needs of all but a small fraction of library users are not for enormous and comprehensive collections of books and journals. The goal of amassing large collections comes from an earlier time when books and journals were fewer in number and less expensive. In the last two decades, the number of titles being published has exploded along with their prices. The task for libraries, now and in the coming years, is to learn to be selective and to build lean, quality collections from the mass of printed and other materials that are gushing forth from the world's publishers. We also need to further develop our capabilities to gain effective access to materials that we do not and cannot have in our local collections as well as to resources in electronic form.

Just as American business is going back to basics, rediscovering the importance of the factory floor and production, so we librarians need to go back to basics and rediscover that our main function is serving users, not building collections. It is not our main function to devise and implement new cataloging codes, or online catalogs, or national networks. Like collection building, these are all means of serving users and not ends in themselves. We have sometimes forgotten this in the excitement of implementing new technology in this time of rapid change.

There is no necessary or significant correlation between the size of a library's collections, staff, or expenditures and the effectiveness of its services or the degree of user satisfaction. Some of our largest libraries are the most difficult and frustrating to use. In library matters, we tend to equate quantity with quality. The bigger the numbers, the better the library. In the past we have accepted that premise without much question. Now, diminishing financial support and expanding technology are forcing us to put quality and user satisfaction ahead of growth and large numbers as the goal of library management.

It's the Results That Count

During the last two decades the management scientists have dominated the management scene. They have had their chance to show what they can do and it has not been much. Now it is time for the practicing general managers to reassert their primacy in the art of management. The management scientists are Woodrow Wilson's thinkers and writers. The general managers are Wilson's "men of action." They have been very busy managing their companies and their libraries. They have neither the time nor the aptitude to write and theorize about management. They express themselves in action.

During these last two decades the people of action, the managers, have allowed themselves to be intimidated and upstaged by the people who write—by the theoreticians. There has been such a tremendous increase in the amount of theory and writing about management that it tends to overshadow and diminish the importance of practice. Theory is supposed to improve practice. The test of the value of a theory or a technique is how well it can be applied by practitioners. Sometimes we say something is good in theory, but bad in practice. That cannot be. If it is bad in practice, it can't be good in theory.

From the time of Machiavelli, managers have used and appreciated the theories and advice that was offered to them by the thinkers and writers. In recent years many new and inexperienced managers have relied too heavily on managing by the book and have damaged their organizations in the process. Practical managers cannot avoid the uncertainties and risks inherent in their jobs by using or misusing these faddish scientific management tools.

Yes, managers learn from theory as well as from experience. The more experienced a manager is the more he or she can learn from theory. Experience teaches managers when (and when not) and how to use the growing variety of theories and techniques that are available to them. But theories and techniques have no value unless and until they are used to enhance and facilitate practice. In the end it is the results that count.

I do not want to disparage the management courses that are offered at library and business schools, and particularly not the people who are teaching them. My point is that there is a big difference between theory and practice in management, between the textbook professional manager and the practical general manager, and between the specialist technician and the generalist. What is being taught in management courses is not general management, but the theories and techniques that are used by management specialists. These management specialists serve useful, and sometimes not so useful purposes, but what they do is not management and should not be confused with it. Practical management is far more human, subtle, and complex than the tools and techniques of management science.

Notes

1. Wilson, Woodrow, *Leaders of Men*. Ed. by T. H. Vail Motter. Princeton Univ. Pr., 1952. p. 19.

2. Plotnik, Art. "75 Years and Two Cents Worth," *American Libraries,* January 1982, p. 6.

3. Abernathy, William & Robert Hays. "Managing Our Way to Decline," *Harvard Business Review,* July-August 1980.

4. De Gennaro, Richard. "Library Administration and New Management Systems," *LJ,* December 15, 1978, p. 2477–82 [reprinted in this volume].

5. Levitt, Theodore. "A Heretical View of Management Science," *Fortune,* December 18, 1978, p. 50.

6. Drucker, Peter. *Management.* Harper, 1974, p. 462.

MATCHING COMMITMENTS TO NEEDS AND RESOURCES

This paper was given initially as the University of Tennessee Library Lecture in 1980 and was published in *Library Journal,* March 1981, 9–13.

The principal thesis of the paper is that librarians are guilty of accepting commitments that are far beyond their ability to fulfill and that this perpetuates the cycle of poverty and failure in libraries. This promises to be an even more serious problem as libraries reach out to take responsibility for information in a wide variety of new electronic formats without demanding the additional financial resources necessary to fulfill that responsibility.

There is a chronic fiscal crisis in libraries which comes from a growing imbalance between the commitments that librarians make and the resources they have to fulfill those commitments. Even during the affluent 1960s—the golden age of education and libraries—librarians never really overcame their traditional poverty. This was because the demands made on them by users and the commitments they willingly and eagerly accepted always exceeded their resources. That chronic imbalance between commitments and resources threatens to become a vast gulf with the soaring inflation and declining budgetary support that will likely characterize the 1980s. The reach of librarians far exceeds their grasp. The promises they make to their users for collections and services far exceed their ability to deliver and this leads to failure and frustration.

In 1975 I said that support for libraries was not keeping

pace with the inflation in book and journal prices, increases in staff salaries and benefits, increases in building operation, and maintenance costs.[1] Subsequent developments have confirmed and reinforced this view. Moreover, these trends will persist through the 1980s, when student enrollments, upon which most financial support is ultimately based, will decline significantly. Librarians must face squarely this growing imbalance between commitments and resources, reexamine their conventional wisdom and goals, and develop new responses to a rapidly changing environment.

Promises and Reality

Much of the current rhetoric that the library profession is getting from many of its leaders on goals and directions for the future is naive and keeps librarians from accepting and dealing with reality. Two examples follow. In 1975 when the National Commission on Libraries and Information Science (NCLIS) published its program and goals for action, it set as its main goal and ideal:

> To eventually provide every individual in the United States with equal opportunity of access to that part of the total information resource which will satisfy the individual's educational, working, cultural, and leisure-time needs and interest, regardless of the individual's location, social or physical condition, or level of intellectual achievement.[2]

The authors of the document do not tell us where the money will come from to fulfill that simplistic and extravagant promise, but it is obvious that they see it as the responsibility of the federal government to assure the equal opportunity of access to information that they advocate.

Not to be outdone by NCLIS, an American Library Association (ALA) presidential committee came forward in 1978 with a proposal not only to equalize opportunity of access to information but to equalize access itself. The following proposition was offered in a document entitled "Toward a Conceptual Foundation of a National Information Policy":

> The information needs and aspirations of this nation can be fulfilled only through the attainment of five separate but related universals. All information must be available to all people in all formats purveyed through all communication channels and delivered at all levels of comprehension.

If any of these five qualities is compromised, the whole is enervated, and the national enterprise as a consequence suffers.[3]

The unmistakable implicaion of this proposed policy is that all information must be conveyed to all users at no cost to them and—one is tempted to add—whether they want it or not.

These are samples of the many unrealistic promises that well-meaning library leaders are making.[4] Now what is the reality? The reality is that libraries are nearly everywhere in decline. Many of our great urban public libraries are reducing purchases and services and closing their doors to users. We used to joke about the small town libraries that were open only a few hours on alternate days; now it is the great New York Public Library on 5th Avenue and 42nd Street that is on short hours.

When I worked there in the late 1950s, we proudly boasted that the reference department was open every day of the year from 9 A.M. to 10 P.M.—a total of 91 hours a week. It is now open 49 hours a week and never on Sunday, Thursday, or holidays.

That decline is not limited to public libraries. Large numbers of academic libraries, both public and private, are suffering devastating losses in book funds and personnel from inflation and declining support. Many have lost a substantial portion of the purchasing power of their book and journal budgets in the last several years and are spending an ever-increasing percentage of their shrinking funds maintaining subscriptions to a decreasing number of journals at the expense of monographs.

It should be clear to all of us by now that what we are experiencing is not just a temporary or cyclical decline in support levels, but a serious long-term reduction in our ability to maintain the kind of research collections, services, and facilities that scholars have traditionally demanded and that librarians have tried to provide. The financial pressures we are facing come largely from inexorable economic, social, and demographic trends over which university administrators and librarians have no control. And they will undoubtedly get worse in the decade ahead. Some publicly supported university libraries, particularly in the wealthy sun belt states, continue to receive generous support. But few, if any, large research libraries will be able for long to maintain their traditional exponential growth rates or remain immune to the economic inflation and depression in higher education that is upon us.

This new reality is forcing librarians and scholars alike to reexamine the conventional view of the nature and extent of the collections and services that libraries need and can afford to provide to support the instructional and research needs of their users.

Updating Collecting Policies

We need to refresh and refocus our thinking about libraries and how they should function in the last two decades of the 20th century—a time of rapidly accelerating technological and social change. A good place to begin is with the basic assumptions about building research collections that we inherited from the library readers of the late 19th and early 20th centuries.

Take the New York Public Library as an example. It had a collecting policy that was well suited to the environment and needs of the first half of this century but it is no longer valid today. In an outstanding paper about the Lydenberg era at New York Public Library, Phyllis Dain writes this about its acquisitions policy:

> It was then an unquestioned assumption that an institution like the New York Public Library should try to acquire everything of possible research value in the fields for which it took responsibility, irrespective of actual or potential frequency of use and irrespective of time, language, ideology, or place of publication. It was a maxim that every individual's use, for whatever purpose and of whatever obscure publication, was to be respected and that in obtaining such a wide variety of materials the library was creating and preserving a cumulative record of human behavior. Problems of size and funding, though serious, were not yet so overwhelming as to challenge these assumptions.[5]

Harry M. Lydenberg, the architect of this ambitious and comprehensive policy which made the NYPL the premier research library of his time, retired as director in 1940, a decade or two before "problems of size and funding" became overwhelming and forced the library into a period of decline.

By 1980, his successors were struggling desperately to bring the library's policies and commitments into line with its available resources. In a well-reasoned and hard-hitting report to the Board of Trustees, a Planning and Resources Committee concluded "that the Research Libraries can no longer attempt to be all things to all people; desirable as it may be to collect all materials which our diverse readership might require, we are no longer able to do so, and . . . choices must be made. . . ."[6]

Obviously, no single library—not even the Library of Congress—can continue to try to be all things to all people and apply such extravagant collecting policies to the current output of the world's presses. Lydenberg's goal is still valid today, but it can only be achieved by the collective efforts and resources of all our libraries organized into a nationwide network based on advanced electronic technologies.

The conventional view of collection building in research libraries evolved over the last century in response to an environment that no longer exists. This view calls for acquiring and storing locally as large a portion of the available universe of potentially usable research materials as a library can afford. It fails to take into full account such new factors and trends as the explosive growth in publishing throughout the world; the great post-war expansion of research; the rapid increase in the number and cost of books, journals, and information services; the rapid rise in labor costs and benefits in a labor-intensive environment; the increasing need for and cost of library space to house research collections which tend on the average to double in size every 20 to 30 years; a book and journal paper deterioration problem that has already reached major crisis proportions; and a theft and mutilation problem which has become epidemic. This formidable array of problems comes at a time when research library budgets are being stabilized or reduced by inflation.

No single library or institution can hope to solve these problems by itself. The problems are national and even international in scope, and the solutions must come from new attitudes, new concepts, new organizations, and new technologies. The conventional wisdom and responses of a passing era will not suffice to see us through this transition.

New organizations and capabilities are being developed to permit and encourage libraries to band together to try to fashion cooperative solutions to their common problems of building and maintaining collections and serving the needs of their users. Among these are the Ohio College Library Center (OCLC), the Research Libraries Group with its Research Libraries Information

Network (RLG/RLIN), the Washington Library Network (WLN), the Center for Research Libraries (CRL), and the British Library Lending Division. The development of rapid and relatively inexpensive means of communication and air travel makes it possible and desirable for scholars to travel to the libraries that have special collections of needed research materials. Improvements in telecommunications, micrographics, and computer technologies are beginning to provide alternatives to amassing comprehensive local research collections in all fields of interest in each university.

In sum, librarians and the public they serve need to develop a new consensus about the nature, scope, and cost of library collections and services that is more in tune with the social, fiscal, and technological realities of our time. Library administrators and their staffs are beginning to come to terms with these economic and technological realities. Library users are also going to have to become more flexible and tolerant of change in libraries in the coming years as we move to implement computer-based alternatives to card catalogs and new ways of building and sharing library collections.

The Federal Solution

In recent years, the library profession has begun to turn more and more to the federal government for solutions to its problems. The recent White House Conference on Libraries and Information Science may well lead to additional federal programs and subsidies for libraries as many library leaders fervently hope, but putting our faith in such programs may do more to weaken libraries in the long run than to strengthen them. Robert Wedgeworth, the executive director of the American Library Association, had the foresight and courage to state that unpopular view in his report to the Council at the 1977 ALA Midwinter Convention and was taken to task in the library press for doing so.[7]

With federal subsidies come federal control and a subsequent weakening of local support and responsibility for libraries. In any case, it is doubtful that these federal subsidies will be large enough to make a significant difference to any particular library's budget in the next several years. Let's look at the numbers. In 1980, federal appropriations for academic and public libraries amounted to $12 million under the Higher Education Act, and $67 million under the Library Services and Construction Act. Together they total $79 million. This is less than 1 percent of the estimated $3 billion that are spent annually in support of our academic and public libraries. Given those numbers it is hard to believe that the solution to library funding problems will come from Washington.

Managing Libraries in Hard Times

Many librarians look to new technology, resource sharing, and new and improved management techniques and systems for solutions to our current fiscal problems. But we know now that most computer systems in libraries have improved services more than they have reduced costs. The use of network systems provided by OCLC, RLG/RLIN, WLN, and UTLAS in Canada promises to be much more effective in producing long-term savings, not only in cataloging and processing operations, but also in acquisitions and resource sharing. However, it seems likely that in the next few years those savings as well as the minor savings that come from improved management will be more than offset by inflation and declining support, and our fiscal problems will still be with us.

Minor one-time cutbacks can be met by minor trimming and retrenchment, but what do we do for an encore after the obvious and easy slack has been cut from the library? What do we do if reduced support becomes a way of life?

When faced with a substantial and long-term decline in budgetary support, the only way library administrators can save significant sums of money is to eliminate positions, because from two-thirds to three-quarters of all the money spent in libraries goes for salaries and benefits. To reduce staff in an orderly manner in technical services requires a reduction in the intake of new materials into the library. To reduce staff in public services usually means reducing reference services.

The best way to eliminate positions is through attrition and the worst way is through layoffs. Layoffs, or even the threat of layoffs, can demoralize a staff and undermine the operation and effectiveness of the library. Job security takes precedence over all other issues in the eyes of employees. Even the forced transfer of staff members from less essential to more critical positions can create serious morale problems, but this is difficult to avoid if a no-layoff policy based on attrition is to be followed. By resisting the library administration's efforts to reduce and reorganize the work and eliminate positions, library staff members can delay and undermine the process and even cause management to fail. However, when management fails, the staff suffers. The library staff has as large a stake in a well-managed library as the senior administrators. It is in everyone's long-term best interests to support reasonable and necessary efforts to reduce commitments and increase productivity. But in the end, administrators must earn the support and cooperation of their staff by dealing fairly and effectively with them.

Those of us who are responsible for managing and staffing libraries during this crucial transition decade must avoid defeatism and despair and carry on as professionals. Many of us have already been put through the wringer of retrenchment and have not only managed to survive it but even to turn it into advantage on occasion.

It is nearly impossible, for political and practical reasons, for a library administration to reduce its budget and cut back its commitments and services unless all other parts of the institution are also retrenching and there is a general recognition on campus—and particularly among the faculty—that a real budgetary crisis exists. Once the fact of a crisis is accepted by the library's various constituents including its staff, it is possible to make changes and cutbacks that would have been inconceivable in more affluent times. Periodical subscription lists can be trimmed, marginal positions can be eliminated, and less essential services can be reduced. Indeed, if the situation is serious enough, an aggressive library director with a strong political base may even be able to merge certain departmental libraries or absorb them into the main library. However, on those rare occasions when departmental libraries are merged, it is usually because the department wants to use the space that its library is occupying for other more important purposes rather than in response to library budget pressures.

When faced with budget cuts, some directors may try to get them rescinded by using such obvious but dangerous (and dishonest) tactics as drastically reducing library hours or declaring that the library will become a third-rate operation totally incapable of adequately serving the needs of its users. Since most academic libraries are staffed largely by students during evening and weekend hours, no significant cost savings can be made by reducing these hours. Moreover, the institution has a substantial investment in the library buildings and book collections and the librarians should give the highest priority to maximizing their use. Keeping the libraries open on a normal schedule is always a "best buy" and it is also good politics. For a librarian to declare publicly that his or her library will be forever doomed to mediocrity or worse if the budget is not increased by some amount is a risky scare tactic. If the crisis is real, it will not work and then it may take a long time for the librarian and the staff to repair the damage to the library's image on campus. Faculty will remember that the director himself said the library was inadequate. It is nearly always preferable for librarians to stress the library's quality rather than its deficiencies. If the financial crisis is real and severe, it is better for the library administration, and the staff, to accept this new reality and deal with it in an honest and professional manner.

During the affluent 1960s when book and journal budgets were being increased, librarians were quick—and right—to point out that it was not enough to increase the book budget but that it was also necessary to increase the technical processing staff required to acquire and catalog the additional materials that would be purchased. And those were the days when only a third of the materials budget was being spent on serials. Now during the not-so-affluent 1980s, when the book and journal budgets are growing less rapidly and inflation is seriously eroding purchasing power, librarians should be conceding that it may be possible to reduce the size of their technical processing staffs to compensate for the reductions in acquisitions.

During the period of rapid growth in the 1960s, colleges and universities expanded and added a variety of new programs which were necessary and appropriate at the time, and libraries expanded to support them. Many of these academic programs and the library support for them continue to exist long after the actual need for them has greatly diminished or even ceased. For example, the tremendous need we had for school teachers and professors with doctorates has passed, yet many universities and libraries continue to support those programs as though nothing had changed. But needs have changed. A New York State Department of Education report cited in the *Chronicle of Higher Education* predicts that:

In the 1980s, all the academic jobs for Ph.D.'s in English, including jobs in two year colleges, could be filled by doctorate-holders from the 15 biggest graduate schools. In Philosophy, the jobs could be filled by Ph.D.'s from the 10 biggest schools, and in history, by the Ph.D.'s from the six biggest schools. . . . During the same period, five of every six new doctorates in the humanities from "elite" graduate schools would not get academic jobs. From the less prestigious graduate programs, nine of ten new doctorate holders would not find academic jobs.[8]

Austerity and Change

It will be more difficult to make changes and be innovative during this period of austerity than it was during the time of relative affluence we experienced during the 1960s and early 1970s. To do something new then one simply got new money. To do something new now may require deemphasizing or discontinuing something old and reallocating the existing resources. Inevitably, the something old will be someone's vested interest.

In those libraries which still have some budgetary flexibility, the most feasible way of getting together a large enough sum of discretionary money to launch a new program or project is to review carefully each vacancy that occurs and to reassess the need for the position. The money from one or two positions or their transfer can be enough to permit a library to change a direction or embark on a significant new program. However, many budget systems have become so rigid that it is extremely difficult or even illegal to transfer positions or funds from one department or budget category to another. The unfortunate consequence of this growing budget inflexibility is that it turns the director into a bureaucrat rather than permitting him or her to be a manager, and even, on occasion, an entrepreneur.

The amount of discretionary money in a library budget, the money that can be allocated for new or different purposes among or within different categories, is exceedingly limited. Well over half the book budget is committed to subscriptions and continuations, and much of the remainder is committed formally or by tradition to specific departments. The personnel budget is even more rigid with line-by-line allocations to each specific position, and all positions are assigned specific functions in the various units. In many institutions, money from unfilled positions reverts to the university comptroller. At best it is difficult to transfer, eliminate, or change the duties of positions that are not vacant.

And when vacancies occur, the elaborate, costly, and time-consuming procedures dictated by the federal government's affirmative action regulations must be followed. In libraries with civil service or unionized staffs, the situation can be particularly inflexible. Nevertheless, since more than two-thirds of the budget is devoted to personnel, this is the only category that can be tapped if management wishes to reallocate significant sums of money to new or different functions.

As library jobs are made more secure by a rapidly expanding body of rules and regulations, and as personnel policies and grievance procedures are spelled out in increasing detail, this continual reallocation of resources will become more difficult, and the library's capacity to respond to changing times and needs will be further diminished. In time, the larger publicly supported libraries may become as rigid and conservative as units in other mature bureaucracies such as government agencies, postal services, and public school systems. It seems that as we try to remove administrators' authority to act arbitrarily or unwisely, we gradually remove their ability to act at all.

Despite these ominous signs, I remain optimistic about our ability to guide our libraries through the difficult times ahead. Just as periods of expansion and affluence bring their special opportunities for embarking on new and exciting initiatives, so periods of austerity and even severe retrenchment can also create opportunities for beneficial changes and innovations.

It is commonplace that a little austerity after a long period of affluence can be good for an organization. It creates a climate where minor cost cutting of frills and nonessentials can be carried out. While this kind of minor budget pressure helps trim bits of fat, the organization tries to carry on all existing functions and commitments at slightly reduced levels.

It is equally true, but less generally recognized, that a more severe retrenchment may also, on occasion, be beneficial for an organization. It frequently happens during these times of extreme financial crisis that leaders are enabled, or even forced, to be courageous and strong enough to propose and implement the bold changes or programs that really make a difference in the long run. It took a climate of crisis for the Research Libraries of NYPL to revamp its collecting policies totally and try to regain control of its future. It will take a similar crisis for some of our university library systems to close out or consolidate a number of their marginally effective departmental libraries and services. These extraordinary actions, which can contribute greatly to the long-term health of a library system, are politically feasible only under extreme conditions and not in response to minor austerities. People expect to weather minor difficulties by making minor adjustments, but it is generally accepted that major problems call for bold and unusual solutions.

The point I am trying to make is that we should not give up trying to improve our libraries during this period of austerity. It is harder to be innovative and creative when funds are limited, but the opportunities are there and we should not use tight budgets as an excuse for standing pat. But libraries cannot survive for long by simply reducing commitments or trimming and fine-tuning their existing systems however necessary and useful these steps might be in the short run. What is required for survival is a thoroughgoing change in the basic objectives, orientation, and technology of research libraries. In the words of Patricia Battin, "We must reinvent the research library in the network environment."[9] I am confident that we will succeed.

Notes

1. See Richard De Gennaro, "Austerity, Technology, and Resource Sharing," *Library Journal,* May 15, 1975, pp. 917–23; "Escalating Journal Prices: Time to Fight Back," *American Libraries,* February 1977, pp. 69–74; and "Copyright, Resource Sharing and Hard Times," *American Libraries,* September 1977, pp. 430–35 [all reprinted in this volume].

2. National Commission on Libraries and Information Science, *Toward a National Program for Library and Information Services: Goals for Action* (Washington, D.C.: U.S. G.P.O., 1975), p. xi.

3. David Kaser, Chairperson, *"Toward a Conceptual Foundation for a National Information Policy,"* document prepared by the ad hoc Alternative National Policy Drafting Committee of the American Library Association, distributed at the ALA midwinter meeting, January 1978.

4. For an excellent critical analysis of these and other proposals for a national information policy see: Don R. Swanson, "Libraries and Growth of Knowledge," *Library Quarterly* 50 (January 1980): 112–14.

5. Phyllis Dain, "Harry M. Lydenberg and American Library Resources: A Study in Modern Library Leadership," *Library Quarterly* 47, (October 1977): 451–69, (see especially pp. 458–59).

6. Report of the Planning and Resources Committee to the Board of Trustees, The New York Public Library, Astor, Lenox, and Tilden Foundations, March 1980, p. 3.

7. Robert Wedgeworth, State of the Association Report to ALA Council, ALA midwinter meeting, February 1, 1977, Washington, D.C.

8. Malcolm G. Scully, "In Grad Schools, Unhappy Trends," *Chronicle of Higher Education,* April 24, 1978.

9. Patricia Battin, "Research Libraries in the Network Environment: A Case for Cooperation," *Journal of Academic Librarianship* 6 (May 1980): 68.

LIBRARY STATISTICS AND USER SATISFACTION: NO SIGNIFICANT CORRELATION

Reprinted from *Journal of Academic Librarianship,* May 1980, 95.

Library administrators are caught in a dilemma. On the one hand, they are deeply committed to reducing the rate of growth of their operating costs, staffs, and collections through efficient management, automation, and participation in resource sharing networks. On the other hand, they are equally committed to making their budgets, staff, and collections grow as large and rapidly as possible. The dilemma is that significant success in reducing the rate of a library's growth may well result in a reduction in the various traditional statistical and rank indicators that librarians use to measure their success and the relative standing of their libraries among their peers. But up to now, the growth ethic was always more powerful and more rewarding than the cost-conscious management ethic, and there has been no real conflict between these seemingly conflicting goals.

But now the game is changing. We are entering a time of crisis when rampant inflation in book and journal prices, soaring personnel costs, and declining budgets will force library managers to reduce their commitments to match their declining resources. Those librarians who succeed in coping with this new reality by making substantial reductions in their staffs, acquisitions, and expenditures through good leadership and skillful management will find that this success plays havoc with the traditional library statistical indicators and ranking systems and may actually be perceived by their user communities as a sign of failure.

For example, up until a few years ago, if an ARL library dropped a significant number of places in such key ARL Rank Order Tables as Gross Volumes Added, Current Serials, Materials Expenditures, and Size of FTE Staff, we might have assumed that the library was in trouble or in decline and the director was in some measure responsible for it. But if it happens now, we can't be so sure anymore. It could mean that the library is making a necessary and successful budget retrenchment and adjustment to a lower standard of living and that the director and his or her staff are doing a commendable job. They may in fact be commended for their efforts, but it is far more likely that they will be blamed for the apparent "decline" of their library just like before. This is because our faculties will continue to live by the library growth and rank ethic (which we helped instill in them) long after we librarians have been forced by fiscal realities and new technologies to deemphasize it or perhaps even abandon it.

All libraries attach importance to their vital statistics, but university libraries have an excessive concern with them. The annual ARL Statistics with their rank order tables are eagerly awaited and scanned by librarians and academics in universities throughout the country to see where their library ranks in relation to the competition. The bottom line is in the rankings and in the tables that record volumes in the library, gross volumes added, number of serial subscriptions, total staff (FTE), materials expenditures, and total expenditures.

Sure, we know that these statistics and rankings are misleading for comparative purposes and totally inappropriate as qualitative measures, but we take the attitude that they are all we have and that they are better than nothing. That attitude was understandable and justified in the 1950s and 1960s when rapid growth and relative affluence were the norm, but it is increasingly at odds with the spirit and needs of the 1980s when we are being forced to limit our growth, reduce our costs and expenditures, and strive for quality.

I have an untested theory, or perhaps it is just a hunch, which says that there is no necessary or significant correlation between the size of a library's expenditures, collections, or staff and the effectiveness of its services or the degree of user satisfaction with that library. In library matters, the traditional and conventional view is to equate quantity with quality. The bigger the numbers, the better the library. Generations of librarians, faculty members, and academic administrators have accepted that basic assumption without much question. But now we have entered a period of diminishing financial support and expanding technology and it is no longer fruitful or even possible to continue making that assumption. It is time to put quality and user satisfaction ahead of big numbers as the goal and guiding concept of library management.

Declining support in the 1980s first will permit and then force some courageous librarians not only to cut costs and withdraw their institutions from the numbers game, but also to make the case to their constituents for doing it. Many of the attitudes that faculty members and administrators have about the need for massive libraries come from our own efforts to "educate" them. Now we have to begin to educate them to new and more appropriate attitudes about the need for and advantages of lean, flexible, and responsive libraries. But first we have to change our own attitudes. We have to accept the fact that we can't continue to provide 1960's collections and services on 1980's budgets and perhaps more importantly, that we may not really need 1960's budgets or collections to provide for the *essential* needs of our users. Then we should try to find the courage and the skill to sell our constituents on that idea openly and honestly. But let's not kid ourselves. It won't be easy.

LIBRARY ADMINISTRATION AND NEW MANAGEMENT SYSTEMS

This paper has become a minor classic. It was first published in *Library Journal,* 15 December 1978, 2477–82. It was reprinted in *Library Lit. 10—The Best of 1979;* in *Strategies for Library Administration,* edited by C. R. McClure and A. R. Samuels. (Littleton, Colo.: Libraries Unlimited, 1982); and also in *Management Strategies for Libraries, A Basic Reader,* edited by Beverly P. Lynch (New York: Neal-Schuman, 1985).

Monsieur Jourdain, Molière's *Bourgeois Gentilhomme,* was surprised and pleased to learn that he had been speaking prose all his life without knowing it. I felt the same way when I finally learned that I had been a manager for 20 years without knowing it. Well, I always knew that I was a library *administrator,* but somehow I never thought of myself as a *manager* because that term connoted a kind of modern professionalism that the more familiar term *administrator* lacked.

Ten years ago I attended the University of Maryland's excellent two-week development program for library administrators and was deeply impressed by the introductory courses and readings which covered the full range of subjects like McGregor's Theories X and Y, Management by Objectives (MBO), Program Budgeting (PPBS), Decision Theory, Cost-Benefit Analysis, Mathematical Modelling, Management Information Systems, etc. I came away thinking, somewhat naively, that business and other managers had mastered and were routinely using that arsenal of sophisticated management systems and techniques in their daily work, and that it was only library and perhaps academic administrators that were struggling along with the traditional methods. It was clear that we librarians had a lot of catching-up to do.

It was with some hesitation that I accepted the directorship of a large library in 1970 because I believed that research libraries were becoming increasingly costly and complex organizations and that I lacked the formal management training and skills that the job required. Determined to remedy my lack of formal training, I enrolled in the Harvard Business School's Advanced Management Program, a prestigious and expensive three-month program especially designed for high-level business, government, and military executives. I thought the "B-School" would work its magic and convert me from a self-taught library administrator into a certified modern manager, but I was disappointed.

Early in its history, the Harvard Business School developed the case method of instruction and it has used it almost exclusively in its teaching ever since. The case method can be very effective, but it was overused in the executive development program. In three months, we never read anything but cases, and since the cases were all efficiently reproduced and distributed in convenient packets, we never had the need or the occasion to use the rich resources of the Baker Library. In fact, we seldom had to read from a real book or journal. The classics of management science were rarely mentioned, and with the exception of a few sessions on decision theory and computer simulation, almost no mention was made of any of the new management systems that had been developed and were presumably being used routinely everywhere but in libraries. The Harvard program was useful, but it did not give me the management knowledge and skills that I needed and wanted; so I continued to read about management and to attend management institutes and workshops. (Among the best and most useful are the short programs offered by ARL's Office of Management Studies.) This reading and supplementary training helped me to develop and sharpen my management skills over the years. At the same time, I was gaining confidence and maturity and getting a lot of practical on-the-job experience.

I was also called upon to serve on a number of boards, commissions, and committees; this gave me the opportunity to work closely with and observe a peer group of top managers and executives, not only in libraries, but in universities, business firms, and government offices. I found that most of them, like me, had no special management training or education and were struggling, each in his or her own unscientific way, to do the management jobs to which they had been appointed. Some were more competent and effective than others, but previous formal management training seemed not to make any significant difference. Indeed, it was hard to tell who had training and who didn't. I noticed that there were few trained management experts in top level management positions. Instead, they were working as specialists in staff positions or as teachers, researchers, or consultants.

I could not see any real difference in what I was doing as a library director and what my peers in other fields were doing. After a while, I began to suspect that the reality of what we managers were experiencing in our day-to-day activities had more validity than the theoretical world of management that was being described in books and articles written by management professors and social scientists.

I was confirmed in that view when I read Henry Mintzberg's *The Nature of Managerial Work*.[1,2] Mintzberg, a McGill University management professor, had a much different view of management and the way managers worked than the conventional authors; that view checked with my own experience as a library administrator. In order to find out and describe what managers actually did, he conducted a number of studies and also scanned the literature to integrate and synthesize the findings of other studies with his own.

How Do Managers Manage?

The studies by Mintzberg and other researchers showed that from street gang leaders to the President of the United States, managers do not spend their time planning, organizing, coordinating, and controlling as the French industrialist, Henri Fayol said they did in 1916 and as most writers on management have continued to repeat ever since. They are not like the orchestra leader who directs the component parts of his organization with ease and precision. Instead, they spend their time reacting to crises, seizing special opportunities, attending meetings, negotiating, talking on the telephone, cultivating interpersonal and political relationships, gathering and disseminating information, and fulfilling a variety of ceremonial functions. Mintzberg says:

> I was struck during my study by the fact that the executives I was observing—all very competent by any standard—are fundamentally indistinguishable from their counterparts of a hundred years ago (or a thousand years ago, for that matter). The information they need differs, but they seek it in the same way—by word of mouth. Their decisions concern modern technology, but the procedures they use to make them are the same as the procedures of the 19th Century manager. Even the computer, so important for the specialized work of the organization, has apparently had no influence on the work procedures of general managers. In fact, the manager is in a kind of loop, with increasingly heavy work pressures but no aid forthcoming from management science.[3]

The Mintzberg view is by no means unique. There is a growing number of management scholars who are questioning the conventional view of management and what managers do. In a critical review of *On Management* (Harper, 1976), a book of articles selected from 25 years of the *Harvard Business Review,* Albert Shapero, a management professor at the University of Texas, strikes a similar note:

> The term "management" conjures up images of control, rationality, systematics; but studies of what managers actually do depict behaviors and situations that are chaotic, unplanned, and charged with improvisation. The Managerial life at every level is reflexive—responding to calls, memos, personnel problems, fire drills, budget meetings, and personnel reviews. Occasionally, however, we find at managerial levels individuals who go 24 hours without being interrupted by meetings or phone calls. They are the long-range planners, the people in O.R., E.D.P., financial or market planning, or market research. Management is really for them. The bulk of the articles in *On Management* are concerned with ideas from the world of the staff functionary.[4]

Are Management Systems Really Used?

What about the claims of widespread use of new scientific management systems and techniques? Is it really true that managers in business, government, and other institutions are using them extensively while we library administrators are lagging far behind?

Let's first look at what a few of the management experts say about the use of these systems in general, and then we will look at their use in libraries.

William R. Dill, dean of the Graduate School of Business

Administration at New York University, makes this sober assessment:

> For all the progress we have made in developing good approaches to planning, forecasting, budgeting, and control, and for all the enthusiasm we in schools of management have helped to build for these approaches, their use has been fitful and sporadic, even in the most analytically sophisticated and goal-oriented institutions. In corporations that are pointed out as models for what can be accomplished, the outputs of planning, budgeting, and modeling staffs are often quietly ignored by operating people when times are good; these outputs often seem irrelevant in times of sudden challenge or change. Analysis and planning are still far from foolproof ways to anticipate change and potential crises.[5]

Aaron Wildavsky, dean of the Graduate School of Public Policy at the University of California, Berkeley, has written a number of articles in which he argues convincingly, citing evidence and authorities, that the major modern information systems like PERT, MBO, PPBS, Social Indicators, and Zero Based Budgeting have not worked and cannot work. About PERT (Program Evaluation Review Technique), he says that "the few studies that exist suggest that outside of construction, where one activity tends to follow another, PERT is rarely successful."[6]

On MBO (Management by Objectives), he says: "The trouble with MBO is that the attempt to formalize procedures for choosing objectives without considering organizational dynamics leads to the opposite of what was intended—bad management, irrational choice, and ineffective decision-making."[7] "The main product of MBO, as experience in the United States federal government suggests, is, literally, a series of objectives. Aside from the unnecessary paper work, such exercises are self defeating because they become mechanisms for avoiding rather than making choices. Long lists of objectives are useless because rarely do resources remain beyond the first few."[8]

On PPBS, Wildavsky is equally harsh. He says that "Program budgeting does not work anywhere in the world it has been tried," and that "no one knows how to do program budgeting."[9] His assessments of Social Indicators and Zero Based Budgeting are in a similar vein.

These realistic assessments that we are getting from authorities like Mintzberg, Shapero, Dill, Wildavsky, and others should serve to remind us to maintain a healthy skepticism whenever we read about the effectiveness and widespread use of new management systems and techniques. We librarians should guard against the tendency we have to look for panaceas and to accept uncritically the claims and promises made on behalf of each new management theory or system that appears.

Consider the minimal impact on libraries as compared with the initial promise, for example, of PPBS, Operations Research, MBO, and even Participative Management.

To the best of my knowledge, PPBS has not been successfully implemented in a single library and I doubt that it ever will be.[10] Interest in it is rapidly waning.

The practical application of Operations Research in libraries has been extremely limited to date. One of the earliest and best known economic analyses of library decision making was done in the MIT Libraries in 1969. The report of that study came to this sobering conclusion: "Although helpful, an economic analysis of a university (or public) library is insufficient because libraries operate as political systems and thus improving libraries requires political analysis."[11] In an excellent article on library decision making, Jeffrey Raffel, an economist and co-author of the MIT study begins by saying that "in general, the more important the decision, the less beneficial a cost-benefit analysis is to library decision makers," and concludes by saying that "it is time that we all recognized the politics of libraries and acted accordingly."[12]

In a classic paper on Management by Objectives in academic libraries, James Michalko, after a thorough, critical review of the literature, recommends against the use of MBO in libraries on the grounds that it is a limited approach which is costly and difficult to implement and which yields uncertain results.[13]

Participative management is another "new" management technique that has been particularly oversold in the last decade. In fact, it is considered by many librarians to be the perfect management system. Good management has always included consultation and participation, it is just the name, the faddishness, and some of the formal structures that are new. When used properly and honestly, participative management is a useful process at all levels, and not just by top managers on major decisions as is sometimes assumed. It is essential that there be appropriate consultation and participation of interested and competent staff members on important decisions affecting them. But participative management will not bring on the management millenium in libraries.

Participative management is not decision making by committee or by staff plebiscite. Good management requires that when all the facts have been gathered and analyzed and all the advice is in, the appropriate administrator has to make the decision and take responsibility for it. Knowing when and how to seek and take advantage of consultative advice and prior approval of decisions where appropriate is one of the most important managerial skills. Decisions should be made at the lowest competent level. The library's critical strategy decisions involve a world outside the library and must usually be made by the director and his chief associates. Staff committees can give good advice on such matters, but they simply do not have the information, the knowledge, or the perspective required to make those decisions—and they cannot take responsibility for the results.

One extreme form of participative management, the collegial or faculty system of governance, was developed for academic departments; it works badly there and worse or not at all in libraries. Where it appears to work, it is because those involved have tacitly made concessions to traditional hierarchical systems and the demands of the environment while preserving the collegial form. A library is not an academic department, it is a service organization and should be so administered. A librarian by any other name is still a librarian and it is time for mature acceptance of that fact.

Perhaps the reason that participative management has been embraced so enthusiastically and uncritically by librarians in recent years is not because of its management benefits, but because it appears to be the model that best justifies faculty status. It is assumed that because faculty members participate in a collegial academic decision-making process, that model is the appropriate one to use in libraries—if librarians are to achieve faculty status. Much of the library-based management literature since 1970 is self-serving and reflects a direct or indirect preoccupation with matters of staff status and benefits frequently hidden behind arguments for participative management. It is time that we recognized this natural bias and took steps to overcome it by giving more attention and weight to the more objective management literature from outside the library field.

Two recent articles on participative management in libraries, one by James Govan and the other by Dennis Dickenson, give encouraging evidence that the library profession is beginning to take a more realistic and balanced view of the advantages and limitations of participative management and collegial governance. Govan reminds us that:

> Librarians cannot afford to degrade services or alienate their users in an effort, however enlightened or well-intentioned, to make their jobs more challenging and satisfying. Participation and consultation cost time and money and often, like faculty deliberations, produce rather conservative results. In this connection, it is useful to remember Maslow's belief that Theory Y is possible only in periods of affluence. It is also healthy to recall Drucker's statement that service institutions do not operate for the people who work in them.[14]

In his perceptive article, Dickenson tries to provide "an antidote for some of the more extreme and sometimes naive interpretations of participative management that appear from time to time in library literature."[15]

Peter Drucker summed up an important truth about management when he said in response to an interviewer's question about the efficacy of new management techniques: "The young people today expect to see business run by theory, knowledge, concepts, and planning. But then they find it is run like the rest of the world—by experience and expediency, by who you know, and by the hydrostatic pressure in your bladder."[16]

This is not just the way business is run, it is the way libraries are run as well. And it is the way they will continue to be run despite the current rhetoric about the managerial revolution that is being ushered in by the use of new quantitative and psychological management systems and theories.

Why? Because a library operates in a political environment and nearly all the really important decisions that are made at the highest levels have an overriding political component. They are rarely the product of cost-benefit analysis or Operations Research where the various factors are weighed and compared and the "best" or most cost-effective course is chosen. These management techniques can be useful sometimes to implement a program or a project in the most effective manner *after* the political decision to proceed has been made. They can also be useful in providing a rationale to support some essentially political decision that is being proposed or advocated, or to impress higher authorities or constituents with the competence of the managers and the rationality of their decision making process. Management systems, particularly PPBS, ZBB, and PERT are used in government and military bureaucracies largely because they are mandated by law or regulation.

In the library world, as in education, business, and government, few major program decisions are made solely or even largely on the basis of careful studies of needs and costs. Consider, for example, decisions to build a new library building, to open a new departmental or branch library, to achieve excellence in some special subject discipline, or to embark on a major automation program. These program decisions are usually the result of an initiative or vision by an imaginative and powerful person, perhaps a library director, a dean, a president, a mayor, or other official. They are political, emotional, or even personal decisions—justified, rationalized, and perhaps implemented with the assistance of various kinds of analyses and studies, but seldom derived from them.

It is important that librarians understand how and why these really critical decisions are made so that they will not be disillusioned or discouraged when they discover that the "best," the most efficient, or the least expensive solution frequently loses out to the one that is the most politically expedient or attractive.

The Quantitative Approach

I think it is important to make a distinction between the claims made on behalf of complex quantitative management systems such as Operations Research and Cost-Benefit Analysis, and the collection and analysis of quantitative data in libraries to assist in rational decision making. I am questioning the validity and usefulness of these complex systems, but I am not questioning the need for and use of quantitative studies for measuring and evaluating library services. Quite the contrary, we need to know more about libraries, their resources, and how they are actually used. We have relied historically upon input data, e.g., the number of books acquired, the numbers of serials subscribed to, the number of books circulated, the dollars spent, etc. The qualitative characteristics of these data are dubious; we desperately need reliable measures of library effectiveness.

Following the pioneering work by Fremont Rider[17] in 1940 on the growth of research libraries, there has been an increasing number of extremely valuable quantitative studies like those by Fussler,[18] Lancaster,[19] Buckland,[20] and other works of solid quality. The findings of such studies provide the theoretical foundations and practical knowledge that working library managers need to draw on to help them think clearly and creatively about library management and to make sound decisions based on valid data. This is especially true in this time of transition when the conventional wisdom of our profession will not suffice to see us through.

As one of the library managers for whose benefit and use such studies are presumably made, I thank the authors and urge them on to greater productivity and precision. I also urge them to try to keep their studies as simple as possible and to summarize their findings in readable English.

Unfortunately, a good deal of the quantitative research that is done in the library field is unintelligible, irrelevant, or too complicated and theoretical for any practical use in libraries. Much of it is written in the language of higher mathematics which is incomprehensible to most managers. This is particularly true of studies that are made by academics outside the library field such as statisticians, economists, psychologists, Operations Research people, etc. Their goal is not necessarily to do studies that are useful, but to demonstrate their mathematical prowess, to test theories and methodologies, to get published, and to award doctoral degrees to deserving graduate students. They select the library as their laboratory because it is convenient and because they think it is virgin territory ready for easy exploitation. They are more interested in the process than in the results.

The most useful library research is done by librarians or others with a serious long-term interest and involvement in libraries who work with librarians in a spirit of genuine collaboration. They are trying to make an impact. It is the difference between a class assignment and the real thing, between war games and war.

A notable exception to this criticism of academics is the landmark work by William J. Baumol and Matityahu Marcus, *Economics of Academic Libraries* (American Council on Education,

Washington, D.C., 1973). These two economists went to unusual lengths to explain their statistical methods and to summarize their conclusions with refreshing brevity and clarity. As a consequence, their work is widely read and frequently cited.

Management scientists and other quantitatively oriented researchers frequently wonder why the results of quantitative research studies are not used more by practicing library managers in the decision making process.[21] One reason is that the mathematics and the methodologies required are far too complex and difficult for operating managers to learn and apply in their busy work environments. Few senior library administrators have the kind of staff support needed to successfully carry out complex analyses. Another and equally important reason is that the quantitative approach does not and cannot take into sufficient account the complex of political, organizational, and psychological factors that characterize the real world where people are more potent than numbers or logic.

The quality of many decisions could be significantly improved if we had more and better data, but many of the more important decisions have a relatively small quantitative component. As a library director, I seldom have a critical need for more quantitative data than are available from regularly kept statistics or by having someone make a special and usually simple survey and analysis of the problem. When the data are simply not available or too difficult to assemble, I can usually find a satisfactory way to manage without them. My real problem has nearly always been to correctly assess the political rather than the economic or quantitative factors. It is fairly easy to determine the most cost-effective course of action with or without detailed data. It is much harder to map out and implement a successful strategy for achieving it, to assess how the various persons and groups affected will perceive the manager's intentions, and how they will react to the decision. Someone said that quantification is not synonymous with management. Finding the best or most cost-effective course of action is not the same as getting it accepted. Sometimes the quality of a decision is critical, other times, it is acceptance.

Effective decision making processes in large academic and public libraries involve complex sets of policies, procedures, and problems which require a variety of different kinds of information and approaches. Some decisions will be authoritarian, some will be collegial, some will be made by committees, and some will be made by combinations of the above. Library directors are not all-knowing, nor are the collective judgments of library faculties and committees infallible. Different situations call for different approaches. There are no simple formulas and no easy answers.

The new management systems that I have been discussing in this article divide into two general categories. There are *quantitative systems* such as Operations Research, PPBS, and ZBB, and *psychological* or *behavioral* systems such as Theory Y (and its variants) and MBO. In each system, there are a number of concepts, ideas, tools, and techniques that have validity and can be used to advantage by library managers, but as comprehensive systems they are all far too theoretical, complex, and simplistic to be applied successfully by ordinary managers in the day-to-day work environment. Few managers have the time or the specialized knowledge and skills required to make these systems work, and those that do are probably astute enough to manage as well or better without them.

In the hands of amateurs—and this is most of us—the quantitative systems frequently produce misleading and wrong solutions, while the psychological or behavioral systems can lead to the manipulation and misuse of people. The real danger with both kinds of management systems is that they offer mechanistic formulas for dealing with complex realities and keep us from thinking about and solving our management problems in practical, realistic, and common sense ways.

Despite the many claims to the contrary, management is not yet a science. It is still an art, but is very much an art that can and should be mastered and practiced by librarians.

Notes

1. Henry Mintzberg, *The Nature of Managerial Work,* Harper, 1973.

2. A very readable summary of Mintzberg's findings and views appeared in a much cited and reprinted article by him entitled "The Manager's Job: Folklore and Fact," *Harvard Business Review,* July-August 1975, p. 49–61.

3. Mintzberg, "The Manager's Job . . . ," p. 54.

4. Albert Shapero, "What Management Says and What Managers Do," *Fortune,* May 1975, p. 275.

5. William R. Dill, "When Auld Acquaintance Be Forgot. . . .

From Cyert and March to Cyert vs. March," in: Richard M. Cyert, *The Management of Nonprofit Organizations,* Heath, 1975, p. 67.

6. Aaron Wildavksy, "Policy Analysis Is What Information Systems Are Not," Working Paper #53, July 1976, copy of a typescript of a paper delivered at the ASIS Conference, October 1976, p. 3.

7. Wildavsky, "Policy Analysis . . . ," p. 5.

8. Wildavsky, "Policy Analysis . . . ," p. 6.

9. Aaron Wildavsky, "Rescuing Policy Analysis from PPBS," *Public Administration Review,* March/April 1969, p. 193.

10. The reasons can be found in an authoritative study by Guy Joseph De Genaro, "A Planning-Programming-Budgeting System (PPBS) in Academic Libraries: Development of Objectives and Effectiveness Measures." Ph.D. dissertation, University of Florida, 1971.

11. Jeffrey A. Raffel, "From Economic to Political Analysis of Library Decision Making," *College & Research Libraries,* November 1974, p. 412.

12. Raffel, "From Economic to Political Analysis . . . ," p. 412, 421.

13. James Michalko, "Management by Objectives and the Academic Library: a Critical Overview," *Library Quarterly,* Vol. 45, No. 3, 1975, p. 235–52.

14. James F. Govan, "The Better Mousetrap: External Accountability and Staff Participation," *Library Trends,* Fall 1977, p. 264.

15. Dennis W. Dickenson, "Some Reflections on Participative Management in Libraries," *College & Research Libraries,* July 1978, p. 261.

16. Thomas J. Murray, "Peter Drucker Attacks: Our Top-heavy Corporations," *Dun's,* April 1974, p. 40.

17. Fremont Rider, *The Scholar and the Future of the Research Library,* Hadham Pr., 1944.

18. Herman H. Fussler & J. L. Simon, *Patterns in the Use of Books in Large Research Libraries,* Univ. of Chicago, Pr., 1969.

19. F. W. Lancaster, *The Measurement and Evaluation of Library Services,* Washington, D.C., Information Resources Press, 1977.

20. Michael K. Buckland, *Book Availability and the Library User,* Pergamon, 1975.

21. See for example: A. Graham McKenzie, "Whither Our Academic Libraries?" *Journal of Documentation,* June 1976, p. 129.

THE CHANGING FORTUNES OF RESEARCH LIBRARIES: A RESPONSE TO "PITT AND THE PENDULUM"

Reprinted from *Library Journal,* 1 February 1978, 320–21.

This was a response to an editorial by John Berry entitled "Pitt and the Pendulum" suggesting that the funding problems of research libraries were temporary and would pass with the next swing of the pendulum.

The editorial, "Pitt and the pendulum" (*LJ,* November 15, 1977, p. 2295), by John Berry does not help us think clearly and realistically about the problems of research libraries in this time of change and uncertainty. His use of the mechanical image of the swinging pendulum to characterize the changing fortunes of research libraries is misleading. It suggests that our funding problems are temporary and will solve themselves if we can be patient and frugal for a time. There are short-term fluctuations in library support levels, but there is no discernible pattern to them. We need to focus on the more important and clearly discernible long-term forces—economic, social, and technological—that are transforming research libraries and they resemble more the unfolding of history than the swings of a pendulum.

The facts don't support Berry's view that the fortunes of research libraries peaked at the time Fremont Rider declared (in 1940) that research library collections were doubling in size every

16 years and that the pendulum started its swing back toward poverty then. Academic research libraries, like their parent institutions, have grown at fairly steady exponential rates during the last hundred years, but they experienced an extraordinary surge in funding, growth, and development after the War and after Sputnik during the decades of the fifties and sixties. Growth in funding as well as volumes added began to level off and decline in the early 1970's with the coming of the current depression in higher education.

Based on my professional experience and my reading of the various signs and indicators, I am saying that support for research libraries is not keeping pace with 1) inflation in book and journal prices, 2) increases in staff salaries and benefits, 3) increases in building operation and maintenance costs, and that this trend may well persist through the 1980's when student enrollments, upon which most financial support is ultimately based, are expected to decline even further. Demographers are predicting an upswing in enrollments in the 1990's, but it will be a changed world by then. I am urging librarians to face squarely this growing imbalance between commitments and resources and re-examine their conventional wisdom and received ideas and develop new and appropriate responses to a changing environment. (See my recent articles: "Austerity, Technology, and Resource Sharing," *LJ,* May 15, 1975, p. 917–23; "Escalating Journal Prices: Time to Fight Back," *American Libraries,* February 1977, p. 69–74; and "Copyright, Resource Sharing, and Hard Times," *American Libraries,* September 1977, p. 430–35 [all reprinted in this volume].)

Berry says I am pessimistic; others say I am negative. Yes, I am pessimistic and negative about the ability of research libraries to carry on business as usual with late 19th and early 20th Century concepts and technology, but I am very optimistic and positive about our ability to develop and implement new concepts, new technology, and new ways of fulfilling our mission to users in the future despite declining support and growth rates. My optimism is fueled by developments such as the rapidly increasing use of on-line computer technology in libraries, the movement toward closing card catalogs in the research library world, and the findings of the Pittsburgh and other use studies.

Some people think I am advocating austerity. I'm not. Austerity, or reduced support, is simply a fact of life for me and many other library directors and we are trying to face its problems and challenges in a realistic and hard-nosed way.

Some idealistic and well-meaning librarians would have us use a portion of the library's financial resources to help solve some of our society's most pressing social and economic problems—to assist the poor and the disadvantaged, or to help sustain full employment. There are many other institutions, agencies, and programs in our society whose mission it is to serve these laudable purposes. The mission of the academic research library is to provide library collections and services to support the instructional and research programs of the university it exists to serve. The resources available are barely sufficient to achieve these limited goals and cannot be diverted to other purposes, however worthy they may be.

Berry advises us not to "capitulate to austerity," but responsible library managers can't avoid making difficult choices. We can't adjust to changing needs and a serious long-term decline in support levels by "giving a little" on the acquisitions budget but "holding firm on staff and services" as Berry advocates. We can't bargain away our budget pressures. Libraries are labor intensive, particularly in technical services, and if we must make substantial cost reductions, we will not only have to reduce acquisitions, but also the technical services staff that exists to acquire and process the materials that we are no longer buying. The importance of the University of Pittsburgh use study and others like it is that they can help dispel some of the mythology that we live by and provide useful tools for those who are being forced to reassess their acquisitions policies and reallocate their diminishing resources. The findings of use studies have to be interpreted correctly and used appropriately.

Berry says that many don't share my view that research libraries can no longer afford to maintain the collections, staffs, and service levels that we became accustomed to in the last two affluent decades. He is right. Some libraries have been hit sooner and harder than others. Many libraries continue to receive generous support and can postpone making hard choices for several more years. Eventually, however, all will have to face the fact that exponential growth rates cannot be sustained indefinitely and when they do, they will be confronted by the same difficult problems and choices that many of us are facing now. If professional library managers can't muster up the courage and the competence to deal with these problems and make these choices, others will be brought in to do so. No difficult or challenging job ever lacks for takers.

IMPACT OF ON-LINE SERVICES ON THE ACADEMIC LIBRARY

Reprinted from: *The Online Revolution in Libraries,* Proceedings of the 1977 Conference in Pittsburgh, Pa., edited by Allen Kent and Thomas J. Galvin (New York: Dekker, 1978).

In 1973, I wrote a paper to try to counter the view that was widely held at that time that academic research libraries were going to have to begin subscribing to the growing number of tapes of bibliographic data bases in machine-readable form and to provide current awareness and other services from them for their local users. (The paper was published in the December 1973 issue of the *Journal of Library Automation* with the title "Providing bibliographic search services from machine-readable data bases; the library's role.") In the paper I said that high costs and the nature of the demand would make it unfeasible for libraries to subscribe to tape services and to establish local processing centers, and that it looked as though the newly available on-line commercial services would become the dominant means of gaining access to these data bases and that librarians would become brokers for on-line services. The critical question then (and now) was: will the user be charged for the services he/she uses or will the costs be absorbed by the library? The answer to that question would determine how and to what extent the on-line services would be used in the future. If they were free, the use would be high. If the user had to pay, then use would be more moderate. I predicted that a combination of institutional subsidy for indirect costs and individual charges for direct costs would evolve as the dominant method of paying for computerized bibliographic services.

My purpose then was to try to put these powerful emerging capabilities into perspective for library decision makers—and that is my purpose today. Like all the other speakers, I, too, believe that on-line search services are going to revolutionize libraries, but there are other revolutions competing for our attention. Now I don't want to appear old and wise or cynical, but I have been experiencing revolutions in libraries ever since I got my first job at NYPL in 1956. At that time, the current revolutionary technology was microphotography. We were told it would solve our space problems and transform our way of servicing readers. The use of microfilm has become routine since then, but we can hardly call it a revolution. Ultrafiche was going to revolutionize libraries in the late 1960's but that didn't pan out either.

Actually, the closest thing we had to a revolution in libraries in the 1960's was the Xerox machine, but no one called that one in advance; it just happened quietly and was taken for granted. But no other technology has had as much impact on libraries and the way they are used as the copying machine.

There were other revolutions. In the 1960's, the second generation batch processing computers were going to revolutionize libraries and many technologists were predicting that the contents of the Library of Congress would soon be converted to computer tapes via optical scanning and would be made instantly accessible to anyone anywhere. The conventional library with books and journals would go the way of the dodo. Then came the MARC tapes revolution, the OCLC on-line revolution, the network revolution, the participatory management revolution, the media revolution, the minicomputer revolution, the resource sharing revolution. No one would deny that we are living in a period characterized by rapidly accelerating technological change in libraries (by now it is a cliché), but we have to learn to take these changes in stride. We live in a real world where we have to make day by day and week by week decisions in a political environment where the people are real and demanding and where funds and choices are limited.

The situation we are in today with on-line search services reminds me of the mid 1960's when we were facing the "computer revolution" in libraries. Engineers, information scientists, and even some librarians were predicting the end of libraries. No thinking person can deny that fundamental change (call it revolution if you like) was coming in the next decade or two in libraries from new technology such as computers, telecommunications, and microtechnology. That is obvious but not very helpful to those of us who have responsibility for managing libraries. The important questions are: when and how are these developments going to be implemented in the working library environment? Timing is everything.

Theoreticians can and should take the long view. They can look ahead and try to tell us what is coming five or ten years hence, and if they are off by a few years in their predictions—no harm is done and no one can fault them for it.

In the case of library technology, the rate of development proved to be slower than was predicted by many in the 60's. The job of automating the library proved to be more difficult than was anticipated, and in fact is happening in ways that were totally unforeseen 15 years ago. OCLC started the on-line revolution in 1971 and over 1,200 libraries are on-line today. Nevertheless, those libraries that tried to go on-line in 1968 failed because the technology and state of the art were not yet ready. A two or three year error in forecasting for a theoretician or anyone without responsibility for acting on his predictions is not serious. However, for those of us who have to act and commit ourselves and our limited resources to a new technology, a mistake in timing of one or two years can be a minor catastrophe. (Larry Buckland of Inforonics used to say that it was the fate of pioneers to get arrows shot in their rears by the Indians.)

Anyone who has pioneered the development or implementation of a new computer-based system knows how serious the consequences can be of a poor choice of equipment or a mistaken conceptual design. Those who planned and built libraries in the early 1960's without expansion space because they believed that microfilm was the storage medium of the future know the consequences of bad timing. Those who built libraries in the 1960's with large rooms in the basement to house the massive computer that would be required for the library in the 1970's also know the consequences of bad timing. One library uses the space to store a collection of little used books. Prudent managers know that it is better to be a year late in adopting a new technology than a year too early.

Fortunately, there are virtually no risks for a library that wishes to get a terminal and offer search services. The investment is small and the systems work. The only mistake you can make is to exaggerate the importance of the service and lose perspective on your other needs.

The first commercial search services came on-line only four years ago in 1973, and now we are told that they are going to revolutionize libraries. We believe it; but when is it coming? How long will it take, five years, ten, or twenty? And what are the various impacts that it will have on journals, A&I services, on libraries, on research? When and in what ways will they be impacted? Nobody really knows for sure. That is the subject of this conference and this panel. My role is to try to forecast the impact that on-line search services will have on research libraries. It is a risky assignment, and I will limit myself to a time frame of three to five years.

At Penn, we were one of the first academic research libraries to begin offering on-line search services with SDC, Lockheed, and the *New York Times* Information Bank. We started in September 1973. Our policy is to subsidize the indirect costs and change for direct. The impact to date has been slight when viewed in the perspective of the University Library as a whole. We increased our reference staff by one and trained the entire reference staff to use the technique. They loved it. It increased their skills, broadened their horizons, and increased their already heavy workloads. Less than a hundred searches a month are provided for a small but satisfied and ever-increasing number of library users. Despite our best efforts at advertising and selling, the majority of our faculty and researchers have not yet tried the new service and most of them know only vaguely that we are offering it or what it could do for them. In the next few years, the services will continue to expand but the overall impact will continue to be modest.

Perhaps by 1980 the cumulative effects will begin to be felt at an accelerated rate—not just or even primarily at the various reference desks but in the acquisitions department, in the science libraries, and in the budget. On-line services could become one of the important driving forces in a larger context of change. Why?

Rising prices, declining budgets, and increased resource sharing will help bring about the demise of many journals. Libraries may soon begin to rely on on-line searches to turn up a demand for particular articles in lieu of having increasingly expensive subscriptions. This could lead to basic changes in the allocation of library acquisitions funds away from large numbers of subscriptions to little used journals and more reliance on on-demand acquisitions of specific articles and reports through NTIS and ISI's OATS service.

Many libraries can be expected to cancel some hard copy subscriptions to expensive A&I services in favor of relying on on-line searches. This could cause A&I services to raise their prices both of the hard copy editions as well as the tape versions they provide to the vendors. The vendors may have to raise the prices of their services, and this could cause a serious decline in the use of such services by libraries. A price increase could also exacerbate the already bitter debates about whether libraries should give these services free to all their users or only provide them to those who can pay for them. Those libraries which are fully or partially subsidizing these services now may be hard put to continue the subsidies if the prices go up.

A sharp increase in the cost of on-line searching is not merely idle speculation on my part. Donald W. King, President of King Research, Inc., has expressed the dilemma as follows:

> My major concern is that increased use of the on-line services at the sacrifice of subscriptions to printed forms will not yield enough return to A&I services. The reason is that current on-line service prices are simply not structured to recover the very large input costs of bibliographic data bases. If A&I services get caught with a sharp decrease in their traditional subscriptions and without appropriate return on the on-line services, they could be in serious difficulty. Just as NTIS increased microform prices, the price of on-line services must also increase as users switch from printed form to on-line services. However, if the bibliographic search services charge a sufficiently high price to recover the large input cost, there is a good chance that libraries in turn will begin to decrease use of on-line services and these services will not recover their costs. This is a dilemma which I consider to be the most pressing issue in our field at the current time since it has such far-reaching implications on current services as well as on development of future systems . . . (BASIS, June 1977, p. 40).

We have to guard against the very human tendency we have to see the future as a continuation of present trends. Because we have seen a 20% annual increase in on-line searches in the last few years, we assume that it is bound to continue and increase indefinitely. Anyone who has experience in the stock market knows that this is a dangerous fallacy. Who could have predicted the depression in higher education that began in 1970 or the energy crisis in 1974?

It is not at all certain at this time that libraries will be the primary searchers of on-line data bases in the future. This is an area where commercial information brokers who have no qualms about charging could take over a substantial part of the market. They could perhaps do the searches more efficiently by having skilled subject specialists working on a high volume basis.

Perhaps libraries, as a result of political and philosophical considerations, will not be able to charge their users enough to cover the high cost of these searches or they simply may not have the money to subsidize them.

There are indications that suggest that over the course of the next decade academic research libraries will undergo substantial changes. Their acquisitions policies may be greatly restricted and their growth rates may diminish. This will be partially caused by and will cause in turn a substantial diminution in the size of library staffs. Increasing staff salaries and benefits will cause some operations and services to be priced out of the market and on-line search services could be among them in many poor libraries.

AUSTERITY, TECHNOLOGY, AND RESOURCE SHARING: RESEARCH LIBRARIES FACE THE FUTURE

First published in *Library Journal,* 15 May 1975, 917–23. It was reprinted in *Library Lit. 6—The best of 1975,* edited by Bill Katz (Metuchen, N.J.: Scarecrow Press, 1976).

This article was my first attempt as a library director to take a comprehensive view of the major trends and issues facing academic libraries in the coming decade.

During the last two decades academic libraries, in parallel with their parent institutions, experienced the greatest period of growth and affluence that they have ever known. The watchword was "more"—more money, more books and journals, more staff, more space, and more technology. Many new research libraries were created, and those that already existed experienced unprecedented growth. Although libraries got more of everything during those years, they still could not keep pace with the growth of new fields of research, new doctoral programs, and the increasing production of books and journals. Two decades of affluence not only failed to help solve the many problems that were brought on by exponential growth—they exacerbated them.

This extraordinary period peaked around 1970. A decline began which was further accentuated in 1974 by declining enrollments, reduced budgets, rising costs, and the energy crisis.

Recent demographic forecasts point to a further leveling off or even an absolute decline in undergraduate and graduate student enrollments in the 1980s.[1] Undoubtedly the cycle will turn up again; cycles always do, but it is unlikely that those of us who lived through that period of affluence and growth will ever live through another comparable one. It almost seems that the normal condition of libraries is austerity. That is the way it was up to the 1950s, and that is the way it is again now that the boom is over. The last two affluent decades may well have been a temporary aberration or perhaps the glorious end of an era in the history of the growth of research libraries.

Faltering Growth

The significance of the changes that have taken place in the library economy in the last five years should not be underestimated. There is mounting evidence that the long-accepted exponential growth rate of research libraries which has been causing them to double in size every 16 years or less has begun to level off and even decline. In the 1971–72 (ninth) issue of the standard statistical study of 58 academic research libraries compiled at Purdue University, the projections in the key indicator of *volumes added* showed a distinct faltering by the year 1971–72.[2] There was a positive decline when the 1973–74 *volumes added* category in the Association of Research Libraries (ARL) annual statistics are compared with those of 1971–72.[3] Out of 58 libraries compared, 36 showed a decline between 1971–72 and 1973–74. The total volumes added in the 58 libraries was about 6,114,000 in 1971–72, and 5,538,000 in 1973–74, a decline of 476,000 volumes or 7.8 percent for the two year period. The current acute budget crisis which is affecting many of these libraries will accelerate this trend and cause a turndown in other indicators such as the size of staff and total expenditures. Obviously, further statistical evidence is required before definitive conclusions can be reached, but it seems reasonable to suggest that these signs foreshadow a basic change in research library growth patterns rather than an insignificant cyclical decline.

The Numbers Game

Even during those affluent decades, librarians continued to talk poor and be poor. No matter how rapidly their budgets increased, the demands made on them and the commitments they assumed always exceeded the available resources, and it was taken for granted that this should be so. One of the main reasons for this chronic fiscal crisis in libraries—this chronic imbalance between resources and commitments—is that librarians have all been caught up in a kind of involuntary numbers game where success, progress, and achievement are measured by comparing their vital statistics with those of other academic libraries. Since no valid measures of quality are available, prestige and recognition go to those libraries with the largest numbers. Membership in the prestigious Association of Research Libraries is awarded on the basis of various measures of size.

These statistics are extremely important in many ways, but they do not tell us how good a library is or how well it is satisfying the real needs of its various user groups. There is frequently a significant difference between what library users say they want and what they actually need and use—between their real needs as opposed to their expressed needs. (They are not unlike people who insist on living near a large city for its cultural benefits but then seldom go into town to take advantage of them.) Moreover, the presence of a few great libraries like Harvard and Yale and a few growth leaders like Toronto and Texas at the top of the annual ARL statistical listings has set an impossible standard and caused an unhealthy competition among academic libraries. Unfortunately, even these leaders are now having serious difficulties maintaining their previous commitments and roles.

It should be clear by now that the goal of self-sufficiency or even comprehensiveness is unrealistic and unattainable. Librarians must act on that knowledge and begin to put an end to the numbers and growth game. Instead of trying to keep up with the Harvards and the Torontos and sustain the extraordinary growth of the last two affluent decades, we should be searching for ways to achieve a new kind of orderly and healthy growth pattern which is more commensurate with the resources and needs of our own institutions and in tune with contemporary economic realities. A basic change in attitude about growth and numbers is needed in research libraries as in other spheres of our lives. The natural tendency to equate high expenditures, high growth rates, and large collections with library effectiveness should be resisted.

The Promise of Technology

One of the principal reasons why we have not yet begun to end the numbers game and to accept the new economic reality is that we have had the hope, or the illusion, that new technology would somehow save us, or that it would at least permit us to sustain our traditional growth and development patterns for an additional period of time. We thought that computers would help control processing costs and that microforms would permit filling the gaps in library collections *en bloc* at reasonable costs. It is now apparent that the cost-effectiveness of the localized type of library automation that characterized the 1960s was marginal or even nonexistent for some applications, and that micropublishing is merely creating a whole new class of little-used research materials which librarians are pressured to purchase from their already inadequate book budgets.

The era of localized library automation is passing. Experience has shown that it is not economically feasible for any but the very largest libraries to afford the heavy costs of developing, maintaining, and operating complex local computer-based systems. Many libraries are abandoning this approach in favor of joining cooperative networks such as OCLC and its affiliates, or purchasing turn-key minicomputer systems for specific local applications from commercial vendors. It is becoming acceptable even for major libraries to have no in-house automation program or staff. In-house systems staffs are not essential to implement the local interfaces to these centralized networks or to install and operate the package systems.

Although these new approaches to library automation promise to be much more effective and produce greater savings, particularly in cataloging and processing operations, these savings will be rapidly offset by inflation and diminishing budgets, and libraries will still be left with serious long-term fiscal problems. This is because these problems originate in over-ambitious acquisitions policies and are only exacerbated by costly traditional processing routines. Computer technology will have its greatest payoff for libraries as it is more widely used as a tool to assist librarians in developing and operating networks and other new mechanisms for sharing research resources on a national and international scale. The growing use of the OCLC data base and network of interlibrary loan location purposes foreshadows the high potential of this approach.

There are still some technologists who continue to predict that research libraries as we know them will soon be superseded by rapidly developing large-scale on-line, interactive data and textual access systems based on computers and telefacsimile systems, but such views no longer enjoy the vogue they once did. The lesson that has been learned after ten or 15 years of experimentation and development is that technology alone is not going to save us, nor permit us to continue to build library collections as before, nor solve our problems by putting us out of business. Technology will help in time and in very significant ways, but we should not allow its promise and glamor to keep us from coming to grips with the immediate and critical problems of exponential growth. The solution to these problems lies in the adoption of more realistic acquisitions policies and the development of more effective means of resource sharing, not only through computerized networks but also through the creation of new and improved national resource centers.

Realism in Acquisitions

Long before libraries receive the relief and benefits that the increasingly effective use of technology promises, librarians will be forced to learn the harsh truth that the current economic recession in higher education is teaching us—namely, that no matter how good a case we make for it, the money we will need to continue to build and maintain the comprehensive research collections in the old image of Harvard and Yale is simply not going to be forthcoming. Our institutions do not have the money, and our society cannot or will not provide it.

Moreover, it is time for a serious questioning of the need for building and maintaining the rapidly growing number of multimillion-volume research collections all across the land. In 1951, for example, there were only 14 academic research libraries in the United States and Canada with collections exceeding 1,000,000 volumes, three with 2,000,000 or more, and two with over 3,000,000. By the end of the year 1973–74, there were 76 libraries with over 1,000,000 volumes, 25 with over 2,000,000, and 14 with over 3,000,000. The growth rates in collections such as these range between three and six percent compounded annually, which causes a doubling in size every 12–24 years and requires steadily increasing investment in material, processing, and space costs. Even with this investment, libraries cannot keep up with the estimated 5–15 percent annual growth rates in the world's output of publications and the 10–20 percent annual increase in book and journal costs, nor is there any way they can hope to fill in the retrospective gaps in their collections.[4]

Unfortunately, many of these recently created research libraries serve better to satisfy the prestige needs of their universities and the status needs of certain academic departments and faculty members than the actual research needs of the scholars who use them. The two categories of research materials that are most frequently acquired to satisfy these prestige and status needs are foreign language and microform collections.

There is an increasing awareness among librarians of the great disparity that exists between the money and manpower that are expended to acquire and process foreign language materials and the actual amount of use that is made of them. Large academic research libraries typically spend at least half of their book and journal budgets for foreign language publications, and these are the most troublesome and expensive materials for a library to acquire and process. Harvard estimates that 60 percent of its acquisitions are in languages other than English.[5] At the University of Pennsylvania Library foreign language materials account for less than 15 percent of the total use, and half of this is in language and literature classes with French and German predominating. Studies of titles requested on interlibrary loan in the U.S. show that a median of 86 percent are for materials in English.[6] The British Lending Library reports that over 95 percent of the items requested are in English. This merely confirms what everyone knows quite well, namely, that English-speaking people generally do not read foreign languages. This is not to minimize the importance of and need for foreign language research materials in U.S. libraries but merely to point out that they are not heavily used and could be shared to a much greater extent than they are now.

During the last two affluent decades some libraries—particularly those in the newly created or rapidly expanding universities—spent significant sums of money purchasing and processing collections of research materials in various types of microform in an effort to catch up and compete with the older and more established institutions. Experience has shown that many of these collections are seldom used, and we now see that their purchase by individual libraries was frequently unwarranted. In recent years librarians have become more selective in their purchases of microform collections and are relying increasingly on the Center for Research Libraries for the loan of specific titles or collections upon request by a user. Even with the rapid expansion of its membership in recent years, the Center receives surprisingly few requests for its microform holdings.

The scholars who need to make use of extensive collections of research materials in any form can rarely be satisfied by the holdings of any one library—even including the largest ones. This is more true today than ever before, despite the continued growth of collections, as the following statement by the Harvard Librarian so aptly attests: "Research interests have become so broad and the quantity of printed materials useful to research has increased so greatly that the Harvard Library today, with its 7,000,000 volumes, is more frequently reminded of its inadequacies than it was 60 years ago when it had only 1,000,000. It is less nearly adequate now than it was then to meet all the demands of Harvard professors and students."[7] That statement was made in 1963; since then 2,000,000 additional volumes have been added and Harvard has fallen farther behind.

From Holdings to Access

It is becoming increasingly clear that the long-term solution to the chronic fiscal, staff, space, and other problems besetting research libraries lies in setting aside the old models of Harvard and Yale and developing new and more realistic sets of goals, including especially more selective acquisitions policies designed to meet the actual needs of particular institutions and their library users. These old established libraries with extraordinary collections should serve as resources for other libraries, not models. The traditional emphasis on developing large local research collections must be shifted toward developing excellent local working collections and truly effective means of gaining access to needed research materials wherever they may be. Since a substantial percentage of all library costs ultimately stem from acquisitions, this reordering of priorities will have beneficial effects throughout the library. The ordering and processing backlogs which plague most libraries could be reduced or eliminated, storage areas could be cleared, space problems alleviated, and library staffs could begin to enjoy the feeling that comes from knowing that they can cope with their workloads as they shift their emphasis from processing materials to serving readers—from *holdings* to *access*.

Such a drastic change in goals would not have been politically feasible before because senior faculty members and administrators, most of whom were trained at the few leading research universities whose libraries we use as our models, are just as committed to the traditional concept of research libraries as are librarians. However, two new factors have emerged which will permit and even force librarians to adopt new goals and new models. One is a change in attitude on the part of administrators and faculty members brought on by the new climate of austerity, and the other is the growing awareness that viable and acceptable alternatives are or may soon be available as a result of advances in resource sharing concepts and capabilities.

To make it politically and practically feasible for academic research libraries to abandon finally the traditional models and the chimeric goal of self-sufficiency while at the same time improving their ability to fulfill their research functions, an effective national library network will have to be created. An excellent design for such a network, complete with a national resource system, a national bibliographic system, and a network communication system, has already been submitted to the National Commission on Libraries and Information Science.[8] However, this is a complex undertaking from political, organizational, and technical points of view, and its implementation, if approved, will necessarily be in stages over a period of years. In the meantime, there is one element in the proposed national resource system which is of such paramount importance to all libraries that it should be singled out for priority implementation. This is the concept of a national library resources center, which has been an important ARL concern in recent years.[9] Modeled after the British Library Lending Division, this center would assume responsibility for acquiring and making available to libraries, through loan and photocopying, a comprehensive collection of periodicals and monographs in all subjects except medicine. It could start with periodicals and later be expanded to include monographs. The existence of such a center would extend the resource base of all libraries by permitting them to be more selective and to expend their resources on materials which are of particular interest in the local environment. We will return to this concept again in the discussion of strategies for resource sharing which follows.

Strategies for Resource Sharing

Two highly successful models for effective resource sharing already exist—the Center for Research Libraries (CRL) in Chicago, and the British Library Lending Division (BLL) in Boston Spa, England.

The Center for Research Libraries is a nonprofit libraries' library with over 100 members and a collection of over 3,000,000 volumes of research materials. The Center is to its member libraries what a local library is to the individual scholar. Just as the scholar tries to acquire for his personal library the materials he uses regularly and can afford, and depends on the university library for the materials he uses less frequently or cannot afford, so the individual member library draws on the Center for little-used and expensive collections of research materials which extend and supplement its own local resources.[10]

Unlike other libraries, the CRL has no local constituency to serve and is therefore able to provide assured and rapid access to its materials to all of its members on an equal basis. Its effectiveness is measured not only against the relatively modest amount of material that its members borrow each year, but also, and more importantly, by the savings they make by being able to forego the purchase and storage of those materials which they would otherwise be called upon to acquire.

Unfortunately, the Center for Research Libraries is filled to capacity and requires substantial new funding to expand its space and functions. Founded in 1949 by a group of ten midwestern universities and with the assistance of foundation grants, it has reached a critical stage in its existence, and the nature and direction of its future development are undergoing a thorough review by its board of directors.

The British Library Lending Division, formerly the National Lending Library for Science and Technology, has also achieved remarkable success in building an organization to provide a national and even international lending and copying service for libraries. In contrast to the Center for Research Libraries, which started with the concept of providing access to little-used research materials, the BLL started with the concept of providing rapid and assured access to a corpus of the most useful and frequently requested periodicals, first in science and technology, then expanding to the social sciences and humanities and including monographs as well as periodicals. It now receives some 44,000 periodicals and 60,000 monographs a year in all subjects and languages, but its main strength is still largely in science and technology.

The government-funded BLL's sole mission is to provide these extramural services, and since its founding in 1962 it has been increasingly successful in meeting the interlibrary loan and copying needs of libraries of all kinds in the United Kingdom by pioneering new and more effective methods of acquiring materials and handling and expediting orders. In fact, the BLL has been so successful in Britain and Europe that it recently instituted a new Overseas Photocopying Service for journal articles. BLL officials suggest that the BLL may be capable of handling the overseas need for certain categories of low demand materials on a cost and time competitive basis with traditional internal interlibrary loan services and that it may be unnecessary for the U.S. and other countries to replicate these collections and services. A survey has shown that the BLL's services to foreign countries compare favorably for speed with any national system that is not based on a central loan collection.[11]

A single facility in Britain is probably not a viable long-term solution to our resource sharing needs. Nevertheless, a number of U.S. libraries are beginning to make use of the BLL's services, and their experience, if successful, could stimulate interest in the creation of a similar government-supported and nationally oriented, centralized facility to support library resource sharing in the U.S.

The University of Pennsylvania Library recently became one of the first U.S. libraries to make regular use of the BLL's Overseas Photocopying Service. In an effort to maintain the total periodical resources available to its users in the face of continuing inflation in book and journal prices and a declining budget, the Penn Library adopted a policy of offering free photocopies of articles from journals that are not available in its libraries. By absorbing the costs, rather than passing them on to the users, the library encourages the use of the service and avoids the expense and difficulties inherent in billing and collecting small sums of money. While it still continues to use neighboring libraries and the Center for Research Libraries as sources, the BLL serves as the prime source for science and technology, in which its chief strength lies. Requests are sent by teletype to the BLL and orders are promptly filled and dispatched by air mail. The charges, which amount to about $1.50 for each ten pages, are billed to a Pennsylvania account and paid for from a special library fund. The goal is to provide easy access to the specific articles that users need in the infrequently used periodicals that the Library can no longer afford to acquire.

The British Strategy

The key to the success of the BLL is that it started as a completely new entity in 1962, building its specialized collections and services on a centralized basis independent of the British Museum and the great university libraries. Thus it had no other conflicting mission, commitments, goals, or traditions and was free to develop new services in new ways. Moreover, it relied entirely on simple and available communication technology—mail and telegraph.

In contrast, we in the U.S. are committed to the seemingly logical idea that an effective national resource sharing system must take maximum advantage of and be based squarely on our existing great research libraries, and that it requires the prior development of a complex computer-based telecommunications network to make it function. Paradoxically, it is our insistence on these points that has most inhibited the development of an effective resource sharing system in the U.S. while the British built a parallel structure without complex technology and succeeded to a point where they are serving an international market.

The reasons for this divergence are clear. In the first place, the development of our computer-based bibliographical system and telecommunications network, despite the excellent progress that is being made, will require considerable additional time and resources. In the second place, the strength of the great research libraries lies in their retrospective holdings, and it is precisely the weight and legacy of these holdings that will keep them from becoming efficient resource libraries for the vast and increasing quantity of contemporary materials that are in the greatest demand. These libraries, like great department stores, were designed to serve patrons on their premises; what we urgently need now are more facilities like the CRL and the BLL which resemble warehouses and which are designed to serve other libraries in the manner of mail order merchandise distribution centers. The great research libraries can also draw on the recent materials in these new facilities; they in turn can serve, with compensation, as sources for needed retrospective titles which cannot and should not be duplicated.

U.S. Strategy

The present approach to resource sharing and interlibrary loan in the U.S. (apart from the CRL) has been oriented theoretically in a hierarchical system extending from locality to state and region, with a handful of the largest research libraries at the apex serving as the collections of last resort. In practice, borrowing libraries, in an effort to save time, commonly bypass the system and send their requests directly to the larger libraries which they hope and expect will have the needed titles. Since these major resource libraries are expected to provide interlibrary loan service in a spirit of *noblesse oblige* and without compensation of any kind, they have never had any incentive to give priority to this costly and difficult activity. Indeed, the more efficient one of these libraries becomes at filling requests the more requests it will attract, until its service again deteriorates to a point where further traffic is discouraged. It is a no-win situation. Filling free interlibrary loan requests has always been treated by the large netlenders as a troublesome extra, and this, along with the cumbersome nature of the decentralized system, accounts to a large extent for the relative slowness and inefficiency of this activity in the U.S.

With the promise of federal aid as an incentive, there is increasing acceptance of the concept of decentralized sharing and state-oriented systems of compensated interlibrary lending. This concept has worked rather well for certain states such as New York, Illinois, and others which have substantial bibliographical resources, but for many states it will only result in a pooling of poverty until an effective national library network becomes a reality.

If we continue to put our faith in building and improving hierarchical interlibrary loan systems with existing resource libraries at the apex, it is because we have not yet assimilated the findings of recent interlibrary loan studies and the lessons that have been learned by the National Library of Medicine and the BLL. The evidence shows that more than half the requests are for items published in the previous ten years; many are for items alreadly owned by but not available in the requesting library for a variety of reasons; 85–95 percent are in English; and more than half the requests to academic libraries are for serials. These findings suggest that such requests can be more easily satisfied from a centralized and specialized facility such as the British Library Lending Division whose sole function is to serve this need. Contrary to library folklore, exotic and obscure retrospective materials are not what are most commonly requested on interlibrary loan. Requests for such items constitute a small percentage of the total and could be easily handled by the existing large research libraries if they were freed from having to cope with routine requests and if they were adequately compensated for it—preferably by a federal subsidy of some kind.

The Case for an NLRC

The traditional hierarchical system for sharing retrospective resources by interlibrary loan, even after it is forged into a national system and improved (as it should be) by adding a compensation feature to it, may still fall short of filling the need that research libraries have for an effective system for gaining access to recent and current materials and particularly periodicals. The time appears to be ripe for a melding of the Center for Research Libraries' experience with little-used materials and the British Library Lending Division's success and experience with interlibrary lending and copying of the most-used materials. These two functions are essential, and ideally they should be in the same organization so they can better complement each other. There is an urgent need for the Center for Research Libraries to expand its functions to include a national library resources lending facility along the lines of the BLL but with initial emphasis on periodicals. In order to do this, the Center will require a new source of funding and substantial new space. The obvious solution which has been suggested is that the Center be made into a federally funded component of the national library system. If this proves to be an unfeasible line of development for the Center, then a completely new beginning could be made as it was in Britain. Perhaps a surplus military or other government facility could be pressed into service to meet this urgent need.

It would be difficult to overestimate the importance of creating a national library resources center. Consider the following factors:

- Serials subscriptions consume more than half of library expenditures for materials, and the percentage is rising at an alarming rate as journal prices continue to rise at a faster rate than monograph prices. Some departmental libraries in science and technology are now expending 80–100 percent of their book funds for subscriptions, leaving little or nothing for the purchase of monographs. Serials are not only expensive to buy, but they require substantial additional expenditures for cataloging, check-in of issues, binding, and storage.
- Bibliographical identification and location tools are more advanced and more effective for serials than for monographs, and they make it easier to fill requests. Since we have the *Union List of Serials, New Serials Titles,* and countless computer-produced published lists of the serials holdings of libraries of all types, the need for a computerized data base and telecommunications system for interlibrary loan of serials is less pressing than for monographs.
- Over half of all interlibrary loan requests are for periodical materials, ranging from a third in public libraries to 85 percent in governmental and special libraries. About 85 percent of periodical requests are filled by photocopies of articles.[12]
- The designers of the proposed national library program estimate that within a period of less than ten years a national periodicals resources system could provide a substantial proportion of the article photocopies which make up a high percentage of all interlibrary loan requests.[13]
- The BLL estimates that it is now handling about three-quarters of all interlibrary loan traffic in the United Kingdom and that 83 percent of the requests are satisfied from stock, with a further eight percent from other libraries, including some abroad.[14]

In view of these factors, it is hard to escape the conclusion that the creation of a national library resources center modeled after the British Library Lending Division should be a prime objective of U.S. library planners. It provides an efficient and immediate way to increase the total resources available to all libraries and would be an indispensible element in the national library network that is rapidly emerging. Unfortunately, no mention is made of this concept in the second draft (September 15, 1974) of the NCLIS program document,[15] nor does it appear in the list of priorities at the conclusion of the proposed design of a national library system that was prepared for the Commission by Westat, Inc.[16]

Copyright

The growing concern that publishers and copyright holders have about this kind of library resource sharing will have to be allayed in some way. The Westat report just cited suggests that concentrating copying service at a single national center might facilitate a resolution of this problem. Perhaps the British experience could again serve as a model. Britain revised its copyright law in 1956 permitting libraries limited fair use privileges, and the BLL has been operating completely within its provisions with little apparent adverse effect on publishers. Libraries continue to purchase those books and journals most in demand by their readers. The BLL serves only a backup function, and if it did not exist borrowers would simply have to do without since much of the material requested has gone out of print or is otherwise unobtainable in the book trade.

Publishers have the idea that if they can discourage interlibrary loan and photocopying, libraries will be forced to spend more money to buy books and journals. The fact is that with or without effective sharing mechanisms, and with rising prices and declining budgets, libraries simply will not have the money to maintain their previous acquisitions levels. Publishers may suffer some losses. Some journals may go under, others will never be published because it will be foreseen that there would be insufficient demand for them. In the end, it may not be a bad thing if the tremendous number of journal titles currently being published were to decrease significantly. This could occur without a serious loss to scholarship since many of them were created to exploit the library market in the affluent sixties.[17] The idea that library budgets should support commercial publishing is a product of the last two affluent decades and is no longer viable, if it ever was.

Library sales have contributed to the support of some scholarly publications, but it is becoming clear that if subsidies are needed, more effective and reliable mechanisms than library book budgets will have to be found.

Conclusion

Academic libraries—and perhaps all libraries—have entered a new era of austerity in which the financial resources available will not be enough to enable them to continue to build their collections and operate as they did during the last two affluent decades. There is evidence that the exponential growth rates of library collections and budgets are declining and the time has come to shift emphasis away from holdings and size to access and service. More realistic concepts of collection building will have to be adopted, and new patterns of service will have to be devised.

The urgent task of developing effective means of library resource sharing has two major components of equal importance. One is to increase the total library resources available, and the other is to improve the organizational and technical mechanisms for gaining access to them. To increase the total resources available involves not only strengthening existing libraries but also creating an essential missing element: a national library resources center modeled after and combining the best features of the Center for Research Libraries and the British Library Lending Division. To improve the mechanisms for gaining access to these resources involves building a national library network supported by a computer-based national bibliographical and communications system. These two major components must go forward together. We should not allow the more glamorous and exciting technological elements to overshadow the more prosaic but equally important resource building elements.

Notes

1. Fiske, Edward B. "Education Feeling No-Growth Pains," *New York Times,* p. 57, 88, January 15, 1975.

2. Dunn, Oliver C., et al. *The Past and Likely Future of 58 Research Libraries, 1951–1980: a Statistical Study of Growth and Change.* Instructional Media Research Unit, University Libraries and Audiovisual

Center, Purdue University, West Lafayette, Ind. 1971–72 (Ninth) Issue, 1973.

3. *Academic Library Statistics 1973–1974.* Washington, D.C., Assn. of Research Libraries, 1974.

4. Fussler, Herman H. *Research Libraries and Technology.* Univ. of Chicago Pr., 1973, p. 34.

5. Buck, Paul. *Libraries and Universities.* Harvard Univ. Pr., 1964, p. 72.

6. Stevens, Rolland E. "A Study of Interlibrary Loan," *College and Research Libraries,* September 1974, p. 336–343.

7. Bryant, Douglas W. "A University Librarian Looks Ahead." 1963. 48p. (Mimeographed)

8. *Resources and Bibliographic Support for a Nationwide Library Program.* Final Report to the National Commission for Libraries and Information Science. August 1974. (WESTAT, Inc., Rockville, Md.)

9. For the original expanded version of this concept see: Palmour, Vernon E., et al. *Access to Periodical Resources, a National Plan.* For the Assn. of Research Libraries, Washington, D.C., WESTAT, Inc., February 1974. (NSF Grant GN 35571)

10. This was paraphrased from the Introduction, *Handbook, the Center for Research Libraries, 1973.* Chicago, Ill.

11. *The British Library First Annual Report* 1973–74, p. 7.

12. *Resources and Bibliographic Support* . . . op. cit., p. 107.

13. *Loc. cit.*

14. *The British Library,* op. cit., p. 7.

15. *A National Program for Library and Information Services,* 2nd Draft. (Rev.) Prepared by the National Commission on Libraries and Information Science. September 15, 1974. Washington, D.C.

16. *Resources and Bibliographic Support* . . . op. cit. p. 147–48.

17. This point is nicely underscored by a letter addressed to *Chemical & Engineering News* (December 10, 1973) and signed by 11 distinguished chemists from Europe, Britain, and the U.S. urging librarians to refrain from purchasing "unnecessary" chemistry journals. It was reprinted in *College & Research Libraries,* July 1974, p. 268–69, under the title "Too Many Chemistry Journals."

LESS IS MORE: THE UNIVERSITY OF PENNSYLVANIA REORGANIZES ITS LIBRARY SUPPORT FOR REGIONAL STUDIES

Reprinted from *South Asian Library Resources in North America, Papers from the Boston Conference, 1974,* edited by M. L. P. Patterson and M. Yanuck, Zug, Switzerland: Interdocumentation Co. AG.

In the 1950s and 1960s great stress was put on building comprehensive research collections to support the growing foreign area studies programs. Funds from Public Law 480 supplied a flood of publications from South Asia. As we entered the austere 1970s it became clear that libraries would never have sufficient resources to process these materials and it was essential to reduce drastically the flow and the level of commitment. The presentation that I made to this Conference was part of a campaign I mounted to make the PL 480 South Asia program more selective and to stem the tide of materials that were overwhelming the participating libraries. It was a real-life example of "matching commitments to needs and resources."

Reorganization

In June of 1971, after a thorough review of all library policies and operations in support of Asian studies, a basic change in policy and a thoroughgoing reorganization of library resources and procedures were implemented at the University of Pennsylvania. The library's newly created Oriental Department was restructured back into its three component parts, namely, South Asia Regional Studies, Middle East, and Chinese-Japanese. The South Asian and Middle Eastern collections, which had been withdrawn from the main stacks and shelved in a separate sequence as an Oriental collection, were completely reintegrated back into the library's regular stack collection. The library's attempt to create a separate Oriental catalog was also abandoned and full reliance was placed on the main public catalog for access to holdings in these subjects. Since the Chinese-Japanese vernacular language collection was classified by the Harvard-Yenching system, it was not affected by the decision to reintegrate.

These physical and organizational changes were accompanied by a decision to apply the same rigorous criteria for selection and processing materials from the PL 480 South Asia program as were applied to other subjects and areas in which the library had serious and long-term collection-building commitments. In other words, materials from South Asia were upgraded from a special category of low-grade ore-type resources for the use of a small number of regional studies specialists to an important part of the library's permanent collections for the use of the entire university community now and in the future.

Nearly three years have passed since this reorganization took place and these policies were adopted. In that time, the University of Pennsylvania Library has processed all its backlogs of PL 480 materials (except those awaiting LC cataloging copy) and all current selections are being added to the main collection after passing through the library's regular processing routines. All this was accomplished in spite of a planned reduction of the staff in 1971 from three librarians and two clerical workers to its present complement of one librarian and one clerical worker.

It is not the purpose of this paper to describe these changes in the abstract or for public relations purposes. Rather, the conference program planners felt that Pennsylvania's rationale for and experience with this new policy and approach would be of general interest to the field. Other libraries are now, or may soon be, under similar pressures to bring their own PL 480 accessions for South Asia into line with those of other major areas and disciplines during this period of declining financial support.

Reassessment

Since the unprecedented period of affluence and growth that took place during the decades of the 1950's and 1960's came to an end around 1970, library administrators have had to begin reassessing the various new programs and commitments which were added during that period of relatively easy money. During these two decades, many new area studies programs were started and libraries had to begin building collections on a crash basis to support them. Money came from government and foundation grants, as well as from the university administration, and PL 480 programs provided a rich and easy source for collection building. By now much of the grant money has dried up and library budgets have effectively ceased to grow. Many universities have had to reduce their area studies programs and some of the PL 480 programs have been phased out. Clearly, the outlook in the decades of the 1970's and 1980's for the development of library collections in general, and regional studies collections in particular, is quite different from what it was in the 1950's and 1960's.

We are into a new period of austerity in libraries, and it is essential that we unburden ourselves of many of the ideas and expectations we acquired about collection development in the era of rapid growth and affluence in which most of us spent our formative professional years. This does not mean, however, that we have to lower our standards, abandon our search for excellence, and resign ourselves to mediocrity. On the contrary, the exact opposite is true; and one of the main points of this paper is to suggest that a little austerity can be beneficial and that in managing library resources and building collections occasions do arise when "less is more." Pennsylvania's experience in the last three years with its regional studies library programs, and particularly with South Asia and PL 480, is offered as a case in point.

The Library at Pennsylvania

In the spring of 1971 when we reviewed our South Asia PL 480 situation, we found that it was failing badly and heading for a total breakdown. The reasons were simply that the goals that had been set for that department of the library were unrealistic and unattainable with the resources that were or could possibly be made available in the foreseeable future. We were apparently trying to acquire, process, and add to our collections the vast bulk of the PL 480 materials that were being received. We were also trying to maintain a separate catalog and shelflist of our South Asia holdings in addition to those maintained by the library. In sum, we were trying to operate our South Asia unit as a kind of separate library within the main library. The rationale for this arrangement probably had its origin in the model of the small seminar library which is commonly used to meet the special and limited needs of an academic department or discipline. The South Asia Regional Studies (SRS) Library at Pennsylvania once fit that description, but by 1971 it had totally outgrown that model because of the size and character of the PL 480 program which was attached to it.

The PL 480 program was bringing in every year over 7,500 volumes, 3,500 serial titles, and 100 newspapers in 23 languages, many of which were unintelligible to all but a handful of persons on campus. At its peak in 1971, the central library was devoting some 20 per cent of its total processing capability to the unsuccessful attempt to cope with this flood of material. No other major discipline or even group of disciplines was receiving anywhere near this level of support, and from no other comparable geographic region of the world—developed or undeveloped—were we acquiring this quantity of material. In spite of this, the SRS Department felt, and quite justifiably, that it was still not getting the kind of library support it needed and deserved. The library administration was equally unhappy with the situation. Over 42,000 PL 480 volumes were backlogged and only marginally available in a storage area, and clusters of the familiar grey bindings of PL 480 books were to be seen backed up at every major work station in the processing department. Quantities of books and journals, whose research value and life expectancy from both an intellectual and physical point of view were extremely limited, were being added because they had arrived in the library, they were "free," and we could not, for various reasons, decide which ones to add to the collections and which ones to discard. This selection problem was complicated by the sheer numbers of books and the variety and difficulty of the languages in which they were printed.

It was clear that the only solution to these problems lay in formulating and implementing a whole new approach to PL 480 and South Asia based on a realistic assessment of the resources available to the library, and the needs of the scholarly community it was designed to serve. It was important to restore a kind of balance to the various parts of the library in order to assure the health and long-term development of the South Asia collections. The extravagant and unsuccessful policies of the 1960's had to give way to more selective, economical and ultimately far more successful policies geared to the needs and the economic realities of this and the next decade.

Pennsylvania's New Policy

With the active assistance of a departmental library committee, a new collecting policy was developed and implemented. PL 480 materials on subjects outside the scope of South Asia Regional Studies were subjected to the same selection criteria as material coming from other regions and from other sources. Serials and newspaper subscriptions were reviewed and pruned.

Of the estimated 42,000 volumes in the PL 480 backlog, approximately 70 per cent were processed and 30 per cent were discarded. The volumes discarded were largely in science and technology, textbooks, and contemporary fiction. Current shipments are now routinely processed except where Library of Congress card copy is not available. Processing statistics indicate a retention rate of nearly 100 per cent for Sanskrit, Pali, Prakrit, and Tibetan; 80 per cent for English; 75 per cent for Bengali, Hindi, Tamil, and Urdu; and 60 per cent for Gujarati, Malayalam, Marathi, Nepali, and Telugu. In 1972, Assamese, Kannada, Oriya, Punjabi, and Sindhi were dropped altogether, but before that the retention rate was 30 per cent for those languages.

The task of dealing with PL 480 will be further eased when the effect of the restructured program which permits a choice of levels of coverage begins to be reflected in current shipments from New Delhi. The University of Pennsylvania elected comprehensive coverage for English, French, Pali, Portuguese, Prakrit, Sanskrit, and Tibetan, and basic coverage for all other languages except the five that were dropped.

All these various changes were not made without a certain amount of discussion and even controversy. The most controversial decision was the one which led to the reintegration of the Oriental collections into the regular library stack shelving sequence. Many good arguments were made for and against this move, but the most compelling factor was that the South Asia and Middle East collections had come of age and now constituted a major and important segment of the library's total resources. Over 40 per cent of the annual accessions of the central library were being classed in the Oriental stacks. Half of that 40 per cent was in South Asia. In time, the library would have been divided into two distinct parts—one for Oriental, and the second for all other subjects. This would have increased operating costs and compounded the complexity and confusion of a stack already divided by Dewey and Library of Congress classification systems.

The time had passed when these regional studies collections could be treated as the private preserves of a small number of specialists and relegated to one floor or one corner of the library for these scholars' convenience. An analysis of the library's computerized circulation records for an 18-month period showed that, while SRS students constituted the largest per capita borrowing group and accounted for 17 per cent of the total library use, the major user group, 83 per cent, were all from other parts of the university. Of the faculty members recorded as using the collections, only 25 per cent were in the Oriental programs. These studies reinforced the view that reintegration of the Oriental collections was in the best interests of all the library's users including the South Asia group. This view has by now won general acceptance among users, including most of the SRS students and faculty.

One primary aim of the various changes that have been described here was to incorporate the bulk of the Oriental collections into the main stream of the university library in order to make them more accessible to the entire university community. At the same time, there was another major thrust in this overall strategy; this was an effort to expand and improve the quality of the reference and working conditions and physical facilities devoted to each of the three regions that had been included in the Oriental Department.

The W. Norman Brown Library, located on the fifth floor of the main building, was completely refurbished, reorganized, and reconstituted as a reference and working collection and study center devoted exclusively to Sanskrit and South Asia Regional Studies. The Library's extensive and unique collection of Indic manuscripts (over 3,400 texts) will be housed in an adjoining room where it will enjoy increased security and accessibility.

The Middle Eastern staff was moved to an office of its own on the first floor, and a seminar room for its reference and working collections was established. The Chinese-Japanese staff space was increased and its reference and working collection was also moved to larger quarters. This entire reorganization of library support for regional studies was accomplished in less than three years. All three components, and particularly South Asia, are operating far more efficiently and effectively and their long-term health and continued development are assured. The lesson we learned from our experience at Penn and which we are trying to share with you is that a little austerity can be a good thing when it forces us to abandon our illusions and set realistic and achievable library goals.

Library Technology and Networking

Integrated Online Library Systems: Perspectives, Perceptions, and Practicalities

A version of this article was presented at the Conference on Integrated Online Library Systems in Atlanta in September 1984. It was published in *Library Journal*, 1 February 1985, 37–40.

The standard keynote speech at library technology conferences begins by describing, in glowing terms, the wonders of the new information processing technology and then exhorts the assembled company to embrace that technology or be left behind on the ash heap of the technological revolution.

Since this paper is focused on integrated online library systems you might expect it to begin by describing how advanced those systems are now and how much better they are going to be in a year or two. Then, of course, it should urge readers to select and install the system that best fits their library's needs. As you may have guessed, that is *not* what it will do.

What I will try to do is offer some help to those currently sorting their way through the maze of information and misinformation on integrated online systems. Many librarians have the feeling that they are being left behind in the current rush toward online catalogs and integrated online systems. Most probably think that the state of the art of those systems is much farther advanced than it really is. I thought the same thing until I really started looking at the available systems with a view to actually buying one before the end of 1984.

I learned that there is a vast gap between promise and reality when it comes to integrated online library systems. I surveyed the market, read the vendors' literature, listened to sales pitches, talked to many smart systems people and consultants, and then used common sense and concluded that there are no finished integrated online library systems available on the market today for any size library. Nor do I expect there to be any in the next year or two, no matter what the vendors are promising.

A Moving Target

It is appropriate to ask at this point: What is an integrated online library system, anyway? What capabilities and functions does a system have to include before it qualifies for that title?

Integrated systems are a moving target. What might have been acceptable five years ago is inadequate today, and what looks advanced today will seem primitive in five years. As technology improves and costs go down, we librarians demand additional functions and capabilities and our requirements and expectations always exceed the offerings.

In one of her excellent *LJ* columns, "Integrated Systems: Dream vs. Reality" (July 1984, p. 1302), Susan Baerg Epstein gives a long list of functions that librarians are asking for in integrated systems. The list starts with the obvious bibliographic functions such as circulation control, public access catalog, cataloging and catalog maintenance, authority control, acquisitions, serials control, materials booking, reserve book room control, and goes on to list another 20 features which cover nearly every activity that takes place in a library. Here are just a few: payroll and check production, budget control, schedules for staff, personnel records, personnel statistics, word processing, spread sheet programs, two way cable television hook-ups, etc.

Clearly, it is neither possible nor desirable to put that long wish list of functions into a single system. Some vendors do offer systems with word processing and spread sheet capabilities, but those offerings predate the microcomputer revolution and rich library of software that it spawned. Library systems vendors will never be able to keep pace with this commercial software market. They should stick to what they know and what they do best.

Word processing, spread sheet programs, and many of the other business functions in Epstein's long list do not belong in an integrated library system. Librarians would be better advised to buy the standard commercial programs for a few hundred dollars and run them on microcomputers.

I would be pleased if I could purchase an integrated system that performed well and reliably the principal bibliographic functions such as the public access catalog, cataloging and catalog maintenance, authority control, acquisitions, serials check-in, and circulation control. I would also like the system to be expandable to handle other bibliographic functions such as title pages, indexes, and full text. I don't know of any system, however, that can handle all these basic functions in good working order or that will be able to handle them within the next year or two.

There are a number of so-called "integrated" systems on the market with excellent circulation modules because they were initially designed to be circulation systems, but their online catalogs and catalog maintenance modules are crude appendages which some libraries accept in their zeal to supersede the card catalog and go online.

With his customary logic Mike Malinconico, in "Circulation Control Systems as Online Catalogs" (*LJ,* June 15, 1983, p. 1207–12), refutes the idea that circulation systems can double as online catalogs. He sums it up like this: "With respect to all of the parameters used to characterize an automated system—computing capacity, auxiliary storage, communications, and operating personnel—a circulation control system that can double as an online catalog entails a quantum leap in size, cost, complexity, and sophistication. The result is, thus, an undertaking which is a qualitative departure from the prevailing situation."

In plain English, what Mike is saying is that there is a world of difference between the hardware and software requirements of a true online catalog and a circulation system that is doubling as one.

Practicalities

Hank Epstein advises anyone who is going to buy an online catalog system to make sure that the system will handle the database size and the number of terminals that they are going to put on the system. The way to do this, according to Hank, is not by asking the vendor and taking his or her word for it, but by making a site visit to a library (approximately the same size or larger than yours) which has the equivalent database and number of terminals. You can actually see how the system is working there. If the vendor has no customer that fits that description, then you should not buy the system. More precisely, you should not buy the system unless you are prepared to be a pioneer and take the possible consequences that go with the decision. One of the worst mistakes you can make is to judge a system by its performance in a demonstration mode which uses a small special database and a limited number of terminals. Anybody who buys such a system should be prepared to experience all the pains and pleasures of pioneers who, as we all learned in school, suffer terrible hardships before they get to the promised land—and many never get there.

Anyone choosing components of an integrated system today faces a dilemma. If one wants to minimize risk and choose a system that operates reliably in a working environment, it will most likely be a 1970s system because they are the only ones that have been around long enough to be properly field tested. Most of those systems that work are considered to be obsolete or out of date by many librarians. If on the other hand one wants to have a system with the latest and most sophisticated design and capabilities, one will have to choose a system that is relatively untested and do business with a new entrepreneurial company that is subject to all the usual problems that beset such companies. Keep in mind that you are not only buying a system, you are entering into a long term dependent relationship with the vendor that sells and supports it. The vendor's troubles become your troubles; the vendor's failures become your failures. Don't think we haven't had our share of troubled and failed companies in the library systems field. It is a mistake to believe that every new company that comes to ALA exhibiting the latest microprocessor-based system is going to be around in two or three years.

Don't believe that it is safe to select an untested or even a tested system because it has been selected by a prestigious library or endorsed by a prominent director in a full-page ad in the library press. That library will have its own good reasons for making that choice; it may be getting a special price or a special deal for various reasons. But your needs and your deal will be different. Prestigious libraries have also been known to make prodigious mistakes. In the end, there is no substitute for doing your own homework.

We need to question the notion that is currently so prevalent in the library field that minicomputer-based library systems are somehow more manageable and less expensive than mainframe-based systems. That assertion may have been true in the past when we were implementing turnkey circulation systems, but it probably is not true today when we are dealing with integrated online systems. As a matter of fact, the traditional distinction between micros, minis, and mainframes is rapidly losing all meaning as the capabilities expand and the prices decline.

Many of the reasons for the preference for minicomputer systems in libraries are no longer valid now, as we move toward complex integrated systems which will require the data storage and processing capabilities of powerful and highly reliable mainframes. Some library systems vendors are expanding the capacity of their microcomputer systems by joining several machines together in a series, but this makes for a very complex system which may cost more to purchase and maintain than a large mainframe. It is no longer a question of preferring micros, minis, or mainframes, but of using the most appropriate and cost effective configuration of software and equipment for the job at hand. The job at hand—an integrated system—is of a different order of magnitude than a circulation system.

A final practicality: selecting and implementing an integrated online system is only part of the job—probably not the most costly part. The other part is to convert the library's retrospective catalog records to machine readable form and create and maintain a quality online database. Computer systems become obsolete and are replaced in time, but the library's catalog database is a permanent asset—or liability—depending on the care with which it is created and maintained.

Visions vs. Reality

How can we explain the tremendous gap that exists between the rhetoric and the reality of integrated systems, or between the promise and the performance? First of all we need to recognize that there is nothing new or unusual about this gap between perception and reality. Making visionary claims is simply part of the birthright of information science and technology.

It all started with Vannevar Bush's famous article, "As We May Think," in the July 1945 issue of *Atlantic Monthly*. The article, a seminal one, was the forerunner of thousands of visionary articles and "blue sky" papers. They have become a regular feature of the literature of information science and technology ever since. In his article, Bush set forth his vision of the Memex, a desk-like device for individual use which could store and retrieve vast quantities of information and would serve as a scholar's library and information system. Despite the fact that Bush postulated a mechanical device with an improved form of microfilm as the storage medium, it has become an article of faith in the folklore of information science that he was visualizing something like the computer-based Scholar's Workstation.

In one sense, Bush was as wrong about the Memex as he was about the intercontinental ballistics missile which he flatly declared to be an impossibility. Nevertheless, his vision of the Memex was accepted as prophetic in 1945 and served as an inspiration and a goal for the pioneers of information science. Now, 40 years later, the Memex is about to become a reality, but it will be based, not on microfilm, but on computer and telecommunications technology that simply could not have been imagined in 1945. Our Memex is a powerful computer linked to optical disks, database machines, and information networks.

The point is that our field thrives on visions. Some of those visions turn out to be pipe dreams; others, like the Memex, eventually become realities—one way or another. The fun and frustration of it all is that it is so hard to distinguish the pipe dreams from the prophetic visions.

When you add the dreams and schemes of hundreds of ambitious and competitive systems designers, entrepreneurs, salesmen, and library directors to those information science visions, you get the current confusing and exciting situation in this little corner of the information world—the integrated online library system market. All the integrated systems will arrive late, some will be obsolete by the time they get here, and others will succeed beyond our wildest expectations. Our task is to pool our knowledge so that we can do a better job of telling one from the other.

Library vs. Information Automation

The new technology presents a paradox. While we still don't have the software required for an integrated online library system, the hardware for the current version of the Memex, the Scholar's Workstation, will soon be a reality.

To understand this paradox, we must recognize that there are two, parallel streams of development of new technology in the library and information field. One stream is the software for what we call "library automation" and that includes integrated online systems. The market for library automation software is limited, so that software develops very slowly. Two decades after the beginning of library automation we are just getting circulation systems that are complete and reliable. Online public access catalogs and related functions are well along in their development, but they are not yet ready for routine installation and operation in a variety of libraries.

The other stream of development, what I call "information automation," uses the new technology to store, process, and access large quantities of information—bibliographic, textual, and numeric. It includes the growing number and range of online search and information services as well as personal computer-based information systems. Information automation is developing at an extraordinary rate because it has a large and lucrative market of which libraries are but a small part. Information automation provides access to information resources outside the library; the goal of library automation is to provide better access to the resources within the library.

Information automation has been developing faster than library automation, but there are signs now that advances in information automation are being transferred to library automation and are speeding its development. The two streams are rapidly converging.

Toward a New Generation of Systems

Nearly all of the integrated online systems that are under development and being marketed today have their origins in the 1960s or 1970s. This is equally true of the library network systems. Those systems were all conceived, designed, programmed, and implemented at a time when experience with computers and automated library systems was rudimentary, when computer equipment was expensive and unreliable, when operating systems and programming languages were limited, and when applications software was painfully difficult to develop and maintain. The result is that most of the systems in operation and available to libraries today are the product of a passing era in computing.

Although, as I said, there are no finished integrated systems available, several seem close to achieving that goal. The impending success of these systems may give rise to the notion that the battle for library automation has been virtually won and all that remains is to complete and use the existing systems. Existing systems are everywhere being enhanced and improved. Many specialized microprocessor-based systems are being developed. Still, there are remarkably few major new integrated systems projects under development.

In the 1960s and 1970s there were dozens of systems groups at work in libraries, networks, and businesses developing their own systems. Each group was certain that it had better ideas and more elegant designs than its competitors, and each was grossly underestimating the amount of time, effort, and expense required to develop, install, and maintain a workable system. The road to original systems development was strewn with technical and financial failures and dead ends. By the beginning of the 1980s, the message had come through loud and clear: original systems development was beyond the capability of individual libraries and could only be done by library networks and commercial vendors.

The maxim that best expressed the spirit of the computer systems pioneers in the exciting 1960s and early 1970s was: "If it works, it's obsolete." Now, after two decades of sobering and frequently traumatic experience on the frontiers of development, that generation of pioneers has grown older and wiser—and more cautious. It has inherited many of the key management and leadership positions in our libraries, networks, and computing centers. Yesterday's pioneers have become today's homesteaders. The maxim that best characterizes the spirit of the veteran systems developers in our time is: "If it ain't broke, don't fix it."

Our generation has been traumatized by its experience with systems development in much the same way that previous generations were traumatized by the experience of the Great Depression or the student protest movement in the 1960s. We are ready to improve, build upon, and expand the systems that we have, but few of us are willing to take the risks involved in developing new systems based on new concepts and new technologies. Ironically, this new wave of conservatism coincides with a veritable explosion in computer hardware, software, and telecommunications capabilities. It comes at a time when a $5000 personal computer is more powerful and versatile than the machines that were used for the early versions of the OCLC and BALLOTS systems.

The world of technology is shifting dramatically and we must shift with it to maintain our equilibrium. We need a new vision of the future that is based on current and future realities rather than on past history and experience.

Computing and information processing technologies have entered an exciting new stage of development similar to the one we experienced in the 1960s. There are new generations of hardware, operating systems, and programming languages. Both the hardware and software have become much more robust and reliable. Prices are plummeting. Mainframe computers are now selling for the price that was charged for minicomputers five years ago, and microprocessors many times more powerful than those minicomputers can now be bought at bargain prices. When those microprocessors are linked to large mainframes, optical and digital disk systems, database machines, local area networks, and the various library and commercial information networks, library automation and information automation will converge and a new wave of synergistic development will take place similar to the one that took place in the late 1960s and early 1970s.

In the next decade, the creative development work will no longer be limited to the small entrepreneurial vendors as it has been in recent years. They will be joined by the systems groups that are now being reconstituted and revitalized in many libraries after a decade of relative inactivity and decline. The work of this new generation of systems librarians will be augmented and supplemented by the efforts of a growing army of enthusiastic volunteers drawn from the rank and file of the professional staff. These irregulars have already begun to use personal computers as a tool for automating functions and activities that are not yet a part of the available integrated systems. This new generation of systems librarians and computerwise irregulars will have the requisite tools and knowledge, and they should be encouraged and supported in their efforts to pioneer the development of a new generation of library and information processing systems.

WILL SUCCESS SPOIL OCLC?

Reprinted from *Library Journal,* 1 April 1984, 626.

Right or wrong, there is a growing perception in the library world that OCLC is isolating itself from the main stream of library cooperation and is becoming increasingly unresponsive to the needs and wishes of the libraries it serves and to which it owes its past and possibly also its future success. OCLC appears to be shedding the last vestiges of its cooperative origins as it evolves into a new kind of not-for-profit high tech information company based on the corporate model. Its management comes from the corporate world, speaks the language of business and law, and measures success by the bottom line. OCLC's view of itself and its place in the library world appears to many to resemble that of former Defense Secretary and GM President Engine Charlie Wilson who said that what was good for General Motors was good for the country. It appears that OCLC's management believes that what is good for OCLC must be good for the library world.

A number of important management decisions in recent years lend credence to that perception. OCLC has taken the position that its principal asset is its database and has moved to copyright it despite a firestorm of objections, not only by libraries that shared in its creation, but by a library community dedicated to sharing bibliographic information. It has also moved to strengthen its hand in the contracts it has with its broker networks and member libraries, and in the process, has put itself into an adversary relationship with them. OCLC also gives the impression of being late and lukewarm in its commitment to participate in national-level cooperation, including especially the vital CLR-sponsored Linked Systems Project.

A Bum Rap?

Does this perception have any validity or is OCLC merely getting a bum rap from those who wish it ill? There is no way of assessing the validity of perceptions. The evidence is impressionistic and inconclusive. OCLC's management, whose dedication and good intentions no one questions, acknowledges its existence, but denies in the most sincere and persuasive terms that there is any basis for it in reality. But the perception is real and widespread, especially among those who wish OCLC well, and it will not be dispelled by denials. OCLC will have to confront the reality that underlies the perception and shape its attitudes and strategies accordingly.

There are those who are untroubled by this perception and believe that it would be no bad thing if OCLC were to become an information company with no pretext of being governed or controlled by its users. OCLC's management would be free to restructure its relations with the networks and to pursue its strategic goal of serving information users directly rather than through the broker networks and libraries. It would also permit OCLC to treat its users as independent customers rather than as members or participants. OCLC would have to satisfy those customers by providing quality services at competitive prices in the marketplace. This might require OCLC to reorder its priorities so as to give its customer base, and the good will that goes with it, a value equal to that which is now accorded to the database. There would be other benefits and losses to both OCLC and its users.

No Turning Back

There are others who would urge OCLC to spurn the corporate model and go back to its cooperative origins, but this is not a realistic option. There is no turning back. OCLC has taken its place as a powerful and successful new player on the library scene. The challenge it faces in the coming years is to sustain its economic success and service capabilities in a rapidly changing business and technical environment while also preserving the loyalty and goodwill of its users and the rest of the library community.

OCLC cannot go back to its origins, but neither can it afford to forget them. It is an enterprise that was built by and is still totally dependent upon libraries. What is good for OCLC is usually good for libraries, but what is good for libraries will always be good for OCLC. If OCLC charts a course which ignores the interests of libraries, librarians will cease to have a special interest in supporting it as one of their own and will deal with it like any other vendor. In the long run, OCLC has far more to fear from its own success and hubris than it does from its critics and competitors in the marketplace.

It is the nature of things that the large and successful organizations which provide our vital services come in for a certain amount of criticism. IBM, Ma Bell, and LC are among the organizations we love to criticize. It is an indication of its importance that OCLC has been added to the list, and like the others, it must learn to ignore the carpers and listen to its friendly critics.

LIBRARY AUTOMATION AND NETWORKING: PERSPECTIVES ON THREE DECADES

Reprinted from *Library Journal,* 1 April 1983, 629–35. A version of this paper was presented at the 1982 Essen Symposium: Increasing Productivity through Library Automation, Essen, Germany. An abridged version in Swedish was published in *Bibliotekariesamfundet Meddelar* 2(1984). A Spanish translation was published in *Notas Bibliotecologicas* by the Biblioteca Benjamin Franklin in Mexico City, 1985.

There is a powerful and well-documented trend in our contemporary world toward decentralization, deinstitutionalization, and localism. Futurist Alvin Toffler describes this trend at length in his book *The Third Wave.*[1] Trends analyst John Naisbitt ranks decentralization and multiple options among the top ten "megatrends" that are moving across the United States. He says:

"The single most dominant trend we find in our research is the rapid and extensive process of decentralization. All the major social, economical, and political forces of the period from 1900 to 1960 supported centralization of power, authority, and responsibility within our private and public-sector organizations. The Great Depression, the World Wars, and the dynamics of a growing industrial economy made hierarchical, top-down structures appropriate and effective for those items. But now the society is creating decentralized alternatives to almost every centralized form of organization.[2]

Advances in computer and information technology increase the speed and force of the trend toward decentralization, and that trend, in turn, has a powerful impact on the way we use those technologies in the larger society and in the field of library automation and networks.

Henriette Avram wrote recently: "Perhaps the most significant point about this new technology is that after pulling the community toward large centralized facilities for 10–15 years—in order to use large machines with accompanying economies of scale—it is now pushing toward decentralization."[3]

William J. Kurmey puts it more specifically; he says: "the major impact of the variety of microcomputers now available is to bring the capabilities of total online processing well within the budget range of all libraries, not just large and medium-sized libraries. There is no longer the necessity to join consortia or contract with service bureaus in order to obtain computing services."[4]

Three Decades of Automation

We are well into our third decade of library automation. The first decade, the 1960's, was dominated by primitive local systems. The second decade, the 1970's, was dominated by large multitype and multipurpose library networks. The current and third decade, the 1980's, will be dominated by a return to local systems. But this time they will be sophisticated multifunction turnkey systems on mini- and microcomputers; and they will have lines to a variety of library and commercial networks on large mainframes.

The dominant trends in library automation during these three decades have been shaped and driven by the cost and capabilities of the computer and communications technologies that were available at the time. Local systems dominated the 1960's because that is all that the then available technology could support. Those early batch processing systems were of limited use, and only large libraries could afford the high costs of experimenting with them. There was no easy way to share systems, and library networks were still the dreams of visionaries.

Three major developments occurred in the early 1970's which had profound and far-reaching effects on the course of library automation and library management: 1) the emergence of the first cheap and powerful minicomputers; 2) the coming of sophisticated online systems; and 3) the development of powerful telecommunications capabilities. Commercial vendors, like CL Systems, Inc., started developing turnkey library systems on minicomputers, first for individual libraries, and then for small clusters of affiliated libraries. They laid the groundwork for this decade's dominant trend in automation—turnkey systems. But the principal achievement of the 1970's was the acceptance and wide use of the MARC format and MARC distribution service followed by the development of OCLC and other library computer utilities and service networks, all of which were based largely on shared cataloging systems.

The coming of powerful but expensive online systems and telecommunications capabilities provided both the technical means and the economic incentives for librarians to band together to develop large cooperative networks. Online systems were too expensive and too complex for individual libraries to develop and operate. Librarians had to build cooperative network organizations and systems in order to distribute the high costs of computer technology among a large number of users. Pioneer utilities like OCLC, Inc., RLG/RLIN, and WLN brought online technology to several thousand libraries, large and small, during the 1970's thereby helping to create and prepare the market for the pervasive use of new technology that is now taking place.

Since the beginning of library automation in the early 1960's, there have been two parallel and sometimes conflicting lines of development, one focused on local systems and the other on network systems. In the 1980's, these parallel lines are coming together in a synergistic way to produce this decade's dominant trend in automation. That trend is toward the rapid proliferation of a variety of powerful and versatile mini- and microcomputer systems in individual libraries and clusters of related or affiliated libraries.

The three major utilities (OCLC, RLG, and WLN) and the more than 20 regional service networks that librarians created in the 1970's primarily to broker OCLC services are now firmly established. A few service networks have gone out of business and a few others may disappear in the next several years as times get tougher for libraries, but the bibliographic utilities are maturing and stabilizing and coming to terms with current economic realities. Increasing financial pressures are moving them from competition to collaboration.

The intense interest that librarians had in building and joining utilities and library networks in the 1970's is subsiding because they exist, and most large and medium-size libraries belong to one. The networks have become essential and accepted organizations in the library world. The interest, energy, and resources that went into network building in the 1970's are now going into buying, and installing mini- and microcomputer-based local systems with particular emphasis on the local online public access catalog and retrospective conversion. These local systems may eventually acquire the capability to link to each other and to the utilities for shared cataloging and ILL purposes.

In the 1980's, large numbers of libraries and many clusters of related libraries will be able to afford to purchase and operate their own computer systems. Libraries no longer need to band together in large cooperative networks in order to share the costs of expensive central computers located in distant places as they did in the 1970's with OCLC, WLN, RLG, and others. There is still a need for large central network systems and databases for shared cataloging and for ILL locations and communications to facilitate sharing bibliographic resources.

The 1970's concept of a centralized national library network consisting of OCLC and a few other major utilities is gone. The 1980's concept will be a more decentralized and pluralistic network consisting of the computer systems of some key libraries and a variety of local, regional, national, and special-purpose networks loosely linked and coordinated in a variety of ways.

The 1960's—The "Total" System

The two parallel lines of development of library automation, local systems and network systems, both had their origins in the early 1960's. The goal of the pioneering library automators of the time was to eventually develop the "total integrated library system" which would include all library functions such as acquisitions, cataloging, serials control, and circulation. Among the advocates of the local systems approach, some advocated developing the total system as a single package, but the more practical ones set out to design and implement the various modules one at a time and to eventually link them all into a total system. In any case, the accepted view was that each large library was going to have its own systems development staff and operate its own systems on its own computer which would be located preferably in the library.

A number of large libraries led the way in this development, including Harvard, NYPL, Toronto, Northwestern, Chicago, and Stanford, among others. When experience showed that it would cost more to develop, operate, and maintain these systems than a single institution could afford, the major thrust of library automators shifted in the early 1970's. It shifted from developing self-sufficient local systems to developing multifunction systems that could be shared by a group or a consortium of libraries in a network environment. The Stanford effort became BALLOTS in a network mode, and the Toronto effort became UTLAS. Chicago and Northwestern persevered in their efforts to develop a total integrated system that would be cost effective for a single library.

Although the main thrust of automation in the 1960's was in developing local systems, parallel efforts to build networks originated in this decade. As early as 1963, Kilgour was proposing an online shared cataloging system for the Yale, Harvard, and Columbia medical libraries as the first stage in a larger effort to automate all the functions of those libraries in an online network mode. In other words, Kilgour's goal, like that of the other pioneers, was to create a total system, but he wanted to do it for a group of libraries in an online network rather than for a single library. However, the technology available in the 1960's would not yet support online networks. Batch processing was the standard mode; there were few operational online systems; computer memory and data storage were extremely expensive; and communicating data over telephone lines was still in its early stages. Moreover, there was no MARC format or distribution service.

Kilgour took his ideas to OCLC in 1967 and eventually succeeded in implementing most of the components of a total system. However, there is a growing consensus among librarians that circulation, acquisitions, serials control, and the public access catalog will be better and more economically provided on local systems rather than by the large networks. I believe the idea of providing total library systems on a large network is no longer credible, such development appears to me to have reached its peak and is now on the decline. RLG has already abandoned that goal, and OCLC soon will. OCLC is developing a stand-alone Local Library System (LLS) to distribute to its members in 1984, in addition to the online components it now offers.

What about the local approach to building a total integrated library system? How has that fared? It has fared much better than the network approach and development continues at an accelerating pace. However, the remarkable thing is that two decades have passed since that goal was articulated and there is, to my knowledge and to the knowledge of Matthews,[5] Boss,[6] and other observers, no total integrated system yet available that a library can purchase and install. In the 1970's, commercial vendors began to displace the large university libraries as the principal developers of computer-based library systems. They have had considerable success with circulation systems and public access catalogs based on circulation records, but none is yet able to deliver a complete library system covering all functions.[7]

Most of the original conceptual and development work on online catalogs is still being done by individual libraries and library networks. The commercial vendors will pick up, perfect, and market these prototype systems as they did with circulation systems in the 1970's.

Thus, the principal goal of the library automators of the 1960's, the development of a total integrated library system, has yet to be achieved. The goal they set for themselves was simultaneously too ambitious and too limited: it was too ambitious for the technology that was available in the 1960's, but too limited for the technology that would be available in the 1980's. The 1960's concept of the total library system was limited to automating the library's internal housekeeping functions. It did not include or even foresee such sophisticated features as online catalogs with full authority control and Boolean searching that today's technology makes possible and which librarians are now demanding as a matter of course. The goal of a total system is a moving target; the definition changes and the requirements expand with each expansion of the technical capabilities available to us. We will never have a finished total integrated library system, because we will never be satisfied to freeze the systems when we know that further improvements will always be possible.

The 1970's—Centralized Networks

When it came online in 1971, the OCLC shared cataloging system marked the beginning of a new era in library automation and library cooperation—the era of large centralized multitype and multifunction library networks. The beginning of the Library of

Congress MARC tape distribution service in 1969 made shared cataloging in the network possible and necessary—because individual libraries could not afford to make use of MARC tapes. OCLC gradually displaced LC's Card Division as the main source for current cataloging copy and cards and also took over many of the functions of LC's National Union Catalog.

The example of OCLC's initial success with an online network system inspired the rapid creation of a score of regional cooperative networks which had as their initial goal the replication of OCLC's computer system or the creation of their own system, but most of them ultimately became regional brokers of OCLC services. Librarians created and joined computer-based utilities and service networks in the 1970's because they saw them as the only technically and economically feasible way to bring the power of computer technology to their libraries. Joining a network was an inexpensive and risk-free way of using technology to cope with the rapidly increasing rates of library costs and even the smaller libraries could benefit. With the instant success of the OCLC interlibrary loan system in 1978, more libraries rushed to join OCLC and other consortia in order to facilitate interlibrary lending (ILL) and other kinds of resource sharing. Declining book budgets and rising prices gave libraries additional incentives to join networks.

Those service networks that are brokering OCLC services have a clear mission and a chance to grow and prosper, but their future depends largely on OCLC's future. A few of those that have no computer capability would like to create one to serve their members, but competition for OCLC, RLG, WLN, and commercial vendors will make successful initiatives in this arena exceedingly difficult. The time for bringing up new centralized main-frame computer systems for large national or regional networks is past. The need for them is being met and the market is saturated. The current and future thrust of development is clearly in decentralized mini- and microcomputer systems and networks. OCLC, RLG, and UTLAS in Canada are all moving to decentralize or distribute many of their functions to the local level.

Cooperation's Golden Age

The turn in the 1970's to large cooperative networks and shared computers and systems was born of economic expediency plus a vision of effective cooperation and resource sharing based on the rapidly developing computer and communications technologies. The 1970's appears in retrospect to be the golden age of library cooperation and cooperative networks. But the drive toward cooperation, so strong in the 1970's, is being tempered by the hard economic realities of the 1980's and the easy availability of local computing power.

Maurice Line, the Director General of the British Library Lending Division (BLLD) and an articulate critic of library cooperation, says that librarians have an irresistible need to cooperate and calls it a psychological need akin to the need that humans and animals have to huddle together for warmth. He says that librarians should recognize the psychological basis of that need "if only to make allowance for it in preferring reason to emotion."[8] Margaret Beckman, Tom Ballard, and Samuel Rothstein are among the growing number of librarians who are questioning the effectiveness of shared computer networks and multitype library resource sharing schemes.[9],[10],[11]

Line is right; librarians have always had an urge to cooperate and to share their cataloging burdens as well as their bibliographic resources with other libraries. The record is replete with initiatives for local, regional, and national cooperative networks and ventures of all kinds. Despite all the rhetoric in favor of library cooperation, however, few of those initiatives yielded significant benefits before the 1970's—that is, before the availability of the powerful online computer and communications capabilities that have enabled some of them to succeed.

OCLC was a state-sponsored cooperative in its early years, but in order to sustain and build upon its initial success, it had to divest itself of its cooperative character and become a not-for-profit corporation managed on sound business principles, which it did in 1978. One of the hard lessons we are learning from our experiences in the 1970's is that cooperation is a difficult, time-consuming, and expensive way to do something, and results are frequently disappointing.

Cooperatives sometimes work well enough and long enough to identify and confirm the need for a particular service or function and show the way to meeting the need. But once the need and the market for the service are established, a more reliable and businesslike organization is usually needed to provide it—as when OCLC became OCLC, Inc. Sometimes the service or function is given to or taken over by a commercial vendor or a government agency. There are many examples of successful cooperative initiatives, but it seems that cooperative organizations have a tendency to falter after a few years—the time that it takes for the spirit of cooperation to be tempered by the cold reality of economics. Self-interest usually replaces altruism and is always a firmer base upon which to build a viable organization or service. Cooperatives, like businesses, must serve their members' interest effectively in order to prosper.

Much of the state and multitype library cooperation that flourished in the 1970's was funded by federal LSCA grants and state appropriations, and that money is running out now. Those consortia and networks that are funded from government grants will be forced to rely entirely on their membership to support their programs and services. That will, in turn, force the members to take a new and more critical look at the costs and benefits of cooperation. When this happens we can expect to see a number of cooperative programs and services disappear or become moribund. For example, the Illinois Regional Library Council was phased out in 1981 when its LSCA funding ran out. The Pacific Northwest Bibliographic Center ceased operations in 1982. Passage of Proposition 13 in California and similar measures in other states are causing painful reappraisals of library cooperative ventures in those states.

Library utilities and service networks were created and thrived in the relatively affluent economic climate of the 1960's and 1970's, but as the economic climate for libraries worsens in the 1980's, the financial outlook of the organizations that serve and depend on them will also worsen. If the utilities and networks falter seriously in their ability to deliver services at favorable prices, members will be forced to seek other alternatives. This could lead to severe financial problems for the networks. However, I am optimistic about the ability of the three major utilities to weather the hard times that are ahead and to adapt themselves to the rapidly changing economic and technical environment of the 1980's and beyond.

We tend to discuss the utilities as though they are alike and share a common future, but this is not the case. Each one is very different from the others and will have a different future. RLG and WLN have more in common with each other than with OCLC in that they are consortia that are owned or controlled by the members and use their computer network to support their various cooperative programs. OCLC, in contrast, is a vendor of services to libraries. An OCLC spokesman said recently that its future business plan was to broaden its customer base beyond libraries and sell a variety of new information services directly to users. This is good business for OCLC, but it could have serious implications for the future of the regional networks that broker OCLC services.

The increasing number of news stories in the library press in the last year reporting on the financial, technical, and management problems of OCLC, RLG, UTLAS, SOLINET, NELINET, PRLC, and a number of other networks is evidence of a healthy and necessary retrenchment and reassessment of the goals and financial bases of these organizations. They are being forced by economic stresses to face reality and make a better match between their goals and commitments and their financial resources. Those that survive will be stronger and more secure. RLG, for example, has emerged strengthened from the technical and managerial problems it experienced in the first part of 1982. It draws its strength from the fact that it supports important programs and is a partnership of the parent universities and not just the libraries. The difficulties being experienced by the utilities and service networks could also be seen as an inevitable reaction against some of the unrealistic expectations we had for library cooperation in the 1970's. These reports also signal, in my opinion, a tilt in favor of increased autonomy and local library responsibility that is more in tune with the economic and technical realities of the 1980's.

The 1980's—Multiple Options

The development and operation of local systems turned out to be too expensive in the 1960's. This provided strong incentives to libraries to form and join a variety of networks and utilities in the 1970's, but now the largest of those utilities (OCLC, Inc. and UTLAS) are in danger of becoming increasingly inflexible and unresponsive to the growing and changing needs of their multitype library users. Their size and governance structures could make it difficult for them to make timely business and technical decisions. The utilities tend to be undercapitalized and overgoverned. The fact that the computer systems have to be up and running all the time in a service mode makes it difficult to develop and test new systems and to abandon obsolete ones. They may have trouble keeping pace with the rapidly changing technology and with the growing competition from commercial vendors with new systems and services and the investment capital needed to develop and market them.

The networks that are sponsored by governments, as they tend to be outside the U.S., can be particularly inflexible and vulnerable to technological obsolescence. It takes so long for governments to act that by the time they decide to do something, it is time to do something else.

Computers are getting smaller, cheaper, and more powerful. Turnkey systems and other packaged software are becoming increasingly available on powerful and inexpensive mini- and microcomputers.[12] It may be possible within the next few years for a library, or a group of affiliated libraries that wants to share bibliographic resources, to buy a mini- or microcomputer-based turnkey system capable of handling most library operations. The long-heralded "total integrated system" may finally become a reality. With this trend toward less expensive local systems, the need that libraries had in the 1970's to join large multitype library networks to get the benefits of automation is diminishing. But the need libraries have to be in a network for sharing cataloging and bibliographic resources is increasing. The shared cataloging and ILL functions are and will continue to be the mainstays of the bibliographic utilities for several more years in the foreseeable future.

In the 1970's, a library had three ways of using computer technology. It could join a network like OCLC, WLN, or RLG; it could develop local systems; or it could buy systems and services from vendors. Many libraries did all three. The systems available from vendors were largely limited to circulation systems which were still incomplete and unreliable. The available network systems were also incomplete and unreliable and were being developed even as they were being used.

In the 1980's, more libraries will buy turnkey systems and the systems will be more comprehensive and more reliable. Some libraries will prefer to purchase and install integrated or multifunction systems, but we will also see an increasing number of vendors which will develop and market functional components for microcomputers. Examples of this "mix and match" approach are the acquisitions systems that are being marketed by Innovative

Interfaces, Inc. and Ringgold Management Systems, Inc. It may be possible—some say even preferable—in the 1980's for a library to put together multifunction library systems from the functional components of several different vendors with appropriate links or interfaces. Thus, as the various subsystem components become obsolete, they can be replaced with the latest and best components on the market.

Two large periodical subscription agencies, Faxon and Ebsco, have recently begun to offer libraries alternatives to both network and local subsystems for serials control. The systems permit libraries to maintain their own periodical and serial order, payment, and check-in files on the companies' computers.

Blackwell North America, Baker & Taylor, and Bowker have been offering a variety of computer-based services to their customers for some time. Other vendors are now or will be offering similar services in the future. It is too early to assess the potential of these initiatives, but indications are that some libraries will find them useful alternatives or supplements to the other systems and services that are now available. Another promising initiative by a commercial vendor is the Carrollton Press REMARC project. Carrollton Press is converting the 5.2 million records of the LC shelflist to machine readable form and is marketing a retrospective conversion capability to libraries.

In sum, commercial vendors have the investment capital, the technical know-how, and the managerial flexibility to take risks and explore new markets and services. They are providing some potentially useful alternatives to existing network services and local systems—and some threatening competition as well.

Network vs. Local Functions

The challenging task facing librarians in the years ahead is to determine which functions and services are best provided by local systems and by commercial vendors, and which are best provided by the utilities and networks. There are no firm answers yet, but it is interesting and useful to speculate.

Up to now the major thrust of library automation has been to computerize the library's circulation, technical processing, and bibliographic systems—first locally and then through the utilities. In the 1980's these essentially local functions will be returned or distributed to local libraries. This will permit the utilities to give more attention to developing and implementing the rapidly emerging new generation of electronic storage communications capabilities. Library automation will continue to be developed and implemented at the local library level, but the utilities will emphasize document delivery and the storage and delivery of textual and numeric data in electronic form.

As part of this shift from the old to the new, individual libraries will get deeply involved in implementing office automation systems including word processing, financial, personnel, statistical, and other similar functions. Word and data processing work stations in the library's principal office and public service desks will soon be commonplace as will be library participation in local area networks.

The utilities will continue to maintain large centralized data bases for shared cataloging and ILL locations as well as network communications, and some form of online retrospective conversion capability. In some cases, notably RLG, network members will look to the network to support shared collection development, preservation, and other shared resources programs. To what extent and for how long acquisitions is or will remain a network function is debatable. I would argue that acquisitions is a legitimate network function as long as the cataloging process is done on the network system, but both functions will probably be distributed to local library systems in the next several years. (In that case the central database would still be used as a source for shared cataloging data.)

One of the most critical issues facing librarians and networkers is whether to try to design and implement automated authority control systems for network databases. Some experts argue that the powerful search capabilities of the computer make authority control unnecessary and that those who want it are merely trying to perpetuate card catalogs in computer form.[13] Others, including Henriette Avram[14] and Michael Malinconico,[15] maintain that automated authority control is essential for a machine readable database and that it can be most efficiently provided at the network level. OCLC, Inc. has neither the interest nor the capability to implement an automatic linked authority control system in its existing ten million record database. RLG initially intended to provide automated authority control in the RLIN data base, but that database will soon exceed five million records. RLIN cannot afford to implement and maintain an automatic authority control system retroactively on such a large, previously unmanaged database, but it does plan to implement authority control for currently cataloged materials. Authority control over a library's retrospective catalog will be a local rather than a network function.

Librarians will look to the utilities for various functions and services for only so long as the utilities can provide them effectively and at a reasonable cost. Should advances in technology or other approaches make shared cataloging on the utilities uneconomical or uncompetitive, their financial viability could be undermined. It is conceivable that optical disk technology or other means will be found in the next several years to distribute economically the MARC database to local and regional sites. Or perhaps one of the commercial database firms such as DIALOG, ORBIT, or BRS will make available a MARC file directly to libraries with the option of copying records out in machine readable form for local uses. Such a service could come as a by-product of an effort by these firms to offer their library customers a comprehensive database which would include citations to books as well as journal articles.

In the 1980's, library administrators will move to regain much of the control over their own operations and decision-making that they gave up to the networks in the 1970's. Experience is teaching them that they cannot afford to be totally dependent on external and sometimes fragile technical systems over which they have little or no control. Library directors cannot give up responsibility for or authority over their key library functions to external agencies which cannot be fully sensitive and responsive to local political and financial concerns and pressures. The general euphoria in favor of cooperation and networking that characterized the 1970's is over. Libraries will continue to participate in networks, but they will want to see the benefits. The networks are going to have to compete successfully with local systems and commercial vendors in the 1980's or they will lose their members and their financial base.

As libraries install their own local online catalogs and convert their retrospective records to machine readable form, they will necessarily give priority to the development and maintenance of their own local systems and databases. Their commitment to the rigid and costly bibliographic standards that the networks impose may weaken.[16] As libraries embark on large scale and expensive retrospective conversion projects in the coming years, they may have to accept a significant percentage of brief entry MARC records for the sake of getting the job done at a price they can afford. The recent Bath University study of full and short entry catalogs points up the advantages of short entries and will doubtless encourage more libraries to use them in their online public access catalogs.[17]

One of the great challenges to the library profession in the 1980's will be to forge a new and more balanced and productive relationship between the networks and their members. Networks were created by libraries to serve certain needs and services that are best provided collectively. They should not be given or allowed to take on functions and services that are better when they are done locally or by other means.

Local Autonomy in Open Networks

Librarians will feel the need to reassert the primacy of the individual library over the network in the 1980's. The decentralizing social, political, and technological trends that I cited at the beginning of this paper will encourage and facilitate that need.

Decentralized networks which preserve maximum local autonomy and put each participating library at the center will emerge to supplement, modify, or even supersede the familiar star networks. Some early examples can be cited. The West Virginia Library Commission recently announced the selection of the Virginia Tech Library System (VTLS) as the basis for a statewide network for automation and resource sharing.[18] Under this plan, identical VTLS systems would be installed in each of eight strategic library centers and their computers and databases would be linked via telecommunications lines. Such a network of local systems and databases requires no large duplicate central database and no expensive overhead organization to support it. Similarly, any cluster of libraries in a region which used the same vendor's system could get the vendor to build the appropriate computer interfaces and form an effective voluntary distributed network with minimal loss of autonomy and expense. Representatives of RLG libraries in the Northeast which already own or are interested in GEAC systems, met recently with GEAC's management to discuss the feasibility of forming a regional network of GEAC systems—with encouraging results. Such system-based networks have significant advantages and could become commonplace in the years ahead.

There is recent initiative in Canada to plan and implement a decentralized national library and information network which would provide easy and direct access from a single terminal to a wide variety of library and commercial information systems. Eventually it would also provide for the direct transfer of bibliographic records from one library computer system to another and would connect the online catalogs of provincial and regional libraries to form an online national union catalog. The National Library of Canada is working with the Computer Communications Group (CCG) of the TransCanada Telephone System which has developed a special DATAPAC communications system for linking computer systems. A pilot effort called the iNet Gageway Project was initiated in July 1982 to link the computer systems of six key Canadian libraries and a variety of government and commercial information handlers in an open network.[19]

This is a variation on the U.S. strategy which is seeking to link and coordinate the RLG, WLN, and Library of Congress systems through a variety of initiatives by the Council on Library Resources and the Library of Congress. (OCLC elected not to participate.) These efforts do not yet include establishing links to other information handlers, but such links are a logical future step. This Canadian approach to an open decentralized information network is generating considerable interest, but it is still too early to assess its potential. If it succeeds, it could serve as a model for open information networks in other countries.

We are rapidly moving beyond the 1970's concept of a hierarchical or centralized national library network based on OCLC and a few other networks with computer-to-computer links. When he was building OCLC in the early 1970's, Kilgour used to say that the National Library was the nation's libraries. The 1980's corollary to that statement is that the National Library Network is the totality of the computer systems and online catalogs of the nation's libraries and networks. They will be linked and coordinated in a variety of ways through the initiatives of the Council on Library Resources, the Library of Congress, the principal networks, and the communications companies. There will be no single hierarchical National Library Network in the U.S.; nor will there be a central government agency planning and directing the pluralistic, multifaceted and ever-changing mosaic of library and commercial systems and networks that will be the national library and information network in reality, if not in name. The rich multiplicity of decentralized systems and services that we see developing are very much in tune with the major trends that are shaping our information society.[20,21]

Notes

1. Toffler, Alvin. *The Third Wave*. N.Y., Morrow, 1980.

2. Love, John, "Search for Tomorrow," *TWA Ambassador*, November 1980, p. 43–48. The author is quoting Naisbitt in the Executive Summary to a 1980 *Trend Report*. Naisbitt's ideas are presented more fully in his recent book: *Megatrends: Ten New Directions Transforming our Lives*. N.Y., Warner, 1982.

3. Avram, Henriette D., "Directions in Library Networking." *JASIS,* November 1980, p. 441.

4. Kurmey, William J., "The Impact of Technology." In: The Future of the Union Catalogue. *Cataloging and Classification Quarterly,* Vol. 2, Nos 1/2, 1982, p. 46.

5. Matthews, Joseph R. "Online Public Access Catalogs: Assessing the Potential," *LJ,* June 1, 1982, p. 1067–71.

6. Boss, Richard and Judy McQueen. *Library Technology Reports*. ALA. March-April 1982.

7. Joseph R. Matthews, "The Automated Circulation Systems Marketplace: Active and Heating Up." *LJ,* February 1, 1982, p. 233–235.

8. Line, Maurice B., "Is Cooperation a Good Thing?" In: *IATUL. Library Cooperation: Trends, Possibilities & Conditions*. Goteborg, IATUL, 1980.

9. Beckman, Margaret, "Local Service: Expectations and Accomplishment," *Cataloging and Classification Quarterly,* Vol. 2, Nos. 1/2, 1982, p. 57–68.

10. Ballard, Tom, "Public Library Networking: Neat, Plausible, Wrong," *LJ,* April 1, 1982, p. 679–683.

11. Rothstein, Samuel, "The Extended Library and the Dedicated Library: a Sceptical Outsider Looks at Union Catalogues and Bibliographic Networks," *Cataloging and Classification Quarterly,* Vol. 2, Nos. 1/2, 1982, p. 103–120.

12. Swanson, Donald R., "Miracles, Microcomputers, and Librarians," *LJ,* June 1, 1982, p. 1055–66.

13. Beckman, Margaret, "Online Catalogs and Library Users," *LJ,* November 1, 1982, p. 2043–47.

14. Avram, Henriette D., "Authority Control and Its Place," 1982, 14p. and Appendix. Unpublished discussion paper.

15. Malinconico, S. Michael, "Bibliographic Data Base Organization and Authority File Control." In: *Authority Control: The Key to Tomorrow's Catalog; Proceedings of the 1979 Library and Information Technology Association Institutes.* Oryx, 1982, p. 1–18.

16. De Gennaro, Richard, "Libraries and Networks in Transition: Problems and Prospects for the 1980s," *LJ,* May 18, 1981, p. 1045–49 [reprinted in this volume].

17. *Full and Short Entry Catalogues: Library Needs and Uses.* Alan Seal, Philip Bryant, Carolyn Hall (BLRRD Report 5669). Bath University Library, 1982.

18. News item in *LJ,* December 1, 1982, p. 2207.

19. Durance, Cynthia J., Edwin J. Buchinski, and Doreen A. Guenter, "iNet and Canadian Libraries: New Telecommunications Facilities for Library and Information Services." *The Canadian Journal of Information Science,* Vol. 7, p. 1–10, 1982.

20. Martin, Susan K., *Library Networks 1981-82.* White Plains, KIP, Inc., 1981. This is a useful survey of networking and I have drawn on it extensively for this paper.

21. Robinson, Barbara M., "Cooperation and Competition Among Library Networks," *JASIS,* November 1980, p. 413–424. This is an excellent overview of the U.S. networking scene. The author stresses the need for coordination and cooperation among networks.

LIBRARIES AND NETWORKS IN TRANSITION: PROBLEMS AND PROSPECTS FOR THE 1980'S

Reprinted from *Library Journal,* 15 March 1981, 1045–49.
A version of this paper was given initially as the keynote address at the LAA/NZLA Conference, Christchurch, N.Z., 19 January 1981.

Library automation, now entering its third decade, has made enormous strides, but the promise of the 1960's—that it would permit us to replace our expensive and cumbersome manual bibliographic systems with more powerful, more versatile, and less expensive computer-based alternatives—is still largely unfulfilled. We have learned that computerizing our libraries is more difficult and will take longer than we thought, and that some functions will be carried out locally and others through networks.

We are also finding that, although computer-based systems are more powerful and more versatile than the manual systems they replace, they can also be more expensive to operate and maintain—at least during this transition period. They impose much higher standards of accuracy on cataloging and catalog maintenance as well as in circulation control and other areas of library operations. While these higher standards are an essential foundation for both networks and local systems, they carry a price—and many libraries are finding it hard to pay that price in the face of crushing budget pressures. Thus, libraries are caught in a dilemma: they must automate to move ahead, but they cannot automate without making substantial capital investments in new technology, higher standards, and expanded capabilities.

With the standardized Machine Readable Cataloging (MARC) formats and the MARC data base as the foundation, with the online networks and utilities providing the advanced systems capabilities, and with *AACR 2* and the pressures to close card catalogs as powerful incentives, libraries have begun in earnest the difficult transition from manual to fully automated bibliographic systems. That transition is proving to be far more complicated and costly than we anticipated. One of the principal reasons is that we have underestimated the difficulties and expense of maintaining our traditional manual systems while trying to implement and operate partially complete, and therefore marginally effective, computer-based systems. Library staffs need to develop and maintain not only the new computer systems and the skills required to operate them, but also their card catalogs and shelflists and all the skills and procedures required to maintain the old manual systems. This parallel operation of manual and automated systems is making our library operations more complex, more expensive, and even more inflexible during the transition period than they were in the manual environment.

Now we need to come to terms with some new realities. Substantial capital expenditures for retrospective conversion and for new electronic equipment and systems will be required to complete this transition to an automated environment. Computerized libraries in a network environment will be more effective because they will provide new and more useful services, but those services will supplement, rather than replace, existing services. Consequently, the automated network libraries of the future, to the extent they are successful, will actually cost more to operate than today's traditional autonomous libraries. But that cost will be considerably less than that which a single library would have to bear in order to sustain the usual exponential growth patterns of traditional research libraries.

Network Cataloging

Before the advent of computers each library had local rules and procedures for adopting Library of Congress (LC) cataloging and for doing original cataloging. Sometimes local original cataloging was done to LC standards, and sometimes corners were cut to improve productivity. Librarians cataloged to serve the needs of their own users; their manual systems easily tolerated local options, inconsistencies, and changing rules. There was little need for or pressure on a library to conform precisely with any national standards.

Computer-based network cataloging came along in the 1970's, with OCLC leading the way. Much of OCLC's instant success was due to the fact that it did not force standardization in cataloging or in catalog card formats on its users. OCLC's founder, Fred Kilgour, used to boast that the OCLC system could provide 3000 variations of card formats—but some hard-line conservatives faulted him for not providing subject headings in red.

As long as OCLC enjoyed a virtual monopoly as a shared cataloging system it could withstand pressures to improve and expand its services, but competition from the Research Library Group (RLG) in 1978 forced OCLC to begin developing more and better quality services for its users. OCLC's data base was its principal asset and the foundation upon which it had to build its new functions and services; however, a full-service utility cannot be built on a data base that has no standards, no quality control, and no authority control. OCLC is now making belated efforts to apply the standards that are in use or being built into the Washington Library Network (WLN), RLG's Research Library Information Network (RLIN) and the Southeastern Library Network's (SOLINET) version of the WLN software, but it may be too late to impose such standards and controls on users or to implement the necessary systems changes.

Cataloging in a sophisticated network environment requires a quality data base as well as high cataloging standards to achieve and maintain that quality. While the networks facilitate the use of LC, MARC, and other derived cataloging—and thus diminish the volume of original cataloging that participants need to do—they do not speed up the process of original cataloging. This is because catalogers become more careful of their work when it is displayed on a network and are subject to a kind of stage fright which has been called "fear of inputting." Every local cataloger now feels obliged, and with justification, to do LC-grade cataloging. No self-respecting professional cataloger wants to sign his or her initials on anything less than perfect copy, and thus each record tends to be treated like a signed original work of art—and costs nearly as much. This slows down the work, with the result that original cataloging in libraries is being done at the rate of three or four books a day per cataloger.

Many large research libraries, which must continue to do a substantial amount of original cataloging, are falling behind and are building large backlogs which are either not cataloged at all or are brieflisted on separate inprocess COM catalogs or in searchable online circulation systems. There is little hope that these libraries will ever go back and recatalog these "temporary" minimal records to full standards on the network data bases.

Ten years ago a task force tried unsuccessfully to design a brief version of the MARC record. The difficulty was that they could not agree on what elements to exclude, so they included everything, or thought they included everything. Even rare books and special collections librarians, initially cautious about participating in computer-based systems, are now eager to add their records, in customary detail, to the network data bases. They are calling for an enriched MARC format with additional access points and information. This could further increase the already exorbitant cost of cataloging rare books and special collections.

Someday I think we are going to discover a fundamental law of cataloging which will reveal that the effort required to catalog any particular book is inversely proportional to the amount of use it will receive. It seems, in other words, that the harder a book is to catalog, the less the likelihood there is that it will be found in the catalog and used.

The Future of Cataloging

Like other library directors, I am asked from time to time to speak to library school audiences on current realities and future trends in the "real world" of libraries. In the 1970's I can remember warning students against becoming catalogers. I used to tell them that catalogers were an endangered species and might become extinct in the 1980's with the effective use of online networks. I thought that with the National Program for Acquisitions and Cataloging (NPAC) the Library of Congress would carry an increasing percentage of the original cataloging load and make it easily available in a timely manner to the networks and vendors on the MARC distribution system. What cataloging LC did not do would be done expeditiously through the networks' increasingly effective online shared cataloging systems.

It has not happened that way. It turns out that small and medium-sized libraries have been well served by shared network cataloging, but local original cataloging in large libraries, like the state under communism, is not withering away. LC's cataloging output peaked a few years ago and is in decline now. Shared cataloging on the networks, after an initial burst of productivity, is slowing down as data bases grow and as standards are raised to perfection levels by conscientious catalogers in response to real or imagined network requirements. Meanwhile, the coming of *AACR 2* is slowing down today's work and forcing us to re-do some of yesterday's. Far from becoming extinct, original cataloging and the catalog maintenance functions in large libraries are now growth industries, and *AACR 2* promises to become cataloging's Full Employment Act. Never before has so much effort gone into cataloging and the maintenance of catalog records.

What we are seeing, however, is not the flowering of cataloging's Golden Age, but an unhealthy growth that must be brought under control. For our immediate needs we must develop more effective network cataloging systems with full authority control. Yet, this may prove to be too expensive, and we may need to devise new and more simplified computer-oriented approaches to cataloging and indexing in the future. We seem to be trapped into perpetuating the concepts of the card catalog in the online environment. We may soon find that the continued use of traditional cataloging rules and standards in that environment is an unneeded and unaffordable luxury.

Traditional cataloging may go the way of hand bookbinding. Hand binding was an art and a craft. The work was beautiful and durable, but the labor costs involved became prohibitive and we had to learn to accept less elegant, but more affordable, machine-made alternatives. With production at a few books a day per cataloger, traditional original cataloging, like hand binding, has also priced itself out of the market.

Most of our attention until recently has been focused on automating the library's cataloging and technical processing operations, but that is only a prelude to and a foundation for the more important task of automating the library's public service operations. The main impact of new technology in the future will be on reference service and access to online catalogs by the public.

Online systems are providing powerful new subject and word search capabilities which will increase access to collections and begin to make many of our traditional subject cataloging and classification conventions redundant or obsolete. It remains to be seen whether cataloging, which is already in some disarray, will be able to recover its former preeminence in the library profession or whether it will be further undermined by its inability to respond effectively to a rapidly changing economic and technical environment.

Problems of Synchronization

The problems of synchronizing and linking parallel manual and machine data bases are serious and growing. An increasing number of libraries are using computerized circulation systems with a brief-entry data base separate from the library's main catalog data base. This approach requires either double keying of records or the development and maintenance of complex and fragile interfaces between the two systems so that data from the catalog system can be transferred by computer to the circulation system. Several computer programs and "black boxes" are available which provide these linkages, but so far no one has devised an efficient way to assure that the two data bases remain in synchronization, i.e., that any changes in one data base are appropriately made in the other.

OCLC users have an additional synchronization problem, which is that of maintaining the currency and accuracy of the records they contributed to the OCLC data base. Archive tapes must be cumulated and "refreshed" periodically if the data they contain is to be used again. The synchronization problem also exists with the computerized serials lists that many libraries maintain.

Retrospective Conversion

The problems that our libraries and networks are facing during this critical transition period are not due to too much computerization, but to too little. The systems we are using are not yet sufficiently advanced to do the job required. We need to develop more powerful and more versatile automated systems so that we can reduce the costs and complexities of maintaining parallel manual and machine systems and the interfaces between our various computer-based systems.

The single most important thing libraries can do to improve management, hasten automation, and reduce the expense and difficulties of maintaining parallel manual and machine systems is to convert their retrospective catalogs to machine-readable form and consolidate all their bibliographic records into a single integrated system. Libraries cannot take full advantage of automation until they can implement integrated systems, and they cannot have integrated systems while a substantial portion of their records are on cards in traditional catalogs.

Ten years ago there was considerable interest in retrospective conversion, but studies by LC and others led to the conclusion that the costs were prohibitive. The conclusion was justified at that time, given the primitive state of input methods and the nonexistence of network cataloging systems with their large online data bases. With the growth of rich network data bases and powerful online conversion capabilities, retrospective conversion may be feasible in this decade for all but the largest and most complex library catalogs. Once conversion is completed, the way is open for a library to install an integrated computer system and replace its manual files and procedures.

Many public and academic libraries in the U.S. have already begun to convert their catalogs to machine-readable form by contracting with input specialists or by using the capabilities offered by the network systems. There is a growing awareness now of the importance of converting records in full MARC format and creating a complete and accurate data base which can serve as the foundation for all future systems. Many librarians have learned through expensive and painful experience that it does not pay to settle for anything less than full MARC records in retrospective conversion projects. They have also learned that it is prohibitively expensive to upgrade to full MARC short records that were created to support a circulation system. Whether libraries will be able to find the additional funds needed to create and maintain such high quality data bases and systems is still an open question.

Carrollton Press has recently embarked on an ambitious project to convert the 5.2 million records in the LC shelflist to machine-readable form during the next several years. Carrollton will use this data base to create a title index to the LC shelflist as well as to facilitate retrospective conversion. Unfortunately, some of the title fields in the records are truncated, and some other fields are incomplete or omitted. This makes it yet another substandard MARC file and diminishes its usefulness to some extent. In addition, instead of being converted in shelflist sequence, the file has been sorted into title sequence and is being converted from A to Z. This makes it difficult to use any part of the file before the A to Z conversion is completed several years hence. In spite of these limitations, the Carrollton Press REMARC file, as it is called, is an important new resource which will greatly facilitate retrospective conversion in the years ahead.

Effectiveness Will Cost More

I have said that libraries are in the midst of a critical transition from manual to electronic systems and from local autonomy to partial dependency on networks. Our present computer systems are not yet capable of handling our complex bibliographic apparatus. Moreover, during this transition libraries cannot close down and retool; they must continue to provide all customary services to their users and do business as usual on their manual systems while they install and learn to use complex computer systems. Both the old systems and the new must be supported during a period of stable or declining budgets.

Librarians have an urgent need to convince their local budget authorities, foundation officers, and corporate donors to provide the capital investment needed to complete the transition from manual to fully automated systems. We cannot bootstrap our libraries into the electronic age. For the last ten years librarians have been trying to build resource sharing consortia and the computer network systems to underpin them almost entirely from income derived from shared cataloging and other network service charges. They have made a good beginning, but income from these sources will not be enough to complete the job. Additional investment capital will be required if libraries are to make effective use of high technology.

The increased benefits and capabilities that computer-based systems offer will not come without increased costs. When we first started to use computers in libraries 15 years ago, we thought we would save money, but we soon learned that there would be no net savings from automation. Then we thought that automation would at least "reduce the rate of rise of library costs," but even this is proving to be illusory as we demand and receive an ever-increasing variety of new and expensive services from our networks and local systems. The sophisticated products of automated systems will cost more than the limited outputs of our old manual systems. We will pay a price for online catalogs of uniformly high standards in our libraries and in our networks. We will pay for the ability to do complex online subject searches of our own or other libraries' catalogs. We will pay dearly to input, maintain, and search the enriched and detailed records required by our rare books and special collections librarians and the demanding scholars they serve.

We are no longer merely automating our traditional library operations: we are multiplying our capabilities and raising the level of expectations of library staff and users alike. As library services become more efficient and more useful, demand for them will increase, and while the unit cost of providing any given service will decline, the total cost of satisfying the increased demand will go up. For example, online search services, such as ORBIT and DIALOG, have increased the capabilities of reference librarians along with the demand for their services. Thus, this new computer-based service is causing an increase in the cost of providing reference service rather than a decrease. Another example is the new online interlibrary loan communications systems provided by OCLC and RLG. They are causing a rapid rise in the volume of interlibrary lending because they increase the speed and reliability of the service. The cost per transaction goes down, but the total cost of providing ILL service goes up. On the other hand, improved interlibrary loan service compensates for reduced acquisition levels and broadens the range of materials available.

In his recent book, *Managing in Turbulent Times* (Harper), Peter Drucker tells us, "Few companies that installed computers to reduce the employment of clerks have realized their expectations; most computer users have found that they now need more, and more expensive, clerks, even though they call them 'operators' or 'programmers' " (p. 25). He goes on to note that the savings of labor in unskilled or semi-skilled work by the introduction of machinery in hospitals was more than offset by increases in skilled labor. "The same thing has happened in the university. And the fact that these institutions, i.e., hospitals and universities which 50 years ago were labor-intensive but not capital-intensive, explains in large measure why the costs of health care and the costs of higher education have gone up disproportionately fast. Yet neither hospital administrator nor university administrator realized this until recently. Both believed that capital investment would 'save labor,' that, in other words, they would 'trade off' 'labor' against 'capital.' It did not work" (p. 27).

It does not seem to be working in libraries and the networks that serve them either. Our new computer systems are increasing and improving the services of libraries, causing a trade off of one kind of position for another within libraries, and a transfer of jobs from libraries to the network organizations that serve them. I have seen no convincing evidence, however, that the use of computers in libraries has resulted in any significant long-term reduction in positions or costs.

Libraries: A "Best Buy"

Librarians should stop apologizing for the alleged "high cost" of libraries in general and our old manual procedures in particular. Libraries can only be expensive (or inexpensive) in relation to some accepted criteria—and there are none. I would confidently assert that libraries are among the best managed services on campus or in town. A university's research library is commonly acknowledged to be fundamental to the purposes of the institution. It is often characterized as "the heart of the university" on ceremonial occasions. Nowhere is it written that the library's budget cannot exceed the customary three or four percent of the total university budget. There are no accepted, objective standards by which the effectiveness or value of a library's collections or services can be measured. The level at which any given library is supported depends on local traditions, aspirations, and expectations.

Information is becoming an increasingly valuable and expensive resource. Our society will have to get accustomed to paying much higher prices for it in the future, as it has with energy in the last decade. Cheap information and cheap research libraries are going the way of cheap energy.

Among our most challenging tasks as librarians in the 1980's are to improve capabilities, raise expectations, and establish new and higher funding levels for information age libraries in a network environment. This will not be easy. The ultimate decisions about academic libraries are made by laymen—trustees, academic officers, and faculty committees—but they cannot be expected to take the initiative in planning for the future. They have neither the time nor the specialized knowledge required to give direction or leadership in library matters. Moreover, universities have little capacity to formulate and follow long-range plans. In fact, they have been characterized as "organized anarchies" where no one has the power or mandate to act. In this environment librarians must take the initiative and set the agenda and the stage for the changes that are needed. They must keep users and funding authorities informed of goals and plans in clear, jargon-free language in order to spark their interest, encourage their participation, and secure their financial support.

But we must be realistic. No amount of persuasion will convince library funding authorities to increase support for traditional libraries at rates sufficient to keep pace with rising costs and increasing demands. The money libraries would need to continue doing what they have been doing in the past simply will not be forthcoming. Libraries need to develop new goals and new strategies based on new technologies, or they will be severely weakened by starvation and retrenchment in the lean years ahead. They must reaffirm their role as vital information agencies or risk becoming mere symbols of culture and museums of the book.

We should heed the wise advice of Daniel Burnham who said, "Make no small plans, they have no magic to stir men's blood. Make big plans, aim high in hope and work." With big plans and dynamic leadership we may be able to persuade our funders to provide the additional capital we will need to make the transition from the autonomous manual libraries of the past to the electronic network libraries of the future. This is not just rhetoric. We are building a new kind of library consortium in the Research Libraries Group, Inc. which gives its members a vehicle for maintaining and expanding their capabilities even in the face of diminishing resources.

The Promise of RLG

The Research Libraries Group is a growing partnership of 25 research universities and independent research libraries. Its members are trying to achieve collectively, and through the use of new technology, what they can no longer afford or hope to achieve individually using traditional technology—namely, the continued provision of adequate research collections and services to their users. Constituted in its present form in 1978, RLG has survived the various financial and other problems that commonly beset new endeavors and is establishing itself on a sound managerial, financial, and technical footing. Its members are firmly committed to using the RLG organizational framework and its online computer and communications network, RLIN (Research Libraries Information Network), as the means for transforming their traditional autonomous libraries into an effective network of information age libraries. The lack of a strong organization and an online computer and communication capability is what has made previous consortia and resource sharing efforts largely ineffective. RLG seeks to meld the collections and staffs of its members into a single voluntary, coordinated library system in which their collective strengths and resources can be managed and mobilized to serve the needs of researchers. In time, the separate collections of the member libraries will be viewed by users as a single large distributed collection to which they will gain efficient access via online systems and the rapid delivery of requested items by electronic and other means as well as by personal visits.

The RLG concept and its vision of the future have captured the imagination and are winning the support of a growing number of librarians, academics, and foundation officers. RLG libraries are taking charge of their destiny: they have clear goals and programs and are working together to achieve them. Let no one, however, expect quick and easy results. Restructuring traditional autonomous research libraries into an effective consortium based on new technology is an exciting challenge, but it will also be a long and difficult process. RLG is only two years old. It should not be judged solely on the basis of present services and recent accomplishments—as extensive as they may be. It must also be judged on the quality of its ideas, visions, and plans for the future, and its potential for fulfilling them. I write as a committed participant and not as an unbiased observer, but I believe RLG is the most significant and promising development on the U.S. library scene today. A successful RLG could serve as a model and inspiration for similar initiatives in other countries.

COMPUTER NETWORK SYSTEMS: THE IMPACT OF TECHNOLOGY ON CO-OPERATIVE INTERLENDING IN THE U.S.A.

This paper was reprinted from *Interlending Review* 9, no. 2(1981). It is a revised version of a paper presented at the International Seminar on National Document Provision, Boston Spa, England, 22–24 September 1980.

In the late 1960s, a consensus emerged among librarians that no library, no matter how large or well-funded, could hope to achieve self-sufficiency in its collections, and that new and more effective strategies and mechanisms for sharing resources would have to be developed. Through resource-sharing, librarians hoped to control the growth of their collections and costs while satisfying a growing demand for access to an ever-expanding universe of publications. A heated and prolonged debate began over the relative merits of resource-sharing strategies and how the costs would be met.

Some librarians argued that the best and most cost-effective strategy would be to develop one or more government-subsidized libraries modelled on the British Library Lending Division (BLLD); others argued for a more decentralized approach based on improving access to existing collections through co-operative computer networks and improved interlibrary lending (ILL) mechanisms; and still others held that a combination of approaches would yield the best results. The debate goes on, but recent developments in the USA appear to have resolved the question in favour of the decentralized network approach and against the centralized resource library.

While librarians were debating and developing these centralized and decentralized strategies for sharing their resources during the 1970s, a number of commercial and not-for-profit information vendors were creating and satisfying a new and growing market for on-line computer information services and rapid document delivery outside the traditional library framework.[1]

Computer Networks

By far the most important characteristic of US libraries, along with the rich variety of consortia, co-operatives, computer networks, interlibrary lending and document delivery systems that they have spawned in the last decade or two, is that there is virtually no central planning, funding, controlling, or co-ordinating authority guiding their development and activities. Our libraries are highly decentralized with each one having its own special mission and getting its financial support from a different government or private source. No agency of the federal government—including the National Commission on Libraries and Information Science and the Library of Congress—plays a commanding leadership or funding role in the development of the nation's libraries or the new network organizations that have come into existence to serve them.

The Council on Library Resources with its Bibliographic Services Development Program and the Library of Congress's Network Development Office have recently begun to exercise some leadership in the co-ordination of networks, but it is not clear yet how effective that leadership can be.

The principal driving force on the US library scene is clearly the extraordinary degree of initiative, flexibility, and freedom of action enjoyed by the managers and governing boards of the several thousand separately funded and independent academic, special, and public libraries in the country. Thus, in a single decade and with no central direction or plan and almost no government funding, those libraries—with academic libraries in the lead—created three major computer utilities or networks and some twenty regional supporting network organizations, which broker computer services to some 2,500 libraries of all types in every part of the country. This is a remarkable achievement.

Except for the National Library of Medicine's biomedical network, US computerized library network systems are entirely the creation of the participating libraries and grew naturally from the need and desire they had to share library and computer resources. Their development was unplanned and pragmatic, but they are proving to be an exceptionally effective vehicle for transferring computer technology to traditional libraries.

The Washington Library Network (WLN), the smallest of the three networks, is a government agency with headquarters in the Washington State Library. It has a highly developed computer system and serves a limited number of libraries in Washington and neighbouring states. The two large utilities, OCLC Inc. and the Research Libraries Group Inc. (RLG) are something relatively new under the library sun. They are tax-exempt, not-for-profit corporations. RLG is owned and governed by its member institutions; OCLC is owned and governed by an independent board which is advised by a Users' Council. Some of their initial start-up capital came from foundation grants and government subsidies, but OCLC is now self-supporting and RLG soon will be. Their operating funds come largely from the sale of services to participating libraries.

OCLC

Founded in 1967 as the Ohio College Library Center, OCLC started as a consortium of academic libraries with an organizational structure and goals not unlike those of RLG. However, as OCLC grew and prospered it changed its goals and structure and took on the characteristics of a commercial vendor operating in an international market-place. OCLC is managed like a business and this is both its greatest strength and limitation. It can borrow money, issue bonds, acquire property, and accumulate capital. It can offer new products and services and make profits that can be ploughed back into the business to fund new developments. This flexible and versatile organizational form is admirably suited to serve the changing needs of libraries in our rapidly evolving technical, economic, and political environment. OCLC is for all practical purposes a commercial enterprise with its own goals and agenda although it is still perceived by most librarians as a library consortium.

OCLC was just another struggling state-wide library consortium until it produced the first successful on-line network system in 1971. When it demonstrated its ability to serve the needs of the members of other consortia, they became regional brokers of OCLC services. There are now twenty such networks throughout the country.

As a by-product of its shared cataloguing system, OCLC is building a comprehensive bibliographic data base, which serves as an on-line union catalogue. It contains over six million bibliographic records with over sixty-five million location symbols and grows at the rate of about 25,000 records a week. Some 2,200 libraries with over 3,000 terminals are users of the system.

As OCLC's data base grew in size, its use as a union catalogue increased; this use was greatly encouraged and facilitated by the implementation of an Interlibrary Loan Subsystem in 1979.[2] This subsystem is designed to speed requests and responses, to facilitate the verification of bibliographic information in interlibrary loan requests, and to maintain records of interlending transactions. It is not a document delivery system. The time and effort involved in fetching the requested books and journals from the shelves and sending them to the requesting library is still a serious bottleneck in the interlending process.

Use of the interlibrary loan subsystem increased rapidly during the first years of its existence, but the number of requests appears to be levelling off at the rate of about 3,500 a day. Even before the implementation of the ILL subsystem, the use of OCLC's on-line union catalogue had begun to increase the volume of interlending and spread the load over a large number of libraries, thus relieving the traditional large net lenders of some of their previous burden.[3] Now the use of the ILL subsystem is further increasing the volume and changing the traditional patterns of interlending. Many small libraries are receiving interlibrary loan requests for the first time and some are becoming net lenders. This gives them some initial satisfaction, but they soon find, like the large libraries, that being a net lender is a burden. Five large public libraries in Ohio recently instituted a $5 charge for each item loaned to out-of-state libraries. This fee, unprecedented for public libraries, was intended to limit the rapid increase in the number of out-of-state requests received since implementation of the new OCLC ILL subsystem.

The working of OCLC's ILL subsystem is a good illustration of "Butler's Law," which states that: "Libraries cannot tolerate marked increases in the 'success level' of their operation."[4] This is true of interlending services. Interlibrary loan, whether manual or computer-assisted, is an expensive and difficult service to provide and its rewards to the lending library are limited. Libraries, like retail stores, are basically designed and run so that local users can serve themselves. Providing the kind of mail-order service that interlending requires will always carry a relatively high unit cost per transaction because of the extra labour costs involved. Free ILL in a multitype library network environment like OCLC's will simply not be possible in the long run, and OCLC's ILL subsystem could possibly serve as the mechanism and clearinghouse for ILL payments.

RLG and WLN Experience

In its goals and structure, the Research Libraries Group Inc. resembles OCLC in its early days, when it was simply a consortium of academic libraries. It is a growing partnership of some twenty-four major research libraries and has four principal programs: cooperative collection development, shared resources, preservation, and the creation of a Research Libraries Information Network (RLIN). RLIN has a high quality data base of nearly three million records, a powerful search capability, shared cataloguing, and other services.

RLIN has an interlibrary message system which is used for interlending and a variety of other network communication needs. It is an interim system designed without the capability to link directly to the records in the bibliographic data base. It will be superseded by a complete system during the next few years.

By common agreement, RLG members waive ILL fees among themselves, but a record of transactions is kept to monitor traffic patterns and to allow the reimbursement of large net lenders in the future as volume rises and imbalances develop. Since actual experience with RLG's resource-sharing capabilities is limited, it is too early to assess the impact of RLIN on interlending activities. However, it appears that an increasing percentage of the members' ILL needs are being met within the network.

The Washington Library Network (WLN) serves some twenty-five academic and public libraries, largely in the states of Washington and Alaska. Founded in 1977, it has a highly developed computer system, which has been purchased by the Australian National Library and more recently by SOLINET

(Southeastern Library Network) in the USA. SOLINET intends to convert and improve the WLN software package, which will be used as the foundation for new network services to replace many of those provided by OCLC to SOLINET members. Like RLIN, WLN has insufficient experience with computer-assisted ILL activity to warrant an attempt to assess the impact of technology on it.

These versatile new network organizations are developing a *de facto* national network and have taken the government and other central planners by surprise and left them behind. There is one government agency that is playing an effective role in networking in a special field and that is the National Library of Medicine. NLM's federally subsidized and centrally administered biomedical network is atypical of US networks because medicine enjoys high priority funding and is not subject to the same constraints as other fields.

Centralized Resource Libraries

Co-operative computer networking was the dominant force in US efforts to build resource-sharing and document delivery systems during the last decade. However, it was not the only one. From the early 1970s there was a strong movement, also led by academic librarians, either to transform the private membership-supported Center for Research Libraries (CRL) in Chicago into a full-scale federally-funded centralized resource-sharing facility modelled on the highly successful British Library Lending Division or to create an entirely new one. The initiative to transform the CRL was quickly superseded by a larger effort to create a National Periodical Center (NPC) as the first step in a more comprehensive government-sponsored centralized resource-sharing system.

The debate on the NPC raged hot and heavy for several years among librarians, publishers, and information industry people. The librarians were weak and divided in their support for the NPC while the publishers and the information industry stood united and firm in their opposition. The opposition prevailed, and it now appears that the proposal for an NPC as the major component of a large National Periodical System has been effectively shelved by the US Congress. It is fashionable to say now that the

NPC was a good idea, but one whose time had come and gone by the mid-1970s. Many have come to believe that the concept was made obsolete by improvements in computer networking and interlibrary loan systems, and by other new technological advances and new market forces. It should be noted, however, that most of the librarians who advocated the NPC were also strong advocates of and participants in computer networks. They held that the two systems would complement rather than duplicate each other, and both were needed.

Stymied in their ten-year effort to gain government support for a BLLD-like central facility, many of the leading academic librarians who backed the NPC are turning their attention back again to the membership-supported Center for Research Libraries. As a tax-exempt, not-for-profit corporation like OCLC and RLG, CRL has the potential for carving out a new and more dynamic role for itself in the coming years with new leadership, additional space, and new approaches. It is formulating plans to transform its Journal Access Service by pragmatic and gradual stages into a full-scale periodical service for its members. CRL could rely on the collections of the British Library and other libraries for lesser-used titles and concentrate on providing prompt and effective service from a core collection of in-demand titles. In additional to its present computer link to the BL Lending Division, it could also be linked to the major US and Canadian utilities and networks. However, even if CRL succeeds in revitalizing itself and becoming a strong component in the growing US computer and resource-sharing network, it will only be one component and not the dominant force that the British Library is in the United Kingdom.

The central resource or pool approach to resource sharing as advocated by Herman Fussler[5] and others during the last ten years is, for better or for worse, something of a lost cause in the USA today. It is a victim of too much planning and too much public debate. The predominant emphasis in the 1980s will be on improving further the decentralized resource-sharing capabilities of existing libraries with the aid of the computer networks. The major thrusts will be towards developing comprehensive network data bases for subject searching and locations, efficient message switching for interlibrary loans, and the transmission of facsimile and digitized textual images.

The New Information Market-Place

This overview of the main trends in US interlending and document delivery would not be complete without a discussion of a third approach that is frequently underestimated or overlooked entirely by librarians. It is an approach that is rapidly increasing in scope, volume, and importance. I am referring to the delivery of documents and information services by a new breed of aggressive vendors such as University Microfilms International, the Institute for Scientific Information (ISI), the Systems Development Corporation (SDC), Lockheed, Bibliographic Retrieval Services (BRS), Information Access Corporation, the New York Times Information Bank, Meade Data's LEXIS, and others. By the end of the decade these commercial vendors, along with the more traditional non-library suppliers of information services and documents, i.e. Chemical Abstracts, Engineering Index, BIOSIS, Physics Abstracts, etc. may well become formidable competitors to traditional libraries and networks as suppliers of certain kinds of documents and information sources.

The major vendors of on-line bibliographic search services, SDC, Lockheed, and BRS, among others, have all begun to offer direct on-line ordering of documents that have been located through their bibliographic data bases and even of documents not found in their files. The search service vendors are middlemen; they transmit the order to the supplier of the documents and the supplier fills the request and bills the requester direct. The entire transaction from initial search to final delivery and payment can take place completely outside the library and the conventional interlibrary loan system. It is too early to tell if this is a profitable business.

A recent report by Arthur D. Little Inc. estimates that private sector back-copy delivery currently represents about 10% of interlending, and that it is growing at the rate of about 15% a year. That rate could accelerate significantly now that the prospect (or threat) of a government-subsidized National Periodical Center or System is diminishing.[6]

Commercial and other non-library suppliers of documents are skimming off the easiest and most profitable parts of the document delivery business and leaving the rest for conventional libraries to struggle with. Thus, we see the Institute for Scientific

Information through the Original Article Tear Sheet (OATS) Service, offering at reasonable prices rapid delivery of copies of the articles that it indexes. However, the number of journals covered and the length of the back files are extremely limited. Even so, we do not know if it is a profitable business. University Microfilms International, a Xerox company, offers microfilms or hard copies of runs of journals or single articles from its extensive and growing archive of journals and other publication in microform.

In the next few years, as the text of journals is computerized in forms that are economical to store, search, and transmit on demand, publishers or their agents will be able to satisfy orders from their electronic files. Thus, the role of the traditional library as the principal repository and supplier of non-current publications may diminish. However, computer networks like RLG and OCLC and central resource libraries like the British Library and CRL could become clearinghouses or middlemen for this electronic traffic.

While these trends threaten to put an early end to the traditional library's monopoly on supplying copies of recent articles, the library will remain for the foreseeable future the principal source of supply for the large body of older, low-use materials in paper form. Satisfying occasional loan or photocopy requests for older material from the small but important group of researchers who request them is a legitimate library service, but it is not likely to become a profitable or even self-supporting business activity.

Conclusions

What I conclude from this brief overview of resource-sharing trends in the USA is that our greatest success has come from allowing the entrepreneurial forces of the private sector, in both the library world and the market-place, to act in our own best interests unfettered by government planning and government control. The private sector entrepreneurs and innovators, with minimal government support and direction, gave us not only the electronic technology upon which our computerized network systems and services are based, but also the new organizational forms and the great variety of information and document delivery services that characterize the US library scene and the growing information market-place.

We succeeded in creating decentralized self-supporting computer networks for resource sharing, but failed to create a government-sponsored central resource-sharing facility modelled on the BLLD. These networks are making rapid progress in computerizing the location and message communication functions involved in ILL, but none has begun to use new technology to improve the actual delivery of documents once they have been located and requested. Our commercial entrepreneurs are creating a variety of new and imaginative information retrieval and document delivery services based on on-line computer technology while government-supported information and postal services struggle to survive.

I am not denying that government has played an important role in fostering the development of high technology and the use of it in library and information services. The first computers were developed under government contract for wartime use. The early use of computers for on-line information retrieval, for computerizing the indexing and abstracting services, and for library automation, were all funded by government contracts or grants. The government continues to encourage and fund research and development in a wide variety of fields. This is where it is most successful. It is less successful when it tries to exploit new technology or to provide direct services to users.

In concluding this overview, I would emphasize that I am not offering the US approach as a model for others, and I am not suggesting that what works best in the USA will work best in other countries and other cultures. I am merely trying to help the bewildered observer understand the principal forces that are shaping the rapidly changing and seemingly chaotic US library and information landscape.

Notes

1. I have addressed many of these issues from other points of view in recent papers: Resource sharing in a network environment, *Library Journal,* 1980, **105** (3), 353–355; Research libraries enter the information age, *Library Journal,* 1979, **104** (20), 2405–2410; From monopoly to competition: the changing network scene, *Library Journal,* 1979, **104** (11), 1215–1217 [all reprinted in this volume].

2. Jacob, Mary Ellen. A national interlibrary loan network: the

OCLC approach. *Bulletin of the American Society for Information Science,* 1979, **5** (5), 24–25.

3. Kilgour, Frederick G. Interlibrary loans on-line. *Library Journal,* 1979, **104** (4), 460–463.

4. Butler, Brett. *Beyond the library—US on-line trends.* Preprint, Third International On-line Information Meeting, London, December 1979. 11–12.

5. Fussler, Herman H. *Research libraries and technology.* Chicago: University of Chicago Press, 1973.

6. Arthur D. Little Inc. *A comparative evaluation of alternative systems for the provision of effective access to periodical literature: a report to the National Commission on Libraries and Information Science.* Washington DC, NCLIS, 1979. V–9.

RESOURCE SHARING IN A NETWORK ENVIRONMENT

Reprinted from *Library Journal,* 1 February 1980. 353–55.

Interlibrary loan started as an occasional privilege, but it is rapidly becoming a necessity and even a right. The tradition of "free" interlibrary loan (ILL) was based on the moral obligation that librarians felt to share their resources with other libraries. Free ILL was feasible as long as it was voluntary and as long as the volume of requests was limited—largely by the inefficiencies of the traditional manual location, request, and delivery systems. But the rationale for free interlibrary loan no longer holds in the new, high volume, and more demanding resource sharing environment that is being created by the successful computerization of the interlibrary loan location and communication functions through OCLC and other online networks and by the growing use of online bibliographic search services.

OCLC's computerized ILL subsystem is increasing the volume and changing the traditional patterns of ILL. For the first time, many small libraries are becoming net lenders, but after the initial glamour of that status wears off they will find that burden no less onerous than the large libraries. In addition, many libraries are finding that ILL requests from distant libraries with which they have no affinity are competing for the same recent in-demand books that their own users require.

Obligation to Pay

Yes, libraries have a moral and practical obligation to share their resources, but in our new electronic network environment borrowing libraries will have to assume an obligation to pay the costs involved. How they pay those costs—whether they absorb them, pass them on to the persons requesting the loans, or get new subsidies to cover them—is a serious local problem just as it always has been for lending libraries. Libraries with close network, political, or regional affiliations may choose to continue to give free reciprocal ILL services where it is mutually beneficial while taking full account of the costs. Where there are no close affiliations, OCLC's ILL subsystem could serve as the clearinghouse for ILL payments. Since OCLC already bills requestors for its own transaction fee, it could possibly expand that accounting capability to include collecting and disbursing ILL fees.

What I am saying, in other words, is that interlibrary loan is becoming too important to be continued as a free service and that it is time to put a realistic price on it and establish it on a more rational and businesslike basis. In our expanding network environment, ILL fees will be necessary and beneficial because they will compensate the lending libraries for the cost of providing the service, they will ration demand, and they will serve as a measure of value for the service.[1] In the coming decade, electronic transmission of text will begin to supplement and supplant traditional ILL and librarians will have to accept the concept of paying fees for this service if they want to continue to play a vital role in the emerging information environment.

In recent years, several large academic libraries, some private and some public, have begun to impose fees of from $5-10 for ILL transactions in order to help cover the costs of this expanding and expensive service. The reaction of some members of the library community to these fees was best summarized by John Berry in an editorial entitled "Interlibrary loan and the network" (*LJ*, April 15, 1978, p. 795). "Document delivery," Berry said, "is hampered by a host of obstacles, not the least of which is the fact that our nation's greatest libraries unilaterally set their own policies and prices for lending to other institutions." He concedes that academic libraries must give priority to serving members of the institution that foots the bill, but points to the "direct and indirect subsidies that society offers through government to help these autonomous libraries stay in business. None of them pays state, local, or federal taxes. From postage rates to copyright protection, the materials they provide are indirectly supported by government. Gifts of money and material are tax deductible." Berry concludes by calling on libraries to agree to accept standard interlibrary loan fees and policies in order to help attract federal funds to subsidize a national library network.

Berry is not the only librarian who is ready to compromise the autonomy and independence of the nation's great research libraries for federal support of resource sharing. For example, the draft legislative proposal by the Chief Officers of State Library Agencies (COSLA) begins with the premise that "effective functioning of American democracy requires access to library and information services for all citizens" and goes on to declare "the new act shall require all libraries receiving federal funds to agree to share their resources in statewide library networks. Wherever federal funds are used to support library activity or service, it is appropriate that the recipient library participate in the State's library network."[2] Thus, in the name of democracy and federal subsidies for statewide library networks, these library leaders seem ready to casually sacrifice the autonomy and independence—not only of our private libraries—but all our libraries, and subject them to government control.

Barbara Markuson, in a keynote address at a recent conference on networking, pointed out that the enormous progress that we have made in the last decade toward building the components of a nationwide resource sharing network based on new organizations and new technologies was accomplished almost completely without federal or even state government assistance.[3] It was done through the voluntary and collective efforts of autonomous libraries and private foundations. To give the federal government a controlling role in building our resource sharing network is both unnecessary and dangerous.

Subsidy Equals Control

I cannot accept the argument that, because private university libraries are tax exempt and enjoy other advantages from government policies, they therefore forfeit their right to continue to be private and set their own lending and access policies. Our system of government exempts religious and educational institutions from taxation and gives them other advantages and freedoms precisely because these institutions are considered to be important to the long-term health of our society and deserve to be encouraged, nourished, and protected. Our research libraries achieved their present status because of these special advantages. It would be foolish of us to negate the wisdom and beneficial efforts of these policies by bringing our private libraries and our great state university libraries under government control in the name of democracy and for some modest subsidies for ILL transactions. With a little subsidy can come a lot of control. It is worth noting that in fiscal 1979 the federal government will spend less than $10 million on college libraries and $6 million on research libraries. These sums together represent just 1.6 percent of the $1 billion total annual expenditures on academic libraries in the United States.

No one would deny that "our great libraries owe society something for its long-standing support and subsidy of them," to use Berry's words. They do have an obligation to make their resources available to society, and they have been fulfilling that obligation voluntarily and in appropriate ways. But it would be a serious mistake to force our great research libraries to function as statewide public libraries. That is not their mission. The special mission of our large research libraries is to serve the needs of scholars and other researchers and as collections of last resort for other libraries. Older books and journals in organized collections are extremely fragile and vulnerable and they cannot be replaced. We must begin to treat the contents of the stacks of our great research libraries as valuable parts of our national cultural heritage because that is what they have become. It has been reliably estimated that a vast majority of the books printed between 1850 and 1950 will be unusable by the end of this century as a result of the destructive effects of air pollution and the presence of acid and other harmful chemicals in their paper and binding.[4] When we add to this the destructive effects of careless use, repeated photocopying, and frequent shipment through the mails, we are facing a crisis of monumental proportions.

We should not ask or expect our beleaguered research libraries to serve the function or take the place of our once proud but now declining public library system. In our enthusiasm to build a nationwide network for sharing resources, we must be vigilant to avoid forcing and homogenizing our incredibly rich and diverse variety of libraries into a single monolithic system or network whether governed directly from Washington, D.C. or Columbus, Ohio, or indirectly through the state capitals. We must try to ensure that each library is only called upon to make its appropriate contribution to the resource sharing network. Each library should be permitted and encouraged to maintain its identity and fulfill its special mission to its primary users who are its reason for being and its source of support. The reason libraries are banding together to establish networks is to permit them to better serve their own users. If one library's users are served at the expense of another's, then the purpose of the network is subverted.

Tempered Idealism

Our idealism must be tempered by economic realities. It is foolish to imagine that we can all become bibliographically rich by pooling our bibliographic poverty, or that we can survive for long by living off and consuming the resources of other libraries. Resource sharing is no answer to galloping inflation, Proposition 13, or wholesale budget cutting. It is no substitute for continued regular and generous support for well-stocked local libraries which are dedicated to satisfying most of their users needs from their own inhouse collections. By itself, the network creates no new resources. It merely facilitates the sharing of existing resources. But we must husband those existing resources and increase them in the future. It would be a tragedy if those who fund our libraries were to misunderstand the purpose of resource sharing and use it as a rationale for further reducing library appropriations. Resource sharing will permit us to do more with less by pooling our resources, but only if we all keep the pool replenished.

Notes

1. For two scholarly treatments of the subject of library pricing policies by economists see: Casper, Cheryl A., "Pricing Policy for Library Services," *Journal of the American Society for Information Science,* September 1979, p. 304; King, Donald W., "Pricing Policies in Academic Libraries," in: "The Economics of Academic Libraries," ed. by Allen Kent, Jacob Cohen, and K. Leon Montgomery, *Library Trends,* Summer 1979, p. 47–62.

2. A COSLA Legislative Proposal, Adopted April 5, 1979, Washington, D.C., p. 2. This typescript document was summarized in *LJ,* June 15, 1979, p. 1302.

3. Conference on Networks for Networkers, held in Indianapolis, May 30–June 1, 1979. The proceedings will be published by Neal-Schuman.

4. Magarell, Jack, "Damage in the Stacks," *The Chronicle of Higher Education,* May 30, 1978, p. 9.

FROM MONOPOLY TO COMPETITION: THE CHANGING LIBRARY NETWORK SCENE

Reprinted from *Library Journal,* 1 June 1979, 1215–17.

A new era in American librarianship began in 1971 when OCLC went on-line with its shared cataloging system. Shared cataloging was to be the forerunner of a full range of subsystems designed to computerize all library functions including the local public catalog. Although the other subsystems have been delayed far beyond their promised delivery schedules, OCLC managed, almost miraculously, to build a $25 million a year business on its highly popular and successful shared cataloging and location service. That service is now used daily by over 1500 libraries and has given the OCLC bibliographic utility a well merited and commanding lead on the national network scene. Although there were other fledgling networks, OCLC had no effective competition during its first eight years of existence.

Stanford University's BALLOTS network had developed what many considered to be a more powerful and versatile technical system, but its somewhat higher prices and less developed marketing capability limited BALLOTS membership to less than 100 libraries.

The Washington Library Network (WLN), after several years of development began to emerge in 1978 as the first truly successful regional network. It has a sophisticated software package that is capable of supporting shared cataloging with authority control, acquisitions, and a number of other desirable features. Although successful in its region, it was no threat to OCLC.

As the unchallenged leader in networking, OCLC could afford to tolerate and even encourage its weak and struggling sister networks and participate as a senior partner in studies and plans to develop protocols for linking electronically the separate networks into a nationwide network system for the common good. This was networking's era of benevolent monopoly. It was brought to an end by two significant recent events.

Competition Begins

One of those events was the merger in 1978 of the Research Libraries Group (RLG) and the BALLOTS system into a single revitalized organization based at Stanford. The weakness of the old RLG was that it lacked the sophisticated computer and communications systems that were essential to carry out its resource sharing, shared collection development, and preservation programs. The weakness of the BALLOTS network was that it lacked a membership base among the research libraries that its powerful system was designed to serve. With the merger, RLG acquired the BALLOTS technical capability, and BALLOTS acquired RLG's resource sharing and other programs and its ability to attract research library members. The BALLOTS system became the foundation for the newly created Research Libraries Information Network (RLIN). When RLG and RLIN made a serious bid in January 1979 to enlist as members a large number of academic research libraries, a new era in library networking began—an era of intense competition.

The second notable event was the successful transfer and implementation by the National Library of Australia of the WLN software. This demonstrated the technical feasibility of using the WLN system to establish regional networks in this country.

Even more recently, RLG and WLN announced the signing of an agreement for broad-based cooperation including the sharing of systems and data bases.

Faced for the first time with serious rivals on the national network scene, OCLC's immediate and quite understandable response was to flex its muscles and mount a vigorous defense of its position of dominance. At its own considerable expense, it invited the directors of all the academic library members of the Association of Research Libraries to its headquarters in

Columbus for a day-long briefing on OCLC's future plans and programs.

OCLC Responds

In an effort to discourage research libraries from joining RLG, OCLC's director used that occasion to emphatically reaffirm OCLC's long-standing policy that only libraries which input all their cataloging would be permitted to use the OCLC system and access its data base. That policy precludes research libraries that join RLG from continuing to enter their holdings in the OCLC data base either by terminal or by tape transfer and could decrease significantly the accessibility of their resources to members of multitype library regional networks. It would also seem to inhibit OCLC from making an effective contribution to the efforts that are being sponsored by the Council on Library Resources and other library agencies to link the computers and data bases of the various networks.

There is some evidence that OCLC is turning away from a strategy of lukewarm cooperation with other networks to one of outright competition. This may seem unfortunate at first glance, but it may be inevitable and even desirable for OCLC and the other networks to submit to the test of the competition of the marketplace.

It is not clear whether this competition will be constructive or destructive. In the short run, it could prove to be extremely destructive to the networks as well as to the goal of a nationwide network comprised of cooperating bibliographic utilities and networks. But there is probably no way to avoid such competition in the next few years because OCLC and the other networks will be compelled by events to act like vendors and compete for members.

We are faced with a dilemma. Viewed realistically, OCLC cannot be faulted for wanting to retain as members the large academic research libraries that RLG is trying to enlist and which are vital to OCLC's continued expansion. Nor can RLG-RLIN be faulted for trying to create a cooperative organization and specialized network designed to address the problems facing large research libraries in the decades ahead. RLG cannot succeed without the technological capability that RLIN provides, and RLIN cannot succeed without a substantial number of libraries that are now members of OCLC.

A similar dilemma faces any regional network that tries to design its own on-line computer system or replicate the WLN system in its region. Can OCLC, Inc. afford to permit a SOLINET (Southeastern Library Network) or a NELINET (New England Library Network) to establish its own regional on-line system and draw off several hundred OCLC member libraries? Can it sustain such a large and sudden loss of revenue? Does SOLINET have a responsibility to continue its present relationship with OCLC to avoid putting it in financial jeopardy? How can regional cooperative networks like AMIGOS (Texas, Arkansas, Oklahoma, New Mexico, Arizona) and PALINET (Pennsylvania Area Library Network) keep from becoming merely subsidiaries of OCLC for marketing and training? How can research libraries join RLG and still continue to play a vital role in regional cooperative networks?

Is it desirable that there be a number of networks in the country, or would it be preferable to permit or even encourage OCLC, Inc. to turn its present commanding lead into a permanent monopoly? To permit one strong network like OCLC to dominate the field may seem expedient now because it avoids unpleasant confrontations, but how will it look to us five or ten years hence? Will OCLC more nearly resemble the telephone company or the U.S. Postal Service?

It is too early to answer these questions, but it is not too early to begin asking them. Library networking is confronted by a number of critical issues; they should be faced squarely and discussed openly.

Competition among the networks is a sign of growth and vitality, and it can be a healthy force for change. We have already begun to see some of its beneficial effects. The RLG membership drive has galvanized a somewhat complacent and imperious OCLC into making a thoroughgoing reappraisal of its service strategy and development plans and to begin paying serious attention to the needs and desires of its members, particularly those of the large research libraries.

Competition can also lead to cooperation. The recently concluded RLG-WLN agreement to undertake joint development and share data bases may have set the stage for effective distributed networking in the regions, and this move could stimulate

OCLC to make beneficial counter moves—either of a competitive or a cooperative nature.

A Loose Confederation

Networking is not a zero sum game where one network's gain is necessarily another's loss. It may appear so in the short term if we consider only the limited services and functions that are currently being offered, but the existing utilities have barely scratched the surface when it comes to delivering services to libraries. The total value of the potential and promised services greatly exceeds the value of those that are being delivered today.

I am convinced that there is a role and a market for a number of general, special, and regional networks. A single monolithic national network embracing all libraries and providing all types of services is neither a realistic expectation nor a desirable goal for this country with its traditions of diversity and free enterprise. It is far more likely that the "national network" will eventually emerge as a loose confederation of general and special purpose utilities and networks, some of which may eventually be linked together by electronic means. Libraries will belong to or purchase services from a number of these utilities and networks. The pattern is already set today when some libraries are using the SDC, Lockheed, and BRS systems for on-line bibliographic searching, OCLC for shared cataloging and ILL locations, and RLIN (BALLOTS) for subject searching and reference.

Library networking is still in its infancy, and not all the players have entered the game. Coordination is desirable, but it is too early to permit or encourage monopolies or to stifle diversity and growth through centralized planning and regulation. If we want to expand and improve the range of services and products available to libraries, the best thing we can do is to encourage variety, competition, and cooperation among the networks and among the commercial vendors of library and information services and products.

Problems of Success

The establishment and growth of library networks, bibliographic utilities, and service centers in the decade of the 1970's has been a remarkable success story, but with that success comes a problem. The problem now is to keep the growth of the network budgets and staffs within reasonable limits so that the administrative overhead costs do not exceed the value of the benefits that individual libraries may realize from network participation. Networks are like our libraries and other bureaucracies; they have a natural tendency to increase their staffs without commensurate increases in productivity. Once jobs are created they tend to become permanent, and as the network organizations grow and mature they will tend to become increasingly expensive, conservative, and self-protective. Survival may replace service as their primary goal. Our task in the next decade is to keep the bibliographic utilities and regional networks or service centers lean and flexible and responsive to the needs and desires of the libraries that created and support them. It will not be easy but healthy competition may help.

THE ROLE OF THE ACADEMIC LIBRARY IN NETWORKING

Reprinted from *Networks for Networkers,* edited by B. E. Markuson and B. Woolls (New York: Neal-Schuman, 1980), 304–8. Proceedings of the Conference on Networks for Networkers, Indianapolis, 1979.

The Contribution of Academic Libraries to Networks

Academic libraries were at the forefront in the development and implementation of early computer-based systems in libraries in the 1960s. Out of these crude systems grew the much more sophisticated and effective on-line systems of the 1970s which made the bibliographic utilities and networks possible. Academic libraries were the pioneers; they supplied the leadership and the entrepreneurial drive. Their staffs contributed enormous amounts of time and effort to the organization, planning, implementation, and governance of the networks. Out of their budgets came the funds needed to develop and operate the expensive on-line utility systems.

Our brief experience with these bibliographic utilities in recent years is teaching us that successful library cooperation and resource-sharing depend in large part on the effective use of on-line computer and communications technology. Before on-line systems came to the library world in 1971, there were numerous library consortia and cooperatives in every region of the country, but few had any significant record of accomplishment. Today, those that have their own on-line systems or those that broker the on-line systems have a sense of purpose and a record of accomplishment, and those that do not are usually vainly struggling to make their resource-sharing and other cooperative programs work.

OCLC, Inc. started out in the late 1960s as a statewide consortium of college and university libraries in Ohio. Its present extraordinary success is due largely to the efforts of its academic librarian-director, Frederick G. Kilgour, and to countless other academic librarians throughout the country.

In the early 1970s, a number of regional consortia of academic libraries were either formed especially for, or adopted as their purpose, the replication of the successful OCLC on-line system. Included among others were NELINET, PALINET, PRLC, SOLINET, AMIGOS, and SUNY-OCLC. When OCLC demonstrated a willingness and a capacity to serve the needs of the members of these academic library consortia in utility-like fashion, the regional consortia set aside the idea of replication and became instead regional service centers devoted mainly to brokering shared OCLC cataloging services.

The BALLOTS utility, now called the Research Libraries Information Network (RLIN) of the Research Libraries Group (RLG), is also the creation of academic librarians. The UTLAS network in Canada is an outgrowth and expansion of the University of Toronto Library Automation System. The Washington Library Network (WLN) is a notable exception to this list of networks that were formed by academic libraries. WLN was formed by the Washington State Library and is a state agency. Nevertheless, it owes much of its success to the strong support of its academic library members.

Academic libraries were not only instrumental in the formation of networks, they also contribute a substantial percentage of the bibliographic entries in the network data bases. Their payments constitute a substantial percentage of the revenues, and their collections carry the bulk of the burden of interlibrary loan.

The Benefits of Networks to Academic Libraries

If academic libraries are the principal contributors to networks, they and their users are also the principal beneficiaries. The larger the library, the greater the contribution and the greater the benefits.

Networking enables academic libraries to share the development and use of sophisticated on-line computer technology without incurring the full burden of development and operational costs. The use of these systems enables libraries—particularly the larger libraries—to significantly reduce their cataloging and technical processing costs. Network participation permits academic libraries to gain timely and efficient access to information about bibliographic resources in other libraries through powerful on-line search capabilities. It also permits more rapid and effective resource-sharing via on-line, interlibrary loan systems.

This increased speed of access and the increased confidence in the availability of resources held elsewhere in the network enables libraries to gain increased flexibility in the spending of their book and journal funds. It permits them to spend their funds on the books and journals that are most used and most needed by their local clientele, and to rely on other libraries for lesser-used materials.

In the next few years, as libraries prepare to cope with the complex and expensive consequences of the adoption of AACR 2 and closed card catalogs, they will rely heavily on their networks to ease the pain and expense of the transition that is being experienced. When academic libraries joined together to form computer-based networks in the early 1970s, they created a structure for effectively pooling their financial and intellectual resources, and for developing a new and powerful library technology based on sophisticated computer and communications technologies. The implementation of this new electronic technology in nearly 2000 libraries during a single decade has made change in libraries a way of life. Its effects will multiply and accelerate, and will lead to a sweeping transformation of libraries in the next decade.

Constraints to Belonging to Networks

Network membership can involve a heavy commitment of the time of key members of the library's staff—this is particularly true when the network is in its early, formative stage, as many of the regional networks were in the early and mid-1970s. Cooperation does not come easy, as anyone who has ever been involved in the numerous and interminable meetings of bylaws committees and governing boards will readily testify. Indeed, the use of staff time and creative energy is a significant hidden cost of network participation and when it is used for networking, other equally, or even more valuable, opportunities may be lost.

Network participation can cost a library some of its local autonomy in decisionmaking and management, particularly in collecting policies, service priorities, and budgetary flexibility. Moreover, the library can become totally dependent on what may be a distant, and sometimes fragile, unresponsive, or unwieldy organization which is subject to the full range of financial, managerial, political, and technical problems. In a crisis, a member library may find it hard to take rapid and decisive steps to solve its own local problems.

Another constraint of network participation is that rapidly accelerating advances in computer and communications technology may make some network systems obsolete. If that happens, organizational inertia, and political and financial pressures could make it difficult for a library to withdraw and join another network, or to implement alternative local systems. Finally, there is the ever-present danger that overselling the benefits of network membership may raise the expectations of academic administrators for unrealistically high cost savings, and thus provide them with a rationale for reducing budgetary support for libraries.

Prognosis for the Future

During the late 1960s and early 1970s when our concept of a national network was forming, computing was going toward ever-larger, more powerful, and more expensive main frames. Our experience with the Chicago, Stanford, and New York Public Library systems taught us that library systems needed large and expensive computers, too large and expensive for any single library to afford by itself. We found that the cost of developing, implementing, and operating computer-based library systems was beyond what even the largest academic libraries could afford. Thus we turned to sharing computing power and system development through utility-type networking.

The central bibliographic utility will probably continue to predominate during the next several years. But parallel with it there will be a growing movement toward distributed computer networks in regions, as well as stand-alone systems in individual libraries. This distribution of computing capability will be made possible by the rapidly increasing power and declining cost of computer hardware and communications capabilities, and by the availability of dependable and transferable network software systems. For instance, WLN has already led the way with the apparently successful transfer and implementation of its system to Australia. These regional and local systems will presumably be connected to, and make use of, the massive data bases that will be maintained by the utilities. These central data bases may function like electronic versions of the National Union Catalog and the Union List of Serials and they will serve as sources for bibliographic data, for reference, location, interlibrary communication, and various other purposes.

Academic libraries will continue to play the major role in fostering and supporting these and other advances in networking in the future as they have in the past.

DOING BUSINESS WITH VENDORS IN THE COMPUTER-BASED LIBRARY SYSTEMS MARKETPLACE

Reprinted from *American Libraries,* April 1978, 212, 221–22.

A growing number and variety of computer-based systems and services have come to dominate the exhibits at recent library conferences. They are being offered by networks, book jobbers, periodical subscription agencies, catalog card suppliers, online search service vendors, custom book and computer output microform catalog producers, catalog conversion specialists, and online circulation system vendors, among others.

Some of these new products of computer technology are simple and cheap and easy to acquire, but others are extremely complex and expensive. Many librarians will want and need to buy the complex systems, but few are equipped by training or experience to assess their value and quality or to do business effectively with the vendors. Eventually, knowledge of these products and the proper procedures for acquiring them will become widely available, but I am suggesting in this article that inexperienced buyers inform themselves and seek expert advice before making decisions to buy some of the more complex and costly systems being offered.

The products attracting the most interest currently are the online circulation systems being marketed by such vendors as

3M, CL Systems, Cincinnati Electronics, DataPhase, Gaylord, Knogo, UTLAS (University of Toronto), and a number of others.

Some of these circulation systems are actually operating in a variety of libraries, others are still under development or are operating as prototypes in one or two libraries. Most vendors are claiming that their circulation systems are merely the first modules of systems that will be expanded to include other library operations such as acquisitions, serials, and even the online catalog. It seems as though that will-o'-the-wisp of library automators of the '60s—the total integrated system—is either here already or just around the corner, that we will be able to buy it off the shelf like a set of stereo components and just plug it in. Well, we are not there yet, not by a long shot. The circulation systems are a promising beginning, however, and merit serious interest and consideration.

The Glamour of Online

Many of us are tired of or bored with our old familiar manual or punched card systems whose quirks, faults, and lacks we know so well from years of coping. We tend to take their good features for granted: the existing data base, patron cards and files, the investment we have made in programs, equipment, and training, and the fact that it is in place and works, more or less. In contrast, the new online systems that we see exhibited at conferences seem amazingly versatile and efficient at first, but we soon learn that they, too, have their own special problems and limitations.

The demonstrations are necessarily crude and simplistic in the hectic and confusing marketplace setting of the conference exhibit, but they are still impressive to the uninitiated—which includes most of us. There is something exciting and glamorous about online interactive systems.

We listen to the salesmen to try to learn about the capabilities and features of these systems so we can compare them, but all we get in the end is a confusing mixture of computer and circulation jargon. We hear about the various bar codes and optical character fonts as each vendor sings the praises of the one he uses and assures us that it will become the library standard of the future. We hear much incomprehensible talk about minicomputers, disc storage, access times, ports, light pans, wand readers, and CRT terminals. It is all gibberish to most librarians.

When we try to compare the features and prices of the various systems we learn right away that there is no simple answer to the question: "How much does it cost?" "It depends on the configuration," they say. Some vendors price their software separately, while others bundle it with the price of the equipment. In all cases the systems are expensive to buy, but probably much less expensive than developing our own custom circulation systems. The hidden cost of these (and other) circulation systems is the conversion cost: creating the data base and patron file and labeling the books. In the end the purchase and implementation of such a system may be the single most expensive purchase a library will make.

Selecting a System

Given our lack of technical knowledge and experience with computers, how are we to decide which of these systems, if any, is most suited to our needs? How do we decide on the configuration we need and how can we negotiate the specifications, the price, the payment schedule, and all the other details that a contract of this nature contains?

None of this can be done at a library conference exhibit. Exhibits are designed to help us keep up with what is being offered, they provide a convenient way of getting an introduction to a number of systems, and they enable us to meet and talk with the vendors and their representatives. This is only the beginning of a long process. There are no shortcuts.

It is particularly dangerous to blindly copy the decision of another library by reasoning that if a particular system was good enough for Library X, then it should be good enough for your library. You may not know that Library X may have been in desperate need of a system; or the vendor may have given it a special price to make a first sale; or that the people in Library X made an uninformed choice which they regret but are loath to acknowledge; or that it was an excellent and informed choice for Library X but for reasons that do not apply to your library.

Time is on your side. If you wait a year and then make a site visit to Library X, you can generally see how well the system works and whether their choice was a good one; but that still provides only partial information about the system's applicability to your library and nothing about the alternatives. As a matter of fact, the site visit is a good and time-honored technique librarians have used for evaluating new systems and procedures, and there is no substitute for it when a library is considering the purchase or use of a system or service already in use in other libraries. The problem is that some of the new systems being offered are not yet in wide use in a variety of libraries and some are completely untried in the field. These are the systems that concern us most here.

The capabilities of the online circulation systems vary, as do the needs of libraries of varying sizes and types. A system that works well in small public libraries may not be adequate for large academic libraries. Promised enhancements are not the same as present capabilities. Just as we cannot rely on other libraries to make the right choice for us, we cannot rely on the vendors to sell us the right system, to give us the most appropriate configuration, or to offer us the most favorable price and contract terms without negotiation.

The vendors are and must be tough and aggressive to survive and prosper in this risky, competitive market. They have an important advantage over their prospective customers: they are knowledgeable and experienced in technical and business matters and their librarian-customers are not, for the most part. At the same time the vendors' representatives are by no means uniformly knowledgeable about the capabilities of their systems or the needs of libraries.

A few years ago I suggested that with the rapidly increasing complexity, cost, and potential use of new technology, most libraries would not be able to afford to develop and maintain their own computer-based systems and would have to use systems that were already available and could be implemented and operated by library staff members without special computer training.[1] The kinds of systems I had in mind were the OCLC and BALLOTS shared cataloging systems, the emerging online search services, the turn-key circulation systems now being offered, and the online catalog access and computer output microform (COM) systems which will provide alternatives to card catalogs in the 1980s.

The number and variety of available systems is increasing rapidly. By now it is clear that not only is original systems development beyond the reach of most libraries, but it is also becoming hard for most libraries to keep up with new developments and to make informed and timely decisions about which systems to choose and how best to acquire and implement them. Not all the systems on the market are actually ready for routine implementation. Some vendors rush products to the market prematurely and expect their first customers to help refine and debug them. Libraries with no pressing need for such systems should wait until they have been tested by others.

There is no need for most libraries to rush to purchase the latest systems. The delay of a year or two is of little consequence and the systems will get better and cheaper with the passage of time. Sooner or later, however, libraries will go to the market to purchase these new products and systems. When they do, they should consider getting the advice of experienced consultants the way businesses and governments do when they are faced with similar complex technical, financial, and managerial decisions.

Using Consultants

Except for building projects, there is little tradition in the library field for using consultants. Most of us realize that planning a new library is a critical task requiring special knowledge and experience. If we don't have it, we are usually willing to admit it and call in a building consultant.

In most other areas of library activity, library administrators feel that they know enough (or they can't admit it if they don't) to make their own decisions without outside advice. Many administrators turn to staff committees to help them make important decisions. Although this is always useful, it may not be enough. Lay committees make good advisors and usually improve significantly the quality of many deliberations and decisions that do not require specialized knowledge or technical expertise. Because technical matters require specialized experience and competence, however, the informed contribution of one expert consultant may be worth more than the consensus of opinions of a director and a staff advisory committee when all are inexperienced lay-people. When all the advice is in, however, the director must still make the final decision and take responsibility for it.

When we buy a house we employ an attorney to search the title and help us close the transaction. When faced with legal or tax problems we turn to attorneys and accountants for help. When we need to analyze our requirements for a new and expensive computerized library system, we should be able to turn to qualified professionals for help and advice. It will cost some money—good advice always does—but chances are it will be worth it several times over. When the vendors realize that librarians are being advised and represented by knowledgeable technical consultants, they will raise their standards and offer better systems at more favorable prices and terms.

Right now the computer-based library systems marketplace is an uneven contest between hard-selling vendors and naive, inexperienced librarian-customers. The vendors are ahead. It is time for the librarians to redress the balance by calling in their own technical experts to advise and assist them in the selection, purchase, and installation of systems and services. There are a number of experienced library systems consultants available now; some are working in libraries and networks, others are with the small but growing number of consulting firms specializing in library and information problems.

Whether we use consultants or not, we still need to increase our technical and business knowledge. We should have ready access to much more consumer-oriented descriptive, comparative, and evaluative information of the kind that is produced and published by *Library Technology Reports.* This information should cover not only online circulation systems, but the whole range of computer-based library systems and services that is available or under development, and it should be updated periodically if it is to serve its purpose. Such a service could be published by a library organization with Council on Library Resources funding or be undertaken as a commercial venture by one of the library consulting firms. In addition, conference programs, institutes, and workshops designed to review and evaluate systems and the procedures for acquiring and implementing them would also be useful.

Mutual Needs of Librarians and Vendors

Finally, I think it is essential that librarians overcome their traditional bias against doing business with the for-profit sector and recognize that commercial vendors are going to be among the principal suppliers of computer-based systems and services to the library field in the years ahead. Vendors are entitled to and must make a profit to compensate for the high risks that they take. On the other hand, vendors need to learn that librarians do not like to be treated as a soft market to be exploited, that they resent it when vendors offer them incomplete or inadequate systems and promise more than they can deliver.

Librarians and systems vendors are going to need each other in the years ahead, and it is essential that they learn how to do business together in a spirit of mutual respect and understanding. Librarians can begin by becoming better informed and more articulate customers, which, in turn, will encourage the vendors to become more responsible and responsive to their needs.

Note

1. R. De Gennaro, "Library Automation: The Second Decade," *Journal of Library Automation,* March 1975, p. 304; and "Library Automation: Changing Patterns and New Directions," *Library Journal,* Jan. 1, 1976, pp. 175–183 [both reprinted in this volume].

WANTED: A MINICOMPUTER SERIALS CONTROL SYSTEM

Reprinted from *Library Journal,* 15 April 1977, 878–79.

In the early 1960's when we first considered using computers in libraries there were two functions that seemed particularly well-suited to computer processing. One was circulation control and the other was serials check-in. Both were troublesome, high volume, repetitive operations with complex record keeping requirements and were, therefore, thought to be the best place to begin library automation by its stalwart pioneers. Some selected circulation because it was easier and safer, others selected serials control because it was more important and more challenging.

Those who selected circulation were wise or lucky; they succeeded in building computerized systems that were somewhat more effective than the failing manual systems they replaced. These primitive early systems were improved and replaced by more advanced versions and now effective computerized circulation systems are fairly commonplace. In fact, there are now several package or "turnkey" on-line minicomputer circulation systems available which appear to be the latest and most promising line of development in this field.

Those who selected serials check-in were less fortunate: they failed miserably and almost without exception. The reasons were many. Serials check-in proved to be a far more complex record-keeping problem than the pioneers had bargained for, especially since they insisted on having automatic claiming and other highly sophisticated features. The state of the art of computer hardware and software was not advanced enough in the mid-1960's to cope with the burdensome task of converting vast quantities of complex bibliographic data into machine readable form and then manipulating it in the cumbersome batch processing mode. Moreover, there was no standardized MARC format for serials to facilitate the conversion of data or for interchanging and reusing serials records that had been converted by others in non-standard formats.

This record of near-universal failure in the sixties gave serials check-in a well-deserved bad press which unfortunately still endures. "Until recently," I cautioned in a 1968 *JOLA* article, "it was fashionable to tackle the problem of automating the serials check-in system as a first project on the grounds that this was one of the most important, troublesome, and repetitive library operations and was therefore the best area in which to begin computerization. Fortunately, a more realistic view of the serials problem has begun to prevail—that serial receipts is an extremely complex and irregular library operation and one which will probably require some on-line updating capabilities, and complex file organization and maintenance programs."[1]

In the nearly ten years that have passed since I wrote that caution, the state of the art of computing and library automation has made enormous advances. On-line computer systems—both maxi and mini—are commonplace in libraries. The MARC Serials format is a reality and the CONSER Project (Conversion of Serials)[2] has created a rapidly growing on-line data base of some 160,000 unauthenticated and 60,000 authenticated records on the OCLC system. There has been at least one notable success with an on-line serials system—the one in the UCLA Biomedical Library designed by James Fayollat.[3] Computer-produced serials lists in printed and COM form have become widespread and demonstrate the need that librarians and users have for more versatile and powerful approaches to serials data. Yet, with the exception of OCLC, I know of no significant ongoing effort to develop an on-line serials control system despite the desperate need that libraries—and especially large libraries—have for information about their serials holdings. Serials prices are escalating and subscriptions costs now account for an alarming and growing percentage of the materials expenditures in many libraries.[4] Serials are also the most used and the most bibliographically complex materials in the library. On-line computer systems are desperately needed both for the internal management of our serials collections as well as to facilitate reference and user access to them.

But what about OCLC's serials check-in system, is that the answer? I don't think so. OCLC's on-line serials check-in capability was tested in Ohio in 1976 and made available to users in January 1977. Although it is still too early to assess the effectiveness of the system with the limited experience we have had with it, the concept of a centralized on-line serials control system to serve the needs of hundreds of libraries in a network environment is questionable. The OCLC system is admirably suited to certain purposes such as shared cataloging, interlibrary loan locations, and as a resource for retrieving and reproducing bibliographic records—including validated serials records—for local use. However, it seems highly unlikely, in the long run, that the OCLC system and data base will be adequate for storing, processing, and retrieving the vast quantities of detailed data that libraries need for managing and accessing their local files and collections. Even now, the OCLC system is cumbersome and inflexible and it is difficult for libraries to obtain usable listings, analyses, or data in formats that are suitable for a variety of local needs.

Although OCLC has long promised its users circulation, acquisitions, and serials sub-systems, the only one available is the serials check-in portion (with no claiming capability) and that came several years after its projected delivery date. Work is in progress on the acquisitions system, but work on the circulation system has not yet begun. It may be possible, in time, for OCLC to make these sub-systems available to its users, but it seems far more likely that its plans will be overtaken and superseded by the rapidly accelerating advances now being made in minicomputer systems.

It is becoming clear that such essentially local functions as circulation, acquisitions, serials control, and catalog access will be done more efficiently, more reliably, and less expensively on local minicomputer systems which draw standard records from and coordinate with the network data bases.[5] This does not mean that individual libraries will or should develop these systems locally. Few will have the staff or financial resources to do so. Most will be better served by adapting or purchasing the package systems that will be developed by a few pioneering libraries with foundation or government funds, or more likely, if recent trends are an indication, by private entrepreneurial firms.

We already have the successful and very promising precedents of the package minicomputer circulation systems developed by Virginia Polytechnic Institute, and such vendors as CLSI Inc., 3M Inc., and others. Both CLSI and 3M promise acquisitions ordering modules as additions to their circulation systems and since the records of both functions can be processed in similar ways, it is likely that these two systems will reside comfortably on the same minicomputer. However, some vendors have the vision or intention of building a total library system by stages until all library functions including the on-line catalog are resident in the same minicomputer system. This may be just sales talk, or it may be an expert forecast of things to come. From my perspective, the goal of a total system for a single library on a minicomputer is as chimeric now and in the next five or even ten years as was the total system on a large computer that was widely heralded but never delivered in the sixties—although the University of Chicago has several components but not serials control.

A total minicomputer system that interfaces with the OCLC, BALLOTS, or RLG network computers and data bases in the 1980's may be the ultimate objective, but developments in computing occur in unexpected ways and forecasting the future in this field is particularly hazardous even for the experts. My view is that it would probably be better for vendors and customers alike if the first versions of the serials control system were designed to operate on a separate minicomputer and sold as a separate system. Treating circulation, serials control, and on-line local catalog access as separate systems in their first versions at least would give desirable flexibility. It would permit separate development, encourage competition, and give libraries the freedom to consider the separate systems on their merits as they are offered. A minicomputer and peripheral equipment that was a good choice for a circulation system in 1970 or 1977 may not be the most suitable for a serials control system in 1980.

There is growing acceptance of the view that card catalogs in large libraries are going to be closed and that they will be superseded by some combination of on-line access and Computer Output Microfilm.[6] The New York Public Library has already led the way. Other large libraries, including the Library of Congress, are planning to do the same as soon as all current cataloging and authority data are being produced and distributed through the MARC system early in the 1980's. But this is a complex problem. The question of how and when serials will fit into this system is still not clear. Ultimately, serials will be an integral part of a total catalog access system, but one possible strategy for achieving this goal might be to adopt a divided catalog approach and deal with serials and monographs initially as separate but related systems.

Many libraries could begin the process of phasing out their card catalogs by putting their serials records and holdings on-line in a minicomputer system using authorized MARC records drawn from the CONSER data base. This would not only give us the experience we need to make a smooth transition from card to on-line and COM catalogs, but it would also give our users an opportunity to learn to use and accept this new form of access in easy stages.

The library automation pioneers of the sixties were right to identify serials control as one of the most attractive and useful targets for computer processing, but they were ten years too soon in their timing. The need now is greater than ever and the timing is right; we have the know-how and the equipment—what we need are the entrepreneurs to do the job.

Notes

1. Richard De Gennaro, "Development and Administration of Automated Systems in Academic Libraries," *Journal of Library Automation,* Vol. 1, No. 1, March 1968, p. 75–91 [reprinted in this volume].

2. Henriette Avram & Richard Anable, "The Next Generation of CONSER," *American Libraries,* January 1977, p. 23–25.

3. James Fayollat, "On-Line Serials Control System in a Large Biomedical Library, Part I. Description of the System." *Journal of the American Society for Information Science,* Sept./Oct. 1972, p. 318–322.

4. For more about the need for better management information about serials see: Richard De Gennaro, "Escalating Journal Prices: Time to Fight Back," *American Libraries,* February 1977, p. 69–74 [reprinted in this volume].

5. For a brief but perceptive discussion of this see: Susan K. Martin, "Trends in Library Networks," in: *Research Libraries and Cooperative Systems.* Minutes of the 88th Meeting of the Association of Research

Libraries, May 6–7, 1976, Seattle, Washington. Washington, D.C., ARL, 1976, p. 2–12.

6. *The Future of Card Catalogs.* Report of a program sponsored by the Association of Research Libraries, January 18, 1975. Washington, D.C., ARL, 1975.

LIBRARY AUTOMATION: CHANGING PATTERNS AND NEW DIRECTIONS

Reprinted from *Library Journal,* January 1, 1976, p. 175–183. Reprinted in *Reference and Information Services: A Reader,* edited by Bill Katz and Andrea Tarr (Metuchen, N.J.: Scarecrow, 1978).

In 1967, the literature of library automation was still very limited in scope and fell into two categories. At one extreme were the detailed technical papers written by systems librarians describing a specific application which was being implemented in a particular library. At the other extreme were general or visionary papers written by information scientists or librarians speculating on how computer technology was going to change libraries in the future. There was little in between to which librarians and administrators could turn for practical guidance on whether and how to plan, implement, and administer automation programs in their own libraries. In an attempt to meet that need the author, who was then responsible for systems development in the Harvard University Library, wrote a paper entitled "The Development and Administration of Automated Systems in Academic Libraries" which was published in the first issue of the *Journal of Library Automation* in 1968. It was reprinted in the ASIS collection *Key Papers in Information Science.*[1]

The paper was in two parts. The first part made it clear that there were no canned formulas for automating a research library that were waiting to be discovered and applied. Each library was going to have to decide for itself which approach or strategy seemed best suited to its needs and resources. Three major approaches were described: 1) the wait-for developments approach, 2) the direct approach to a total system, and 3) an evolutionary approach to a total system. The use of outside consultants and contractors was also considered. The second part of the paper dealt with the important elements of any library automation program regardless of the approach that was used. There was a section on the building of the capability to do automation, including considerations of staffing, equipment, and organizational structure. This was followed by a discussion of the relative merits of the various kinds of projects that could be selected such as serials, circulation, acquisitions, and cataloging, and it concluded with some views on costs and benefits.

Now, eight years later, the author was asked to write another paper on library automation from an administrator's point of view.[2] During those years remarkable progress has been made in automation as well as in the scope and quality of its literature. Gone are most of the hastily written descriptions of applications as well as the worst excesses of the visionaries. They have been superseded by works of solid quality in both areas and the gap in between has been filled by studies such as Herman H. Fussler's *Research Libraries and Technology*, among others.[3,4,5]

In casting about for an appropriate focus for this paper, it seemed essential to review the earlier one to see how well it had stood the test of time and how it could possibly be brought up to date. It came as no surprise that much of what was written there about this rapidly changing and developing field was no longer pertinent or useful. Many of the most important and controversial issues of the sixties have long since been resolved or have simply become irrelevant. However, the main theme of the paper—the identification and discussion of the various approaches to automation and the strategies for pursuing them—has retained its importance as the major current issue in library automation. It seemed appropriate therefore to use the basic approaches to automation that were outlined in the 1968 paper, along with the other issues covered, as a vehicle and framework for highlighting the changes that have occurred and the new approaches and directions that are discernible in library automation in the United States in the mid-seventies.

Library Automation in the Late Sixties

In the mid-1960's there were two highly publicized pioneering projects that did not fit into any of the three most common approaches that were discussed in the paper. One was the Florida Atlantic University project and the other was Project INTREX at MIT. Florida Atlantic, a newly founded university committed to using computer technology to innovate new paths in higher education, decided to build a totally computerized library apparatus in lieu of conventional library card catalogs and other manual systems.[6] While providing some useful experience, the project proved to be entirely premature and was subsequently abandoned. The task was simply beyond the state of the library and computer art and technology of the time. However, the national and even international publicity generated by this project created tremendous interest, incentive, and pressure for other libraries to enter the field. It is hard to assess the legacy of Florida Atlantic, but without it we may have had fewer failures and a more orderly development of the field.

The motivating idea of Project INTREX was that rather than attempt to automate existing libraries it would be far more fruitful to use the advanced technology to build a totally new kind of library which would parallel the conventional one and eventually transform or even supersede it. In the words of its founder, "The goal of Project INTREX is an information-transfer system to be installed by 1975 not only at MIT but at a number of comparable institutions throughout the nation and perhaps the world."[7] After seven years of expertly managed and reported experimentation and development and the expenditure of several million dollars in grant funds, Project INTREX declared that it had achieved its objectives and quietly went out of existence in 1974.[8] On the theoretical side its impact on library and information technology was considerably less than its promise. On the practical side it left little to show for its efforts beyond a handsomely refurbished Engineering Library and a prototype on-line interactive data and textual access system based on computers and microfilm that is apparently still too expensive and experimental for use in an operational environment. In its highly sophisticated way INTREX may have been just as ill-conceived and premature as the more amateurish Florida Atlantic initiative.

The "Wait-for-Developments" Approach

The wait-for-developments approach to library automation was based on the premise that computer-based library systems were still in an experimental stage with questionable economic justification, and that it was unnecessary and uneconomical for every large library to undertake difficult and costly development work. Most libraries should wait until the pioneers with special grant funds had developed workable systems which could be installed and operated at reasonable costs. Princeton was cited as the chief proponent of this approach.

The 1968 paper suggested that this was a reasonable course of action for smaller libraries, but that for larger ones it entailed the risk of being left behind as technology developed, and that in any case it would be difficult to hold to this policy in the face of the then current pressures to automate that were coming from all sides in that decade when technology was riding high. In retrospect, it is now clear that the advice to wait for the pioneers to develop workable systems would have also been appropriate even for large libraries. With the coming of austerity, the pressures to automate subsided. The fear of being left behind proved to be groundless because the technology changed so rapidly that many of the libraries that entered the field early were locked into obsolescent systems while those who waited had little difficulty entering at the current state of the art when they were ready. Princeton joined a fully operational PALINET, the Pennsylvania regional affiliate of OCLC, in 1974, thereby avoiding the pains as well as the pleasures of being in the forefront of a new movement.

In 1975 this cautious approach still seems like the most prudent course for most libraries to follow with regard to original systems development. However, many of the developments that we have been waiting for are here and ready for implementation. The wait-for-developments approach should be in fact an approach to dealing with technology, not just an escape for it.

The Direct Approach to a Total System

This approach was based on the premise that since a library is a single complex operating system and all its varied operations are interrelated and interconnected, logic demands that it be treated as such and that a single integrated or total computerized system be designed for it. The tasks could be designed and implemented as a series of modules, but all must be designed as part of a whole. The University of Chicago and the Stanford University Libraries were cited as the prime examples of this approach and both had received substantial research and development grants from government agencies and foundations.

The 1968 paper suggested that the total systems approach was somewhat beyond the state of the art of both library automation and computer technology; that while trying it was a gamble that could pay off, it seemed doubtful that the first models would be economically and technically viable and that the best that could be hoped for was that they would work well enough to serve as prototypes for later models. It was suggested that while this bold approach would unquestionably advance the cause of library automation it presented serious risks for the library that adopted it. In retrospect, this appears to have been a reasonably accurate forecast of what actually occurred. Only two large academic research libraries, Chicago and Stanford, embarked upon this approach (in 1966 and 1967 respectively) and both are persevering to successful but diverging conclusions. However, each has found the task several times more difficult, costly, and time-consuming than it had originally anticipated.

Chicago's first generation bibliographic data processing system allowed data to be input to an in-process file at the time of ordering or cataloging either from local terminals or from MARC tapes and produced cards and other printed products for the library. Upon completion of this system around 1968, Chicago made a new beginning with an entirely new design concept. The second generation system performs a full range of administrative and reader services via the library's Varian minicomputer, which has direct access to a master data file in the university's large IBM 370/168 computer. Chicago's comprehensive data management system is expected to achieve full operational status in 1976 and be made available to other libraries under the terms of a Council on Libraries Resources grant that it recently received.[9,10] It should be capable of being used either as a standalone system for an individual library or as the central system for a regional network.

Developed at considerably greater expense, the Stanford system, called BALLOTS, is an on-line interactive system with multi-file and multi-index capabilities and using video display units in such a way as to allow for its extension, in phases, from technical processing support to other areas of library operations and eventually to serve as a central system for a library network.[11] Although it has been supporting the day-to-day acquisitions and cataloging operations of the Stanford libraries since November 1972, operational costs in this mode are excessively high and efforts are currently underway, as a result of a recent CLR grant, to make the expansions necessary to permit the system to support a large-scale network for California similar to OCLC.

The original conception of the designers of these systems and the granting agencies that funded them was that they could be transferred to other large libraries when they were completed. There appears to be surprisingly little interest in this possibility now. Experience seems to indicate that these systems are too costly to operate in a single library environment, and most libraries have moved beyond the idea of having their own dedicated system and seem to prefer to join consortia such as OCLC and its affiliates. Stanford is actively trying to promote BALLOTS as a node for a western library network and this is undoubtedly where its future lies. Chicago is still trying to develop a system which can be used either by a single library or by a group of libraries. But in spite of Chicago's efforts, it can be said with considerable justification that the ultimate goal of library automation in the 1960's, the development of a total integrated system for a single library, appears to have been abandoned or at least set aside in the 1970's. However, there are indications that the advent of powerful and inexpensive minicomputers and storage capabilities will lead to a revival of this concept in the next few years. We will return to this point later.

The Evolutionary Approach to a Total System

The ultimate objective of the evolutionary approach was the same as the total system approach but the method of reaching it was different. In the evolutionary approach, the library was supposed to move from traditional manual systems to increasingly complex machine systems in successive stages to achieve a total system over a period of time with a minimum of cost and risk. It was viewed essentially as a series of do-it-yourself projects with librarians and computer specialists working together as a team designing separate batch-processing or on-line systems for various housekeeping functions such as circulation, ordering and accounting, catalog input, etc. This was and still is the most common approach to automation and was adopted by Harvard, Yale, British Columbia, and many others.

In 1968 this seemed to many librarians to be the most reasonable approach to computerizing the operations of a large academic library. By 1972, the state of the art of library automation and computer technology had advanced to a point where the objective of a total system for a single library as well as this conservative strategy for achieving it both seemed irrelevant. Our perception of the task to be done had changed from developing a single comprehensive system to automate or computerize a library to make the most effective use of technology to support library functions. As the technology became more functional it began to lose its aura of glamor, and librarians began to see it more as a tool to do library work rather than as an end in itself. Two new approaches to the use of technology were emerging. The OCLC system had proved itself and the validity of the cooperative on-line network concept for handling bibliographic data while the inexpensive minicomputer package system for handling certain local functions, such as circulation and acquisitions, was showing considerable promise. These new developments and trends will be treated in more detail later.

Building the Capability for Automation

Following the descriptions of the various approaches to automation, the 1968 paper discussed some of the major requirements for a successful automation effort regardless of the approach that was selected. These requirements included staff, equipment, and organizational considerations. This part of the paper has suffered the most most from the passage of time and the course of developments. Much of what was said is no longer relevant because it was assumed that each library had to build an in-house capability to automate its own operations and this basic assumption is no longer valid. This do-it-yourself or localized era of library automation that characterized the 1960's is giving way to new approaches in which libraries join computer networks such as OCLC or its affiliates for some functions and perhaps install package minicomputer systems for others. In either case, a highly qualified in-house technical staff is becoming less essential as regular library staff members develop the competence and confidence to implement and operate these advanced on-line package systems.

Staff—"No one is threatened . . ."

The question of who was to do library automation—librarians or computer people—was one of those burning issues of the 1960's which simply faded away. The paper suggested that a mixture of both types would be needed, but that as systems and equipment became more sophisticated the need for computer expertise would take precedence. This view was sustained by subsequent developments. At present, it is difficult to distinguish the computer people from the librarians as each has taken on the characteristics of the other and no one feels threatened any more. As a matter of fact, many librarians who chose to specialize in computer work during the heyday of the movement in the 1960's are reorienting their careers back to regular library work which they correctly perceive to be the main stream of the profession in the long run.

The concern expressed over the shortage of experienced library systems people in the face of the "ever-growing need and demand" seems particularly outdated in the face of the current shrinking demand for computer specialists in libraries. A small elite of highly skilled and dedicated systems people continues to be needed in the main centers of activity such as the Library of Congress, OCLC, Chicago, Stanford, Minnesota, the New York Public Library, and a number of others.

Equipment—Turning to Networks

Another very live issue of the 1960's was how a library could gain assured access to the computer time that it needed to test programs and run its routine jobs. Computers were changing "generations" every few years and university computing centers were unreliable and unstable. The unresolved question was whether libraries would continue to rely on computing center machines or whether their usage would grow to a point where an in-house library computer could be justified. Since computers were growing in power, size, and cost, and since it was clear that libraries would require the use of powerful on-line systems, it seemed unlikely that a trend toward in-house library machines would develop. This proved to be the case, but instead of using the general purpose machine at the computing center, an increasing number of libraries are turning to the computer-based library network to satisfy their computing requirements. Although few libraries want or need their own full-scale computers, many are casually installing powerful in-house minicomputers for circulation and other applications, and this trend will surely continue.

Organization

It was assumed that large libraries which elected to automate would require a permanent and growing systems group, and it contained a number of ideas on how the group might be organized, administered, and made to fit within the regular library structures. It foresaw a future where the library's automated systems were always being changed, enlarged, and improved, and program and system maintenance were a permanent activity. This is very much the way it was and still is for those libraries that have elected the evolutionary approach described earlier. However, the continued viability of this approach is open to serious question, as has been suggested, and some large libraries have already abandoned it.

Project Selection—End of an Era

This subject was of vital concern to the library automation fraternity in the decade of the 1960's, and the merits of the various projects were widely debated. Some advocated beginning automation with the serials check-in records because the most activity and the largest payoff was there. Others thought that it should begin with the order records because that is where the records first entered the system. Circulation had its advocates because it was relatively risk free. After some discussion of these questions, which are no longer live issues, the 1968 paper suggested that the development and acceptance of the MARC II format in 1967 marked the end of one era in library automation and the beginning of another. In the pre-MARC period, because of the lack of standard format, every system was unique; in the post-MARC period it was foreseen that automation would be facilitated and expanded in the coming years. An input sub-system for cataloging in the MARC format, which individual libraries could use, was promised as an imminent development which would enable libraries to make full use of the MARC tapes to which they would soon be subscribing.

The MARC format and distribution service did in fact signal the beginning of a new era of accelerating development in library automation, but the success of OCLC and other on-line systems dramatically changed the direction of that development. Instead of each major library subscribing to and maintaining a file of MARC tapes and developing a local system for utilizing them as was initially predicted, it turned out that the emerging pattern is for libraries to utilize on-line terminal access systems and MARC data bases that are centrally maintained by networks or even commercial vendors.

Like many other issues which were critical in 1968, the issue of project selection has lost its meaning as library automation has evolved from an experimental localized activity in individual libraries to a service supplied to groups of libraries by a centralized consortium or network.

Costs—Still High

Many of the views about the costs and benefits of library automation in the 1968 paper still retain their validity. Attention was called to the high cost of developing original systems and software, and today one would confirm this and add a warning about the high cost of operating and maintaining such systems. Another major concern at that time was whether or to what extent automation could be justified on the basis of cost effectiveness. The paper suggested that computer-based systems as they then existed would not actually save a library money if all development and implementation costs were included. Their advantage lay in providing better systems with the greater capacity that was thought to be essential to enable libraries to cope with the steadily increasing growth rates and workloads which were over-taxing the traditional manual systems.

Unlike many of the other issues which have faded away with the advances in technology, the issue of costs and benefits has increased in importance. Although the argument that computer systems are needed to take care of increasing growth and workloads has lost some of its strength as library budgets and other growth indicators have begun to level off and decline, rapidly increasing personnel costs caused by rising salaries and benefits have given it a new force and urgency. Nevertheless, it is still possible to say that the actual cost savings of the localized systems that characterized the last decade were either minimal or nonexistent. The first really significant savings that have come to libraries from computerization have come from the OCLC system and its affiliates in the area of personnel costs in cataloging and technical services.

Less easily demonstrated, but still real and increasing, are savings and benefits that will come to libraries indirectly as a result of the successful computerization of services, functions, and tools by organizations that serve libraries. For example, the computerization of the Library of Congress bibliographical apparatus and subject heading list facilitates the production of printed catalogs and lists and other tools upon which libraries depend. The growing capability of the OCLC data base to serve as a location device for interlibrary loan searches is another important example. The computerization of the data bases of various indexing and abstracting services has made it possible for commercial vendors and others to provide libraries with effective on-line search services to expand their reference capabilities.

New Directions

We come full circle and can now summarize and project the four main lines of development that are discernible in the mid-1970's:

1. State and regional computer-based networks or consortia are developing into a national system, not only for sharing on-line processing systems, but also for locating and sharing library resources.
2. Parallel vendor-supplied on-line services and systems both for bibliographic searching and document access as well as for supporting local library processing functions, are developing.
3. Transferable minicomputer systems designed to support a wide range of library functions with a possible future tie-in to the network data bases and systems, have developed and commercially available packaged minicomputer systems for specific functions such as circulation and acquisitions.

4. There is a trend toward in-house development and transfer or adaptation of local systems.

The remainder of the paper will be devoted to a discussion of these four main trends.

Networks—A New Maturity

Since it went on-line in 1971, the OCLC system has profoundly changed the nature and direction and quickened the pace of library automation in the U.S. OCLC has been the most significant development since the establishment of the MARC format and distribution service and has achieved a commanding and well-deserved lead in the area of cooperative computer-based library networks. The parent OCLC network serves Ohio while 11 other affiliated networks serve New England, New York, Pennsylvania and the Middle Atlantic, the Southeastern U.S., and Texas. Several other regional consortia are negotiating terms for participation. The ease with which libraries can participate effectively in the OCLC system has been chiefly responsible for the change in direction of library automation from the development of local systems for individual libraries that characterized the sixties, to the participation in cooperative networks that is dominating the seventies. It is clearly easier and less expensive for libraries to get the benefits of automation by joining networks than by attempting to develop their own stand-alone systems. Even the networks that are affiliated with OCLC, after an initial interest in replicating the OCLC computer system for use in their region, have largely abandoned this idea in favor of continuing to use the central OCLC system which is rapidly expanding its computing capacity to meet the growing demand. This willingness of libraries and even consortia to use an existing system signals a new maturity in library automation where the focus is on the product rather than on the process or the glamor of developing new systems. OCLC's demonstrated capability of serving as an effective library resource-sharing mechanism has also been an important factor in the rapid acceptance and growth of the network concept in the austere seventies.

Although OCLC clearly dominated the eastern half of the U.S., Stanford's BALLOTS system is making a serious bid to become the center of library networking in the West. Several consortia, including the University of California system, are seriously considering affiliating with BALLOTS, which is said to be technically equal or even superior to the OCLC system. Indications are that the University of Chicago system may also be available to support a major network.

As we try to assess OCLC's future, it appears that the two main capabilities upon which its current success is based—shared cataloging and catalog card production and distribution—may be largely superseded by advances in library automation and in the OCLC system itself. As the Library of Congress and other major producers of MARC cataloging abroad step up the currency and broaden the scope of their output until near complete coverage is achieved, the importance of OCLC's shared cataloging capability may diminish because libraries will draw virtually all of their cataloging from the data base and will only contribute original cataloging for limited quantities of retrospective, locally produced, and other special materials. Moreover, as the Library of Congress and other major libraries begin to move in the next several years toward closing their card catalogs and implementing some combination of on-line and computer output microfilm catalogs their need for catalog cards will diminish. Smaller libraries will continue to need cards, but they may be able to obtain them much less expensively from other sources including commercial vendors. Thus, the continued use of the OCLC system as a massive card production and distribution service in the next decade may be seriously open to question.

On the other hand, the use of the OCLC data base and system as a source for machine readable catalog entries for use in local systems will probably assume the same importance that catalog card production and distribution now have. In addition, the use of the system for union catalog and interlibrary loan location and communication purposes as well as for subject searching and other bibliographic reference functions is bound to increase and may well become its dominant functions.

OCLC's ability to deliver and successfully operate the long-promised serials control, acquisitions, and circulation subsystems is not yet certain. Although work on circulation has not yet begun, the serials control and acquisitions subsystems are under development and will soon be available. What is much less certain is OCLC's ability to expand the capacity of the computer system sufficiently to handle the vastly increased storage and processing burden that will be placed on it when several hundred member libraries try to use these additional capabilities. It may well be that such locally oriented functions as serials control, acquisitions, circulation, and catalog maintenance and access will have to be done on minicomputers which may be interconnected to a large regional or national data base such as that maintained by OCLC. This concept will be further developed later.

Vendor-Supplied Services and Systems

While this trend toward vendor-supplied services and systems is not yet as widespread and significant as library networking, it has much in common with networking and is growing rapidly. Just as it is more efficient and cost-effective for libraries to obtain certain services from a network than to try to develop the capability themselves, it may be equally advantageous for them to turn to vendors for other systems and services. Vendors in this context are not limited to commercial firms, they can also be large libraries, professional societies, government agencies, etc. This approach has not been important in the past because few vendors had any fully-tested operational systems for products to offer, but this is changing now. A number of vendors have developed effective systems and many libraries have begun to use them.

The System Development Corporation and the Lockheed Information Retrieval Service, among others, are providing libraries with access to a growing number of on-line bibliographic data bases, including the MARC file, on a fee-for-service basis. The commercial availability of these services appears to be resolving in a highly satisfactory manner what was once considered to be one of the most difficult problems in library automation, namely, how libraries could develop and offer computer-based information retrieval capabilities to their users.[12] Until recently, the end product of these on-line bibliographic searches was a list of citations which created as much frustration as they did satisfaction because they called attention to documents that libraries did not have or could not easily procure. Now it is possible to actually order copies through the on-line terminal of certain of the items that have been retrieved in a search. These are limited for now to National Technical Information Service (NTIS) reports and articles that are available through the Original Article

Tearsheet Service (OATS) of the Institute for Scientific Information, Inc. However, this capability may expand as the indexing and abstracting services embrace the responsibility for providing copies as well as the opportunity for additional revenues that the service appears to afford.[13] The extension of these search services to include convenient access to documents in addition to citations could be one of the more significant developments that has occurred in library and information technology in the last several years. The availability of complete bibliographic access systems through on-line terminals would have a profound impact on traditional library acquisitions policies as well as on the future of scholarly journals. However, the document ordering capability of these systems is still rudimentary and it is too early to assess the long-term significance of these developments. It is quite possible that demand will be limited and that users will balk at paying the high fees that the suppliers will require to make the service profitable and viable.

The large book jobbers use computer systems for their own internal processing and are therefore in a favorable position to offer computer-produced cards, lists, and other services to their customers. Customer libraries will soon be able to tie directly into the jobber's data base and system through on-line terminals and communication lines. By 1980, nearly all catalog data in Roman alphabets will be available through the MARC service, and international standard book and serial numbers will be widely used. This will undoubtedly open new possibilities for system linkages between jobbers and libraries.

Other firms maintain the MARC data base on their computers and offer a variety of products and services including cards, book catalogs, and subject searches, thus making it unnecessary for small libraries to cope directly with any level of automation or technology to benefit from computerization. As technology becomes more complex and cost-effective, and as book and journal prices along with salaries and personnel benefits continue to rise in the face of static budgets, some libraries may find it advantageous to buy products and services rather than to attempt to produce them in-house.

There are, of course, serious risks that come with purchasing vital library services from commercial vendors, and special caution is indicated to guard against the misleading claims and promises of the unscrupulous or incompetent entrepreneurs that exist in this field as in others. Moreover, even reputable vendors with useful products and services can also fail or be forced to abruptly discontinue an unprofitable line, thereby exposing their customers to serious inconvenience and unrecoverable losses.

Minicomputer Systems

A third significant trend is the development of minicomputer systems capable of handling in an on-line mode a variety of library processes such as circulation, acquisition ordering and accounting, serial control, and catalog access. Two projects typify this trend; one is the Minnesota Bio-Medical Minicomputer Project and its application to the main library at the University of Minnesota, and the other is the efforts of CLSI, Inc. of Newtonville, Massachusetts.

The statement was made earlier that the ultimate goal of library automation in the 1960's, the development of a total integrated system for a single library, was largely superseded by the drive toward networking which was sparked by the success of the OCLC system and reinforced by the Chicago and Stanford experiences which showed that the cost of operating such systems was probably too high for one library to bear. Bucking this strong trend, the University of Minnesota Bio-Medical Library is attempting to achieve the total system goal of the 1960's by using the technology of the 1970's—the minicomputer and inexpensive mass storage. With a grant of $360,000 from the National Library of Medicine in 1972, the Minnesota Bio-Medical Library embarked on a three-year project to develop a low-cost, stand-alone, integrated library system which would be suitable for use in other libraries of a similar size. "The premise of the development is that an integrated acquisitions, accounting, in-process control system for all library materials coupled with an on-line catalog/circulation control system can be operationally affordable by a library or system of libraries in the 200,000 volume class using its own computer system."[14] Apart from the usual delays, the project appears to be progressing so satisfactorily that a proposal has been made and approved to apply the same concept to the main university library at Minnesota.[15] The design of these minicomputer systems calls for their being capable of interfacing with and being linked into the regional networks and their data bases. If this concept proves itself, it could become the dominant trend in library automation and networking in the next decade.

The other major line of development in minicomputer systems comes from the commercial sector. CLSI, Inc., of Newton, Mass., appears to be the leader in this field and is already offering standardized circulation and book ordering and accounting modules using its own software package and an off-the-shelf minicomputer and other components. It has installed several circulation systems but the acquisition system is not yet available. The entire system, software and hardware, is sold or leased to the library at prices which may be advantageous when compared with the cost of developing, operating and maintaining a local in-house system. The installation and maintenance of these packaged or "turnkey" systems are the responsibility of the vendor; the library needs no machine-oriented systems staff, it is free from the vicissitudes of dealing with a university computing center, and it retains a measure of independence and flexibility as technology develops. CLSI will soon be joined by Checkpoint-Plessey, Check-A-Book, and other vendors using a similar approach as the market develops. The market for circulation systems appears to be strongest since the networks are not yet offering this capability.

Development and Transfer of Local Systems

Closely related to commercially available packages are complete systems for particular applications that have been developed by certain libraries or centers for their own use and are being offered for sale or transfer at cost to other libraries. A few major examples can be cited. Ohio State University's on-line circulation system is being transferred to the State University of New York System and Purdue University, among others. The Hennepin County (Minn.) Library used the California Bibliographic Conversion System to convert its catalog entries, and then processed them with New York Public Library's book catalog system to produce a book catalog. The New York Public Library is planning to adapt and install the acquisition system originally developed and used by the Columbia University Library. These and other successful ventures suggest that systems transfer, after many years of unfulfilled promise, may finally be possible now that there are some systems worthy of transfer and technical people with the willingness and competence to make the transfer. Libraries are beginning to overcome the "Not Invented Here" syndrome, and systems transfer may occur more frequently than it has in the past.

Many major research libraries, including for example the New York Public Library and those of the universities of British Columbia, California (Berkeley), Minnesota, Northwestern, Ohio State, Oregon, Washington State, and Toronto are continuing to retain systems staffs and to design, implement, and operate in-house systems for various library functions. Others are maintaining and improving existing systems with in-house staff, but are not initiating new systems. Still others, such as the University of Pennsylvania, have completely phased out their systems staffs and are relying completely on networks and outside sources for new systems and for the maintenance of existing ones. This latter course is a trend which may be expected to grow as networks, utilities, and minicomputer systems continue to develop and dominate the field.[16] Naturally, the Library of Congress, because of its enormous size and unique function, will continue as one of the major centers for research and development in library automation.

The Next Phase—Synergy

During the years under review we have seen the main thrust of library automation evolve from building total or integrated systems for individual libraries using local systems staffs and equipment, to building regional library networks using the systems, facilities, and staffs of a few major centers such as the Library of Congress, New York Public Library, OCLC, Chicago, and Stanford. We have also seen the parallel emergence of a new concept at Minnesota, namely, the development of a powerful, flexible, and inexpensive minicomputer system for use in a single library. If this concept proves itself, it could combine some of the best features of the total systems goal of the 1960's with the major success of the 1970's—the cooperative network. This marriage could produce what may become the dominant thrust of the 1980's—the development of cost-effective in-house library minicomputer processing and catalog access systems capable of interfacing synergistically with an effective national library network for sharing bibliographical data and library resources.

Notes

1. Richard De Gennaro. "The Development and Administration of Automated Systems in Academic Libraries," *Journal of Library Automation,* March 1968, p. 75–91. Reprinted in: *Key Papers in Information Science,* ASIS, Washington, D.C., 1971 [and reprinted in this volume].

2. An early version of the second part of this paper with the title "New Directions in Library Automation" was presented to the National and University Libraries Section at the IFLA Conference in Oslo, Norway on August 15, 1975.

3. For example, one excellent and timely source are the proceedings of the annual clinics on Library Applications of Data Processing which are sponsored by the University of Illinois, Graduate School of Library Science, Urbana, Illinois, and edited by F. Wilfred Lancaster. The 9th Clinic in 1972 was on "Applications of On-line Computers to Library Problems," the 10th in 1973 was on "Networking and Other Forms of Cooperation," the 11th in 1974 was on "Applications of Minicomputers to Library and Related Problems."

4. Herman H. Fussler. *Research Libraries and Technology; A Report to the Sloan Foundation,* Chicago, U. of Chicago Press, 1973, 91p. Although this book is not easy reading, it is probably the most thoughtful, authoritative, and comprehensive treatment of the subject currently available.

5. Allen B. Veaner. "Major Decision Points in Library Automation," *College and Research Libraries,* September 1970, p. 299–312.

6. Edward Heiliger, "Florida Atlantic University: New Libraries on New Campuses," *College and Research Libraries,* May 1964, p. 181–184.

7. *INTREX, Report of a Planning Conference on Information Transfer Experiments.* Edited by Carl F. J. Overhage and R. Joyce Harman. Cambridge, M.I.T. Press, 1965, p. 56.

8. Project Intrex. *Semiannual Activity Report,* M.I.T., Cambridge, 15 September 1972, (Intrex PR-14). p. 1–2.

9. Charles T. Payne. "The University of Chicago Library Data Management System." Presented at Clinic on Library Applications of Data Processing, University of Illinois, April 30, 1974.

10. *CLR Recent Developments,* May 1975, p. 1.

11. Project BALLOTS and the Stanford University Libraries, "Stanford University's BALLOTS System," *Journal of Library Automation,* March 1975, p. 31–50.

12. Richard De Gennaro. "Providing Bibliographic Services from Machine-readable Data Bases—the Library's Role,." *Journal of Library Automation,* December 1973, p. 215–22 [reprinted in this volume].

13. James L. Wood. "NFAIS Document Access Activities," Presented at the 17th Annual NFAIS Conference, Arlington, Virginia, March 5, 1975. Mimeo. 9p.

14. "Minnesota Bio-Medical Minicomputer Project," *Journal of Library Automation,* March 1973, p. 66. (Technical Communications).

15. Glenn Brudvig. "University of Minnesota Libraries Automation Program," June 30, 1975. Typescript of an unpublished summary.

16. This point is enlarged upon in my editorial entitled "Library Automation: the Second Decade," *Journal of Library Automation,* March 1975, p. 3–4.

LIBRARY AUTOMATION: THE SECOND DECADE

Reprinted from *Journal of Library Automation* 8, no. 1, (March 1975): 3–4.

Many of the premises upon which research libraries based their decisions to build in-house library systems staffs to automate their internal operations in the late 1960s are no longer valid. Important advances in automation have been made, including the widespread acceptance and use of the MARC format and distribution service, the general success of the co-operative network concept, and the availability of package systems. In addition, many library growth rates such as numbers of users and transactions, volumes received, size of library staffs, and above all, library budgets, have begun to level off or decrease. These developments are causing many libraries to reassess and reformulate their approaches to automation.

In order to illustrate the profound change that has taken place in library automation in the last ten years, it may be useful to contrast the beginnings of library automation in the pioneering decade of the 1960s with the early days of flying the mails in the 1920s. The French author-aviator, Antoine de St. Exupery, captures the feeling of excitement, experimentation, ferment, and accomplishment that characterized that period in his book *Night Flight* (1931). The early aviation exhibits in the Smithsonian Institution communicate something of that same feeling. Those systems librarians who worked in the 1960s may remember what it was like and see the similarities between the two periods.

In the pioneering period of commercial aviation the pilots had considerable freedom to select the best route to their destination; they would follow roads and rivers and "navigate by the seat of their pants." The pilot was up there alone, with no direction or control from the ground. He felt like an eagle, and success depended on his personal initiative and courage. It was a glorious era and a glamorous calling, but it did not last long. The aircraft developed rapidly and became increasingly complex, efficient, and expensive. The pilots needed more and longer training, and the qualities of personal initiative and courage became less important than technical knowledge and the willingness to follow set procedures and orders with precision and skill and to function as a good team member. The early mail pilots were flying poets and adventurers. Today's airline pilots are highly skilled and seasoned executives.

In the early period of library automation, the systems people were encouraged to question all existing library technology and procedures and enjoyed considerable freedom because the administrators for whom they worked knew little about computers or systems analysis and were somewhat in awe of the whole business. Some of the best and most creative systems people did the whole job, from selecting the task to be done to designing, programming, implementing, and sometimes actually operating the computer and coaxing the output off the printer. It was an exciting, creative, and glamorous job, but it has undergone a profound change in a few short years.

What happened in aviation also happened in the library automation field. The day of the one-man or small group library systems development effort is past. The jobs to be done and the equipment required have become complex and expensive, and it requires a team of highly qualified computer specialists to design and implement a viable system. With the increasing sophistication and success of computerized systems for libraries, the need for systems groups in individual libraries is diminishing. The systems librarians of the 1970s are losing much of their old independence and glamour and are becoming more highly professionalized like airline pilots. There will be fewer of them, and they will be, characteristically, managers or members of a team working not for one particular library, but more likely for a library consortium or a national library group. In addition to designing original systems, they will increasingly work on transferring, adapting, and installing systems and software which have been developed by other centers and commercial vendors.

The era of localized library automation has effectively come to an end. Experience has shown that it is not economically feasible for any but the very largest libraries to afford the heavy costs of developing, maintaining, and operating complex localized computer-based systems. Many libraries are quietly abandoning this approach in favor of joining networks such as OCLC or its affiliates or purchasing turnkey mini-computer systems from commercial vendors for specific applications. It is now quite acceptable, even for a large library, to have no in-house automation program and staff. In-house systems librarians are not essential to implement the local interfaces to these centralized networks or to install the turnkey systems. Indeed, they may tend to inhibit such installations by their reluctance to accept the package systems as they are or to give up the existing local automated systems to which they may have a personal commitment. The operating library staff, if given proper encouragement and support, can readily learn to implement and operate these systems and feel a sense of achievement and pride in having done so.

Neither library automation nor library systems people are passing from the scene. What is passing is the localized systems approach that characterized the last decade and provided the knowledge and experience upon which the advanced library automation of the 1970s is based.

LIBRARY AUTOMATION: THE EARLY YEARS

A NATIONAL BIBLIOGRAPHIC DATA BASE IN MACHINE-READABLE FORM: PROGRESS AND PROSPECTS

Reprinted from *Library Trends,* April 1970, 537–50. This article was an attempt to apply the experience we had gained with building a local library data base to building a national data base. It marks the transition from library automation to library networking.

Librarians are gaining experience with localized computer systems, they are struggling with the problem of how to integrate the use of MARC data into their technical processing operations, and they are contemplating the intriguing possibilities of a national library network. As they do so, they are becoming increasingly aware of the necessity for converting their retrospective catalog records to machine-readable form which will be the foundation of the complex automated systems that the future requires. This article will address the question of why retrospective conversion is necessary, and it will attempt to show that it is a feasible objective by citing significant research and recent, continuing large-scale conversion projects. It will explore the means by which retrospective conversion might be accomplished as well as cost and time projections. Emphasis will be placed on the Library of Congress' current and forthcoming activities in this area because they are of particular significance in the creation of any national bibliographic data base in machine-readable form.

Why is retrospective conversion necessary? Most librarians have accepted the idea that conversion of current and future catalog records to machine-readable form is both a desirable and a necessary step in the automation process. Conversion of retrospective records, however, has always appeared to be such a formidable undertaking that few have been willing to face it. The case against retrospective conversion has been made by science and medical libraries on the valid grounds that most of the use of their collections is based on recent or current materials and that time will solve the problem. The same rationale does not hold true for general research libraries because the older materials in their collections are used more heavily and they continually acquire substantial quantities of retrospective materials. If the entire retrospective bibliographical record is not converted, these libraries will always be obliged to maintain their old manual systems along with their machine systems, and they will never get the maximum benefit from automation.

Libraries cannot seriously begin to design and implement "total" or "integrated" systems until they come to grips with and solve the problem of converting their retrospective catalogs into a machine-readable data base. This data base would become the foundation for subsystems for various operations, such as circulation control, searching, cataloging and catalog maintenance, and interlibrary loan service. It would also provide the means of generating the management statistics and information that are needed to improve library operations. Moreover, this comprehensive data base is obviously the foundation upon which networks must be built if the network concept is to become a reality. Actually, few librarians would question the desirability of having their entire catalogs in machine-readable form; they merely cannot believe that conversion can be accomplished, or accomplished at a reasonable cost. Let us discuss feasibility first and costs later.

Six years ago, no major research library had even begun in any serious manner to convert its retrospective catalog records to machine-readable form. There was no standard bibliographical format; the coding and printing of upper and lower case and diacritical marks was still poorly understood and difficult to accomplish with the available equipment. Almost no one had gained any significant experience in converting large files of complex bibliographical data and few librarians would have known how to use the products of such conversion if they had been available.

Today the picture is drastically different. A considerable body of experience has been accumulated and a great deal of solid research and development has been done in the conversion of mass catalog files. Harvard's Widener Library shelflist conversion project was one of the early entries in the field. Routine conversion of its limited-entry shelflist in a local format was begun in 1965, and well over a half million entries of the estimated total of 1.6 million have been converted to data.[1] The Meyer undergraduate library at Stanford and the Ontario New Universities Library Project at Toronto, although more limited in scope, yielded much valuable experience in conversion techniques. The Universities of Toronto, State University of New York-Buffalo, and Syracuse, among others, have converted portions of their shelflists or catalogs. The Library of Congress has developed the MARC II format and complex input systems, and has converted over 100,000 entries into machine-readable form in the two MARC formats. In England, the University of Newcastle-upon-Tyne has converted its entire catalog,[2] and Oxford University has embarked upon a major project to convert the pre-1920 Bodleian catalog using OCR (optical character reader) typewriters as the input medium and a format recognition program to lessen the manual editorial burden.[3]

The Institute of Library Research at Berkeley has done an outstanding job of research, development, and publication on the problems and techniques of mass bibliographic file conversion, principally in connection with its project to develop the design and specifications for a Technical Processing Center for the California State Library.[4] Its publications set a standard rarely equalled in the library automation field. In 1970 it embarked on one of the most ambitious, well-planned, and technically complex conversion projects that has been attempted to date, i.e., the conversion into MARC II structure and subsequent publication in book form of the estimated 900,000 records that form the 1963-67 supplement to the University of California's printed catalog. The project will use OCR-font typewriters and a highly-developed automatic field recognition system to facilitate input and minimize manual tagging and editing. The completion of this project in 1971 will mark the beginning of a new era in file conversion and the experience gained should be of considerable value to LC's Project RECON and other conversion projects.

The body of experience and knowledge gained in all these

projects, together with the many improvements and developments in hardware and software that have taken place in the last few years, clearly indicate that the state of the art is now sufficiently advanced to support the large-scale conversion of complete bibliographical entries in the MARC II format.

While experience has shown mass conversion to be technically feasible at this time, it has also demonstrated that the cost is extremely high—in a range of one to two dollars per entry. Input keyboarding is only one of the costs and by no means the major one. Tagging the elements and editing the copy require the greatest effort and are the most difficult to accomplish since they demand personnel with training and experience in bibliographical work, and such persons are in extremely short supply. Computer and other machine costs are also significant, as well as project direction, administration, space, and other overhead costs. Another major category of expense which is frequently overlooked or underestimated is the very high cost of software development—systems design, programming, and program maintenance. Expense is not the only problem; it is difficult to find and hold the highly-skilled persons who are needed to do this complex technical work.

The issue is no longer whether the retrospective record can or should be converted, but rather how it should be converted and at what cost. Here we come to a critical point. Unless some over-all national plan for centralized conversion of a standard record in a standard format is developed and implemented in the near future, many libraries will begin (as many have already begun) to convert their own catalogs on an individual basis. The result will be the repetitve creation of expensive local conversion systems producing non-standard or sub-standard machine-readable entries. The combined cost of these separate efforts will exceed substantially the cost of a single centralized conversion effort which would provide a common bibliographical data base in the standard MARC II format from which libraries could draw a significant percentage of their catalog entries.

The RECON Working Task Force under the chairmanship of Henriette D. Avram has recently completed and published a comprehensive study entitled, *Conversion of Retrospective Catalog Records to Machine-Readable Form; A Study of the Feasibility of a National Bibliographic Service*[5] (hereafter referred to as the "RECON Study"). This excellent study, which was underwritten by the Council on Library Resources, Inc., has in one stroke raised the prospect of a national centralized retrospective conversion effort from the discussion and speculation stage to a level of systematic analysis and concrete planning. Since the RECON Study is now the basic document on LC-based conversion, this paper will necessarily draw upon and summarize many of its ideas and conclusions. For the serious student of retrospective conversion, library automation, or bibliographic networks, no summary can take the place of the full text of that report.

Most of the arguments that can be made in support of LC's centralized cataloging and card distribution service apply equally well to centralized record conversion. Indeed, if the MARC distribution service is a logical extension of LC's current card distribution service, then creation and distribution of retrospective catalog data in machine-readable form is an equally logical extension of that service as well as of the MARC service itself. Conversion of its retrospective record is essential for LC's own future internal automation as well as for the card distribution service. Most of the experience, development work, and computer software that has been created for the MARC service is directly applicable to an LC-based retrospective conversion project. In short, conversion of LC records in the MARC format by LC is clearly the most reasonable and economical course to pursue; this is the major conclusion of the authors of the RECON Study.

So far, we have argued that retrospective conversion is necessary, that it can be done, and that it should be done centrally at LC with LC records as the starting point. Three other major considerations remain to be discussed: 1) the catalog or data base at LC which would be the most appropriate, 2) the principal technical and cost considerations, and 3) the over-all method of implementing the project.

With regard to the selection of the catalog or master data base to be converted, the RECON Study cites three important factors to be considered. There should be a high rate of duplication between materials covered by the data base selected and the collections of other libraries. The entries should have a high degree of accuracy and completeness, and certain types of entries should be excluded, such as serials and non-book materials. With these and other factors in mind there are only four catalogs which can be seriously considered for conversion: 1) the National Union Catalog, (NUC), 2) the LC shelflist, 3) the LC official catalog, and 4) the LC card division record set (a catalog of printed cards in LC card number and, therefore, roughly chronological sequence).

The NUC seems at first glance to be a likely candidate because of its size and comprehensiveness. In addition to its four million LC records, it contains seven million records that represent analytics, dissertations, local publications, foreign-language titles, etc., which are not on LC cards. These, however, are titles which are not held by many libraries and these entries do not come up to the standards of accuracy and completeness that are desirable in a master data base. Therefore the NUC was eliminated from further consideration.

Drawing on experience gained from converting the Harvard shelflist, the LC shelflist was this author's candidate for conversion in an article in *College & Research Libraries* published in 1967.[6] There would be many advantages to approaching conversion through the LC shelflist if the shelflist were a reasonably accurate, up-to-date, and legible record. When the RECON Working Task Force considered the LC shelflist, it found that this file "contains a mixture of temporary, incomplete, and printed records with essentially no corrective changes beyond revision or updating LC class and book number. Nor are the cards legible enough to be microfilmed to provide a readable guide to locating the master records in the Official Catalog."[7] Because of these deficiencies the shelflist was eliminated from further consideration.

From the point of view of up-to-dateness, completeness, and accuracy, the LC official catalog would appear to be the most desirable candidate for a master data base. However, there are serious difficulties in using it directly for this purpose. The name portion of the catalog contains some twelve million cards of all kinds, and the task of searching out the four million discrete records produced since 1898 would be formidable. These records frequently contain numerous additions and corrections and would be difficult to use as a source document for first conversion. For these reasons the RECON Working Task Force recommends using the LC card division record set for first conversion and then bringing up to date the resulting record after comparing it with the master entry in the official catalog.

The card division record set consists of a master copy of the latest revised reprint of every LC printed card, arranged by card series and, within each series, by card number. The chronological nature of this catalog, its subdivision by series, and its legibility are potent arguments in favor of making it the starting point for conversion. The chief disadvantage is that not all changes in a catalog entry are cause for reprinting and therefore this record will have to be searched, compared with the official catalog entry and corrected to insure the level of accuracy and quality that a machine-readable data base of this nature requires.

Even with this disadvantage, the record set is still the prime candidate for first conversion because, like the shelflist, it has one of the characteristics most essential in a data base for a mass catalog conversion project: it is a large file that can be divided into a series of significant subsets that can be tackled and completed singly and used effectively as they are completed. The importance of this feature should not be underestimated. The Working Task Force recommends that the record set be divided by language categories (a tedious manual process) and that these categories be divided by time spans of card series according to the table below.[8]

TABLE 2: DIVISION OF RECORD SET FOR FIRST CONVERSION

Category	**Time Span of Card Series**	**Number of Records**
1. English language	1960–March 1969	386,000
2. Romance and German languages	1960–June 1970	381,000
3. English language	1898–1959	1,728,000
4. Other Roman alphabet languages	1960–June 1971	137,000
Nonbook materials	1960–June 1971	157,000
5. Slavic languages	1960–June 1972	225,000
6. Other non-Roman alphabet languages	1960–June 1973	256,000
7. Romance and German languages	1898–1959	698,000
8. All remaining catalog records	1898–1959	682,000

This rearranged file would be microfilmed and a copy produced for the project; the original file would then be reconstructed for the card division.

This table clearly demonstrates the advantage of being able

to divide a large file into a series of significant segments to which priorities based on various considerations can be assigned. Such a strategy is a reverse chronological conversion sequence with priority assigned to the categories in greatest demand (and with the fewest problems). It will tie in nicely with the recommended rapid phasing-in of additional categories of current catalog data to be produced by the MARC distribution service. In no language category would retrospective conversion begin until the current records in that category were being produced by the MARC distribution service.

The RECON Study recommends that an initial conversion effort be made with English-language monograph records issued from 1960 to the beginning date of the current MARC service. This would be followed by conversion of Romance- and German-language monographs issued from 1960 to their beginning date in the MARC service (projected for June 1970). Both should be completed within four years. The third category would be English-language monograph records issued from 1898–1959. The conversion of other categories might follow the sequence of the table above or might be modified in the light of experience gained with the first three.

One of the very difficult and important problems that the study recognizes, but rightly reserves for further investigation, is how best to obtain standardized bibliographical records for items that are not now in the LC record set. In other words, how can the master data base be expanded to become a truly national union catalog or data base in machine-readable form? Just as the problem of retrospective conversion had to await certain hardware developments, the establishment of a standardized format, and the accumulation of some practical experience with conversion, so the larger problem of how to create and maintain a true national union catalog in machine-readable form must await additional hardware developments. It must also await the experience and knowledge that will be gained by the conversion, organization, and manipulation of a substantial body of retrospective and current records. The Working Task Force wisely recognizes this and recommends moving rapidly toward the design and implementation of a conversion system capable of handling a non-trivial pilot project of English-language records from 1960–68.

Retrospective conversion is no longer a technical problem awaiting the development of better keyboard input equipment or even the long-heralded advent of direct-read optical character recognition (OCR) equipment. The last few years have seen the development of several input keying devices including the magnetic tape inscriber and the OCR-font typewriter which are well suited to the mass conversion of bibliographic data. One of the most surprising findings of the RECON Study is that the cost of conversion by direct-read OCR equipment, when it is perfected, would be slightly more than conversion of unedited records by magnetic tape inscriber when all systems costs are considered.[9] The reason, according to the RECON Study, is that these devices will not be capable of reading non-Roman characters, diacritical marks, and other special characters. The machine would have to be programmed to reject records with an excessive number of unreadable characters and these records would have to be manually keyboarded. It was estimated that the number of records rejected might be as high as 10 percent. The cost of keyboarding corrections and unreadable records, added to the relatively high estimated cost of the OCR equipment itself, makes this alternative much less attractive than one might think. In any case, the importance of input keyboarding and the selection of input devices have been given more attention in the past than they deserved. These two factors together account for only 16 to 20 percent of the total unit conversion cost in the LC environment and whether one device is slightly more efficient than another is a relatively minor matter. The selection of an input device in a conversion project may well be made on the basis of criteria other than cost.

Thus the need to await further breakthroughs on input equipment before undertaking large-scale conversion of bibliographical records has disappeared. We have the hardware for conversion, and we either have or know how to create the necessary software. The cost per record will probably never be much less than it is now, since 85 to 95 percent of the costs can be categorized as manpower, and only 5 to 15 percent as machine costs, and it is a fact that manpower costs are rising and machine costs are falling. It should be stressed that these cost ratios apply to the LC environment where the data has to be edited and corrected to the highest standards possible in order that it be acceptable for a national data base. In local environments where less complex procedures could be adopted and lower standards of accuracy could be tolerated, the total unit conversion cost might be significantly less and the manpower-to-machine cost ratio might be more nearly even. Indeed, a greater utilization of automatic format recognition programs might yield a more favorable result even in the LC environment. In any event, it appears that the chief obstacles to conversion are no longer technical; they are financial, political, and managerial.

While detailed consideration of technical and cost factors is not appropriate for this general overview, a brief review of these factors is essential for a basic understanding of how the records can be converted and at what cost. The RECON Study considered six input devices: 1) keypunch, 2) paper tape typewriter, 3) magnetic type inscriber, 4) on-line typewriter, 5) OCR-font typewriter, and 6) direct-read OCR (still under development). The keypunch and paper tape typewriter were eliminated as being technically unsuitable. The on-line typewriter and OCR-font typewriter were eliminated after a cost analysis showed them to be more expensive than the magnetic tape inscriber and direct-read OCR. The magnetic tape inscriber was deemed to be the most appropriate and least expensive device now practicable, while the direct-read OCR, although it is not fully developed, was retained as a possibility on the assumption that it might be used for some portion of the file when it is perfected. The elimination of the OCR-font typewriter as being too expensive is probably justified in the LC environment, but there is considerable evidence to suggest that it may well be the most appropriate input device in other environments.

The manpower and machine unit costs of twenty technical alternative methods were analyzed and the four best ones were selected for detailed consideration. They were: 1) direct-read OCR (assuming its perfection in a few years) using a format recognition program, 2) unedited copy using a tape inscriber and a format recognition program, 3) partially-edited copy using a tape inscriber and a format recognition program, and 4) fully-edited copy using a tape inscriber. The resulting copy would in all cases be manually compared against the LC official catalog and corrected. The total cost per entry of the four alternatives ranged from a high of $1.87 to a low of $1.51 in the third alternative with 94 percent of the cost ascribable to manpower and 6 percent to machine costs.[10] Of the manpower costs in this alternative, $0.52 is for partial editing which in this context includes partial coding prior to input, post-editing to correct and augment the output of the format recognition programs, and editing of new data derived from comparing the interim records against the LC official catalog. This study confirms the conclusion that human editing in cataloging conversion projects is one of the most important cost factors and the trained personnel required are in short supply. That fact accounts for the intense interest that has developed in writing and utilizing automatic format recognition programs in such centers of conversion as Oxford, Berkeley, and the Library of Congress.

The format recognition program envisioned by the RECON Study analyzes the data in a partially pre-edited machine-readable record and automatically assigns tags or content designators and coded information which make explicit what is implicit in the textual information on the catalog card. Partial editing means that the records have been pre-processed by a human editor who has supplied some cues which increase the accuracy and reliability of the format recognition program. The utilization of these techniques reduces significantly the cost and difficulty of the conversion process by putting the burden of tagging and coding on the machine where it belongs. The Bodleian Pre-1920 Catalogue Project is successfully using a format recognition program that was initially written by John Jolliffe for the British Museum general catalogue.[11] The Institute of Library Research has successfully tested the ILR Automatic Field Recognition System, on several significant samples. The goal of the System "is to achieve a full MARC II record without any pre- or post-editing/tagging. The computer recognition algorithms work with the existing format of the catalog card, and have no special input requirements."[12] The system was developed for use in the University of California Union Catalog Supplement Project and promises to reduce substantially the amount of human editing necessary and thus reduce the time and the cost of the project. This approach, if it proves feasible in actual operations, could be used for inputting current as well as retrospective records and might even be adaptable to the LC environment.

Applying the unit cost of the least expensive RECON Study conversion method, i.e., $1.51, the 386,000 English-language records in the record set from 1960 to March 1969 could be converted for an estimated $581,000. The cost of converting the 1,728,000 English-language records from 1898–1959 would be $2,602,000. To covert the estimated total of 2,114,000 English-language records would cost nearly $3,200,000. Since this is approximately half of the entire LC record set, the cost of converting the whole set would be on the order of $7 million.

The cost of systems design and software for a conversion system is estimated at $569,000 and is constant regardless of the number of records to be converted. The cost of hardware is based on the total number of records to be converted over a period of years and is therefore an extremely complex factor. However, for purposes of this discussion, the conversion, storage, and manipulation of the four million entries in the record set would require a two-shift computer system costing an estimated $7 million over an eight-year period. This system would support more than mere conversion operations; it would provide equipment for a national bibliographical service.

No matter how it is viewed, the total cost of retrospective conversion, including the cost of the systems design and software to accomplish it and the cost of the hardware necessary to support a national bibliographical service, is formidable. However, as has been said earlier, these costs seem far more reasonable and acceptable when viewed against the alternative, which is for each library to attempt to do its own conversion, a course which would produce a rich profusion of non-standard and incompatible records and systems at an enormous aggregate cost.

Another element in the cost picture which deserves more emphasis than is given by the RECON Study is the fact that full-scale mechanization of the card distribution service, upon which LC has embarked, is dependent upon conversion of major portions of the retrospective record. There is no doubt that this dual use of the machine-readable data base along with dual use of the hardware and software would make the costs a good deal more acceptable. It should also be emphasized that a machine-readable data base will be a valuable property. It can be used to produce many kinds of marketable services and products which could contribute significantly to the support of the initial conversion as well as to the maintenance of the bibliographical system that will be based on it.

The Working Task Force recommended that the MARC distribution service be expanded as rapidly as possible to include all current cataloging done by LC in order to arrest, or at least slow, the growth of the retrospective record. It suggested that the cost of this expansion, along with some of the cost of retrospective conversion, might be budgeted as part of LC's regular operations, supplemented by grants and transferred funds. The research and development costs might well come from grants from private and governmental agencies with an interest in libraries.

Fortunately, planning for retrospective conversion did not end with the completion and publication of the RECON Study. Continuing the momentum that had been generated, the Library of Congress applied for and received an Officer's Grant of $25,000 from the Council on Library Resources, Inc., to implement the first phase of a RECON Pilot Project. This grant was made to convert the 85,000 English-language monograph titles cataloged during 1968 and those English-language titles cataloged in 1969 but not included in the MARC distribution service.[13] The conversion will provide a practical situation to test and study the various conversion techniques as well as the concepts and techniques of partial-editing and format recognition as outlined in the RECON Study so that the best methods for future conversion efforts can be determined. In addition, a representative sample of from five to ten thousand older titles in English and other Roman-alphabet languages will be drawn from the record set for further detailed analysis and testing.

Thus, the important task of retrospective conversion is moving from the study stage to active experimentation in the form of a pilot project. Experience with library automation has shown that this method of proceeding in stages is the one most likely to be successful in accomplishing a difficult and complex task. The development of the MARC II format and distribution service followed a similar pattern with excellent results.

The RECON Study leaves many technical, organizational, and procedural questions unanswered. How can such a massive file be organized and maintained efficiently and effectively? How can the data base be expanded into a true national bibliographical system with locations? How can other libraries draw entries from the data base for their own use and add their unique holdings to it? How will serial entries be handled? In what forms and on what financial basis will the data be distributed to libraries as well as to firms desiring to exploit its commercial possibilities?

Some of these questions will be answered by the first phase of the RECON Pilot Project; others will be answered only in later phases. In any case, despite the numerous problems and islands of ignorance that remain, a significant beginning has been made on the task of converting LC's retrospective bibliographical file to machine-readable form, and cautious optimism is in order.

Notes

1. De Gennaro, Richard. "Automation in the Harvard College Library," *Harvard Library Bulletin,* 16:217–36, July 1968 [reprinted in this volume].

2. University of Newcastle-upon-Tyne. "Catalogue Computerisation Project" (Interim Report, Sept. 1, 1967 to Aug. 31, 1968). Sept. 1968.

3. Brown, Peter. "The Bodleian Catalogue as Machine Readable Records," *Program: News of Computers in Libraries,* 3:66–69, July 1969.

4. Cartwright, Kelly L. and Shoffner, Ralph M. *Catalogs in Book Form; A Research Study of their Implications for the California State Library and the California Union Catalog, with a Design for their Implementation.* Institute of Library Research, University of California, Berkeley, 1967; Cunningham, Jay L., *et al. A Study of the Organization and Search of Bibliographic Holdings Records in On-Line Computer Systems: Phase I* (Final Report Project No. 7-1083, Grant No. OEG-1-7-071083-5068). Institute of Library Research, University of California, Berkeley, March 1969. See especially Chapter IV: "Data Base Development," pp. 75–116; and Sherman, Don and Shoffner, Ralph M. *California State Library: Processing Center Design and Specifications.* 3 Vols. Institute of Library Research, University of California, Berkeley, April 1969.

5. *Conversion of Retrospective Catalog Records to Machine-Readable Form; A Study of the Feasibility of a National Bibliographic Service.* Prepared by the RECON Working Task Force, Henriette D. Avram, Chairman, John C. Rather, ed. Washington, D.C., Library of Congress, 1969.

6. De Gennaro, Richard. "A Strategy for the Conversion of Research Library Catalogs to Machine Readable Form," *College & Research Libraries,* 28:253–57, July 1967 [reprinted in this volume].

7. *Conversion of Retrospective Catalog Records . . . , op. cit.,* p. 25.

8. *Ibid.,* p. 31.

9. *Ibid.,* p. 97.

10. *Ibid.,* p. 99.

11. Joliffe, John. "The Tactics of Converting a Catalogue to Machine-Readable Form," *Journal of Documentation,* 24:149–58, Sept. 1968.

12. Sherman, Don. "Initial Progress Report on Automatic Field Rec-

ognition" (Technical Paper No. 5). Institute of Library Research, University of California, Berkeley, Aug. 18, 1969, p. 1.

13. U.S. Library of Congress. *Information Bulletin,* 28:427–28, Aug. 21, 1969.

HARVARD UNIVERSITY'S WIDENER LIBRARY SHELFLIST CONVERSION AND PUBLICATION PROGRAM

Reprinted from *College and Research Libraries,* September 1970. It was also reprinted in *Book Catalogs,* edited by M. Tauber and H. Feinberg (Metuchen, N.J.: Scarecrow Press, 1971).

This article summed up the progress and prospects of the now mature Harvard shelflist conversion and publication program.

Introduction

In 1964 Widener Library, the central research collection of Harvard University, developed a system for converting its manuscript sheaf shelflists to machine readable form and embarked on a project to computerize the 1.6 million entries in the list. To date, more than 600,000 records from some of the most active classes in the library have been converted and used in various ways, and the project continues as an accepted and important part of the library's automation operations. The project has now come of age; its feasibility and usefulness are firmly established and it seems appropriate at this time to review briefly the essential background of the program and to report on its progress, evolution, and future outlook.

The previous papers on the Widener shelflist project were largely concerned with the strategy and the techniques of converting this large and unique file into machine readable form. This paper will stress the present and potential uses that can be made of the shelflist of a major research library after that conversion (or a large part of it) has been completed. Two main categories of uses will be discussed: (1) the production of publications of various kinds and the provision of other reader services; and (2) library management uses including the generation of statistical and other data for further automation, for managerial purposes, and for general research.

Review of the Project

The justification for embarking on the ambitious project to convert the estimated 1.6 million handwritten entries in the old looseleaf shelflists in Widener Library can be found in an article entitled "A Computer Produced Shelflist" which appeared in *CRL* in 1965.[1] The project was placed in the larger context of the Harvard Library's overall automation program in another article, "Automation in the Harvard College Library" which was published in 1968.[2] A technical description of the operation in its early stages was written by Foster M. Palmer in 1966.[3] No detailed technical descriptions of the computer systems have been published since that time, although specific information can be obtained from internal working documents. The preparation for publication of technical descriptions of a rapidly evolving system of a local nature is time-consuming and difficult to justify. This article will merely sketch in enough of the project's background to make it comprehensible without reference to the earlier papers. No technical material will be included.

A library shelflist is a record of the books arranged in the order in which they appear on the shelves. It is maintained primarily as a tool for assigning new and unique numbers to books that are added to the collection and as an inventory record of the books in a library. Since the book collections in most American libraries are arranged in classified order, the shelflist is potentially useful to scholars, particularly if it can be made available in convenient form and if classification schedules and author and title indexes are provided. For most libraries the maintenance of a shelflist is a routine process and involves merely filing a copy of each main-entry card into the card shelflist in call-number order. However, the Widener shelflist, for historical reasons, is largely handwritten in loose-leaf volumes, rather than on cards, and is therefore difficult to use and maintain. In 1964 it became evident that, through the use of computer technology, the library could modernize the shelflist maintenance procedure and at the same time make an expanded version of the shelflist available as an additional approach to the library's holdings. Accordingly, an experimental system was designed to convert the shelflist to machine readable form and, after a successful pilot project, a full-scale conversion and publication program was begun in 1965.

The initial system was somewhat primitive, with input and output limited to the standard uppercase character set that was then commonly available on computer print chains. In June 1966 the system was improved so that the input could be coded with an expanded character set to produce output with both upper- and lowercase letters and the required diacritical marks. The output for the published volumes continued to be produced by photo offset from a computer printout until further improvements in the system made it possible, late in 1969, to produce graphic arts quality printer's copy in double columns by computerized photocomposition techniques. The evolution of the output format is virtually complete; all further improvements will be in the input, processing systems, and development of new products.

To date, more than 600,000 entries of the total 1.6 million in the shelflist have been converted. Twenty-two volumes have been published in the *Widener Library Shelflist* series and a dozen more are scheduled for publication in 1970. An estimated twenty-five to thirty additional volumes will be required to complete the series. Several of the classes that were initially keypunched in the limited uppercase format have been converted by a combination of computer program and manual editing to the new standard expanded character set and format, while the rest will be completed by the end of the year. Thus, all the records in the system will soon be in a single uniform and compatible machine format. The master files are arranged in classified or shelflist sequence on magnetic tape. Widener call numbers are machine processable and, since the numbers are unique, they also serve as identification numbers for the machine records.

The entries in the old manuscript shelflists are not bibliographically complete. They were limited to call number, volume count, author, title, place, and date of publication. Frequently the author's forenames were not spelled out and the titles were shortened. Notes, added entries, and subject headings were not included. The strategy of the conversion project is to accept the entry essentially as it is with some few exceptions; obvious errors are corrected, authors' full names are added when easily obtainable, abbreviations in titles are spelled out, and a language code and a code distinguishing serials from monographs are added. All elements present are tagged so as to permit machine manipulation. The average number of characters per record is 100, while full LC records are estimated at 350–450 characters. This enforced limitation on the quality and completeness of the records is unfortunate for many reasons, but it has made the conversion and publication projects economically and technically feasible. Had the shelflist contained complete bibliographical records, the project would not have been attempted, for various reasons.

Since clean and accurate copies of the Widener classification schedules are a necessary prerequisite for the preparation of the published shelflists, a major program was undertaken in 1966 to revise and edit the schedules. The schedules are being converted to machine readable form, and a computer program used to facilitate editing as well as to format them into the two distinct forms that are required for the published lists.

All shelflist conversion and editorial work is done in the library with regular library funds by a staff of eight nonprofessionals. It has become a routine activity of the Data Processing Division and funds for the completion of the project within the next several years seem assured.

The design and programming of the system has been accomplished entirely by librarians trained as systems analysts. The routine computer work has been done for the most part on an IBM 1401 which has 8,000 positions of core storage and four tape drives and is located in the library. In 1970 the 1401 will be phased out after the entire system has been redesigned and reprogrammed to run on an IBM 360-65 located in the University's Computing Center. The system conversion will be done by the library's data processing staff. The occasion will be seized to convert the local shelflist system into a more permanent and standardized system based on the MARC II format. When the present system was designed, the MARC II standard format for bibliographic entries in machine readable form did not exist. That format has now been completed and widely accepted internationally, and programs are being written at several centers to manipulate bibliographic data in that format in various ways and for various purposes.

Although Harvard shelflist entries are not as complete as

full LC MARC II entries, the elements that are present can be tagged and put into the format, and those that are not can be left blank. When the library develops a system to input its current cataloging in the MARC II format, those entries can be integrated into the new shelflist system, since the machine format of the two kinds of entries will be compatible even though they differ in the amount of data included.

In the more distant future it is expected that the present brief shelflist entries will be superseded by standard bibliographical records in MARC II format. Given the growing interest in retrospective conversion at the national level, it is reasonable to foresee that a central bibliographical agency will convert and distribute these entries and that Harvard may be able to substitute them for its own incomplete entries.[4] But this is a distant and as yet uncertain possibility. Meanwhile, Harvard will have realized a satisfactory return on its investment in converting its abbreviated shelflist entries. The nature and extent of that return is the subject of the remainder of this paper.

Uses of the Machine Readable Data Base

The present and potential usses of the Widener shelflist data base fall into two broad categories. The one involves creating and publishing new or special listings of the holdings of the library for the use of scholars, bibliographers, and librarians at Harvard and elsewhere. The prototype is the published shelflist series; this series and its possible future variations will be discussed first. The other involves using the machine readable data base to improve or facilitate certain library operations such as shelflist maintenance, circulation control, collection building, and the generation of statistical and other information for management and analysis purposes.

Publications and Reader Services

The publication of the Library's shelflist was one of the principal justifications for converting the shelflist to machine-readable form. The rationale is stated succinctly in the preface to the published volumes:

> In the absence of a classified catalog, the shelflist has long been used by librarians and experienced library users as a means of systematically sur-

veying the library's holdings in a particular subject. When perusing the shelflist one sees all the titles that have been classified in a given area, and not merely those which happen to be on the shelves and whose spine lettering is legible. In addition, one can take in at a glance the essential bibliographical description of a book—author, title, place and date of publication. However, the potential usefulness to readers of the Widener sheaf shelflist in manuscript form has never been realized because it existed in only one copy. Moreover, it was kept in a relatively inaccessible area, was awkward to read and frequently difficult to interpret. Computer technology has made it possible to enlarge the concept and to expand the uses of the shelflist while improving the techniques of maintaining it and making it available to readers. . . . The development and publication of the shelflist in this form is an attempt to equip the serious reader with a copy of the classification scheme that has been used to organize the collection, together with lists in classified, alphabetical, and chronological order of the books and journals in each class.

After each class and its corresponding classification schedule have been converted to machine readable form, a three-part catalog of the holdings in the class is published in the *Widener Library Shelflist* series. The first part contains the classification schedule and a list of the entries in the class in call number (i.e., classification) sequence with subclass headings (derived by program from the machine readable classification schedule) interspersed throughout the list. The second part is an alphabetical listing by author and by title and is obtained by a programmed computer sort of the original entries, and the third part lists each entry again chronologically by date of publication. Thus, each entry is listed four times.

The first twenty volumes in the series were produced by photo-offset from photographically reduced computer printouts and averaged about seventy entries per single-column page. Beginning with volume 21, all page copy has been set in 6-point Times Roman type in double columns by a computerized photocomposition technique, with approximately 140 entries per page. Volumes are 8 1/2 inches x 11 inches, printed on durable paper, and cloth bound. The library is the publisher.

The published volumes are extensively used in the Harvard libraries in a variety of ways by both readers and staff. Sets of the entire series are located in reading rooms for reference and in the stacks for circulation to readers. Copies of the volumes covering particular classes are located in special boxes attached to the end panels of the stacks in which the class is located and are used by readers as browsing guides and as convenient finding lists. The availability of the series also tends to reduce somewhat the objections to shelving infrequently used books by size in storage areas outside the library, because these titles are retained in the shelflist with a symbol showing the actual location of the book in storage. The volumes are also used by book selectors in building collections as well as by inter-library loan staff, both at Harvard and in other libraries. Since the shelflist volumes form subject catalogs of specific portions of the collection, and since, unlike book catalogs of entire libraries, they can be purchased separately, many individual scholars acquire personal copies of the volumes covering their field.

All costs of the shelflist conversion project, including systems development, conversion, editing and machine costs, have been borne entirely by the library from regularly budgeted funds. All costs incurred in the actual publication of the series, including final computer sorts, photocomposition, printing, binding and distribution, are met from sales receipts. Within this framework the published series has been self-supporting from its inception. The rationalization for this large expenditure of library funds is that conversion of the old manuscript shelflist is a necessary improvement of the library's record-keeping operations and that the investment in conversion (an estimated thirty cents per entry) will be amply justified by long-term savings in shelflist maintenance and other library management gains. Other savings—impossible to measure—are in the time and effort of readers and staff who use the printed shelflist catalogs in lieu of going to the card catalogs. James L. Dolby makes this point nicely in his recent book on computerized book catalogs:

> In particular, we claim that no careful study is necessary to show that a printed catalog on the desk of the user, or at least in the immediate vicinity of his office, is a sufficient advance over the present card catalog to provide a substantial time advantage in his use of the catalog. At the very least, the user is saved a trip to the library for all those searches that prove to be fruitless. Further, in an automated catalog it is feasible to produce many more different orderings of the catalog (and subsets thereof) than is feasible in a card system. This in turn increases the number of access points to the library collection and the over-all utility of the catalog to the user. It may be difficult to put a precise dollar

figure on the value of added access, but at the first level it is certainly sufficient to offset minor cost increments in the cataloging operation.[5]

The selling price of the individual volumes ranges from $10 to $45 and is based on the number of pages, the estimated sales potential of the particular volume, the manufacturing cost, and in special cases, such as the Slavic class, the amount and cost of extra editorial work.

Since the shelflist in this form was a new and unfamiliar kind of bibliographical tool, and since the promotion efforts were deliberately limited, sales were initially slow and tended to be limited to the larger American research libraries, many of which placed standing orders for the series. Sales have increased as the series has become larger and better known and as the format has been improved. The market for volumes has ranged from four to eight hundred copies, depending on the subject covered; while further improvement is possible, it is unlikely that the sales of any volume will exceed a thousand copies. There has been a market for these volumes because they list the holdings of one of the world's great research libraries and as a result are valuable tools for librarians and scholars.

In 1968, after a thorough analysis of the cost and other factors, a decision was made to change the output system to produce printer's copy by a computerized photocomposition process and to discontinue using line-printer output for publication. The logic behind the decision was that the increased page density of photocomposed text would reduce the number of pages in a volume by approximately one-third thus reducing printing costs by a similar amount, while increasing the quality and legibility of the book. Although the cost of creating a photocomposed page is several times the cost of a line-printer page, the increase would be more than offset by the reduction in printing costs. Experience proved that this was the case but the savings were not as great as anticipated because the cost of the additional computer time required to prepare the tapes for input into the photocomposition machine were underestimated. It costs slightly more to produce the photocomposed volume, but this added cost is justified because it improves the quality of the finished book immeasurably. The slight increase in cost for producing printer's copy in this manner is a temporary penalty only; a significant drop in photocomposition costs can be expected in the next few years as the equipment improves, as the volume of business increases, and as the industry becomes more competitive. Even at current prices, photocomposition is a minor cost breakthrough for the production of book catalogs, particularly in large editions where the savings in printing and paper costs are important.

The relatively new COM (computer-output-microfilm) technology may well provide the solution to the problem of producing small editions of book catalogs at acceptable costs. This process produces output from a magnetic tape onto 16 or 35 mm microfilm at tape running speeds.[6] The cost of producing the film is considerably less than line-printer output, and the quality of the print image is somewhat superior to that of the line printer. However, it does not compare with photocomposed copy, which is significantly better but several times more costly.

The COM output can either be used in microfilm or automatically enlarged to full-sized master copy for reproduction in small editions. Because of the poorer quality product and other uncertainties, the COM process is not being considered as a possible alternative to the present photocomposition process. However, it is being considered as a means of maintaining the official shelflist and more will be said about this later.

In the longer range, and particularly after the entire shelflist has been converted, COM will offer many interesting possibilities for exploiting the shelflist data base so that a whole variety of listings in different sequences and for different purposes can be published in small, inexpensive microform or even full-sized editions depending on the need and use to be made of them.

The problem of issuing supplements or revised editions of the volumes in the current *Shelflist* series is a difficult one. The publication and distribution of supplements to the individual volumes is questionable from the point of view of both costs and usability. It has been rejected in favor of issuing new and enlarged editions when the basic volume has become seriously outdated, generally after five or more years. Thus, the contents of the first volume, *Crusades,* will be included as part of the *General European and World History* volume; volume 2, *Africa,* which was published in 1965, will be revised, enlarged and reissued in 1970 in the new photocomposed format; other early volumes in the series will be treated in a similar manner. In the future, the problem of publishing subsequent editions may well be solved by advances in technology and improvements in the economics of publishing. COM and reductions in the cost of photocomposition and computing are reasonable expectations in the near future.

As has already been suggested, these developments may make possible the publication of special or even custom listings of great usefulness, but of relatively limited demand. For example, upon completion of conversion of the entire shelflist it might be desirable and feasible to produce, by COM at an acceptable cost, an up-to-date microform edition of the entire file in classified, author and title, and chronological sequence. Listings by language would also be possible as would a listing of all serials and journals in the collection arranged in a single alphabetical sequence. Current accessions lists would be another useful product.

The technique of merging several related classes into a single sequence has already been accomplished with excellent results and could be further exploited. An example of this would be to expand the Slavic History and Literature class into a comprehensive Slavic area studies catalog by adding the Slavic titles from other classes such as Education, Folklore, Philology, Sociology, Government, etc. The technique could be applied to other areas such as Africa and Latin America. New shelflist-type catalogs of Judaica and other subjects might be created by pulling together the bibliographic entries that are located in the various country and literature classes as well as in Sociology, Folklore, etc. Miscellaneous scattered titles might be located by searching the tapes for certain key words in titles. The results would have to be edited to eliminate false drops but the process might be useful as a first pass. Similar techniques could be used to search the data base and create special or custom listings for individual scholars or groups on request.

When it becomes economically feasible to store such a large data file in a direct access device and to search and manipulate it from a cathode ray tube console, the possibilities for making interesting and novel uses of the data will be expanded enormously. While mass storage and on-line direct access is an operational technology today, it will probably be several years before it will be economically feasible in the research library environment.[7] It seems idle, therefore, to speculate about these interesting but relatively remote possibilities in an article set in the context of current economic realities in libraries. Recent experience indicates that improvements in computer and photographic technology are occurring at an ever-accelerating rate, and the possibility of dramatic advances and cost breakthroughs in the next few years should not be discounted.

A long range but still realistic idea is the possibility of turning the conventional library shelflist into a kind of classified catalog once it has been converted and is maintained in machine readable form. The basic difference between a conventional shelflist and a classified catalog is that the shelflist treats a book as a single physical object and records it only once, no matter how many subjects it covers, while a classified catalog records the book in as many places as its subject requires. With a computerized shelflist, the reason for this limitation no longer exists; a book can be given one number to record its physical location, and several other class or base numbers to indicate facets of content. Thus, a single book could appear several times and in various classes. The two types of call numbers would be distinguished by a symbol or other means, and these added entries could be printed or suppressed depending on the use to be made of the list. The introduction of this innovation in shelflisting can only be done after conversion has been completed and it has, therefore, not yet been proposed for the Widener shelflist.

Library Management Uses

The present system for adding entries to the official copy of the computer-produced printout shelflists is identical with the system for adding to the old manuscript shelflists. The machine lists are printed with five blank lines between the entries in order to leave space for writing in new additions. Periodically, and as the pages become crowded, all new entries and changes in the list are keypunched and added to the master tape file and a new printout replaces the old one. The inefficiencies of this procedure are obvious, but they were tolerated in the early stages of the conversion project on the grounds that it was preferable to have a single shelflisting procedure for both manuscript and machine-produced shelflists until such time as the proportion of machine lists increased to a point where a second system would yield significant savings.

Now that more than a third of the shelflist, including many of the most active classes, is in machine form, the conceptual design of a machine based system for maintaining official copy has been developed and is being considered. It can briefly described as follows: all classes in machine format would be updated and produced in an efficient single-spaced format on microfilm or microfiche using a COM (computer-output-microfilm) technique. This film would serve as the official shelflist copy along with a temporary card supplement. Book numbers for new books would be assigned by consulting both the film and the card supplement. The number would be preempted by making a temporary slip for it in the supplement, and this slip would be replaced by a unit card after it had been produced. Periodically the contents of the card supplement would be converted to machine form, merged with the master tape, a new cumulated official film or fiche version would be produced by COM, and a new card supplement would be started. This procedure could be further simplified after developing and implementing a system to input current cataloging into machine readable form, but even in the interim the savings would be substantial. Assuming a cost of five cents per frame of microfilm containing 80 entries, the entire shelflist of 1.6 million entries would require 20,000 frames and could be produced for about $1,000 on approximately 12 reels of film. A microfiche version would require only 250 4 inches × 6 inches fiche.

Computer printing and other costs would be substantially less than in the present system. Shelflisting now requires a staff of four persons and an area of 600 square feet. It could probably be reduced to a single work station located in the cataloging room where it logically belongs, while reference copies could be maintained in other locations.

The completed shelflist file can be made to serve many of the purposes of a central bibliographical record in machine form. By running call numbers against this file a variety of products could be produced such as machine readable book cards for an automated circulation system, lists of overdue books, missing books, and books to be replaced or purchased in duplicate. In short, any list of call numbers could be expanded into full shelflist type entries by simply key-punching them and matching them with the data file by the aid of a program.

The records of the one and one-quarter million circulation transactions made in Widener since 1965, when the machine system was installed, have been preserved on five reels of magnetic tape and constitute an invaluable and unique data base from which statistical analyses of the use of the collection have been made.[8] One of the chief limitations of this file comes from the fact that the bibliographic data in the charge records is limited to call numbers. This limitation can be overcome by using the call numbers to extract the complete entries from the shelflist file. Thus, for example, listings of the most frequently used titles could be obtained by sorting the charges in the order of frequency of use and using the resulting call numbers to obtain a listing of the bibliographical entries from the master shelflist file. Decisions about where to locate material in the library and which material to send to deposit collections can be made on the basis of these statistics. Such potentially useful management information has never before been available to library administrators.

Another area of statistical analysis that is opened by the existence of the master shelflist is the analysis of the collections themselves, their make-up, their rate of growth over the years and in various subject areas. Detailed and accurate counts can be obtained of the individual classes and of the collection as a whole, e.g., counts by class, by language, by place of publication, by date, as well as counts of serials, monographs, and volumes. Many of these statistics have already been obtained from the converted classes and used for management purposes.

The general research value of the bibliographical data contained in large research library catalogs has already been recognized and exploited to some extent by Dolby, Forsyth, and Resnikoff.[9] They have used data from one of the published volumes of the Widener shelflist and are currently working with the computer tapes of other classes.[10] Their views on the statistical uses of catalogs in machine readable form have been summarized as follows:

> Library catalogs contain a wealth of information about the historic development of the many fields of human endeavor and the interrelations that bind these activities. Mechanization of the catalog permits exploitation of this information by workers in many fields of research. Analysis of the same information can greatly assist librarians in studying their own collections and in managing the acquisition of materials for the library. Many studies of this type can be conducted on random samples of the catalog, though more detailed work requires access to the entire collection in machine-readable form.[11]

Conclusion

In 1968 this author concluded a description of the shelflist conversion project with this statement:

> As it now stands, the Widener shelflist program, like many other present library computer systems, is regarded as an interim system designed to extract the maximum return from a simple existing bibliographical record of the contents of the Library. It is expected that in time the system will become obsolete and the imperfect shelflist entries will be superseded by standard bibliographical records in the emerging Library of Congress MARC II format. . . . The expectation is that a central bibliographical agency will convert and distribute these entries. It seems reasonable to suppose, however, that this conversion effort is still some years in the future and that, in the meantime, Harvard will have realized a satisfactory return on its investment in converting an abbreviated bibliographical record.[12]

Developments during the two years that have passed since that statement was made only serve to confirm this brief assessment of the program.

Notes

1. Richard De Gennaro, "A Computer Produced Shelflist," *College & Research Libraries* 26, 4:311–315, 353 (July 1965) [reprinted in this volume].

2. ———, "Automation in the Harvard College Library," *Harvard Library Bulletin* 16:217–236 (July 1968) [reprinted in this volume].

3. Foster M. Palmer, "Conversion of Existing Records in Large Libraries, with Special Reference to the Widener Shelflist," in *The Brasenose Conference on the Automation of Libraries, Proceedings of the Anglo-American Conference on the Mechanization of Libraries held at Oxford . . .* 30 June–3 July 1966. (London and Chicago: Mansell, 1967), p. 57–80.

4. *Conversion of Retrospective Catalog Records to Machine Readable Form, A Study of a National Bibliographical Service;* prepared by the RECON Working Task Force, Henriette D. Avram, Chairman. (Washington, D.C.: Library of Congress, 1969); see also, Richard De Gennaro, "A National Bibliographical Data Base in Machine-Readable Form: Progress and Prospects," *Library Trends* vol. 18, no. 4: 537–50 (April 1970) [reprinted in this volume].

5. James L. Dolby, V. J. Forsyth, and H. L. Resnikoff, *Computerized Library Catalogs: Their Growth, Cost and Utility* (Cambridge, Mass.: M.I.T. Press, 1969), p.25.

6. Don M. Avedon, *Computer Output Microfilm* (NMA Monograph No. 4). (Annapolis, Md.: National Microfilm Association, 1969).

7. The Institute of Library Research at the University of California, Berkeley, is operating such a system in a research environment, as are several other groups.

8. Foster M. Palmer, *Widener Library Circulation Statistics 1965–1969: Book Use and Stack Space* (Unpublished working paper. March 1970). 18p.

9. Dolby, *Computerized Library Catalogs* (Chapter 6: "On Economic Growth of Nations and Archival Collections"). p.115–33.

10. Ibid., (Chapter 1), p.1–19.

11. Ibid., p.17.

12. De Gennaro, "Automation in the Harvard College Library," p.229.

THE DEVELOPMENT AND ADMINISTRATION OF AUTOMATED SYSTEMS IN ACADEMIC LIBRARIES

Reprinted from *Journal of Library Automation* 1, no. 1 (March 1968): 75–90. Reprinted in *Key Papers in Information Science* (Washington, D.C.: ASIS, 1971).

This was the lead paper in the first issue of the *Journal of Library Automation*. It was one of the first major papers on the organization and management of library automation and was well received and widely cited.

Since most computer-based systems in academic libraries at the present time are in the development or early operational stages when improvements and modifications are frequent, it is difficult to make a meaningful separation between the developmental function and the administrative or management function. Development, administration, and operations are all bound up together and are in most cases carried on by the same staff. This situation will change in time, but it seems safe to assume that automated library systems will continue to be characterized by instability and change for the next several years. In any case, this paper will not attempt to distinguish between developmental and administrative functions but will instead discuss in an informal and non-technical way some of the factors to be considered by librarians and administrators when their thoughts turn, as they inevitably must, to introducing computer systems into their libraries or to expanding existing machine operations.

Alternative approaches to library automation will be explored first. There will follow a discussion of some of the important elements that go into a successful program, such as building a capability, a staff, and an organization. The selection of specific projects and the matter of costs will also be covered briefly.

Approaches to Library Automation

Devising a plan for automating a library is not entirely unlike formulating a program for a new library building. While there are general types of building best suited to the requirements of different types of library, each library is unique in some respects, and requires a building which is especially designed for its own particular needs and situation. As there are no canned library building programs, so there are no canned library automation programs, at least not at this stage of development; therefore the first task of a library administration is to formulate an approach to automation based on a realistic assessment of the institution's needs and resources.

Certain newly-founded university libraries such as Florida Atlantic, which have small book collections and little existing bibliographical apparatus, have taken the seemingly logical course of attempting to design and install integrated computer-based systems for all library operations. Certain special libraries with limited collections and a flexible bibliographical apparatus are also following this course. Project INTREX at M.I.T. is setting up an experimental library operation parallel to the traditional one, with the hope that the former will eventually transform or even supersede the latter. Several older university libraries, including Chicago, Washington State, and Stanford, are attempting to design total systems based on on-line technology and to implement these systems in modules. Many other university libraries (British Columbia, Harvard, and Yale to name only a few) approach automation in an evolutionary way and are designing separate, but related, batch-processing systems for various housekeeping functions such as circulation, ordering and accounting, catalog input, and card production. Still other libraries (Princeton is a notable example) expect to take little or no action until national standardized bibliographical formats have been promulgated, and some order or pattern has begun to emerge from the experimental work that is in progress. Only time will tell which of these courses will be most fruitful. Meanwhile the library administrator must decide what approach to take; and the approach to automation, like that to a building program, must be based on local requirements and available resources.[1,2]

For the sake of this discussion the major principal approaches will be considered under three headings: 1) the wait-for-developments approach, 2) the direct approach to a total system, and 3) the evolutionary approach to a total system. The use of outside consultants will also be discussed.

The Wait-for-Developments Approach

This approach is based on the premise that practically all computer-based library systems are in an experimental or research-and-development stage with questionable economic justification, and that it is unnecessary and uneconomical for every library to undertake difficult and costly development work. The advocates of this approach suggest that library automation should not be a moon race and say that it makes sense to wait until the pioneers have developed some standardized, workable, and economical systems which can be installed and operated in other libraries at a reasonable cost.

For many libraries, particularly the smaller ones, this is a reasonable position to take for the next few years. It is a cautious approach which minimizes costs and risks. For the larger libraries, however, it overlooks the fact that soon, in order to cope with increasing workloads, they will have to develop the capability to select, adapt, implement, operate, and maintain systems that were developed elsewhere. The development of this capability will take time and will be made more difficult by the absence of any prior interest and activity in automation within the adapting institution. The costs will be postponed and perhaps reduced because the late-starters will be able to telescope much of the process, like countries which had their industrial revolution late. However, it will take some courage and political astuteness for a library administrator to hold firmly to this position in the face of the pressures to automate that are coming from all quarters, both inside and outside the institution.[3]

A major error in the wait-for-developments approach is the assumption that a time will come when the library automation situation will have shaken down and stabilized so that one can move into the field confidently. This probably will not happen for many years, if it happens at all, for with each new development there is another more promising one just over the horizon. How long does one wait for the perfect system to be developed so that it can be easily "plugged in," and how does one recognize that system when one sees it? There is real danger of being left behind in this position, and a large library may then find it difficult indeed to catch up.

The Direct Approach to a Total System

This approach to library automation is based on the premise that, since a library is a total operating unit and all its varied operations are interrelated and interconnected, the logic of the situation demands that it be looked upon as a whole by the systems designers and that a single integrated or total system be designed to include all machinable operations in the library. Such a system would make the most efficient and economical use of the capabilities of the computer. This does not require that the entire system be designed and implemented at the same time, but permits treating each task as one of a series of modules, each of which can be implemented separately, though designed as part of a whole. Several large libraries have chosen this method and, while a good deal of progress is being made, these efforts are still in the early development stage. The University of Chicago system is the most advanced.[4]

Unlike the evolutionary approach, which assumes that much can be done with local funds, home-grown staff, batch processing and even second generation computers, the total systems approach must be based on sophisticated on-line as well as batch-processing equipment. This equipment is expensive; it is also complex, requiring a trained and experienced staff of systems people and expert programmers to design, implement, and operate it effectively. Since the development costs involved in this approach are considerable, exceeding the available resources of even the larger libraries, those libraries that are attempting this method have sought and received sizable financial backing from the granting agencies.

The total systems approach has logic in its favor: it focuses on the right goal and the goal will ultimately be attainable. The chief difficulty, however, is one of timing. The designers of these systems are trying to telescope the development process by skipping an intermediate stage in which the many old manual systems would have been converted to simple batch-processing or off-line computer systems, and the experience and knowledge thus acquired utilized in taking the design one step further into a sophisticated, total system using both on-line and batch-processing techniques. The problem is that we neither fully understand the present manual systems nor the implications of the new advanced ones. We are pushing forward the frontiers of both library automation and computer technology. It may well be that the gamble will pay off, but it is extremely doubtful that the first models of a total library system will be economically and technically viable. The best that can be hoped for is that they will work well enough to serve as prototypes for later models.

While bold attempts to make a total system will unquestionably advance the cause of library automation in general, the pioneering libraries may very well suffer serious setbacks in the process, and the prudent administrator should carefully weigh the risks and the gains of this approach for his own particular library.

The Evolutionary Approach to a Total System

This approach consists basically of taking a long-range, conservative view of the problem of automating a large, complex library. The ultimate goal is the same as that of the total systems approach described in the preceding section, but the method of reaching it is different. In the total systems approach, objectives are defined, missions for reaching those objectives are designed, and the missions are computerized, usually in a series of modules. In the evolutionary approach, the library moves from traditional manual systems to increasingly complex machine systems in successive stages to achieve a total system with the least expenditure of effort and money and with the least disruption of current operations and services.[5]

In the first stage the library undertakes to design and implement a series of basic systems to computerize various procedures using its own staff and available equipment. This is something of a bootstrap operation, the basic idea of which is to raise the level of operation—circulation, acquisitions, catalog input, etc.—from existing manual systems to simple and economical machine systems until major portions of the conventional systems have been computerized.

In the process of doing this, the library will have built up a trained staff, a data processing department or unit with a regular budget, some equipment, and a space in which to work: in short, an in-house capability to carry on complex systems work. During this first stage the library will have been working with tried and tested equipment and software packages—probably of the second generation variety—and meanwhile, third generation computers with on-line and time-sharing software are being debugged and made ready for use in actual operating situations.

At some point the library itself, computer hardware and software, and the state of the library automation art will all have advanced to a point where it will be feasible to undertake the task of redesigning the simple stage-one systems into a new integrated stage-two system which builds up the designs and operating experience obtained with the earlier systems. These stage-one systems will have been, for the most part, mechanized versions of the old manual systems; but the stage-two systems, since they are a step removed from the manual ones, can be designed to incorporate significant departures from the old way of doing things and take advantage of the capabilities of the advanced equipment and software that will be used. The design, programming, and implementation of these stage-two systems will be facilitated by the fact that the library is going from one logical machine system to another, rather than from primitive unformalized manual systems to highly complex machine systems in one step.

Because existing manual systems in libraries produce no hard statistical data about the nature and number of transactions handled, stage-one machine systems have had to be designed without benefit of this essential data. However, even the simplest machine systems can be made to produce a wide variety of statistical data which can be used to great advantage by the designers of stage-two systems. The participation of non-library-oriented computer people in stage-two design will also be facilitated by the fact that they will be dealing with formalized machine systems and records in machine readable form with which they can easily cope.

While the old stage one of library automation was one in which librarians almost exclusively did the design and programming, it is doubtful that stage-two systems can or should be done without the active aid of computer specialists. In stage one it was easier for librarians to learn computing and to do the job themselves than it was to teach computer people about the old manual systems and the job to be done to convert them. This may no longer be the case in dealing with redesign of old machine systems into very complex systems to run on third or fourth generation equipment in an on-line, time-sharing environment. There is now a generation of experienced computer-oriented librarians capable of specifying the job to be done and knowledgeable enough to judge the quality of the work that has been done by the experts. There is no reason why a team of librarians and computer experts should not be able to work effectively together to design and implement future library systems. As traditional library systems are replaced by machine systems, the specialized knowledge of them becomes superfluous, and it was this type of knowledge that used to distinguish the librarian from the computer expert.

Just as there is a growing corps of librarians specializing in computer work, so there is a growing corps of computer people specializing in library work. It is with these two groups working together as a team that the hope of the future lies. The question of who is to do library automation—librarians or computer experts—is no longer meaningful; library automation will be done by persons who are knowledgeable about it and who are deeply committed to it as a speciality; whether they have approached it through a background of librarianship or technology will be of little consequence. Experience has shown that computer people who have made a full-time commitment to the field of library automation have done some of the best work to date.

Stage-two, or advanced integrated library systems, may be built by a team of library and computer people of various types working as staff members of the library, as has been suggested in the preceding discussion, but this approach also has its weaknesses. For example, let us assume that a large library has finally brought itself through stage one and is now planning to enter the second stage. It may have acquired a good deal of the capability to do advanced work, but its staff may be too small and too inexperienced in certain aspects of the work to undertake the major task of planning, designing, and implementing a new integrated system. Additional expert help may be needed, but only on a temporary basis during the planning and design stages. Such people will be hard to find, and also hard to hire within some library salary structures. They will be difficult to absorb into the library's existing staff, administrative, and physical framework. They may also be difficult to separate from the staff when they are no longer needed.

Use of Outside Consultants

There are alternative approaches to creating advanced automated systems. The discussion that follows will deal with one of the most obvious: to contract much of the work out to private research and development firms specializing in library systems.

What comes to mind here is an analogy with the employment of specialized talents of architects, engineers, and construction companies in planning and building very large, complex and costly library buildings, which are then turned over to librarians to operate. When a decision has been made to build a new building, the university architect is not called in to do the job, nor is an architect added to the library staff, nor are librarians on the staff trained to become architects and engineers qualified to design and supervise the construction of the building. Most libraries have on their staffs one or two librarians who are experienced and knowledgeable enough to determine the over-all requirements of the new building, and together they develop a building program which outlines the general concept of the building and specifies various requirements. A qualified professional architect is commissioned to translate the program into preliminary drawings, and there follows a continuing dialogue between the architect and the librarians which eventually produces acceptable working drawings of a building based on the original program. For tasks outside his area of competence, the architect in turn engages the services of various specialists, such as structural and heating and ventilating engineers.

Both the architect and the owners can also call on library consultants for help and advice if needed. The architect participates in the selection of a construction company to do the actual building and is responsible for supervising the work and making sure that the building is constructed according to plans and contracts. Upon completion, the building is turned over to the owners, and the librarians move in and operate it and see to its maintenance. In time, various changes and additions will have to be made. Minor ones can be made by the regular buildings staff of the institution, but major ones will probably be made with the advice and assistance of the original architect or some other.

In the analogous situation, the library would have its own experienced systems unit or group capable of formulating a concept and drawing up a written program specifying the goals and requirements of the automated system. A qualified "architect" for the system would be engaged in the form of a small firm of systems consultants specializing or experienced in library systems work. Their task, like the architect's, would be to turn the general program into a detailed system design with the full aid and participation of the local library systems group. This group would be experienced and competent enough to make sure that the consultants really understood the program and were working in harmony with it. After an acceptable design had emerged from this dialogue, the consultant would be asked to help select a systems development firm which would play a role similar to that of the construction company in the analog: to complete the very detailed design work and to do the programming and debugging and implementation of the system. The consultant would oversee this work, just as the architect oversees the construction of a building. The local library group will have actively participated in the development and implementation of the system and would thus be competent to accept, operate, maintain and improve it.

Success or failure in this approach to advanced library automation will depend to a large extent on the competence of the "architect" or consultant who is engaged. Until recently this was not a very promising route to take for several reasons. There were no firms or consultants with the requisite knowledge and experience in library systems, and the state of the library automation art was confused and lacking in clear trends or direction. It was generally felt that batch-processing systems on second and even third generation computing equipment could and should be designed and installed by local staff in order to give them necessary experience and to avoid the failures that could come from systems designed outside the library.

Library automation has evolved to a point where there is a real need for advanced library systems competence that can be called upon in the way that has been suggested, and individuals and firms will appear to satisfy that need. It is very likely, however, that the knowledge and the experience that is now being obtained in on-line systems by pioneering libraries such as the

University of Chicago, Washington State University and Stanford University, will have to be assimilated before we can expect competent consultants to emerge.

The chief difficulty with the architect-and-building analog is that while the process of designing and constructing library buildings is widely understood, there being hundreds of examples of library buildings which can be observed and studied as precedents, the total on-line library system has yet to be designed and tested. There are no precedents and no examples; we are in the position of asking the "architect" to design a prototype system, and therein lies the risk. After this task has been done several times, librarians can begin to shop around for experienced and competent "architects" and successful operating systems which can be adapted to their needs. The key problem here, as always in library automation, is one of correct timing: to embark on a line of development only when the state of the art is sufficiently advanced and the time is ripe for a particular new development.

Building the Capability for Automation

Regardless of the approach that is selected, there are certain prerequisites to a successful automation effort, and these can be grouped under the rubric of "building the capability." To build this capability requires time and money. It consists of a staff, equipment, space, an organization with a regular budget, and a certain amount of know-how which is generally obtained by doing a series of projects.

Success depends to a large extent on how well these resources are utilized, i.e., on the overall strategy and the nature and timing of the various moves that are made. Much has already been said about building the capability in the discussion on the approaches to automation, and what follows is an expansion of some points that have been made and a recapitulation of others.

Staff

Since nothing gets done without people, it follows that assembling, training, and holding a competent staff is the most important single element in a library's automation effort. The number of trained and experienced library systems people is still extremely small in relation to the ever-growing need and demand.

To attract an experienced computer librarian and even to hold an inexperienced one with good potential, libraries will have to pay more than they pay members of the staff with comparable experience in other lines of library work. This is simply the law of supply and demand at work. To attract people from the computer field will by the same token require even higher salaries. In addition, library systems staff, because of the rate of development of the field and the way in which new information is communicated, will have to be given more time and funds for training courses and for travel and attendance at conferences than has been the case for other library staff.

The question of who will do library automation—librarians or computer experts—has already been touched upon in another context, but it is worth emphasizing the point that there is no unequivocal answer. There are many librarians who have acquired the necessary computer expertise and many computer people who have acquired the necessary knowledge of library functions. The real key to the problem is to get people who are totally committed to library automation whatever their background. Computer people on temporary loan from a computing center may be poor risks, since their professional commitment is to the computer world rather than that of the library. They are paid and promoted by the computing center and their primary loyalty is necessarily to that employer. Computer people, like the rest of us, give their best to tasks which they find interesting and challenging and by and large, they tend to look upon the computerization of library housekeeping tasks as trivial and unworthy of their efforts.

On the other hand, a first-rate computer person who has elected to specialize in library automation and who has accepted a position on a library staff may be a good risk, because he will quickly take on many of the characteristics of a librarian yet without becoming burdened by the full weight of the conventional wisdom that librarians are condemned to carry. The ideal situation is to have a staff large enough to include a mixture of both types, so that each will profit by the special knowledge and experience of the other.

To bring in computer experts inexperienced in library matters to automate a large and complex library without the active participation of the library's own systems people is to invite almost certain failure. Outsiders, no matter how competent, tend to underestimate the magnitude and complexity of library operations; this is true not only of computing center people but also of independent research and development firms.

A library automation group can include several different types of persons with very different kinds and levels of qualifications. The project director or administrative head should preferably be an imaginative and experienced librarian who has acquired experience with electronic data processing equipment and techniques, and an over-all view of the general state of the library automation art, including its potential and direction of development.

There are various levels of library systems analysts and programmers, and the number and type needed will depend on the approach and the stage of a particular library's automation effort. The critical factor is not numbers but quality. There are many cases where one or two inspired and energetic systems people have far surpassed the efforts of much larger groups in both quality and quantity of work. Some of the most effective library automation work has been done by the people who combine the abilities of the systems analyst with those of the expert programmer and are capable of doing a complete project themselves. A library that has one or two really gifted systems people of this type and permits them to work at their maximum is well on the way to a successful automation effort.

As a library begins to move into development of on-line systems, it will need specialist programmers in addition to the systems analysts described above. These programmers need not be, and probably will not be, librarians. Other members of the team, again depending on the projects, will be librarians who are at home in the computer environment but who will be doing the more traditional types of work, such as tagging and editing machine catalog records.

In any consideration of library automation staff, it would be a mistake to underestimate the importance of the role of keypunchers, paper tape typists, and other machine operators; it is essential that these staff members be conscientious and motivated persons. They are responsible for the quality and quantity of the input, and therefore of the output, and they can frequently do much to make or break a system. A good deal of discussion and experimentation has gone into the question of the relative efficiency of various keyboarding devices for library input, but little consideration is given to the human operators of the equipment. Experience shows that there can be large variations in the speed and accuracy of different persons doing the same type of work on the same machine.

Equipment

One of the lessons of library automation learned during the last few years is that a library cannot risk putting its critical computer-based systems onto equipment over which it has no control. This does not necessarily mean that it needs its own in-house computer. However, if it plans to rely on equipment under the administrative control of others, such as the computer center or the administrative data processing unit, it must get firm and binding commitments for time, and must have a voice in the type and configuration of equipment to be made available. The importance of this point may be overlooked during an initial development period, when the library's need for time is minimal and flexible; it becomes extremely critical when systems such as acquistions and circulation become totally dependent on computers.

People at university computing centers are generally oriented toward scientific and research users and in a tight situation will give the library's needs second priority; those in administrative data processing, because they are operations oriented, tend to have a somewhat better appreciation of the library's requirements. In any case, a library needs more than the expressed sympathy and goodwill of those who control the computing equipment—it needs firm commitments.

For all but the largest libraries, the economics of present-day computer applications in libraries make it virtually impossible to justify an in-house machine of the capacity libraries will need, dedicated solely or largely to library uses. Even the larger libraries will find it extremely difficult to justify a high-discount second generation machine or a small third generation machine during the period when their systems are being developed and implemented a step or a module at a time. Eventually, library use may increase to a point where the in-house machine will pay for itself, but during the interim period the situation will be uneconomical unless other users can be found to share the cost. In the immediate future, most libraries will have to depend on equipment located in computing or data processing centers. The recent experience of the University of Chicago Library, which is pioneering on-line systems, suggests that this situation is inevitable, given the high core requirements and low computer usage of library systems. Experience at the University of Missouri,[6] suggests that the future will see several libraries grouping to share a machine dedicated to library use; this may well be preferable to having to share with research and scientific users elsewhere within the university. A clear trend is not yet evident, but it seems reasonable to suppose that in the next few years sharing of one kind or another will be more common than having machines wholly assigned to a single library; and that local situations will dictate a variety of arrangements.

While it is clear that the future of library automation lies in third-generation computers, much of their promise is as yet unfulfilled, and it would be premature at this point to write off some of the old, reliable, second-generation batch-processing machines. The IBM 1401, for example, is extremely well suited for many library uses, particularly printing and formatting, and it is a machine easily mastered by the uninitiated. This old workhorse will be with us for several more years before it is retired to Majorca along with obsolete Paris taxis.

Organization

When automation activity in a library has progressed to a point where the systems group consists of several permanent professionals and several clericals, it may be advisable to make a permanent place for the group in the library's regular organizational structure. The best arrangement might be to form a separate unit or department on an equal footing with the traditional departments such as Acquisitions, Cataloging, and Public Services. This Systems Department would have a two-fold function: it would develop new systems and operate implemented systems; and it would bring together for maximum economy and efficiency most of the library's data processing equipment and systems staff. It will require adequate space of its own and—above all—a regular budget, so that permanent and long-term programs can be developed and sustained on something other than an *ad hoc* basis.

There are other advantages to having an established systems department or unit. It gives a sense of identity and esprit to the staff; and it enables them to work more effectively with other departments and to be accepted by them as a permanent fact of life in the library, thereby diminishing resistance to automation. Let there be no mistake about it—the systems group will be a permanent and growing part of the library staff, because there is no such thing as a finished, stable system. (There is a saying in the computer field which goes "If it works, it's obsolete.")

The systems unit should be kept flexible and creative. It should not be allowed to become totally preoccupied with routine operations and submerged in its day-to-day workload, as is too frequently the case with the traditional departments, which consequently lose their capacity to see their operations clearly and to innovate. Part of the systems effort must be devoted to operational systems, but another part should be devoted to the formulation and development of new projects. The creative staff should not be wasted running routine operations.

There has never been any tradition for research and development work in libraries—they were considered exclusively service and operational institutions. The advent of the new technology is forcing a change in this traditional attitude in some of the larger and more innovative libraries which are doing some research and a good deal of development. It is worth noting that a concomitant of research and development is a certain amount of risk but that, while there is no such thing as change without risk, standing pat is also a gamble. Not every idea will succeed and we must learn to accept failures, but the experiments must be conducted so as to minimize the effect of failure on actual library operations.

Automated systems are never finished—they are open-ended. They are always being changed, enlarged, and improved; and program and system maintenance will consequently be a permanent activity. This is one of the chief reasons why the equipment and the systems group should be concentrated in a separate department. The contrary case, namely dispersion of the operational aspects among the departments responsible for the work, may be feasible in the future as library automation becomes more sophisticated and peripheral equipment becomes less expensive, but the odds at this time appear to favor greater centralization.

The Harvard University Library has created, with good results, a new major department along the lines suggested above, except that it also includes the photo-reproduction services. The combination of data processing and reprography in a single department is a natural and logical relationship and one which will have increasingly important implications as both technologies develop concurrently and with increasing interdependence in the future. Even at the present time, there is sufficient relationship between them so that the marriage is fruitful and in no way premature. While computers have had most of the glamour, photographic technology in general, and particularly the advent of the quick-copying machine, during the last seven years has so far had a more profound and widespread impact on library resources and services to readers than the entire field of computers and data processing. Within the next several years, computer and reprographic technology will be so closely intertwined in libraries as to be inseparable. It would be a mistake to sell reprography short in the coming revolution.

Project Selection

No academic library should embark on any type of automation program without first acquiring a basic knowledge of the projects and plans of the Library of Congress, the National Library of Medicine, the National Library of Agriculture, and certain of their joint activities, such as the National Serials Data Program.

As libraries with no previous experience with data processing systems move into the field of automation, they frequently select some relatively simple and productive projects to give experience to the systems staff and confidence in machine techniques to the rest of the library staff. Precise selection will depend on the local situation, but projects such as the production of lists of current journals (not serials check-in), lists of reserve books, lists of subject headings, circulation, and even acquisitions ordering and accounting systems are considered to be the safest and the most productive type of initial projects. Since failures in the initial stage will have serious psychological effects on the library administration and entire staff, it is best to begin with modest projects. Until recently it was fashionable to tackle the problem of automating the serials check-in system as a first project on the grounds that this was one of the most important, troublesome, and repetitive library operations and was therefore the best area in which to begin computerization. Fortunately, a more realistic view of the serials problem has begun to prevail—that serial receipts is an extremely complex and irregular library operation and one which will probably require some on-line updating capabilities, and complex file organization and maintenance programs. In any case, it is decidedly not an area for beginners.

A major objection to all of the projects mentioned is that they do not directly involve the catalog, which is at the heart of library automation. Now that the MARC II format has been developed by the Library of Congress and is being widely accepted as the standardized bibliographical and communications format, the most logical initial automation effort for many libraries will be to adapt to their own environments the input system for current cataloging which is now being developed by the Library of Congress. The logic of beginning an integrated system with the development of an input sub-system for current cataloging has always been compelling for this author—far more compelling than beginning in the ordering process, as so many advocate. The catalog is the central record, and the conversion of this record into machineable form is the heart of the matter of library automation. It seems self-evident that systems design should begin here with the basic bibliographical entry upon which the entire system is built. Having designed this central module, one can then turn to the acquisitions process and design this module around the central one. Circulation is a similar secondary problem. In other words, systems design should begin at the point where the permanent bibliographical record enters the system and not where the first tentative special-purpose record is created. Unfortunately, until the advent of the standardized MARC II format, it was not feasible, except in an experimental way, for libraries to begin with the catalog record, simply because the state of the art was not far enough advanced.

The development and acceptance of the MARC II format in 1967 marks the end of one era in library automation and the beginning of another. In the pre-MARC II period every system was unique; all the programming and most of the systems work had to be done by a library's own staff. In the post-MARC II period we will begin to benefit from systems and programs that will be developed at the Library of Congress and elsewhere, because they will be designed around the standard format and for at least one standard computer. As a result of this, automation in libraries will be greatly accelerated and will become far more widespread in the next few years.[7]

An input system for current cataloging in the MARC II format will be among the first packages available. It will be followed shortly by programs designed to sort and manipulate the data in various ways. A library will require a considerable amount of expertise on the part of its staff to adapt these procedures and programs to its own uses (we are not yet at the point of "plugging-in" systems), but the effort will be considerably reduced and the risks of going down blind alleys with homemade approaches and systems will be nearly eliminated for those libraries that are willing to adopt this strategy.

The development and operation of a local MARC II input system with an efficient alteration and addition capability will be a prerequisite for any library that expects to learn to make effective use of the magnetic tapes containing the Library of Congress's current catalog data in the MARC II format, which will be available as a regular subscription in July, 1968. In addition to providing the experience essential for dealing with the Library of Congress MARC data, a local input system will enable the library to enter its own data both into the local systems and into the national systems which will begin to emerge in the near future. Since the design of the MARC II format is also hospitable to other kinds of library data, such as subject-headings lists and classification schedules, the experience gained with it in an input system will be transferable to other library automation projects.

Costs

The price of doing original development work in the library automation field comes extremely high—so high that in most cases such work cannot be undertaken without substantial assistance from outside sources. Even when grants are available, the institution has to contribute a considerable portion of the total cost of any development effort, and this cost is not a matter of money alone; it requires the commitment of the library's limited human resources. In the earlier days of library automation attention was focused on the high cost of hardware, computer and peripheral equipment. The cost of software, the systems work and programming, tended to be underestimated. Experience has shown, however, that software costs are as high as hardware costs or even higher.

The development of new systems, i.e., those without

precedents, is the most costly kind of library automation, and most libraries will have to select carefully the areas in which to do their original work. For those libraries that are content to adopt existing systems, the costs of the systems effort, while still high, are considerably less and the risks are also reduced. These costs, however, will probably have to be borne entirely by the institution, as it is unlikely that outside funding can be obtained for this type of work.

The justification of computer-based library systems on the basis of the costs alone will continue to be difficult because machine systems not only replace manual systems but generally do more and different things, and it is extremely difficult to compare them with the old manual systems, which frequently did not adequately do the job they were supposed to do and for which operating costs often were unknown. Generally speaking, and in the short run at least, computer-based systems will not save money for an institution if all development and implementation costs are included. They will provide better and more dependable records and systems, which are essential to enable libraries simply to cope with increased intake and workloads, but they will cost at least as much as the inadequate and frequently unexpansible manual systems they replace. The picture may change in the long run, but even then it seems more reasonable to expect that automation, in addition to profoundly changing the way in which the library budget is spent, will increase the total cost of providing library service. However, that service will be at a much higher level than the service bought by today's library budget. Certain jobs will be eliminated, but others will be created to provide new services and services in greater depth; as a library becomes increasingly successful and responsive, more and more will be demanded of it.

Conclusion

The purpose of this paper has been to stress the importance of good strategy, correct timing, and intelligent systems staff as the essential ingredients for a successful automation program. It has also tried to make clear that no canned formulas for automating an academic library are waiting to be discovered and applied to any particular library. Each library is going to have to decide for itself which approach or strategy seems best suited to its own particular needs and situation. On the other hand, a good deal of experience with the development and administration of library systems has been acquired over the last few years and some of it may very well be useful to those who are about to take the plunge for the first time. This paper was written with the intention of passing along, for what they are worth, one man's ideas, opinions, and impressions based on an imperfect knowledge of the state of the library automation art and a modest amount of firsthand experience in library systems development and administration.

Notes

1. Wasserman, Paul: *The Librarian and the Machine* (Detroit: Gale, 1965). A thoughtful and thorough review of the state of the art of library automation, with some discussion of the various approaches to automation. Essential reading for library administrators.

2. Cox, N. S. M.; Dews, J. D.; Dolby, J. L.: *The Computer and the Library* (Newcastle upon Tyne: University of Newcastle upon Tyne, 1966). American edition published by Archon Books, Hamden, Conn. Extremely clear, well-written and essential book for anyone with an interest in library automation.

3. Dix, William S.: *Annual Report of the Librarian for the Year Ending June 30, 1966* (Princeton: Princeton University Library, 1966). One of the best policy statements on library automation; a comprehensive review of the subject in the Princeton context, with particular emphasis on the "wait-for-developments" approach.

4. Fussler, Herman H.; Payne, Charles T.: *Annual Report 1966/67 to the National Science Foundation from the University of Chicago Library; Development of an Integrated, Computer-Based, Bibliographical Data System for a Large University Library* (Chicago: University of Chicago Library, 1967). Appended to the report is a paper given May 1, 1967, at the Clinic on Library Application of Data Processing conducted by the Graduate School of Library Science, University of Illinois. Mr. Payne is the author, and the paper is entitled "An Integrated Computer-Based Bibliographic Data System for a Large University Library: Progress and Problems at the University of Chicago."

5. Kilgour, Frederick G.: "Comprehensive Modern Library Systems," in The Brasenose Conference on the Automation of Libraries, *Proceedings.* (London: Mansell, 1967), 46–56. An example of the evolutionary approach as employed at the Yale University Library.

6. Parker, Ralph H.: "Not a Shared System: an Account of a Com-

puter Operation Designed Specifically and Solely for Library Use at the University of Missouri," *Library Journal,* 92 (Nov. 1, 1967), 3967–3970.

7. *Annual Review of Information Science and Technology* (New York: Interscience Publishers), 1 (1966). A useful tool for surveying the current state of the library automation art and for obtaining citations to current publications and reports is a chapter on automation in libraries which appears in each volume.

AUTOMATION IN THE HARVARD COLLEGE LIBRARY

Reprinted from the *Harvard Library Bulletin* 16, no. 3 (July 1968): 217–36.

This article provides a state-of-the-art view of library automation as it was in 1968.

This article will begin by outlining the basic approach that has been followed in introducing computer and other machine systems into the Harvard College Library and by explaining why this approach was adopted. It will then describe the specific projects that have been undertaken since 1963 in the Widener Library, with some indication of their present status and their prospects. A third section will attempt to view in perspective what has been accomplished thus far, point out both the immediate and practical gains that have been realized and the more general, long-term benefits that can be anticipated. Against this background, the concluding portions of the article will briefly consider the outlook for future developments in automation at the national level and will suggest how these developments can be expected to affect the Harvard Library.

This is an account of automation in the Harvard College Library, not the Harvard University Library as a whole. The Countway Library of Medicine (then the Library of the Harvard Schools of Medicine and Public Health) entered the field two years before Widener in a pioneering cooperative project with the medical libraries at Yale and Columbia; it continues to develop systems for its own use and, as the Regional Medical Library of New England, is a major participant in projects sponsored by the National Library of Medicine. An excellent list of serial holdings has been developed by Baker Library at the Harvard Business School, which also entered the automation field before Widener. These efforts deserve separate treatment and they are not directly related to developments in the College Library; consequently it has seemed desirable to confine this article to the series of projects based in Widener.

The Harvard Approach to Automation

The Harvard University Library consists of nearly one hundred separate units with approximately 8,000,000 volumes and an annual budget of more than $8,000,000. The Library adds some 200,000 volumes each year, and approximately half of its holdings are in languages other than English. It has a staff of more than 600, of whom 200 are professional librarians with language, subject, or other special qualifications. The staff has had a long history and tradition of providing excellent library service to the Harvard community.

Widener Library is the central unit of the library system. It has nearly 2,500,000 volumes in the Widener building, with another 500,000 in two storage areas outside. It acquires some 50,000 new volumes each year. Because of its age and other special circumstances, it developed its own cataloguing, subject headings, and classification systems either previous to, or concurrently with, the Library of Congress, whose systems are becoming the national standard. In a library as old, as large, and as complex as Harvard's, the problems of automation must necessarily be approached with a mixture of conservatism and boldness.

The Library has much to conserve, including outstanding collections of books and journals in many areas, and a first-class bibliographical apparatus that has been built up carefully and at great expense during the last century. The Harvard Library must build on its strength and make the past investment continue to pay dividends at an increasing rate in the future.

It now operates successfully on traditional lines, and it expects to become a successful automated library in the future; but the transition to this future library must be made without disrupting the organization and crippling current services to users. The established systems cannot be abandoned until new ones have demonstrated their superiority. One the other hand, a bold approach is also needed to counteract the natural tendency of an institution such as this to resist change. There is no question that profound changes in the Library must be made during the next decade if it is to continue to fulfill its traditional mission and to respond to the new and increasing demands that will be placed on it in the future. Library automation is not a luxury to be indulged in for the sake of glamour; it is essential for the survival of the Library as a vital force in the University. The term "automation" in this context is not limited to computers but also comprehends the rapidly developing field of reprography (the aggregate of processes and methods used for copying documents) for it is the combination of these two technologies that will effect the coming revolution in libraries and information handling.

Most of the tools and concepts currently in use in academic libraries, including the card catalogue, the standardized 7.5 by 12.5 cm. cards prepared and distributed by the Library of Congress, subject headings, and classification systems, were developed and introduced in the second half of the nineteenth century. Since then, many great libraries have been doubling in size every twenty years, and the only response that has been possible to increasing growth and workloads has been to add manpower and build more space to house the books, staff, and catalogues.

Using traditional methods, libraries apparently cannot respond to the demands of modern scholarship unless they continue to grow at this geometric rate, yet it is obvious that this course would soon call for buildings and for costs of impossible dimensions. New techniques and concepts are needed, and a period of innovation in libraries was begun during the present decade with the development of new technology in reprography and computer-based systems. Much of the new technology is not yet reliable and inexpensive enough to be introduced into library operations, but some of it is. Developments in computer technology occur so rapidly, moreover, that it seemed essential at Harvard to prepare for fundamental changes as soon as possible by introducing as much of the new technology as could be used. In this way the Library could take advantage of early systems to improve its services and, more important, could become capable of developing and adopting more sophisticated systems as technological advances made them practicable.

Three basic approaches to automation in the Harvard College Library were considered. The first, which can be characterized as a cautious "wait for developments" approach, can be supported on the grounds that computer-based library systems are still in the developmental stage, that they are still of dubious value from an economic standpoint, and that it is wasteful and unnecessary for every library to undertake the costly and difficult work of development. In effect, this approach would leave automation to others. It was rejected on two counts. It seemed unworthy of an outstanding library, and it assumed, mistakenly, that Harvard could afford to wait for the situation to shake down and stabilize (which may never happen) before beginning to benefit from machine systems.

The second can be characterized as a direct approach to a total or integrated system. Here the premise is that, since a library's operations are all interrelated and interconnected, the logical procedure is to design a total system from the start to include all machinable operations in order to make the most efficient and economical use of the computer. This approach is reasonable and other libraries are attempting it.[1] It was rejected by Harvard, however, because of the size and complexity of the library and because neither the state of library automation nor the state of computer technology seemed to be sufficiently advanced to justify the risks that would be involved. It has been said facetiously that the total system concept would be right for Harvard if we could get God to design it.

The third approach can be characterized as an evolutionary approach leading eventually to an integrated system. It takes a long-range and conservative view of the problem of automating a large and complex library. The ultimate goal is the same as with the total systems approach, but the method of reaching it is more cautious and pragmatic. This is the approach that Harvard chose. It sees the introduction of automated systems into the Library as progressing in stages, each building on its predecessors. Harvard is still in the first stage of this approach—a stage in which, using its own staff to operate the equipment that is available, the Library undertakes a series of projects for designing and utilizing basic systems to do particular jobs. The immediate aim is to raise the level of each "housekeeping" operation, such as circulation, shelflist maintenance, book ordering and accounting, catalogue input, etc., from its manual stage to a relatively simple and economical machine system.[2]

During this first stage, which started in 1963 with the design and implementation of the Widener circulation system, the Library has recruited and trained a competent staff and has created a Data Processing and Photographic Services Department with a regular budget, equipment, and space in which to work. In short, it has been acquiring essential experience and building a capability to do the more sophisticated systems work that will be required in the next stages of development.

An attempt will now be made to describe the various specific projects that have been undertaken to date. Each is interesting in itself, and each needs to be understood if the total effort is to be seen in the perspective of future developments at both the local and the national level.

The Development of Specific Projects

Circulation System

The College Library's introduction to data processing equipment and techniques came with the design and installation of a punched card circulation system in July 1963. The old manual system could no longer cope with the steadily increasing load that had been placed upon it in the previous decade. The staff had been augmented to a point of diminishing returns and it was obvious that the Library needed a new system with greatly increased capacity and accuracy. A few other large academic libraries had already successfully introduced data processing techniques in this area, but no system then in operation exactly suited Widener's needs.

Foster M. Palmer, then Associate Librarian for Reference and Circulation, investigated the possibilities, and within a few months designed and installed a circulation system based on punched cards and electric accounting machines.[3] Several refinements and improvements were made, certain operations were computerized during the first year of operation, and a major improvement—conversion of the circulation file (currently on IBM cards) to a daily computer printout—is now under development.

The punched-card circulation system accomplished several

things: it substantially improved the accuracy and reliability of the circulation records, it provided a system capable of handling a greatly increased circulation load at a stable cost, and, perhaps the most important of all, its outstanding success proved the value of data-processing techniques in the Library and gave the staff the experience and confidence to proceed with development of applications in other areas.

Current Journals in the Sciences

In the spring of 1964 the Library undertook a modest project to create a ready-reference tool which would list in a single alphabet the journals currently received in seven departmental science libraries. The Library's data processing unit, under the supervision of an assistant director, then consisted of a single intern, Mrs. Susan K. Martin, who gathered, coded, and keypunched more than 3,000 entries for journal titles from seven libraries. After she had also written the necessary programs for the IBM 1401, the first edition of the list was issued in one hundred copies in January 1965.[4] A third enlarged edition is now in preparation. This list is primarily for use within the University, but a few copies have been made available for outside distribution.

Current Journals is looked upon as a useful interim reference list and will probably be continued in its present form and scope until it can be replaced by a more comprehensive and versatile union list of serials produced by more advanced techniques with a considerably greater expenditure of effort and resources.

The IBM-Sponsored Education Program and Systems Study

In June 1964 the IBM Corporation embarked on a study with the assistance of the Library staff to determine how computer technology might be used to assist in performing certain "housekeeping" operations. In addition to this systems study, IBM sponsored a week-long orientation program in Cambridge during September for twenty-five senior members of the University Library staff. This educational program was extremely effective in creating an understanding of computers and an interest in the role that they may eventually have in the Library.

The IBM systems study concentrated on four principal areas: circulation, acquisitions, serials control, and cataloguing; it concluded with a recommendation that the Library embark on a major automation program. The proposal was set aside by the Library administration in consultation with representatives of the Harvard Computing Center because it was overly ambitious and prohibitively expensive. However, the IBM study and proposal produced valuable indirect results by stimulating key members of the Library staff to consider various alternative approaches to the problem of introducing computer systems into the Library and to make certain basic decisions. In the first place it was decided that, given the lack of experience and the primitive state of the library automation art at the time, it would be unwise to attempt a "total systems" approach—particularly in an institution as old, large, and complex as the Harvard Library. It was also decided that concentration of initial efforts on the simpler applications would be desirable in order to provide experience and that special attention to problem areas in the Library's operation ought to bring to light opportunities for projects that would produce a significant return on the investment. Obviously the staff was not sufficiently large or experienced to undertake work on more than one or two areas in the initial stage. The prevailing view was that preference should be given to a bibliographical project which would have direct value for the Library's readers as well as the staff. Since there was general agreement that automation efforts in university libraries ought not to assume the characteristics of a moon race, it seemed preferable to avoid duplication of the efforts and resources that were being invested by several other libraries in certain areas such as serials control.

With these factors in mind, the five areas of library operations in the Harvard Library situation which seemed susceptible to computerization were reviewed. They were as follows:

1. *Catalogue-card production.* This is an area of fundamental importance in the long run because computerization would create cataloguing copy in machine-readable form which could then be used in a variety of important ways, particularly in book catalogues. Reproduction of cards, however, was not a problem at Harvard, and the Library was reluctant to undertake the input of catalogue data into computers before the Library of Congress and the research library community as a whole had been heard from on standard-

ized formats, etc. In addition, the Harvard Medical Library was involved in this area with Yale and Columbia, so it seemed wise to wait and learn from their experience.

2. *Serials control.* This was—and continues to be—a problem for the Library, but it appeared to involve such complex systems and conversion problems that it was not well suited for an initial project with relatively inexperienced and limited staff. Moreover, as has been noted already, several other libraries with less complex records were working on this problem and again it seemed wise to wait and benefit by their experience.
3. *Acquisitions ordering and accounting.* This was a serious problem area in 1964, and it seemed to be a function which could be computerized by the staff then available. While other libraries had tackled this problem, it seemed unlikely that their efforts would be of much value in Harvard's particular situation. This, therefore, was assigned a high priority.
4. *Circulation control.* This did not present problems in 1964. As reported above, the Library had already installed an economical and efficient punched card circulation system, and it seemed best to let this activity alone for a few years.
5. *Shelflists.* Since the Widener Library had continued to use the old sheaf shelflists that were started in the nineteenth century, shelflist maintenance was a very severe problem. There seemed to be no question about the desirability or the technical feasibility of converting the sheaf shelflist to machine-readable form and replacing the manuscript volumes with computer printouts. This would be a complex but manageable systems problem, and the staff had or could acquire the competence to do the job. The real difficulty was to convert more than 1,600,000 shelflist entries (mostly handwritten and in many languages) to machine-readable form. It appeared, however, that conversion would cost much more than it was worth if a shelflist produced and maintained by the computer continued to serve the same limited functions that it

> had always served in the past, i.e., use in the assignment of book numbers and occasional consultation by library staff and readers.

Thus, after a thorough review of the five potentially interesting areas, it seemed that the best prospect for application of computer techniques in the Harvard Library would be in the acquisitions ordering and accounting functions, and there was some reluctance to make this the initial effort because its impact would be felt only indirectly by the library's users. A second and more imaginative review of the shelflist problem was then made, and the idea developed that, with the aid of the computer, the traditional shelflist might be transformed into a kind of classified catalogue with alphabetical and chronological indexes, which would be useful to readers and staff alike. The paragraphs that follow will briefly describe this idea and explain how the initial pilot project developed into a major program of shelflist conversion and publication. Something will also be said of this program's potential for further development.

The Shelflist Conversion and Publication Project

A library's shelflist is a record of the books arranged in the order in which they appear on the shelves. Since book collections in most American libraries are arranged according to logical and detailed subject classification schemes in order to facilitate browsing and retrieval (rather than by size or order of accession), it follows that the shelflist should have great potential value to readers if it can be expanded and made available to them in some convenient form. A conventional shelflist differs from a classified catalogue in two principal respects: it records each book only once, no matter how many subjects the book covers, and it lacks author and title indexes. The Widener shelflist conversion and publication project has been an attempt, with the aid of computer technology, to develop the conventional shelflist into a new kind of classified catalogue of the Library's collections for the use of scholars, and at the same time to facilitate the task of maintaining the official copy of the shelflist for the use of the Library staff.

Shelflists have traditionally served two main purposes: as an inventory record of the books in a library and as an indispensable tool for assigning new numbers to books that are added to the collection. For most libraries the maintenance of a shelflist is a fairly routine process and involves merely filing one copy of each main-entry card into the card shelflist in call-number order. However, the Widener Library shelflist (with the exception of a few recently created classes) is handwritten in loose-leaf volumes rather than on cards and is therefore a difficult record to use and maintain. This was the standard form for a shelflist in the nineteenth century when Harvard Library's shelflist was started. Conversion of the shelflist to card form had been considered and rejected several times in the past on the grounds that cost of conversion would not be worth the advantages to be gained, and these advantages were always thought of in terms of the traditional uses of the shelflist.

As has been explained more fully elsewhere,[5] in September 1964 when the IBM proposal was under review, it was realized that conversion of the Widener manuscript sheaf shelflists to machine readable form could do much more than improve the official copy for internal use; it could enable the Library to publish an expanded version for public use. Computer technology had made it possible to reconsider the question of converting the shelflist, because significant additional uses could be made of the information once it was in machinable form.

The plan envisaged a class-by-class conversion of the shelflist and creation for each class of a computer printout to replace the existing official copy. In addition, a four-part catalogue of each class would be produced and published as part of a series. The first part would contain a copy of the classification schedule which would serve as a table of contents or key to the second part. The second part would be a listing of the titles in the class in call-number (i.e., classification) sequence with subclass headings interspersed at appropriate places in the lists. These two parts together would serve as a kind of classified catalogue or browsing guide to the books in the particular subject area covered by the classification schedule. Part three would be an alphabetical listing by author (by title, in the case of anonymous works) and would be obtained by a programmed computer sort of the original entries. This third part would provide an additional approach to the class and would serve as a brief finding list for books in the subject area. By using this list the reader would avoid some of the inconvenience of consulting a 6,000,000-card catalogue to find the call numbers of books in a specific field. The fourth part would list the entries (excluding periodicals and serials) chronologically by date of publication. This chronological list would obviously be of some value as a reference tool, and could also yield information about the quantity and rate of publication in a field and help to determine patterns of development as well as strengths and weaknesses in the collection.

Before converting the estimated 1,600,000 entries in the shelflist, it was necessary to undertake a small pilot project to determine the feasibility and cost of shelflist conversion and to gauge the usefulness of the new alphabetical and chronological arrangements. Historical works on the Crusades have been placed in a special classification in Widener, and this small segment of the shelflist, containing 1,200 entries, was selected as the pilot project to test formats and provide experience, because it was the smallest meaningful class in the Widener stacks and yet contained an excellent representation of the handwriting, language, and conversion problems that would be encountered in the larger classes.

In the pilot project and in the initial phases a decision was made to accept the standard upper-case computer print. This reduced the time and cost of keypunching and the writing and testing of programs, and, while less attractive and less legible than would have been preferred, upper case was believed to be adequate for shelflist requirements. Keypunching proved to be less difficult than had been anticipated, however, and in June 1966 the input requirements were changed to include upper and lower case and diacritical marks. Unfortunately, the available computer print chain, though it can print upper and lower case characters, does not have the diacritical marks.[6] This defect will be remedied in the future either by acquiring an expanded print chain or by using a photocomposition process for the production of printer's copy.

Two versions of the classification schedule were made. For the pilot project the existing form of the schedule was edited, typed, and reproduced by offset to serve as the table of contents to the list. (This process was later computerized.) In addition, each heading in the schedule, together with its corresponding call number, was keypunched on cards which were then merged by machine with the main deck of cards containing the shelflist entries. Finally, all cards were converted to magnetic tape, which is used for sorting and printing and serves as the master record.

The programming for the pilot project and subsequent upper-case work was done in Autocoder by Foster M. Palmer,[7] Associate University Librarian. The family of programs for upper and lower case work was written by Mrs. Susan K. Martin and Charles W. Husbands, systems librarians. A canned sort program (IBSYS) is used to obtain the alphabetical and chronological lists on the IBM 7094 computer; the rest of the processing is done on an IBM 1401 computer in Widener.

The pilot project, which was completed by January 1965, proved that conversion could be done at an acceptable cost. In order to test formats, printing costs, and the reaction of users, a paper-cover edition of the four-part Crusades shelflist was produced by offset in January and distributed to professors and librarians both in Cambridge and elsewhere. This first shelflist was received with considerable interest and enthusiasm and it was decided to continue conversion operations and to publish the completed classes in a numbered series entitled the *Widener Library Shelflist*. Arrangements were made with the Harvard University Press to handle the sale and distribution of the volumes.

To date twenty volumes have been published and several others are in preparation.[8] The volumes are priced to cover some computer costs and all costs of printing and distribution, but the Library is absorbing all conversion and editorial expenses as part of its regular budget. At the present time, six keypunchers or paper-tape typists, an editor, and a systems librarian are working full-time on shelflist conversion. Sales and subscriptions for the series (largely to libraries both domestic and foreign) have reached a level that provides a secure financial base for the venture, and continuation of the series seems to be assured.

Shelflist conversion at its present level has become an established activity and thus far more than 300,000 entries, nearly 20 percent of the total, have been converted. As the number of titles in the machine system grows to a critical size, the Library will have a data bank large enough to make possible meaningful experiments in manipulating the data in various ways and for various purposes. Each entry has its basic elements tagged and has been assigned a language code, a volume count, and a serial or monograph code. Some possible future uses for this data bank that suggest themselves are production of book cards for a circulation system, production of classified accessions lists, and the creation of new finding lists based on combinations of language, date, and place of publication. The merging of several related classes into a single list has already been accomplished with excellent results. The production of updated editions for internal use and, whenever it seems desirable, for publication is a simple matter. One line of development which is particularly interesting is the possibility of turning the Library's shelflist into a true classified catalogue by assigning as many base classification numbers to current books as their subject content would require. One number would indicate the physical location of the book and the others would merely indicate facets of content. A single book could then appear several times and in various classes. With slight modifications the existing system can accommodate this innovation. Another interesting potential development is the attempt of the Institute for Latin American Studies at the University of London to use the Latin American shelflist tapes as the basis for building a union list in machine-readable form of Latin American holdings in British libraries.

As it now stands, the Widener shelflist program, like many other present library computer systems, is regarded as an interim system designed to extract the maximum return from a simple existing bibliographical record of the contents of the Library. It is expected that in time the system will become obsolete and the imperfect shelflist entries will be superseded by standard bibliographical records in the emerging Library of Congress MARC II format about which more will be said later. The expectation is that a central bibliographical agency will convert and distribute these entries. It seems reasonable to suppose, however, that this conversion effort is still some years in the future and that, in the meantime, Harvard will have realized a satisfactory return on its investment in converting an abbreviated bibliographical record.

As an important by-product, the Widener shelflist project has provided a firm foundation upon which to build other library automation projects. It provided the initial justification for having the Harvard Computing Center locate one of its IBM 1401 systems in the Widener building. It also helped justify the creation of a Data Processing Department with a regular budget, an experienced staff, input equipment, and a sizable block of space in which to work. The existence of this staff, equipment, and organization have made it possible for the Library to take on new projects in a routine manner. The shelflist project also provided incentive and the means for embarking on an important program for rehabilitating the basic tools that are used by the Catalogue

Department, such as the classification schedules and the cumulative supplement to the subject-headings list, both of which are being converted to machine readable form and produced in multiple copies for internal use. These and other projects will be briefly described in the following paragraphs.

Classification Schedules and Subject-Headings List

The book and journal collections in Widener are classified according to a unique scheme which was developed and is maintained by the staff of the Catalogue Department. In 1965 the class schedules for the scheme existed in only two typewritten copies which had a large accumulation of corrections and additions and were badly in need of revision. Since clean and correct copies of the schedules were wanted in connection with shelflist publication, a major program was undertaken in 1966 to revise and edit the schedules and to use computer technique to facilitate the process. The schedules are converted into machine readable form and a computer program[9] is used to facilitate editing and to format and print them for internal use as well as for publication in the shelflist volumes.

The *List of Subject Headings Used in the Public Catalogue* was in a state similar to the classification schedules. It is a system unique to Harvard (but following closely that of the Library of Congress); the last typescript edition had been completed in 1931 and numerous additions and changes had been made. A new edition in multiple copies was badly needed and work on this, which began in January 1964, was completed in July. All headings in the list were typed on tabulating cards, one line per card, and the cards were then photographed by a high-speed automatic (Listomatic) camera to produce masters for printing a limited edition for internal use.[10]

The Listomatic process was selected because upper and lower case typography with diacritical marks was essential, and in 1964 the available computer print-chains at Harvard were limited to the standard 48 character upper case font. The plan also called for maintaining the list by issuing periodic cumulative supplements by Listomatic, but this was discontinued because the supplements were too small for efficient production by this high-volume-oriented process. When an upper and lower case computer print-chain became available in 1966, a system for producing the supplement to the list was designed and a program was written for printing the supplements in an efficient two-column format. Conversion of data for the supplement to machine-readable form and production by this method on a quarterly basis have become routine. The same system can be used to format and print the basic list when it becomes sufficiently out-of-date to warrant a new edition.

Acquisitions Ordering and Accounting

The old manual system of ordering and accounting for books had been put under considerable strain in recent years because of the increasing volume of work and because of the necessity for obtaining greater fiscal control over the Library's limited book funds. The system was geared to an earlier period when the rate of acquisitions was somewhat lower and funds were sufficient to cover normal demands upon them. By 1966, with needs in many subjects exceeding the available resources, it was clear that the loose existing system was no longer adequate and a new approach was needed. The experience of several other academic libraries with computer-based systems indicated that mechanization was both technically and economically feasible and would produce the kind of stringent control over outstanding orders and book-fund accounts that was required. In the spring of 1966, Colin McKirdy, a librarian experienced in computer-based acquisitions systems, joined the staff and was assigned the task of designing a computer-aided ordering and accounting system for Widener. Since an IBM 1401 computer was to be installed in the Library before the end of the year, it was decided to design the system around that machine. Certain limitations of this computer, which has only 8,000 positions of core storage and no random access (disc) capability, and a limited budget for computer time dictated that the initial system should be as simple and economical as possible.

The system was put into effect in September 1967 with a minimum of change-over problems and has proved to be as valuable as was anticipated; refinements are being added in the light of this experience. The new system provides more rapid, more comprehensive, and more accurate information on the status of accounts and funds than had been available, and eliminates a good deal of drudgery, such as the manual conversion of foreign currencies. The next step will probably be expansion of the system to include periodical subscription data.

Participation in the MARC Experiment

All of the projects previously described were local developments without direct relationship to activities on a national level. This was necessarily the case because, until late in 1966 when the Library of Congress launched the MARC experiment,[11] there had been no significant program linking research libraries in a common effort to solve library automation problems. The advent of the MARC experiment marked the beginning of a line of development which will eventually culminate in a network linking the nation's research libraries in a communications system based on computers and reprography.

One prerequisite to a network of this kind is the development of a standardized format for recording bibliographical data in machine-readable form. The Machine Readable Catalog experiment (MARC) was an effort by the Library of Congress to take the first step in designing and testing such a format. The first version of the format, known as MARC I, was a system for tagging and identifying the many elements in a catalogue entry so that they could be manipulated by machines in various ways and for various purposes. The Library of Congress undertook to convert its catalogue data for current English-language books into machine form in the standard format and to distribute magnetic tapes containing this data to sixteen participating libraries on a weekly basis. The experiment ran for a year and Harvard was one of the participants. The basic goal was to discover and investigate the problems involved in distributing and using catalogue data in this form; as a result, there is now a foundation upon which to build an improved standard format and distributing system. The experimental system has been continued and is evolving into an operational one; during July 1968, using magnetic tape, the Library of Congress will begin to distribute much of its catalogue data in an improved format (MARC II) on a regular subscription basis.

Harvard made a substantial contribution to this common effort and gained considerable experience in manipulating tape files of complex data. Since this was an experimental project, the

Library made no attempt to integrate the MARC data into its routine cataloguing operations, but rather limited itself to studying the promptness of receipt of the data and to writing programs for retrieving entries for books in particular subject areas and for creating name and title indexes to the tapes.[12]

The MARC experiment as conceived by the Library of Congress was limited to a one-way flow of catalogue data, from the Library of Congress to the sixteen participants; however, since the network that can be expected to evolve from MARC will evidently require two-way exchange of data, the Harvard Library applied to the National Science Foundation for a grant to enable it to supplement its participation in the MARC project by experiments with input and transmission of data.[13] Funds from this grant, which was approved in December 1966, were to be used to pay for adapting the systems design and programming developed at the Library of Congress and for using the same equipment (a Dura Mach-10 paper-tape typewriter) and similar editing and production methods to put into machine-readable form data produced by Harvard cataloguing. Thus Harvard would be able to put samples of its original cataloguing on magnetic tapes and send them to the Library of Congress in order to study the problems involved in making the MARC concept a two-way exchange. In a secondary but related experiment, the Library also proposed to use the same equipment in comparing the efficiency and cost of paper-tape input with the IBM 029 Keypunch which was being used for the shelflist conversion project. The latter study was completed on schedule but the former—adaptation of the MARC input system—was considerably delayed when the MARC I format was superseded by MARC II. This made it necessary for the Library of Congress to redesign its input system, a task which is still in progress at this writing.

Benefits of Work to Date

The Library's work in automation has produced some results of immediate practical value; it has also prepared the Library to undertake further work from which it should benefit greatly in the long run. It has already provided more efficient circulation and acquisitions systems, and has renovated basic records, including the subject-headings list, classification schedules, and the official copy of the shelflist. Useful bibliographical tools such as the published volumes of shelflists and the list of current journals in the sciences have also been produced. Even so, these products of work to date are less significant than the foundation for future advances that has been provided by the development of a general approach to library automation in the Harvard context, the building of a capable and experienced professional and clerical staff, the procurement of various pieces of electronic data-processing equipment including card-handling machines, keypunches, paper-tape tyepwriters, and an IBM 1401 computer system, as well as the fitting out of an adequate space in an already overcrowded building for this staff and equipment. Moreover, all these elements were welded into an effective organizational structure with a regular annual budget when a combined Data Processing and Photographic Services Department was created in 1966. In short, the projects described above have served as the vehicle for building a capability to undertake increasingly complex automation activities in the coming years.

The merging of the Photographic Services unit with Data Processing may at first glance seem somewhat premature, but this is a natural and logical relationship and one which will have increasingly important implications as both technologies develop concurrently and become increasingly interdependent in the future. One initial result of this merger has been the utilization of experience gained in shelflist publication and distribution to create book catalogues by photographing cards in languages which cannot yet readily be processed by computers. *The Catalogue of Hebrew Books in the Harvard University Library* in six volumes is currently in preparation, and production of a catalogue of Arabic books in four volumes will be undertaken shortly. Other projects drawing upon this experience with photographic technology and data processing are under consideration.

Future Developments

The development of a MARC II input system for current cataloguing at Harvard is the Library's most important project and deserves the highest priority for the immediate future, because this is the foundation upon which future automation of the bibliographic apparatus will be built. The acceptance of the MARC II format as the standardized communications format for bibliographical data marks the beginning of a new era in library automation. This has international as well as national implications.[14] In the pre-MARC II period, every system was unique; all the programming and most of the systems work had to be done locally. In the post-MARC II period, libraries will begin to benefit from systems and programs that will be developed by the Library of Congress and elsewhere, because they will be designed around the standard format. The effect will be to accelerate and facilitate library automation. An input system for current cataloguing will be the first package available, and this will be followed by programs to sort and manipulate the data in various ways. The task of the Harvard Library will be to adapt these sub-systems and programs to its own particular operating environment in order to develop the capability for inputting local cataloguing data in the standard format. It will also have to develop an efficient means of altering, adding to, and making effective use of the catalogue data on tapes that will be supplied by the Library of Congress on a regular basis beginning in July 1968.

Work on the MARC II format has been brought to a point where this format can be used for monograph entries, but a considerable amount of development remains to be done before it can be used to describe serial entries with their detailed holdings statements. This work is actively in progress as part of the recently organized National Serials Data Program sponsored jointly by the Library of Congress, the National Library of Medicine, and the National Agricultural Library.[15] A standard serials format within the MARC II framework is expected to emerge within a year, and work will then proceed on a national serials inventory in machine-readable form. This is a program which will have a significant influence on the direction and rate of library automation in all libraries, including Harvard. To adopt fully the MARC II system and its serial variant in the Harvard context will be a formidable task; but the potential return will make it well worth the investment of time and energy that will be required over the next several years. Once this central and basic module of the bibliographical system has been designed and put into operation, the present acquisitions, circulation, and shelflisting modules can be redesigned to make them all mesh into a single integrated system.

Ultimately the entire retrospective bibliographical record will have to be converted to machine-readable form in these standard formats before a truly integrated bibliographical system can be implemented in large research libraries. For each library to undertake to convert its own catalogues would be prohibitively expensive, and it seems reasonable to assume that procedures will be developed and financial resources provided for organizing this conversion at a national bibliographical center with a central data bank that each library can use to recreate its own catalogues in machine-readable form.[16]

Developments in the field of library automation since 1960 have been extremely rapid and somewhat chaotic, with an orientation toward purely local systems. With the advent of the MARC experiment two years ago and other developments on a national level, the orientation is beginning to shift toward national or standard systems, and some trends and guidelines are beginning to emerge. Though it is still too early for a library such as Harvard to attempt to lay down a rigid plan and timetable for the development of a master integrated system, Harvard has been able to adopt a general approach toward automation. That approach can be characterized as evolutionary or pragmatic, and this paper has attempted to describe it. Harvard is building a flexible capability for developing increasingly complex systems and for contributing to and capitalizing on developments on a national and even international level while continuing to get the maximum practical benefits from its locally oriented systems.

Notes

1. The libraries of the University of Chicago, Washington State University, and Stanford University are notable examples.

2. The various approaches to library automation are discussed at greater length in Richard De Gennaro, "The Development and Administration of Automated Systems in Academic Libraries," *Journal of Library Automation,* I (Spring 1968) [reprinted in this volume].

3. Foster M. Palmer, *Punched Card Circulation System for Widener Library—Harvard University* (Cambridge, Harvard University Library, 1965). 29 1. A gift from Alexander M. White, '25, helped to defray expenses of installing the new system.

4. Harvard University Library, *Current Journals in the Sciences* (Cambridge, 1965). 90 p.

5. Richard De Gennaro, "A Computer Produced Shelflist." *College & Research Libraries,* XXVI (July 1965), 311–315, 353 [reprinted in this volume].

6. Harvard University Library, Data Processing and Photographic Services Department, *Input Procedures for Widener Library Shelflist Conversion; Classification Schedule Conversion; Subject Heading List and Supplement* (January 1968). 24 l.

7. For a technical description of the project in its early stages, see Foster M. Palmer, "Conversion of Existing Records in Large Libraries, with Special Reference to the Widener Library Shelflist," pp. 57–80 in *The Brasenose Conference on the Automation of Libraries, Proceedings of the Anglo-American Conference on the Mechanization of Libraries held at Oxford . . . 30 June–3 July 1966* (London & Chicago, Mansell, 1967).

8. Published classes include: *Crusades; Africa; Twentieth Century Russian Literature; Russian History Since 1917; Latin America; Bibliography; Reference Collections; American History; China, Japan and Korea; Periodical Classes; Education; Literature; Southern Asia . . . Canadian History and Literature . . . Latin American Literature; Economics;* and *Slavic History and Literatures.*

9. The initial computer program was written by Foster M. Palmer and a later expanded version was written by Charles W. Husbands.

10. Harvard College Library, *List of Subject Headings Used in the Public Catalogue* (Cambridge, Harvard University Library, 1964). 817 p.

11. Henriette D. Avram and Barbara Markuson, "Library Automation and Project MARC," pp. 97–127, in *The Brasenose Conference* . . . (see note 7).

12. Cf. the summary by the officer of the Library chiefly responsible for Harvard relations with the project: Foster M. Palmer, *Harvard University Library Participation in the MARC Project* (February 1, 1968). 18 l. and Appendix, 200 p.

13. *Implementing the Marc Project Input System for Current Cataloguing in the Harvard University Library, A Proposal Submitted to the National Science Foundation, Office of Scientific Information Services,* Richard De Gennaro, Principal Investigator (November 2, 1966). 9 l.

14. The *British National Bibliography* has adopted a MARC II compatible format as a standard and is developing a computerized bibliographical input and distribution system for British publications coordinated with that of the Library of Congress.

15. Elaine W. Woods, *National Serials Data Program (Phase I), A Working Paper* (Washington, Library of Congress, August 1967). 12 l.

16. One possible method has been suggested by Richard De Gennaro, "A Strategy for the Conversion of Research Library Catalogs to Machine Readable Form," *College of Research Libraries,* XXVIII (July 1967), 253–257 [reprinted in this volume].

A STRATEGY FOR THE CONVERSION OF RESEARCH LIBRARY CATALOGS TO MACHINE READABLE FORM

Reprinted from *College and Research Libraries,* July 1967, 253–257. This article and the one that proceeded it were probably the first articles ever published advocating and presenting a strategy for converting library catalogs to machine readable form by converting the shelflist. It seems obvious now, but the idea of using the computer to recreate the catalog from the shelflist rather than converting all the cards in the public catalog from A to Z was a new and exciting idea in 1965. It helped to convince librarians that catalog conversion was both a necessary and a feasible foundation for library automation.

Until a few years ago librarians were rather skeptical about the technical and economic feasibility of converting the massive catalogs of multi-million volume research libraries into machine readable form. The view was generally held that while current input into these catalogs could be computerized the problem of converting the retrospective file into machine readable form was so enormous that future technological advances would have to be awaited before it could be undertaken. The science and medical librarians, citing the rapid obsolescence of their literature, concentrated their efforts where the most immediate payoff was available—in computerizing the record for current acquisitions. While librarians of humanistic collections could not completely turn their backs on the bibliographical heritage of the past, many of them were prepared to settle either for maintaining the retrospective catalog in its traditional format or for reproducing it in book form by offset photography. Thus, the computer would give us a powerful handle on current acquisitions but could not relate them to the total record. These views are beginning to change.

Many librarians are now becoming less pessimistic about the technical feasibility of converting mass catalogs. Practical experience in conversion has been acquired, photocomposition devices and print chains with upper- and lower-case and diacritical marks are available, keyboarding equipment has been improved, and new online keyboarding devices and techniques are being introduced. The extremely high cost of converting mass catalogs still remains a chief obstacle, but even here the picture is beginning to change and there is reason for optimism. With the federal government's growing interest in research libraries it seems reasonable to hope that funds may eventually be made available to convert to machineable form certain library catalogs or bibliographical records of national importance. Since the National Union Catalog is the largest and most comprehensive and therefore potentially the most useful record available, attention has been focused on it as the most likely candidate for conversion. One study has already been made of the feasibility of such a project and the techniques by which it might be accomplished, and a committee of the Association of Research Libraries is presently exploring the problem.

While there are many advantages to starting with the NUC there are also some serious disadvantages. It is an alphabetical file of fifteen million cards, all of which would have to be converted before much real use could be made of it, since a portion of an alphabet is of limited utility. The conversion of fifteen million entries complete with notes and added entries is a formidable undertaking and would require several years and a considerable investment of editorial effort, which might spell the death of the project if allowed to get out of control. The end product, in spite of its tremendous usefulness, would still be incomplete and inaccurate by the standards that are used to judge the catalogs of large research libraries. Advances in computer and communication technology will tend to make these standards even less acceptable in the future than they are now.

The purpose of this brief paper is to suggest as a possible alternative a method of converting the retrospective catalogs of the nation's research libraries and eventually creating a national union catalog in machine readable form as a byproduct of that effort. The strategy would be to avoid a frontal assault on a multi-million card dictionary catalog and a straight A-to-Z conversion, and to divide this massive single conversion project into a series of smaller and more manageable projects, each of which would utilize and build on the experience gained in the previous ones, generating useful outputs as the effort progresses. A similar approach is being used with considerable success in the Widener library shelflist conversion project at Harvard.[1]

The starting point for this conversion effort would be the shelflist of the Library of Congress, a bibliographical record that is relatively accurate and up to date. Since it is a unit-card shelflist, each entry is complete with notes, subject, and added entries, and once converted to machine form would serve as the basic record from which all other secondary records could be generated by computer. What is being suggested here is that the LC shelflist might be converted class-by-class to form the basis for constructing a master machineable bibliographical record in LC classification order and alphabetically in main entry order within each class. Other libraries could compare their shelflists against these basic LC lists, adding their own location symbols and unique titles to the master file and pulling from it machineable catalog copy for their own holdings in each class. The resulting augmented LC master record would eventually become an accurate and serviceable national union catalog in machine readable form. The problem is to develop strategies and techniques to facilitate not only the conversion of the basic LC file, but also for comparing and adding the new titles and locations for the titles held by each succeeding library as it enters the system and for enabling a library to extract catalog entries for its own holdings from the record.

If we can assume that a MARC-type standardized format for inputting bibliographical data into a system will have been developed and adopted within the next few years, then one could envisage a project being funded to re-create LC's catalog in machine readable form using a class-by-class shelflist approach. Initially, a subdivision of a science class such as physics or geology, and a part of a history of literature class might be selected as pilot projects to test assumptions and develop techniques. For the sake of discussion, however, let us suppose that LC started its conversion with the E-F or American history class. Upon completion of the conversion of the entire class or a logical segment of it such as U.S. history, a printout would be produced listing the entries alphabetically by main entry. The American or U.S. history holdings of another research library, that of a university for example, could then be compared with this list. One possible way of doing this would be to search the entries of the university library's American history shelflist against this alphabetical main entry printout. Each time a match was encountered, the local call number would be noted on the main entry printout. At the end of this comparison, the local library would have an annotated printout accounting for a large proportion of the titles in its collection. It could then pull those entries held in common with LC from the master tape by simply keyboarding the LC card number (or a special machine-assigned identification number) together with its own call number and other local information, and having the computer create a new local tape combining the LC entries with the local ones.

The entries present in the university library's shelflist that were not present in the LC list could be duplicated by photography and converted, using the standard input format that had been used for the LC list. This could be done at the university library, but it might be preferable to send them to a central facility for further searching and conversion and for entry into both the master LC file and the university library file. These entries would also have to be assigned LC class numbers. The university library would then have in its tape file the bibliographical information it needs to re-create its shelflist and catalog and to produce other listings either in hard copy or machine form. The central master file would now be augmented to certain titles in the local library that were not held by LC along with locations for all the titles held by the local library. Several problems remain, such as reconstructing the syndetic apparatus or the complex of cross references in the catalog, and accounting for the titles in American history held by the university library but classified elsewhere for local reasons such as in reference or rare books collections, etc. The latter problem would be the responsibility of the local library while the former one would have to be dealt with by the central authority.

The same techniques could be applied to each successive segment of the LC shelflist as the conversion effort progressed.

As classes were completed the computer could sort them into a single main entry list and eventually re-create a version of the dictionary catalog. After the contents of several major collections had been compared with and added to the augmented master LC file, the comparison and conversion effort of each additional library would be made increasingly easier because the number of titles not found in the master file would be decreasing. The comparison procedure would be easiest for those libraries which are classified according to the LC system because there would be a relatively close correlation of scope in the two shelflists. For this reason it might be better if the pilot comparison effort took place in such libraries rather than in those which do not use LC.

This problem of scope of shelflists could well be one of the most serious objections to the strategy being suggested. Many of the older libraries with rich collections, such as the New York public library, Harvard, Yale, etc., have classification systems which may be difficult to correlate effectively with LC's classes. This difficulty might not be as serious as it may seem at first glance if one bears in mind that the comparison or searching is done in a printout of a class of the LC shelflist that has been sorted by computer into main entry alphabetical order rather than the list in classified order. Thus the American literature class of a library with its own scheme would be searched against the equivalent part of the LC schedule arranged by main entry. Nevertheless, the problem remains and should not be minimized. On the other hand, the catalogs of these libraries, because of their uniqueness, age, size, and complexity, are going to present serious problems of compatibility in any future national bibliographical system based on computers and sooner or later these problems will have to be tackled and solved.

The techniques outlined for comparing, searching, annotating, and adding to files are here described in terms of today's familiar technology for the sake of clarity. In an actual project the whole process would presumably be considerably streamlined by the use of advanced online computer technology with visual display consoles, mass random access storage, and sophisticated means of communication. Thus, instead of actually producing a computer printout of the segment of the LC shelflist to be used for comparison, it could be in random access storage and accessible through a cathode-ray tube or visual display console. The local card shelflist entries would be searched in sequence by calling for the appropriate part of the alphabet on the console display unit. Each time a match was encountered a symbol would be added to the machine record together with the local call number and any other necessary local information. This would greatly facilitate the entire process and reduce keyboarding to a minimum.

The ultimate goal of the effort is to create in machine readable form an inventory of the holdings of the nation's major research libraries. The method suggested looks toward building this record in a gradual, orderly, and economical manner. Each bibliographical record would be in a standardized format, and the master file would be the basic record which would be put into mass random-access storage for online long-distance consultation when these techniques become economically feasible in the future. The file would serve as a data bank from which extracts of various types and for various uses could be drawn. While it is theoretically possible to produce the entire contents of this file periodically in printed form, this would be extremely expensive and probably unnecessary. It might be far more useful to produce a large variety of shorter and more specialized lists based on class, subject, language, date of publication, etc.

Some of the principal advantages of this conversion strategy are summarized below.

1. The master record is based on a relatively accurate and solid foundation, *i.e.*, the current inventory records of LC and the participating libraries—their shelflists.
2. It is a gradual process which can be changed, developed, and improved with experience. It is flexible, unlike the single frontal assault required for an A-to-Z conversion of fifteen million entries.
3. It would not only give LC a tremendous impetus in its total systems effort but would also make possible a parallel development for the entire research library community by removing the chief bottleneck—conversion of the retrospective file.
4. The cost and effort of keyboarding a bibliographical entry would only occur once and in a favorable environment.

5. The funding of this single but segmented effort might be facilitated because the subject approach would create interest and enthusiasm among the various segments of the research community including user groups as well as funding agencies. The E–F classes would interest historians, scientists would be eager to see the Q class done, etc.
6. The strategy and techniques could be inexpensively and meaningfully tested and costed in one or more pilot projects, such as the conversion of the Physics or Geology subdivision of the Science class, and a segment of a history or literature class. A decision to proceed with, modify, or abandon the strategy could be made on the basis of the experience and information generated in these pilot efforts.
7. There is no reason why, after suitable pilot projects, several classes could not be converted simultaneously. The work could be geographically decentralized by duplicating portions of the LC shelflist by photography and having the conversion work done outside of Washington, where space and personnel might be more readily available.
8. Useful lists of all kinds, such as shelflists, classed catalogs, subject bibliographies, chronological, alphabetical, and language listings, etc., could be created as each portion of the list is completed. There is no need to wait until the entire Library of Congress shelflist has been converted and augmented to obtain products of this kind.
9. Eventually the complex of cross references that tie a catalog together could be reproduced and all classes merged by computer into a single dictionary catalog in machine form.

The conversion of the present NUC or the re-creation of it in a new form is obviously an extremely complex and costly undertaking and one which has tremendous implications for the future development of libraries. This brief paper is not meant to give pat answers as to how it should be done nor does it pretend to be a detailed and carefully constructed master plan. The most that can be said for it is that it offers an idea for a strategy which may be worth considering along with others that are being discussed.

Whatever the strategy, the job of converting the massive retrospective record can and should be done, but it need be done only once in a standard format providing for full access. These millions of bibliographical entries were keyboarded several times before they came to rest as printed LC cards, and it is not unreasonable to suggest that they be keyboarded once more in machineable form to put the nation's research libraries firmly into the computer age.

Note

1. Richard De Gennaro, "A Computer Produced Sheflist," *CRL*, XXVI (July 1965), 311–15, 353 [reprinted in this volume].

A COMPUTER PRODUCED SHELF LIST

Reprinted from *College and Research Libraries,* July 1965, 311–53. This was my first published article and it described one of the first library shelflist conversion projects. Ritvars Bregziz started a similar project about the same time at the University of Toronto Library.

The 2,225,000 volumes in the Widener library are represented by an estimated 1,600,000 entries in what is probably the only remaining sheaf shelf list in any large American library. A few of the two hundred classes in the Harvard classification scheme are on cards, but the major portion of the shelf list continues to be maintained on handwritten or typewritten sheets in looseleaf binders. This type of list is difficult to maintain, and errors tend to accumulate each time the contents of a full page have to be transcribed to several fresh pages to permit the addition of new entries. The disadvantages of maintaining a shelf list in this antiquated and inefficient form are obvious, but there are two important advantages that are worth citing—it takes less space than a card list, and it is easier to consult.

The shelf list was designed to serve two essential purposes. It is an inventory record of what is in the library, and it is an indispensable tool for the assigning of class numbers to new books. The first function is no longer as important as it once was, because the library has now virtually ceased taking inventory or reading shelves from the shelf list.

In the absence of a classified catalog the shelf list has long been used by librarians and a few other sophisticated library users to provide a means of systematically surveying the library's holdings on a particular subject. When perusing the shelf list one sees all the titles that have been classified in a given segment, and not merely those which happen to be on the shelves or whose spine labels are legible. In addition, one can take in at a glance the essential bibliographical description of a book—its author, title, place and date of publication.

It is not surprising that this potential usefulness of the shelf list to readers has been generally unrealized. The shelf list was never meant for the use of readers—it exists in only one copy, and that copy has always been located in staff areas that are relatively inaccessible to the public. While readers have always been permitted to use the shelf list, they have never been encouraged to do so, and the staff has made no special effort to explain how it could be used. A card shelf list is not easy to consult because the cards can be viewed only one at a time; the sheaf shelf list in Widener is for the most part handwritten and difficult to read. To use a shelf list intelligently and efficiently a reader needs access to the classification schedules to serve as a guide, index, or table of contents of the list. The classification schedules used in Widener have never been published and are available only in typescript form in the catalog department—one floor above the room in which the shelf list is located.

Conversion of the shelf list to standard library cards has been considered and rejected on a number of occasions in the past on the grounds that the expense involved would not be worth the advantage gained—and the advantage was always thought of in terms of the present limited function of the shelf list as a classifier's tool. Computer technology now makes it possible to enlarge the concept and to expand the uses of the shelf list while improving techniques of maintaining it and making it available. This consideration has supported the idea that it would be desirable to convert the shelf list to machine readable form, and a plan for doing this has been formulated and is being tested.

The plan calls for converting the shelf list class by class and using a computer to produce a new kind of three-part list for each class. The first part consists of a printout of the classification schedule, which will serve as an index or key to the second part. The second part is a listing of the titles in the class in call number or classification sequence with class headings interspersed at the appropriate places in the list. These two parts together serve as a kind of classified catalog or browsing guide to the particular subject area covered by the class.

Part three is a printout in alphabetical sequence by main entry of the entries in the list and is obtained by a programmed computer sort. This provides a new approach to the books in a classification and serves as a brief finding list for books in a subject area. By using this list the specialized reader might avoid much of the frustration of consulting a six million card catalog for the call numbers of the books he would like to consult. The entries in the Widener shelf list are frequently much less complete than those in the public catalog, but in most cases they will be adequate as a quick reference or finding entry. Readers would use the public catalog when they needed more complete bibliographical entries. It should be emphasized that these class lists will supplement rather than replace the subject approach of the public catalog.

Once they have been converted into machine readable form, the shelf lists can be produced in multiple copies at a reasonable cost, or if a demand for them materializes, they can be photographically reduced and published in small editions. Copies of the lists of a particular class will be located and prominently displayed in the stack with the class in order to provide a guide to intelligent and systematic browsing. Professors and graduate students could obtain copies of the lists for classes of particular interest to them, and could use these to do a good deal of preliminary bibliographic work and to familiarize themselves with the holdings of the library in their own fields. Copies of the lists could be made available to scholars or libraries away from Cambridge; in fact, a significant demand might materialize for lists in subject areas where the Widener library is particularly strong, such as American history, Slavic, and the various other literature classes.

Obviously these lists will have their deficiencies. No classification is perfect, and books are not always placed where the reader would expect to find them or brought together as would be desirable. Rare books in the Houghton library, infrequently used books in the New England deposit library, and related works in other Harvard collections will not be listed; important material contained in journals will not be analyzed. There are errors and inconsistencies in the shelf list, most of which will not be eliminated in the process of keypunching.

All catalogs are incomplete and incorrect to some extent,

however, and it seems clear that these lists would be useful; indeed, they could be expected to contribute to the education of the library's patrons and might even instill in them increased respect and understanding for the bibliographical apparatus that librarians have so laboriously constructed during the last century. It is a well known fact that readers appreciate the privilege of browsing in a stack of classified books, but unfortunately it is also a fact that few readers ever succeed in grasping anything more than the barest outlines of a classification system. A large part of the effort and intelligence that librarians have invested in devising and using classification systems is lost because we have never found a satisfactory way of sharing knowledge of the system with the readers for whom it is designed and maintained. With the new three-part shelf list that has been described, the librarian will equip the reader with a copy of the ground rules that he is using to organize the collections, together with lists in classified and main entry order of the books and journals in the various classes. The effect should be to convert library stack browsing from a frustrating hit-or-miss activity to a systematic and effective intellectual experience. Indeed, it will also provide the possibility of browsing conveniently in a list without actually having to go into the stack at all. This might reduce the objections to shelving infrequently used books by size in storage, because these titles could be retained in the classified shelf list with a symbol showing the actual location of the book.

The preceding paragraphs have emphasized the value of a computer-produced shelf list to the library's readers. The benefits to the catalog department will be equally dramatic. A machine-produced shelf list will be a vast improvement in accuracy and legibility over the present handwritten sheets, and it will facilitate the process of assigning numbers to new books. The continuing and tedious process of recopying pages that have been filled in the existing lists will of course be eliminated once the initial conversion has been completed. Accurate volume counts of the collection will be automatically obtained and analysis of classes by language and date of publication will also be possible. This latter might be a useful tool for aiding in identifying categories of books which are deteriorating or which might be transferred to the deposit library. Since serial entries will be identifiable as such it will be possible to get printouts of serial titles in the various classes and in the library as a whole once the conversion is completed.

It might once again be practicable to undertake a regular inventory because printed lists that could be marked up would materially facilitate such a project.

In the first phase of the project the official copy of the shelf list will be a special printout with several spaces between entries. The procedure for adding a new entry is to copy it by hand into the appropriate place at the time the class number is selected and pre-empted. A card will also be punched and the new cards will be accumulated and periodically merged by machine into the master tape before an updated version of the list is to be printed. At a later phase, random access disc storage might replace the magnetic tapes, and file maintenance would be greatly simplified. Since maintenance of the lists will not be an on-line operation initially, it will be convenient and economical to rent time on equipment in the university's computation center.

The process of producing catalog copy in machine readable form is under study, and when such a system is implemented the shelf list copy might become a by-product of this process. Also under consideration is the feasibility of generating book cards from the shelf list conversion project in order to computerize the present punched card circulation system. It will be a simple matter to produce monthly accession lists in classified order from the punched card entries that are created for shelf-listing purposes.

The chief difficulty to be overcome is the actual conversion of an estimated one million six hundred thousand handwritten or typed entries in the shelf list to machine readable form. This is being done by manually keypunching the entries on cards. The process is a tedious one and other possible methods are being studied. The shelf list entries are not as complete as the entries that appear in the public catalog, and nearly 80 percent of them occupy only one line in the machine printout. The conversion problem is formidable but not nearly as formidable as would be the case if the project were to convert the one million six hundred thousand main entries in the public catalog. These entries are not only more detailed, but they would have to be identified and the entire file would have to be converted before any use could be made of them. The shelf list treats the collection as a series of separate units, each of which is complete and useable by itself. The classes can be converted one at a time, and there is no need to wait until the entire shelf list is finished before realizing full benefits from the work that has been done. Indeed, some of the larger classes, such as American history, could be subdivided and converted a portion at a time. Several other advantages arise from the fact that it is possible to deal with the shelf list one segment at a time—it may be easier to get financial support for a series of separate projects, priority can be given to active and otherwise exceptional classes, and improvements in techniques, format, type fonts, etc. can be introduced as they are developed.

This same "divide and conquer" strategy that is used in shelf list conversion may very well prove to be the answer to the problem of converting, or more properly, re-creating the dictionary catalog in machine readable and hence book form. The prospect of mounting a project to convert a large dictionary catalog by copying main entries in a straight alphabetical sequence is not one that inspires prudent librarians with enthusiasm. If however, instead of focusing on converting the catalog, we focus on converting unit card shelf list entries with tracings and re-creating the catalog by manipulating these entries in the computer we have reduced considerably the hazards of such a project. An analysis of circulation statistics will show that a significant proportion of the total use of a collection is centered in a small number of classes. The most active classes also tend to be the most rapidly growing. Thus, by converting the shelf lists of the several most active classes and creating machine readable entries for current accessions, one can begin to create a machine-produced book catalog of the most used and most interesting segments of a collection. It might be possible to account for a large percentage of the use of a traditional card catalog by converting a relatively small number of shelf lists. The goal should be the eventual conversion of all or nearly all of the shelf lists so that a complete catalog could be constructed, but the effort should be carried on over a number of years.

This strategy is intriguing, but unfortunately the Widener shelf lists are not of the unit card type, and before the strategy could be used there considerable time and resources would have to be invested in assembling, by one means or another, the information that is contained in a unit record shelf list. The problem of converting the catalog by this method is receiving serious study but the decision has been that the payoff in computerizing the manuscript shelf lists is significant enough to warrant a reasonable expenditure of effort. It was decided that, initially at least, Widener would content itself with shelf lists that were in the standard upper case machine font. This reduced the time and cost of keypunching very considerably, and it was felt that the appearance and legibility that would be obtained with upper case were commensurate with the level of quality that prevails and is required in the present shelf lists.

Early in the effort it was evident that a small pilot project would give valuable experience which would make it possible to refine estimates of the time and cost involved in converting handwritten shelf lists to machine readable form and would also serve as a test of the formats and programs that would be required to produce the lists. The Crusades classification was selected as the pilot project because it is the smallest class in the Widener stacks and yet it contains an excellent representation of the handwriting, languages, and problems that would be encountrered in most of the other classes. There were 1,170 titles (1,400 volumes) which were keypunched at the rate of about thirty entries per hour. Some proofreading was done, but the entries were not machine verified, and it is doubtful that such verification would be worth the effort. Two versions of the classification schedule were made. The existing form of the schedule was reproduced to serve as the contents and index to the list. In addition, each heading in the schedule together with its corresponding call number was keypunched on a card, and these cards were merged by machine with the main deck of cards containing the shelf list entries.

The Harvard College library call numbers lend themselves fairly well to machine coding, since they follow a predictable pattern, usually with a mne-monic letter prefix, a base number, and one or more dot numbers, *e.g.,* Econ 7042.35.10. The dot numbers are whole numbers, not decimals. The notation can be quite long, however, particularly when the necessary blanks are left to preserve logical order. For instance, Phil 35.9 cannot simply be punched as such, because other prefixes may require five letters, other base numbers up to five digits, and other dot numbers up to four. It is thus necessary to punch the number as Phil [4 spaces] 35 [3 spaces] 9. A particular problem arises with certain dot numbers beginning with zeros, *e.g.,* US 50.02, which is supposed to file ahead of US 50.1. Since zeros follow blanks in machine filing, this presented a complication which was solved by leaving one field blank before the zero dot number. This preserves correct filing order, but necessitated some reprogramming in order to avoid printing two dots, which are not keypunched but are reinserted in the numbers by programming in the printout. Programming steps can also recompact the call numbers so that they will appear in their normal format in the printout. Most of the problems involved in making the call numbers susceptible to machine filing were faced and solved at the time the unit record circulation system was installed in the library.

The call number, card code, volume count, language code, and other necessary fixed fields require over thirty columns of the eighty-column card, but insofar as this information is printed, it is printed only once for each entry. Therefore, a large portion of the 132-position print line seemed likely to be wasted, and it was decided to print two cards on one line and thus utilize all 132 positions. The call number, etc., occupies columns 1–33 on all cards. As formatted for printing, the corresponding information, with blanks needed for visual spacing, occupies the first 38 print positions. Columns 34–80 of the first and other odd-numbered cards go into print positions 39–85, and columns 34–80 of the second and other even-numbered cards occupy positions 86–132. Normal word division is used at the end of even-numbered cards, while odd-numbered cards normally end in the middle of a word. A dollar sign appears in column 80 of the last card as an end of record code, but it is not printed. Non-printing marks were placed before the title and date of imprint for future uses, such as chronological printouts of certain classifications for special purposes. With a maximum of 94 positions for author, title, date, etc. on each line (minus one for the dollar code), it has been found that a very large proportion of the entries require only two cards and will go on one line. The programs are written in Autocoder. The classified list program, after certain initializing steps such as printing a title page, reads a card, determines whether it is a regular card (for a book or journal) or a classification heading card, and formats and prints it accordingly. Error checks are provided to point out any call number duplicated or out of sequence, and any cards missing or out of sequence within a set. The classification headings are programmed to overprint so that they stand out on the page like bold face. The alphabetical list is produced by a program which reads the data onto tape and prepares it to be sorted by a canned sort program on the IBM 7094. The list itself is printed from a tape on the IBM 1401.

In order to test formats, printing costs, and user reactions, a small edition of the three-part Crusades shelf list will be produced by offset and distributed to interested faculty members, graduate students, and others. This will mark the end of the pilot project phase and the beginning of routine conversion operations. Two small periodical classes have already been converted, and keypunching of the Africa classification is now in progress.

INDEX

M

N

O

P

R

S

T

U

V

W

THE AUTHOR

Richard De Gennaro is director of the New York Public Library. Previous to this appointment he was director of libraries and adjunct professor of English at the University of Pennsylvania from 1970 to 1986.

He started his professional library career at the Reference Department of the New York Public Library in 1956. He went from there to the Harvard University Library where, for the next twelve years, he held a number of increasingly responsible positions, including assistant librarian, associate university librarian for systems development, and finally, senior associate university librarian. He established the Library's automation program and initiated and directed the computer-based Widener Library shelflist conversion and publication project. During a leave from Harvard in 1968–69 he was a visiting professor at the University of Southern California. He assumed his present post in 1987.

After serving four years in the Navy in the Pacific in World War II, Mr. De Gennaro earned a B.A. and M.A. at Wesleyan University. He also studied at the universities of Paris (Sorbonne), Poitiers, Barcelona, Madrid, and Perugia from 1951–55. He is a graduate of Columbia University's Graduate School of Library Service and the Harvard Business School's Advanced Management Program.

Mr. De Gennaro participates in a wide variety of professional activities. He is on the Board of Governors of the Research Libraries Group, Inc., and served as its chairman in 1984–85. He was president of the Association of Research Libraries in 1975, president of ALA's Information Science and

Automation Division, and chairman of the ASIS Special Interest Group on Library Automation and Networks. He has served on numerous other committees, councils, and advisory boards.

Richard De Gennaro is an internationally recognized authority on library and information technology and library management. He is the author of over forty papers and has completed over sixty consulting assignments. He was awarded the American Library Association's Melvil Dewey Medal in 1986.